ON GREAT FIELDS

ON GREAT FIELDS

The
LIFE *and* UNLIKELY HEROISM *of*
JOSHUA LAWRENCE CHAMBERLAIN

RONALD C. WHITE

RANDOM HOUSE
NEW YORK

Published in the United States by Random House, an imprint and division of
Penguin Random House LLC, New York.

RANDOM HOUSE and the HOUSE colophon are registered trademarks of
Penguin Random House LLC.

LIBRARY OF CONGRESS CATALOGING-IN-PUBLICATION DATA
Names: White, Ronald C. (Ronald Cedric), author.
Title: On great fields : the life and unlikely heroism of
Joshua Lawrence Chamberlain / Ronald C. White.
Other titles: Life and unlikely heroism of Joshua Lawrence Chamberlain
Description: First edition. | New York : Random House, [2023] |
Includes bibliographical references and index.
Identifiers: LCCN 2023008048 (print) | LCCN 2023008049 (ebook) |
ISBN 9780525510086 (hardback) | ISBN 9780525510093 (ebook)
Subjects: LCSH: Chamberlain, Joshua Lawrence, 1828–1914. |
Generals—United States—Biography. | United States—History—Civil War,
1861–1865—Biography. | United States—History—Civil War, 1861–1865—
Campaigns. | United States—History—Civil War, 1861–1865—
Regimental histories. | United States. Army. Corps, 5th (1862–1865) |
Brewer (Me.)—Biography.
Classification: LCC E467.1.C47 W55 2023 (print) |
LCC E467.1.C47 (ebook) | DDC 973.7092 [B]—dc23/eng/20230428
LC record available at https://lccn.loc.gov/2023008048
LC ebook record available at https://lccn.loc.gov/2023008049

Printed in the United States of America on acid-free paper

randomhousebooks.com

2 4 6 8 9 7 5 3 1

First Edition

Title-page art by Mary Evans/Classic Stock/CHARLES PHELPS CUSHING

As ever, for Cynthia Conger White

In great deeds, something abides. On great fields, something stays. Forms change and pass; bodies disappear; but spirits linger, to consecrate ground for the vision-place of souls . . . generations that know us not and that we know not of, heart-drawn to see where and by whom great things were suffered and done for them, shall come to this deathless field, to ponder and dream.

—JOSHUA LAWRENCE CHAMBERLAIN, SPEECH AT DEDICATION OF MAINE MONUMENTS AT LITTLE ROUND TOP, OCTOBER 1889

CONTENTS

LIST OF MAPS

A Courageous and Controversial Leader

*I*T'S JULY 1, 1863. THE MEN OF THE TWENTIETH MAINE REGIMENT *have just entered Pennsylvania. Over the course of a long, hot, and humid day, women and children step out of their modest homes to cheer on the Union soldiers as they march, and to offer them water and milk.*

The Twentieth Maine finally stops just after midnight, four miles southeast of the market town of Gettysburg. They've walked nearly thirty miles since waking up that morning. Bedding down for the night, they hear the recurring boom of cannon. The soldiers don't know what they might face on July 2, but they know their colonel. He has earned their trust.

The colonel of the Twentieth Maine was thirty-four-year-old Joshua Lawrence Chamberlain, husband of Frances Caroline Adams, known as Fanny, the love of his life, and father of six-year-old Grace and four-year-old Wyllys. Chamberlain stood five feet ten and a half inches tall, but with a ramrod-straight posture that made him appear closer to six feet. A handsome man with a lean, strong build, sandy-colored hair, and a ferocious mustache, Chamberlain's sparkling blue eyes conveyed his interest and affection for the volunteer soldiers he led. Yet he was an unlikely military leader.

Mild mannered, soft-spoken, amiable, and good-humored, Chamberlain worked as a professor at small Bowdoin College in far-off Brunswick, Maine, before enlisting. He was a man of intellectual curiosity and deep Christian faith, fluent in nine languages, who interspersed his lectures with allusions to Athens and Rome and quotations from Dante and Goethe. No one would have predicted that this learned professor from a quiet northern town would become a confident Union officer prepared to lead his men in the epic battle of Gettysburg.

Chamberlain prized duty as a central ethical imperative. He was an ardent believer in the Union. Born only fifty years after the nation's founding, for him the idea of the Union was not simply a political reality but a spiritual and transcendent truth.

He did not initially rush to enlist in the Union army in the spring of 1861, but in the months that followed, as he watched his Bowdoin students join up, with some ending up captured or killed, duty called him to offer his service.

Chamberlain was idealistic, ambitious, high-spirited, loyal, and courageous. He could also be impetuous and stubborn. At Gettysburg, he would need to draw upon every one of his qualities. He and the men of the Twentieth Maine would be tested at a place called Little Round Top, defending the far left of the Union line.

In a fierce battle, Maine lumbermen, farmers, and small shopkeepers battled Alabamians led by William Oates, also a courageous colonel. As the combat, fought with bayonets and pistols and hand-to-hand, surged back and forth, the Twentieth Maine volunteers began to run out of ammunition.

With the outcome of the deadly struggle in doubt, Chamberlain called out: "Bayonet!" After a breathless silence, as if a spark had lit a fire, first a few men on the left wing sprang forward; then a few more men on the right wing leaped into the fray. Now shouting, the Maine soldiers plunged down the tree-lined, boulder-strewn slope, surprising the stunned Confederate troops, who either surrendered or ran in defeat.

Outnumbered, and out of ammunition, Chamberlain had led the Twentieth Maine to victory. The victory at Little Round Top on July 2, 1863, would change his life forever.

One year after Gettysburg, at Petersburg, Virginia, Chamberlain suffered such a grievous wound that physicians told him he would die. General Ulysses S. Grant promoted him on the spot so that his family would be honored by his well-deserved recognition.

Accepting this verdict, Chamberlain wrote his wife Fanny a remarkable letter about his faith and his love for her. He did not in fact die, but would live in constant pain from his war wounds and their infections for the remaining years of his life.

CHAMBERLAIN'S HEROIC FEATS were largely forgotten in the passage of time, but they received an unexpected national rebirth in 1974 when he was featured as a main character in Michael Shaara's Pulitzer Prize–winning historical novel, *The Killer Angels*. Then, in 1990, celebrated filmmaker Ken Burns featured Chamberlain in the now-classic PBS television documentary *The Civil War*. And in 1993, actor Jeff Daniels portrayed Chamberlain in the popular Civil War movie *Gettysburg*, based on Shaara's novel.[1] That literary, television, and cinema trifecta generated for Chamberlain a huge following among Civil War aficionados and beyond. By the mid-1990s, Little Round Top had become the most visited place at Gettysburg, thanks in significant part to Chamberlain's newfound fame.

I LEARNED EARLY on in my research that writing a biography of Chamberlain would be a prickly task. Chamberlain has legions of admirers but also, more recently, critics who are convinced he was culpable for embellishing if not fabricating his role in the Civil War. I ultimately disagree with this theory, but in the 1990s, reports circulated that under their official uniforms, National Park Service staff at Gettysburg wore T-shirts bearing the cutting question "Joshua Who?"

Even with the renewed interest in Chamberlain, the focus on his biography has remained largely on the Civil War years. There is so much more to his life. After the war, he would go on to occupy more varied positions than any Civil War veteran: professor, governor, college president, popular lecturer, and author. I have come to believe it is not simply his heroism in the Civil War, but the diverse vocations he held that make his story so compelling.

In living with Chamberlain daily, I confronted a puzzle of many pieces. How to reconcile the bookworm college and seminary student with the risk-taking Civil War soldier? How to understand the proud beneficiary of a classical education in contrast with the young professor willing to challenge both the curriculum and the teaching methods of his revered college? How to balance the soldier who believed his military accomplishments made him deserving of promotion with a man steeped in an ethical framework that taught him never to push for advancement? How to appreciate a patriot who believed fervently in the Union—a powerful concept that can be hard for people to appreciate today—in concert with his magnanimity toward soldiers who fought for the Confederacy?

To meet Chamberlain is to encounter an American of enormous gifts but also great insecurities. His self-doubt began with an intense period of youthful stuttering, appeared frequently in his letters while courting Fanny, and surfaced in diverse ways as he served as soldier, governor, and then president of Bowdoin College.

A central piece of the puzzle is Chamberlain's wife, Fanny, and their marriage. Bright, talented, and artistic, with a lifelong struggle with depression, Fanny was a woman who exhibited both vast strength and vulnerability. The inner workings of her marriage to Lawrence have long defied full comprehension, but I became convinced that a careful reading of her voluminous letters would be the best way to gain access to her aspirations and frustrations.

As WITH MY biographies of Abraham Lincoln and Ulysses S. Grant, several convictions guided my approach to writing this book.

I believe many modern biographies move too quickly through their subject's younger years. The assumption is that readers want to get to the story of the subject's adult accomplishments. Yet early years are the formative period of a person's life. Chamberlain's basic values were formed and shaped as the eldest child of Calvinist parents, and then during four years of classical curriculum at Bowdoin College and his oft-overlooked three years of theological education as a Bangor Theological Seminary student.

I also wanted to understand Chamberlain's religious odyssey. His faith story overlaps a Maine Congregational church trying to meet the challenge of New England Unitarianism coming late to the Pine Tree state. A faith journey is never singular. Chamberlain's involves how he responded to the different faith trajectories of both his wife and daughter Grace, as well as the challenge of clarifying the faith position of a changing Bowdoin College during his presidency.

In research for any new biography, I ask how this person will surprise us. A neglected part of Chamberlain's story is the many years he spent as a sought-after public speaker following the Civil War. In the years after 1865, in reunion meetings, speeches, and memoirs, veterans refought the Civil War with words. They passionately jousted on subjects like: What really happened at Little Round Top? Was Philip Sheridan correct in relieving Gouverneur Warren of command of the Fifth Corps at Five Forks? As a professor of rhetoric, Chamberlain's well-crafted speeches quickly set him apart from other Civil War lionhearts. Notably, in speaking about his former Southern foes, he never affirmed their cause but consistently saluted their courage. Reading these speeches today is to enter into Chamberlain's moving logic of reconciliation.

My purpose in writing this biography is neither to lionize nor prosecute Chamberlain, but to try to understand and appreciate the life and times of this courageous and controversial man. This necessitates a fresh encounter with all aspects of his story, including parts that have not always been front and center.

To fully comprehend the unlikely story of Joshua Lawrence Chamberlain at the Battle of Gettysburg in 1863, we need to step back in time thirty-four years and travel north a distance of 675 miles to a family, home, and church in the small town of Brewer, Maine.

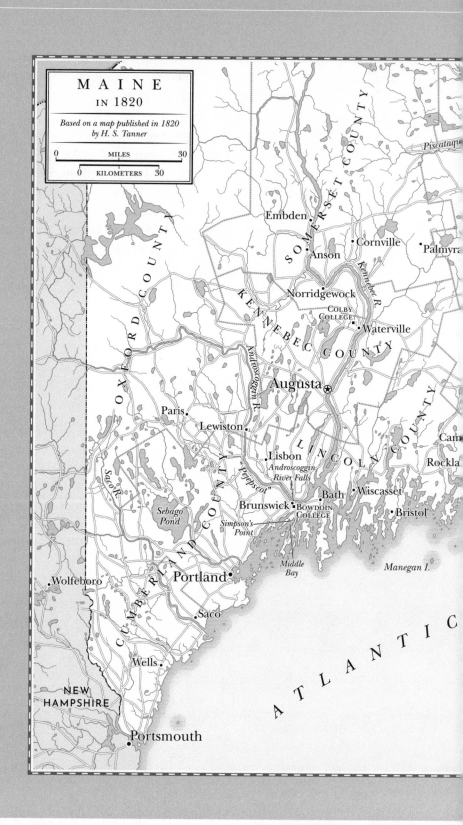

MAINE
IN 1820

*Based on a map published in 1820
by H. S. Tanner*

```
0          MILES          30
0        KILOMETERS       30
```

SOMERSET COUNTY

Piscataqu

Embden

•Cornville   •Palmyra

•Anson

Norridgewock

Kennebec R.

COLBY
COLLEGE

•Waterville

OXFORD COUNTY

KENNEBEC COUNTY

Androscoggin R.

Augusta⊛

Paris•

LINCOLN COUNTY

Lewiston•

Cam

Lisbon•
*Androscoggin
River Falls*

Rockla

Saco R.

"*Pejepscot*"

•Wiscasset

Bath•

*Sebago
Pond*

Brunswick•BOWDOIN
COLLEGE

•Bristol

Simpson's
Point

CUMBERLAND COUNTY

*Middle
Bay*

Manegan I.

•Wolfeboro

Portland•

•Saco

A T L A N T I C

Wells•

NEW
HAMPSHIRE

•Portsmouth

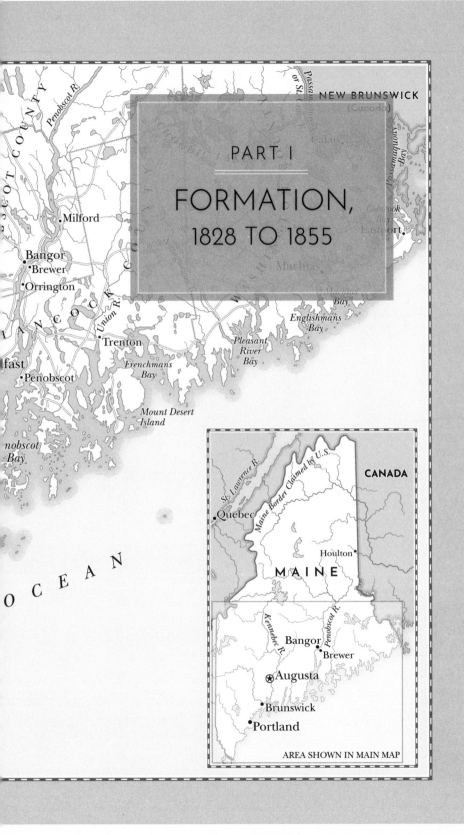

PART I

FORMATION,
1828 TO 1855

ONE

"Do It! That's How!"

A boy's will is the wind's will,
And the thoughts of youth are long, long thoughts.
—HENRY WADSWORTH LONGFELLOW, "MY LOST YOUTH," 1855

Henry W. Longfellow.

O N A WARM AUGUST DAY IN MAINE, A YOUNG BOY PLODS
across his family's farmland, leading two oxen drawing a
wagon heavily loaded with hay. Suddenly the wagon pitches, one
wheel stuck between two tree stumps. It cannot move forward.

"Clear the wheel!" his father, walking behind the wagon, commands.

"How am I going to do it?" the boy replies.

"Do it! That's how!" the father booms.

The son grips the hub of the lodged wheel and shoves and
shoves with all his young might. Finally, to his astonishment, the
cart tongue bumps against the off ox, and the wagon lurches ahead.

Years later, Joshua Lawrence Chamberlain would often recall
this challenge, his father's impossible command, and his own surprise and relief upon success.[1] "'Do it! That's how!' was a maxim
whose value far exceeded the occasion," Chamberlain would recall
in a memoir of his boyhood. It became for him "an order for
life"—an instruction for how to face any obstacle.[2]

CHAMBERLAIN WAS THE first child of Joshua Chamberlain, Jr., and
Sarah Dupee Brastow. Born on September 8, 1828, during the final
months of John Quincy Adams's presidency, his life started on his
family's one-hundred-acre farm in Maine, set at the edge of the Penobscot River next to the village of Brewer in the "Down East" or

eastern coastal part of the state. The Chamberlain house, average in size for that time, stands today at 350 North Maine Street.[3]

Joshua Lawrence Chamberlain birthplace home in Brewer, Maine, c. 1840

Upon their son's birth, Joshua and Sarah inscribed his name as Lawrence Joshua Chamberlain in their large family Bible. Underneath they wrote, "named for Commodore Lawrence of the American Navy."[4]

Captain James Lawrence, commander of the USS *Chesapeake,* a thirty-eight-gun wooden-hulled three-masted frigate, fought the British HMS *Shannon* off the New England coast during the War of 1812. Although Lawrence suffered mortal wounds in a losing naval battle, he would be remembered as an American hero for his defiant final order: "Don't give up the ship."[5] The boy's parents, ardent patriots, wished to honor Lawrence's courage in their naming.

With their son's name, his parents, in good Puritan tradition, also tethered his identity to the biblical Joshua. Chamberlain recalled that his parents admired how the biblical Joshua "left nothing undone which the Lord had commanded."[6] The boy would be the third Joshua in five generations of American Chamberlains.

. . .

CHAMBERLAIN'S FAMILY NAME traced its origins back to the twelfth century, when ancestor Richard de Tankerville became a chamberlain—the officer in charge of managing a royal household—to England's King Stephen.[7]

The first American Chamberlain, William, emigrated from Hingham, a market town in the east of England, to Massachusetts in 1648.[8] Abraham Lincoln's ancestor Samuel Lincoln had left this same town for a new England eleven years earlier. Both became part of "the Great Migration" of hundreds of ships and thousands of people who set their sights on the New World and the opportunities they hoped to find there.[9] Over the next century and a half, the first generations of American Chamberlains worked long and hard to make a living as farmers in the stony land of far northern Massachusetts.

In 1799, Lawrence's grandfather Joshua moved his family to Orrington. Joshua, Jr., was born there the next year. Chamberlain's father grew up in a new nation energized by the spirit of the American Revolution.

ON YOUNG LAWRENCE'S mother's side, Jean Dupuis, a Huguenot from La Rochelle, France, was an ancestor revered for his steadfast faith.[10] French Catholics first used "Huguenot" as a term of derision for French Protestants as the Reformation, sparked by John Calvin, spread across France in the sixteenth century.

In 1685, with prejudice against Protestants rising, King Louis XIV revoked the Edict of Nantes, which had, a century earlier, granted Huguenots substantial rights. This overturning spurred Dupuis to immigrate to Boston that same year to start a new life in America.[11]

Chamberlain's maternal grandfather, Charles Dupuis, fought in the American Revolution. A misspelling of his name on his army unit's muster list resulted in the Americanized name of subsequent generations: Dupee.[12] Chamberlain's mother, Sarah Dupee Brastow—often called Sally—was born in Holden, Massachusetts, in 1803.

Joshua and Sarah married in 1827. Their union has been remembered as the proverbial marriage of opposites. If Chamberlain's father was taciturn, his mother was talkative; Joshua's stern demeanor brought the Maine landscape to mind, while Lawrence remembered how much everyone liked his mother's "joyous freedom of spirit" and "impressible sense of humor."[13]

But the romanticized version of their marriage fails to account for internal tensions, which grew with the years. He of strong, unshakable opinions on all kinds of issues, she wishing to listen to all sides of a question. These tensions would affect the future course of their oldest son, who at times would act with his father's decisiveness, and at other moments would patiently listen to the many sides of an argument.

As the first child, Lawrence received the unfettered attention of his parents until age six, when the family welcomed another son,

Joshua Lawrence Chamberlain's parents: Joshua Chamberlain, Jr., and Sarah Dupee Brastow Chamberlain

Horace, in 1834. The two boys were followed by a sister, Sarah, born in 1836; then John in 1838; and finally, in 1841, Thomas, thirteen years younger than his eldest brother.[14] Throughout his life Lawrence would feel a deep responsibility for his younger brothers and his sister.

To accommodate his growing family, Lawrence's father moved them a short distance, to a larger house at the foot of a slope down from the Pejepscot River; the house still stands in Brewer today.[15]

THE PEOPLE OF Maine, the most northerly continental state, lived in isolation from the rest of America. Boston was 204 miles to the south. Traveling by horse, an animal that can typically walk four miles in an hour, the journey would take four and a half to five days.

The village of Brewer was named for Col. John Brewer from Worcester, Massachusetts, who settled there in 1770. Incorporated in 1812, by 1830, two years after Lawrence's birth, the town could count a thousand residents. It was located on the Penobscot River, the main highway of Maine, called by locals "the Rhine of Maine."

Chamberlain grew up in this much larger house in Brewer.

Bangor, an even larger town located directly across the Penobscot from Brewer, was a successful commercial hub that boasted a population of three thousand. In the nineteenth century, shipbuilding was both Brewer's and Bangor's major industry.[16]

By the time the river reached the two towns, it was so wide and deep that large ships could travel the forty-three miles upriver from Penobscot Bay on the Atlantic Ocean to Bangor and Brewer to load rich harvests of pine forest—Norway, white, jack, and pitch—that lumbermen floated down from the north.[17] McGilvery & Company, Charles Cooper & Co., and Joseph Oakes & Son kept the shipyards humming with activity. Ships were berthed so tightly on both sides of the Penobscot that locals boasted one could skip across the decks from Brewer to Bangor without touching the water.[18] Lawrence, who loved to be around ships, challenged himself to climb every new vessel before it was launched and place his hat on the top of the mast.

This vibrant economic growth coincided with Maine's first years of statehood. Immediately after the American Revolution, settlers began to pour into what people called "the wilderness," a region of Massachusetts known officially as the Northern District of the state. In July 1819, after several abortive attempts by area citizens to separate from Massachusetts, resentful at being ruled by faraway Boston, the citizens voted overwhelmingly to petition the federal government to become the twenty-second state.[19]

The Northern District believed its application to the sixteenth

Congress would be a mere formality. But in Congress, their request became entangled in the Southern states' steadfast determination to maintain a balance between free and slave states in an expanding United States. Powerful leaders, including Speaker of the House Henry Clay of Kentucky, made it clear that Maine would be admitted as a free state only if Missouri was admitted as a slave state at the same time.[20] The debate over the admission of Missouri foreshadowed the increasingly vitriolic controversy over slavery.

Mainers were furious. Their application was being held hostage by this acrimonious debate. In the end, Clay, President James Monroe, and Northern and Southern congressional leaders formed what became known as the Missouri Compromise. On March 15, 1820, Missouri and Maine were simultaneously admitted as the twenty-second and twenty-third states, defusing the congressional debate over slavery—for the moment.[21]

Growing up on a family farm in America's far northern reaches, young Lawrence was insulated from the nation's growing unrest over the issue of slavery.

His daily universe centered on school lessons and labor on his family farm. His schooling took place in one of Brewer's common schools. Maine was settled by Puritans from Massachusetts who started schools that shared a close relationship with the church. This meant that the hiring of teachers was as much concerned with their moral character as their educational credentials.

The teachers in the schools taught "the three R's,"—reading, writing, and arithmetic—along with history, grammar, and rhetoric. Additionally, the teachers were to inject a robust dose of moral teaching, aimed at instilling civic virtues and forming Lawrence and his fellow students into patriotic citizens.

As a boy, he completed barn chores. He cut wood to prepare for the long Maine winters. He cleared, planted, weeded, mowed, hoed, and joined in harvesting the rock-strewn fields of his family's and neighboring small farms. His slender frame grew strong and fit.[22]

Yet his boyhood was not all work. As the Penobscot River arose from four tributaries, so four tributaries of Lawrence's early years—Christian faith, a love of music, an adventuring spirit, and a commitment to education—came together to create the values that would shape his life.

Lawrence's religious values were shaped by growing up in Brewer's Congregational church. Congregationalists in the nineteenth century traced their origins to the Puritans who came to New England in the seventeenth century. This Protestant tradition took pride in its congregational form of church government. The Bible as the Word of God was the wellspring of its theological thinking. New England Congregationalism believed education to be the chief safeguard of the Christian faith. A central purpose in the founding of the two earliest colleges, Harvard (1643) and Yale (1701), was the education of Congregational ministers. To understand Chamberlain is to know he grew up among Congregationalists who had no sympathy for ignorance or anti-intellectualism.

The Brewer First Parish, organized in 1800, grew quickly in number. In 1828, the year of Chamberlain's birth, the church decided to erect a new building and elected Chamberlain's father the moderator (leader) of the Brewer Meeting House Association, a sign of the community's respect and appreciation for Joshua.[23]

Also in 1828 the "Great Revival" came to Brewer. Like many Congregational churches in New England, the leaders of First Parish believed the present generation fell short of the faith of earlier generations. The remedy: the church regularly prayed for revival, that the fresh winds of the Spirit would revive the dry bones of tradition with vital faith.

Though small at the start, Brewer's Great Revival grew in zeal through protracted gatherings that included singing, prayer, and preaching. Soon people were walking five miles from their farms to attend meetings at the Brewer church. As the effect of the revival spread, as more people joined the congregation, "religion was the subject of conversation wherever people met."[24]

In the early 1830s, in these first years of young Lawrence's life, the Great Revival eventually faded, but First Parish remained faithful to its Puritan heritage, recognizing the centrality of the Bible as the Word of God; sitting under learned preaching by educated clergy; honoring the Sabbath as a day set aside for rest; and encouraging congregants to conduct daily family Bible reading and prayers, which the Chamberlain family did.

Church and Sunday school were "strictly attended." If Lawrence missed either meeting, he knew he must make up for it by memoriz-

ing one of the Psalms, or a portion of the Beatitudes, or a hymn—
and repeat it at "mother's knee before sunset Sunday evening."[25]

Puritanism has often been characterized as a repressive
religion—stern and stiff—but Lawrence did not experience it that
way. His parents, and Brewer's First Parish, encouraged a life of the
mind. For young Lawrence, in both home and church, this meant
a growing love of books and music—and a thoughtful understanding of the Christian faith that encouraged a love of learning.

Catechesis, growing from the sixteenth-century Protestant Reformation, was a central practice for learning the Christian faith.
Catechesis was a form of religious instruction rooted in the memorization of the Westminster Shorter Catechism, composed by a
synod of English and Scottish church leaders in the seventeenth
century to structure the life and work of a reformed English
Church.[26] Its 107 questions and answers aimed to teach the meaning of the Christian faith to the young in the formative period of
their life. As a boy, Lawrence learned the well-known first question:

Q. What is the chief end of man?
A. Man's chief end is to glorify God and to enjoy him forever.[27]

While some later critics would decry this practice as rote learning, its adherents believed memorization to be the foundation for
fostering love of the Christian faith. Advocates also claimed memorization fortified the workings of the brain through enhanced elocution, and helped improve speech through exposure to elevated
literature and language.

At the height of his youthful church participation, Chamberlain
memorized the Westminster Shorter Catechism "from cover to
cover."[28] His commitment to memorization—of the Bible, the Westminster Catechism, and poetry—would become a signature practice of his adulthood. It undergirded his disciplined character.
Although this practice might appear to be strictly a mental exercise,
Lawrence described this learning as "by heart."[29]

On June 23, 1845, at the age of sixteen, Chamberlain joined the
Brewer church in the traditional Congregational manner: by giving
a narrative of his Christian faith.[30] Lawrence knew he could not give
a dramatic story of a conversion experience; instead, he empha-

sized needing "saving grace and a loving, divine brotherhood." In this significant milestone in his young life, he claimed not to be a "sudden saint," but evinced a steady nurturing of Christian faith.[31] The wellsprings of the Christian faith, formed in his youth, would go on to shape all aspects of his adult life.

CHAMBERLAIN'S LOVE OF music, his second tributary, grew alongside his faith and was nurtured in a congregation that sang. From an early age, Lawrence discovered that his love of music could lift his spirit. He joined his congregation enthusiastically in singing from eighteenth-century English hymn writer Isaac Watts's *Hymns and Spiritual Songs*.[32] Watts's most famous hymns include "Our God, Our Help in Ages Past" (from his paraphrase of Psalm 90).

> *Our God, our help in ages past,*
> *our hope for years to come,*
> *our shelter from the stormy blast,*
> *and our eternal home.*

Other popular Watts hymns that Lawrence would have sung include "Jesus Shall Reign Where'er the Sun" (part of his version of Psalm 72), "When I Survey the Wondrous Cross," and "Joy to the World."

As Chamberlain's love of music grew, he became interested in learning to play the bass viol. In tiny Brewer, it was not possible to purchase such an instrument, so he constructed his own from a stout cornstalk. He carefully cut places at proper distances for the strings and frets and fashioned a smaller stalk for a bow.[33] He rejoiced at accompanying the church choir with his homemade bass viol, remembering years later, "That was mastery; that was power."[34]

In his later teenage years, Chamberlain would start a "singing school" in a nearby village. Originating in New England Congregational churches in the early eighteenth century, "Yankee singing schools" taught both old and new hymns. A "singing master" instructed students of all ages to sight-read music. The music was often unaccompanied—performed a cappella—but Lawrence had his rustic bass viol sent from home for accompaniment. Although the stated goal of the schools was to improve their congregations' singing to enhance their faith, the singing schools also became popular as social gatherings and opportunities for courting in small towns.[35]

A THIRD TRIBUTARY, Lawrence's spirit of adventure, shone through in myriad facets of his life. He enjoyed exploring the magnificent natural surroundings of forests and streams. Lawrence delighted in being alone in the woods, possessing a keen eye and ear for the sights and sounds of animals and birds. He liked to take long walks along "the high crest above the [Pejepscot] river."[36] Years later, he recalled his younger self: "A solitary schoolboy stopped to see the wondrous beauty and stood before it wrapped in thought."[37]

He enjoyed visiting the Indians who lived in birchbark wigwams in the woods a mile from the back of the family farm. The boy learned some of the language of the Penobscot tribe—his first endeavor in what would become a lifelong passion for languages. Lawrence was mesmerized by the stories of the tribe's long history in the region, and he admired the beautiful beadwork and "curiously braided baskets" that the Penobscot women would sell his household.

Lawrence also felt a connection to horses. They responded to his voice and touch. At thirteen, he delighted in riding a frolicsome mare he described as "that indomitable desert-queen." Spurning saddle and bridle, he rode bareback across endless fields and through pine forests "at a speed that suited the mad mood of both."[38]

He enjoyed swimming across the Penobscot River where fresh water mingled with ocean tides coming up from Penobscot Bay. It wasn't an easy traverse; he had to take care to avoid the multiple boats coming and going from both sides of the river. But he met the challenge skillfully, often swimming the several hundred yards from Brewer to Bangor and back again. When he was older, the "severer" test became swimming there with a twenty-five-pound rock under one arm, then swimming back with the rock under the other arm.[39] A biography published toward the end of his life, entitled A Sketch, called this "bold swimming" a "school of self-command."[40]

Lawrence's family embarked on frequent sailing adventures. As the oldest boy, he helped crew the sloop *Lapwing* on trips down the Penobscot River for special occasions, such as the annual outings held two weeks after haying. Lawrence relished the day he first received permission from his father to take the tiller and command his younger brothers as his crew among the islands of Penobscot Bay.[41]

His father taught him and his brothers to shoot, what the boys called "gunning." A spectacular diversity of animals and birds lurked close by their home. But unlike his friends and siblings, at an early age Chamberlain decided he would not shoot a gun to kill animals. When asked why by other boys, he found it difficult to put his answer into words; he just knew he could not kill for sport. Years later, he was able to articulate his feelings: "It is a mean thing to snatch a pleasure at another's loss."[42]

THE FOURTH AND final tributary sprang from the Chamberlain family's commitment to education. But as Lawrence neared the end of his common schooling in Brewer, tensions grew within his family over what kind of further education he should pursue. The conflict emanated from the very different hopes his father and mother held for him.

Lawrence's father never tired of reminding his eldest son that he came from a lengthy line of soldiers. His great-grandfather Ebenezer served as a New Hampshire soldier in the Revolutionary War. His grandfather served as a colonel in the War of 1812 with England. His mother's grandfather, Thomas Brastow, Jr., served as a private in the French and Indian War and as a captain in the Revolutionary War.

As an eleven-year-old boy in 1839, Lawrence watched proudly as his father marched off to lead a regiment in the Aroostook War, a conflict precipitated by a boundary dispute with the British Canadian province of New Brunswick. In the end, it was a war with no deaths on either side, earning the name the "Bloodless Aroostook War."[43]

Hoping his son would follow in the family military tradition, when Lawrence turned fourteen, his father enrolled him in Whiting's Military and Classical School, located in Ellsworth, a town twenty-six miles down east from Brewer. Major Charles Whiting, a Mainer who graduated from West Point fourth in his 1835 class, had just founded the school the year before, in 1841.[44]

"Classical" meant Chamberlain studied Latin, rhetoric, and French (French being the language of the military literature growing out of the Napoleonic era). He quickly proved himself to be an

eager learner. Drawing on his catechism skills, he learned French by practically memorizing a 450-page book of French grammar.

Major Whiting made sure his students studied the physical arts as well. Military drills were held every day. The boys learned to handle a variety of weapons dating from the earlier French and Indian wars. On Sundays, they even marched to church in columns of four.[45]

Lawrence's father hoped Whiting's school might lead to his son's appointment at West Point and eventually a military career. But the boy's

Major Charles Whiting, a West Point graduate, founded the Military and Classical School.

time there ended unexpectedly, after just one year. His father, not always wise when it came to his finances, lent money to new local businesses in hopes of making a quick profit. Now, significant financial losses compelled him to bring his son home from boarding school.[46]

LAWRENCE'S MOTHER MAY not have been too disappointed by this turn of events, for she wanted her firstborn son to pursue a quite different vocation. The Brewer congregation was known for its support of foreign missions. They had sent members to Micronesia and Turkey through the American Board of Commissioners for Foreign Missions. The Chamberlain family, especially Sarah, strongly supported this emphasis on missions.[47]

Her hopes that her eldest son would become a minister or missionary were strengthened by the nearness of Bangor Theological Seminary, located directly across the Penobscot River in Bangor. Chartered in 1814, its founders aimed to provide the first opportunity for theological education in far northern New England.[48] Seminary faculty and students often supplied the Sunday preaching at Brewer's First Parish.[49]

Wedged between his parents' quite different wishes for his future, Lawrence decided to postpone his decision and try his hand at teaching. Villages hired schoolteachers for a term of six to eight weeks in January and February, when it was too cold for boys to be out in the fields. Pay was minimal, but expenses were few as the "master" boarded with families in the village. The "scholars," both boys and girls, ranged in age from four to twenty-four.

That first winter Chamberlain was posted in the village of Wiscasset, a seaport town eighty-seven miles south of Brewer. In his new role, he discovered how much he liked teaching. He enjoyed the challenge of working with students of different ages in the same classroom, although some parents complained that Chamberlain did not have enough "snap"—he needed to be tougher on the "scholars."[50]

The next winter, Chamberlain, now seventeen years old, received an invitation to teach at a school fourteen miles upriver in Milford. He accepted, knowing that for the past three years the school had been "broken up" by the students. The previous winter, the "scholars" had gone so far as to toss the "master" through the window. After "fortifying the spirit with a few texts from the 'Westminster Catechism,'" Lawrence set out to face the challenge.[51]

Chamberlain arrived at the Milford school on a Monday morning. He spoke to the class about the rights and obligations of both master and scholars. To emphasize his message, he laid a sturdy beechwood stick on his desk.

After the midafternoon recess, the girls returned promptly, but the boys lingered outside. They finally started dribbling in after fifteen minutes, loitering at the stove.

"Take your seats, boys!"

"We'll go when we are ready."

"Go!"

Corporal punishment was a part of nineteenth-century school

culture, and Chamberlain punctuated his words with his right fist, smashing the spokesman for the recalcitrant boys underneath his left jaw. The scholar sprawled backward, lying stock-still on the floor.

The other students looked on, astonished.

Chamberlain commanded two boys to carry the troublemaker home and tell his parents the master would arrive at their house after school.

It is easy to imagine butterflies in the seventeen-year-old's stomach as he knocked on the parents' door. The disruptive boy was subdued, but the father was not. He threatened to bring "the law" against the teenage teacher.

Lawrence screwed up his confidence and replied, " 'Law' is just what I am here for," reminding the man that he was hired specifically to quell the annual ritual of breaking up the school.

Surprisingly, the father backed down. "You're right, master. The boy was rightly punished. You'll not have any more trouble from him, and we guess not from anybody else!"

The young teacher's visits did not stop there. He called on the wayward scholar at his home every afternoon to show his concern until the boy returned to school, where the way was now "clear for good earnest work."[52]

To be sure, Chamberlain, who would later become a highly respected educator, recounted this story through the long lens of memory. What might Chamberlain have wished for us to take away from his initial youthful ventures into teaching? He said nothing about the academic subjects he taught but instead emphasized his growing attention to and relationships with his students.

IN 1846, WITH his eighteenth birthday approaching in September, Lawrence found himself at what he would later call "the fork in the road." One path would lead to West Point and a military career; the other to Bangor Theological Seminary and a vocation in ministry.

The debate about Chamberlain's future now came to a boiling point within the family. His father advocated the military, for it would offer a "manly honorable career." His mother believed a military career would end up being "narrowing and enervating." Plus, to be a soldier in this present time of peace presented nothing "noble." His mother counseled that the ministry offered her son "the Lord's own service."

Chamberlain would remember that he "was not much inclined to either course." He reasoned "that both alike offered little scope and freedom," and worried he would be encircled by inflexible expectations in both vocations.[53]

To forestall the decision once again, he decided to apply to Bowdoin College. In Chamberlain's day, it was not unusual for young men to enroll in college and enter West Point later. If he chose to attend Bangor Theological Seminary, it would be after receiving a college degree.

For sons of Maine, Bowdoin was the top destination for higher education. Chartered in 1794, and located in the town of Brunswick, a little over one hundred miles south of Brewer, Bowdoin was Maine's oldest institution of higher learning.[54] Yet for the sons in Brewer, to attend college instead of going to work for their fathers was an unusual decision.

At the time, the Bowdoin "terms of admission" included the aptitude to "write Latin grammatically, and to be well versed in Geography, Arithmetic, six sections of Smyth's Algebra, *Cicero's Select Orations,* the *Bucolics, Georgics,* and *Aeneid* of Virgil, Sallust, the Gospels of the Greek Testament, and Jacob's (or Felson's) Greek Reader; together with Latin and Greek Prosody." Students applying for admission must also "produce certificates of their good moral character."[55]

To pass the entrance exam, Lawrence knew he needed to brush up on his Latin, as well as learn Greek. Classical languages and literature constituted the foundation of a liberal education in nineteenth-century colleges. The trouble: for him, "Greek was an unknown world."[56]

Young Lawrence prepared for Bowdoin with determination and a particular study regimen. He designated a room in the attic as his study. There, he hung a daily schedule on the bookshelf; it split a seventeen-hour workday—from 5 A.M. to 10 P.M.—into hourly commitments.[57] For month after month, he shut himself in his study, his only companion William Hyde, a tutor he hired from the money he had earned from teaching to augment his efforts in both Latin and Greek. Hyde, a Bowdoin alumnus nine years older than Lawrence, was pursuing a degree at Bangor Theological Seminary and possessed the added advantage of familiarity with both Bowdoin's curriculum and entrance requirements.[58]

Each day the two drilled, memorized, and tested. During his hours alone, Lawrence dedicated himself to memorizing all 573 pages of Rafael Kühner's *Grammar of the Greek Language*.[59] To this he added Homer and Herodotus, as well as the Romans: Caesar, Sallust, and Cicero. He recited passages from their writings to the silent walls of the attic in preparation for the day he would be asked to do so in front of a faculty committee at Bowdoin.[60]

But there always seemed to be so much more to learn. Earlier in the year, he wrote his cousin, Sara Shapard, "All things are fleeting, we are fleeting. *Time,* how it flies. We are no longer children." He added pensively, "I sometimes wish myself a child always, for then it is that sport is the most innocent and joy most unbeclouded."[61]

A believer in the importance of balancing mental and physical work, as fall turned to winter, Lawrence split wood—rock maples and yellow birch—and carried the heavy wood up the stairs to his study to keep him warm while he studied.

His father also helped break up the long days of studying by giving Chamberlain lessons with broadswords. Popular in the nineteenth century, these were large basket-hilted swords with double-sided blades. Five years earlier, Abraham Lincoln, a young Illinois legislator, had been challenged to a duel, and chose broadswords as the weapons. At six feet four inches tall, Lincoln knew that his height and reach would give him a decided advantage over his shorter opponent, James Shields. In the end, cooler heads, helped along by Lincoln's clever choice of weapons, prevailed. The duel was called off. In the dueling in Brewer, Lawrence and his father decided that a "perpetual peace" was the wiser course.[62]

DESPITE HIS FULL year of preparation, as September approached once more, Lawrence admitted to himself that even with his rigorous study regimen, he "was not more than half ready."[63] He faced a daunting question: should he charge ahead and face the Bowdoin entrance committee, or should he delay? With his nineteenth birthday approaching on September 8, 1847, he felt behind his peers.

After much agonizing, he finally settled on a compromise: he would apply to enter in February, at the beginning of the second term. If he succeeded, he would try his hardest to overtake the first-year class that would enter in the fall so he could stay in his class year. Having reached a decision, he redoubled his attic efforts, musing it would "take a good deal of wood splitting and head splitting" to prepare himself.[64]

TWO

A Bowdoin Man

We must learn to think in their own language as the Greeks
thought before we can inhale the glorious and inspiring atmosphere
of Athenian wisdom—and we must learn to feel as the Romans felt
before we can become participants in the profound and practical
sagacity of ancient Rome.

—GEORGE FREDERICK HOLMES, 1849[1]

Gro. Fredk Holmes.

T HE YEAR 1848 BROUGHT HEIGHTENED ACTIVITY IN THE CHAM-
berlains' Brewer home. Six months after his nineteenth birthday, the eldest child prepared to leave the nest for the first time.

Early on a cold February day, Lawrence and his tutor, William
Hyde, climbed into a sturdy sleigh. With the young man's favorite
mare at the front and a large wooden trunk lashed to the back, they
set off on the one-hundred-mile trek downstate to Bowdoin College.
They avoided the main stagecoach road through the Dixmont Hills,
which was almost certain to be covered with large snowdrifts, and
opted instead for the longer "shoreline" route. Traveling via the sea-
ports of Belfast, Rockland, Wiscasset, and Bath, their winter journey
brought them along the Bath Road to Brunswick and Bowdoin's
small red brick campus just as the sun was rising on the second day.[2]

THAT VERY AFTERNOON, Lawrence stood before a committee of
professors for the infamous oral entrance examination. The faculty
questioned Lawrence on Latin and Greek grammar and composition and asked him to recite passages from the works of various
classical authors from memory. The questions felt more like an in-

FACING PAGE: *Bowdoin College in the 1840s*

terrogation than an exam, inducing what he later described as "mingled sensations of awe and awkwardness."[3] He had diligently studied for the past eighteen months, but the formal college setting felt completely different from the attic where he'd taken mock exams. Working to keep his nerves in check, he put his best effort forward before these august educators.

He passed. All of his self-discipline, hard work, and memorization, day after day in the attic in Brewer, was rewarded at Bowdoin.

The college's newest student was told to report for his first class the next morning at 6 A.M.

IN 1848, BOWDOIN College stood in the first tier of American colleges. Chartered by the General Court of Massachusetts at the end of the eighteenth century, Bowdoin was established after seven years of petitions from citizens in northern Massachusetts who wanted a college more geographically accessible for their sons than Harvard College in Cambridge, a full five-day ride by horseback.[4]

The college was named for James Bowdoin, a former Massachusetts governor whose son, James Bowdoin III, offered to endow the school in his father's name. The younger Bowdoin's great-grandfather, Pierre Baudouin, who was, like Sarah Chamberlain's ancestor, a Huguenot from La Rochelle, France, immigrated to the United States in 1686 and became a successful merchant in Boston. After his death, his eldest son anglicized "Baudouin" to "Bowdoin"— pronounced "Bo-dun."[5]

Eight Massachusetts towns courted the founders to become home to the new college. In 1796, the trustees selected Brunswick as the winner. First settled in 1628, Brunswick was the eleventh town incorporated in what would become the state of Maine.[6] Located in the southern midcoast region of the state, close to Maine's future capital, Portland, by the nineteenth century Brunswick had developed into a major producer of lumber, powered by the Androscoggin River Falls.

In 1802, eight students enrolled for Bowdoin's first classes, taught by a single professor.

. . .

BY THE TIME Chamberlain arrived nearly a half century later, Bowdoin had grown in all categories: number of students, faculty, physical size, and intellectual scope. The college buildings formed a row fronting Maine Street. Now the faculty consisted of eight men. One hundred and five undergraduates, all male, made up the student body. The large majority of the student body came from Maine, but by 1848 it included students from Massachusetts, New Hampshire, and Rhode Island.[7] Bowdoin even had a medical school, bringing professionalism to a then-underappreciated vocation, as well as medical services, to a largely rural state.[8]

LAWRENCE ARRIVED AT the college near the beginning of the twenty-seven-year presidency of Leonard Woods. Appointed in 1839 at age thirty-two, Woods had previously served as professor of biblical literature at Bangor Theological Seminary, just across the river from where Lawrence grew up. Like his three presidential predecessors, Woods was a Congregational minister. As president, he would lead Bowdoin into its maturity as the college gained increasing respect in and beyond Maine.

THE COLLEGE ASSIGNED Lawrence to room 21 of Maine Hall. He lugged his trunk up the stairs to his cramped lodging on the fourth floor.

At age nineteen, Chamberlain stood one and a half inches shy of six feet. He had a long, slender face, wide forehead, and slightly protruding cheekbones, and his blue-gray eyes sparkled when he spoke. He

Leonard Woods would serve as president of Bowdoin College for twenty-seven years.

liked to refer to the three parts of his name—Joshua Lawrence Chamberlain—as his scriptural, medieval, and modern names, but he introduced himself as Lawrence, the name his parents would call him throughout his life.[9]

. . .

As LAWRENCE WENT to sleep in his dorm that first night after achieving his long-sought admission to Bowdoin, he surely wondered what the next chapter of his life would bring.

Before sunrise the next morning, Lawrence entered the tall door at the end of Winthrop Hall, named for John Winthrop, the legendary first governor of the Massachusetts Bay Colony.[10] His first day of classes had begun.

FRESHMAN CLASS CURRICULUM

1. TERM. MEMORABILIA OF XENOPHON.
Greek Grammar.
Folsom's Livy.
Lacroix's Arithmetic, Smyth's Algebra.
Weekly Exercises in Latin Composition.

2. TERM. MEMORABILIA.
Greek Grammar.
Livy.
Smyth's Algebra.
Eschenburg's Manual; translated by Fiske.
Weekly Exercises in Latin Composition.
Arnold's Greek Prose Composition.

3. TERM. ODYSSEY (OWEN'S EDITION, COMMENCED).
Greek Grammar.
Excerpta Latina. (Paterculus and Quintus Curtius.)
Eschenburg's Manual.
Smyth's Algebra.—Hedge's Logic.
Exercises in Elocution.
Weekly Exercises in Latin Composition.
Arnold's Greek Prose.
Review of the studies of the year.[11]

Lawrence settled in comfortably to a course load steeped in classicism, the principal intellectual commitment of colleges at the time along with Protestant Christianity.

Americans at the time were fascinated by the ancient Greeks and Romans. The nation's founders had looked to the classical past for political and ethical ideals at the end of the eighteenth century, and fifty years later, Chamberlain's professors still believed that anyone who wished to be truly educated needed to be immersed in ancient texts.[12]

As young Lawrence had learned during his year of preparation in his Brewer attic, the language aspect of this study was difficult—but that was the point. It was not meant to be easy.

But learning Latin and Greek was never intended to be simply the study of language; it was a means to enter the wider world of Latin and Greek culture: the study of words became the study of worlds. The ultimate goal was to form in students the "spirit" of the culture of classicism.[13]

The intellectual achievements of the Greek civilization of the fifth century B.C. were presented as an antidote to modern American dangers. Harvard professor Cornelius Conway Felton, in writing about "on becoming Greek," railed against a "self-indulging age" that tolerated "a constant reference to self."[14]

To be sure, Bowdoin's Protestant professors averred that Christianity was superior, but they accepted Greek and Latin authors and their texts as also valuable, written centuries before Christ. Whether graduating aspiring ministers, lawyers, or politicians, Bowdoin's mission was to form the characters of young men who would be ethical Christians and principled American citizens. The school's faculty believed both the classical and Christian traditions were essential to this task.

HAVING MISSED THE fall term, Lawrence knew he would need to work hard in the winter and summer terms to catch up to the other freshmen. His classmates were not the only ones Lawrence would have to try to keep up with. The Bowdoin professors came with impressive reputations.

Professor Parker Cleaveland, one of the best-known members of the faculty, taught chemistry and physics.

Alpheus Spring Packard, one of Chamberlain's favorite professors, taught ancient languages.

Parker Cleaveland, a Harvard graduate, was in his forty-third year of teaching at the college. The ageless Cleaveland taught chemistry, but was best known for his 1816 book *Elementary Treatise on Mineralogy and Geology*, a pioneering study that brought early prominence to the college. The German poet Goethe, fascinated by mineralogy, admired Cleaveland and made him an honorary member of the prestigious Jena Mineralogical Society.[15]

Alpheus Spring Packard was the first alumnus to teach at the college. A handsome man with gold-bowed spectacles when Lawrence was a freshman, he would go on to be at Bowdoin in various capacities for sixty-five years. Packard taught ancient languages. Lawrence took several classes from Packard in his freshman year and became good friends with his son William Alfred. The Packard house would become a second home for young Chamberlain.

Professor William Smyth, an 1822 graduate, began teaching mathematics in 1828. Lawrence took algebra from him in the winter term and found Smyth's lectures dense and difficult to follow. He surely joined other students' laughter in observing the professor walk briskly across campus, his black coat covered with chalk, earning him the nickname Professor "Chalkboard" Smyth.[16]

Smyth also taught Sunday school at First Parish, where he was moderator [lay leader] of the congregation in 1848 and 1849. Smyth was present every Sunday in pew number twelve in the south tran-sept of the sanctuary, the area set aside for Bowdoin faculty and students.[17]

Through Smyth, Chamberlain would be exposed to a strong an-tislavery position for the first time.[18] Smyth's home was a station on the Underground Railroad, where he helped escaped enslaved persons traveling north to Canada. A decade before Chamberlain's arrival, conser-vative Brunswick's concern about Smyth's antislavery stance led to a failed attempt to remove him from his post. In the 1840 presidential election, Smyth was reportedly the only Brunswick resident to vote for the antislavery Liberty Party. Smyth's son would recall that in those years his father was "standing almost alone" as he expressed his antislavery con-victions "with fearless power."[19]

Professor William Smyth taught mathematics at Bowdoin, and Sunday school at First Parish, and was an ardent antislavery advocate.

LAWRENCE WAS PARTICULARLY drawn to Thomas Cogswell Upham, professor of mental and moral phi-losophy, who shared with Smyth an abhorrence of slavery and worried about what the future held for an in-creasingly divided nation.[20] A gradu-ate of Dartmouth and Andover Theological Seminary, Upham was a prolific writer. In 1843 he wrote *Prin-ciples of the Interior or Hidden Life.*[21]

In Upham's classes, and in his book, Lawrence was introduced to a number of Catholic mystics, includ-ing Thomas à Kempis, *The Imitation*

Professor Thomas Cogswell Upham, professor of mental and moral philosophy, authored Principles of the Interior or Hidden Life.

of Christ; William Law, *Spirit of Prayer;* and Francis de Sales, *Introduction to the Devout Life.*[22]

Yet even with his superb work ethic, Lawrence struggled with an affliction that sapped his self-confidence and turned him in upon himself: he stammered.

Stammering, or stuttering as its often called today, is involuntary. Lawrence's stammering came upon him without warning; it forced him to repeat words or prolonged the pronunciation of words. He particularly stammered when pronouncing words beginning with the letters b, p, and t. Unfortunately, the harder he tried not to stammer, the worse it became, often leaving him exhausted and embarrassed.

His problem was especially acute because he grew up in an oral culture in which teachers and textbooks proceeded from the supposition that learning public speaking would be key to successful participation in public life. Large chunks of Chamberlain's early education would have been speaking aloud passages from the Bible, Shakespeare, and Byron.

American colleges at this time typically offered no electives. Much instruction took the form of tutorials—one-on-one teaching between the professor and student. At Bowdoin, oral recitation was the expectation. Rhetorical exercises terrified Lawrence because of his stammering.

The first-year class on elocution held special terror for Lawrence. He stumbled early on when asked to recite the first line of Virgil's *Bucolics:* "Tityre tu patulae recubans sub tegmine fag." ("You, Tityrus, 'neath a broad beech-canopy reclining.") There were those terrible triplets of letters.[23]

He tried deep breathing as he approached one of the abominable words. When that didn't work, he began to skip meetings where he knew public debate would take place, but later called this tactic "humiliating." He considered his struggle with stammering as a student at Bowdoin "one of the miseries of his life."[24]

BUT EVEN STAMMERING was not the greatest of Lawrence's social challenges. He arrived at Bowdoin at a time when rowdiness charac-

terized student behavior across American colleges. Students were
supposed to abide by *The Laws of Bowdoin College:*

> If any student shall be guilty of profaneness, intoxication, or
> dissoluteness; of lying or purloining; of challenging, assault-
> ing, or fighting with any person; or shall sing indecent songs,
> or be indecent in conversation; or shall lead a dissipated life;
> or shall associate with any person of known dissolute charac-
> ter; or shall be guilty of any other violation of good morals; he
> shall be admonished, suspended, dismissed, or expelled.[25]

In addition to these laws, students were not to play cards or any
games of chance, smoke or chew tobacco, or have a gun or pistol in
their room.[26]

Despite these many rules, a committee of the college's trustees
and overseers one year before Chamberlain's enrollment expressed
alarm at the "vices and lack of morals on the part of the students."[27]
The report criticized the hard drinking that sometimes turned dangerous. Wood stacked about the campus to heat the college's buildings disappeared at regular intervals. The previous fall, students
had even burned the main woodshed to the ground.

The residence halls had become the province of the young. Stu-
dents in Winthrop Hall renamed the two ends of their building
"Sodom" and "Gomorrah." A Sodom County Court in Winthrop
Hall regularly handed out judgments against freshmen.[28]

Bowdoin students often arrayed themselves against what they
called the "government"—the administration and faculty of the
college. Student pranks included an annual extravagant funeral
procession each May, replete with printed programs with Latinate
titles. The procession culminated in the burning of books from Professor Smyth's dreaded mathematics classes.[29]

IN THIS RAUCOUS spirit, a group of sophomores decided to "welcome" Lawrence's new class of freshmen. In the fall, they had
hazed Lawrence's roommate, George Hayes, by tying a rope
around his waist and running him to the top of a Bowdoin pine

tree. Left there, with little clothing, he had to use his own devices to get down.[30]

The sophomores targeted Hayes so aggressively because they deemed him a "defiant" freshman. Lawrence presented a meeker demeanor; perhaps that's why his initiation rite was more practical joke than full-on hazing. The sophomores made what they called a "visitation" to his room when he was not present and engineered a "smoke out." Closing the doors and windows, they smoked pipes of peace until, Lawrence recalled, his lamp "looked like a red moon on a foggy night."[31] By not complaining to "the government," Chamberlain passed a different sort of examination, this time graded by his peers.

IN THE MIDST of this boisterous student behavior, Lawrence was determined to live out the Christian beliefs and practices he had learned in Brewer.

If religion played a central role in the founding of American colleges, Bowdoin was an interesting case study. It was started by citizens rather than a denomination; nonetheless, Congregational ministers dominated among the first trustees and overseers, leaving no doubt as to the college's religious moorings.

Bowdoin required Lawrence and his fellow students to attend religious services twice daily. President Woods, as was true of many college presidents, presided at a weekly evening chapel service.[32]

Each Sunday morning, Lawrence attended Brunswick's First Parish Church along with all the Bowdoin students, located directly next to the Bowdoin campus. It cannot be overstated how thoroughly the college and the congregation were interrelated in these years. Lawrence would become deeply involved in the life of the congregation.

The congregation traced its origins to 1735 when residents of Brunswick erected a small Congregational meetinghouse built in the New England Puritan tradition. As the town and congregation grew, in 1806 a second, larger meetinghouse was completed, paid for by residential taxes and used not only for religious but community purposes, as well as some functions of the college. In September 1806, the Bowdoin commencement was held in the new meetinghouse.[33]

When Chamberlain arrived at Bowdoin in 1848, he entered the congregation's third meetinghouse, dedicated two years earlier. A striking example of Gothic Revival architecture, it was built of wood, with a buttressed tower, doors with lancet-arched openings, and vertical board-and-batten paneling. The interior—timber, plastering, and panels—was all oak, and the building was topped with a beautiful slender spire. Members exulted that it could be seen for many miles across the region. The building, partially paid for by funds from the college, accommodated one thousand people in a town of fewer than four thousand residents.[34]

Though the beautiful wood sanctuary of First Parish has received acclaim through the years, it initially sparked some controversy. The building was designed by noted American architect Richard Upjohn. During his lifetime, Upjohn would design nearly one hun-

First Parish, a handsome church of Gothic Revival architecture, was dedicated in 1846, two years before Chamberlain arrived as a student.

dred churches, most of them Episcopal churches. He would be best remembered as the architect of Trinity Church on Wall Street in New York.

When the plans for the new church were made public, critics charged that First Parish was departing from the centuries-old architecture of New England meetinghouses. What's more, the new church would be built in the form of a cross. "Popery," critics cried. An anonymous writer named "Pilgrim" complained to *The Boston Recorder,* the leading periodical of the New England Congregational churches, that a Bowdoin student would now have to "'doff his cap' and 'practice genuflections' on pain of expulsion, every time he passes the venerable sign of the Cross."[35]

Rev. George E. Adams, an excellent preacher, was in his nineteenth year as minister of First Parish when Chamberlain arrived as a student at Bowdoin in 1848.

The architectural uproar quickly faded, and on Sundays, Chamberlain would listen to the preaching of the Reverend George E. Adams. The Congregational minister had been called to the congregation in 1829 at only twenty-eight years old. A graduate of Yale and Andover Theological Seminary, he came to Brunswick from Bangor Theological Seminary, where he served as professor of biblical literature and sacred rhetoric.[36]

Prior to Adams, the Brunswick church had endured years of short, ineffective ministries, so both town and gown appreciated the leadership of the handsome, well-read Adams. He was an energetic preacher; a contemporary spoke appreciatively of his "reserved fund of humor." Now in his twentieth year leading the congregation, he was an important and influential member of the Brunswick community and also served as an overseer of Bowdoin.[37]

Attendance by Bowdoin students at First Parish on Sunday morning was required; monitors were even placed to "take attendance." Chamberlain would have seen plenty of disruptive behavior from students. In a favorite tactic, boys in the front row put their feet up on the railing, a practice that, over the years, came to be called "Dr. Adams Boot & Shoe Display."[38]

All around him, fellow students were questioning—if not fully rebelling—against the exacting religious expectations at Bowdoin. Chamberlain's letters from this period, by contrast, give no evidence of any restlessness or rebellion.

In addition to the required religious services, Lawrence embraced a variety of voluntary religious activities and organizations. He attended a Thursday evening Bible study and a Saturday evening "Prayer Circle." In the summer term, Chamberlain walked two miles on Sunday afternoons to teach Sunday school in a yellow schoolhouse.[39]

He also joined the Praying Society, a meeting that convened after the first bell on Sunday morning and before Sunday church services in town. Founded in 1815, it was modeled after similar societies at Harvard, Brown, Yale, Princeton, Dartmouth, Williams, and Amherst. To join, a new member needed to give "charitable evidence that he is a real Christian" and be voted in by all the members. The society aimed to bring students without regard to their denomination: there were Congregationalists, Baptists, Methodists, and Presbyterians.[40]

The society supported the emerging modern missionary movement, and a number of its members volunteered for the mission field. This emphasis surely appealed to Lawrence, given that he'd contemplated becoming a missionary.[41]

But the primary focus of the Praying Society was on religious life at Bowdoin. Both Brunswick and Bowdoin were caught up in the winds of the Second Great Awakening, a wave of revivals accompanied by social reform emphasizing abolition and temperance, which swept through New England in the 1840s. Lawrence and students in the Praying Society took their places as leaders in meetings both on campus and at Brunswick's First Parish Church.[42]

IN MAY 1848, Lawrence took stock of his first term at Bowdoin in a letter to a minister friend: "I really think I have never been so faithful to myself and my duty since I have been at college."[43]

He mentioned to his friend that, in addition to the Bible and Greek text, Professor Upham's *Principles of the Interior or Hidden Life* was a central pillar of his intellectual and spiritual development. In it, Upham presented principles by which followers of Christ can move toward "a greatly advanced state of religious feeling."[44] Upham's principles included "the life of the soul, incorporated into the life of Christ;" and "the hidden life of religion is not identical with the place and formalities and observances of religion."[45]

Chamberlain's faith wasn't something he felt the need to hide. He has not left behind a significant record of his friendships, but to his minister correspondent he wrote, "My classmates seem to understand me now." After a few months, they knew that if they smuggled in a cask of wine, Lawrence would not help drink it. At his home in Brewer, he occasionally joined his parents in enjoying a glass of cider. But in the very boistrous environment of Bowdoin, he decided that, during college, he would abstain from alcohol "without putting on superior airs."[46] "If there is to be a class cut or *spree*, 'O! No! Chamberlain won't go into it.' " He concluded, "They seem to understand my duty pretty well. I have found myself sometimes alone, but all came out right."[47]

IN AUGUST 1848, freshmen examinations were held to test all that students had learned during the previous year. Lawrence studied particularly hard because the exams would cover the whole of the year, including the fall term that he missed while preparing for the entrance exam. His shortcomings were most severe in Professor Smyth's mathematics courses, so he determined to put in all-night study sessions to make up for them.[48]

He approached the exams with mixed emotions: confidence because he had put in all the preparation he could, nervousness because would it be enough?

But again, he passed. He mused, "The laggard was abreast of his class."[49]

After so much physical, mental, and emotional stress, the three-week vacation and reunion with family and friends in Brewer must have passed in the blink of an eye.

. . .

IN SEPTEMBER 1848, Chamberlain returned to Brunswick and Bowdoin for his second year. The railroad had arrived in June, offering the town a crucial link to Boston, New England's primary city. What had previously been a three-day carriage trip was now reduced to six hours by rail. Two years later, the Kennebec and Portland Railroad would finish a line connecting Portland, Brunswick, and Augusta, the state capital.

Chamberlain eagerly entered into the fixed curriculum of his sophomore year:

SOPHOMORE CLASS.

1. TERM. ODYSSEY, CONTINUED.
Horace (Odes.)
Legendre's Geometry.
French Language, (Guizot's History of European
    Civilization)
Newman's Rhetoric

2. TERM. ELECTRA OF SOPHOCLES COMMENCED.
Horace, (Satires and Epistles)—Terrence, (Andria.)
Smyth's Trigonometry.
Cam. Math., (Heights and Distances, Surveying, and
    Navigation.)
French Language. (Guizot continued, and Moliere.)

3. TERM. ELECTRA, FINISHED.
Cam. Math., (Projections, Leveling.)
Smyth's Application of Algebra to Geometry.
French language, (Moliere.)
Review of the studies of the year.[50]

In his second year Lawrence began his love affair with languages. He had learned Greek and Latin for the college entrance exams, but

now he immersed himself enthusiastically in French, a newer offering at Bowdoin. During the college's growth spurt in the 1820s and
1830s, various changes had been proposed to the curriculum. The
college adopted only one: the introduction of modern languages.[51]

In 1829, a recent graduate, Henry Wadsworth Longfellow, destined to become one of America's great poets, returned to his alma
mater from Europe to launch the new course. He taught at Bowdoin until 1835 when he accepted an appointment at Harvard, but
the modern language program he left behind flourished.

Daniel Raynes Goodwin, an 1832 Bowdoin graduate, was offered
Longfellow's position. Before he assumed the role, the college sent
him to Europe for two years so that he could immerse himself in
French.[52]

There is nothing like a great professor to encourage a student.
Goodwin won over students, including Lawrence, with his teaching
and approachability. Chamberlain would remember Goodwin fondly:
"French under Professor Goodwin was something altogether new."
He emphasized philology and helped Lawrence understand the relation of French to Latin, so students began to be able to visualize the
structure and development of languages. Lawrence enthused, "He
did more than 'hear' lessons, or even to teach; he broadened; he inspired; he integrated knowledge, and animated it, vitalized it."[53]

Goodwin, who also served as librarian of the college, gave Lawrence his first academic honor at Bowdoin, appointing the young
student one of his assistant librarians. The selection signified a
"high rank" in the department of modern languages. It also brought
with it invitations to socialize with Goodwin and his family in their
home.

Most importantly, the library helped expand Lawrence's reading
habits. The Bowdoin Library shared the peculiarity of nineteenth-
century college libraries in that it opened to students only one day
a week. Lawrence took advantage of the expanded library privileges
his assistantship carried.

Lawrence later admitted that reading "was a department too
much neglected in [his] boyhood." The restrictive notions present
in his family, especially concerning novels, had not left much room
for reading "that was interesting."[54]

Before entering Bowdoin, he had wanted to read James Fenimore Cooper's *The Deerslayer,* the story of Natty Bumppo, a young frontiersman in early-eighteenth-century New York, in the Leather-stocking Tales. His parents denied his request; they were uneasy with the title.[55]

Now free to follow his reading interests wherever they led him, Lawrence joined the Peucinian Society. This literary society, orga-nized for "the attainment in habits of discussion and elocution," sponsored fortnightly disputations on statesmanship, political thought, and broader cultural issues. Wishing to distinguish them-selves from other college literary societies, the Bowdoin society took the name Peucinian believing the Greek word for "pine-covered" would claim a local distinctiveness.[56]

In addition to enjoying its debates, Lawrence joined the society because of its wide catalog of books. By his sophomore year Law-rence regularly ventured beyond the Bowdoin curriculum's set of required texts, but the holdings of college libraries reflected the tastes of donors more than the intellectual interests of either the faculty or the students.[57]

So, the Peucinian Society and its rival, the Athenian Society, acted as lending libraries for student members who wished to ex-pand their reading palates. Lawrence and the other members paid regular dues, and additionally, some members purchased and do-nated books to the society's library. A Bowdoin librarian at the end of the nineteenth century observed of the societies, "The amounts contributed by undergraduates for the purchase of books were not infrequently double that appropriated by the Boards for the in-crease of the college library."[58]

IT WAS ALSO during his sophomore year that Chamberlain finally found help with his stammering. Dr. Packard, the professor of an-cient languages, offered to work with him privately. Under Pack-ard's guidance, Chamberlain did advance reconnaissance on difficult texts. Packard also told Chamberlain that the ancient Spar-tans, encountering the same problem, would use a form of singing to get through hard passages. Chamberlain, remembering his "order for life"—"Do it! That's how!"—pushed relentlessly forward, Spartan-like in conquering his persistent problem.[59]

.　.　.

CHAMBERLAIN PUSHED FORWARD socially as well. In his sophomore year, classmates decided to give him a new name. Perhaps wanting to pierce his reserve, they dubbed him the less formal "Jack." He came to like the name, for it symbolized acceptance by his peers.[60]

In the early summer, Bowdoin held the aptly named Class Tree Day, during which each of the four classes was to plant a tree to enhance the campus. Lawrence joined a group of freshmen who decided to turn the assignment into a day of mischief.

They traveled to Lisbon, a town ten miles away, where they would not be known. They dug up a tree in broad daylight and transported it in a two-horse wagon by a circuitous route back to the campus, boisterously drinking alcohol all along the way.

Back at Bowdoin, the revelers planted their purloined tree on the campus at night. But their antics awakened several members of the faculty who reported the affair to President Woods.[61]

Early the next morning, the "summoning" began for the culprits, one by one. Around noon, Lawrence's turn arrived. While Lawrence walked with foreboding to the president's home, the other boys assembled in one of their rooms, nervous about what Lawrence might reveal.[62]

The president began the conversation: "We cannot believe you had anything to do with the disgraceful occurrences on that occasion." By now, Lawrence had earned a reputation as both a good student and an upright young man.

Chamberlain replied that he did not participate in the drinking.

The president told Chamberlain that during the morning interviews he had not been able to identify the guilty parties. "It now becomes necessary for you to discover them."

He replied, "I have conscientious scruples against that, sir."[63]

President Woods was having none of it. "You will be suspended from the college at once."

Chamberlain told Woods he was willing to take punishment for disobeying the laws of the college but would not give the president information about his fellow students. "It makes a boy an informer."

When Woods replied that his response came from a false sense of honor, Chamberlain replied that, to the contrary, the college ought to instill a sense of confidence and trust among students.

He repeated that he was ready to accept whatever punishment the college meted out, even if that meant expulsion. In words that must have shocked the president, he insisted that, in this situation, his father would be proud to have him come home and not return.[64]

Chamberlain returned to the room where his classmates waited anxiously.

"I am going home, boys."

Stunned, someone cried out, "No you are not." As others joined in, the guilty students quickly decided to go to the president's house. "This shan't come on Jack."

The president, upon receiving the boys, reconsidered. He decided to give each boy only a reprimand.

The events of Class Tree Day turned out to be a decisive turning point in Chamberlain's experience at Bowdoin. His decision not to inform on his friends brought him full acceptance from his classmates. His bravery in invoking "conscientious scruples" before the president of the college laid a foundation for future yet unknown courageous actions. If loyalty had been a value in Bowdoin's curriculum of classicism, Lawrence put it into practice in the midst of student hijinks.

BY THE CONCLUSION of his second year, the shy farm boy had begun to find his distinctive voice. He had achieved academic success. He was on the road to conquering his stammering. He had kept his religious faith commitments in a challenging college environment. He was developing both intellectual and spiritual discipline while being awakened to a larger world.

He looked forward to a "triumphant home-returning; great welcome and great rest."[65] But his time back home in Brewer would not turn out as he expected.

THREE

"Be Virtuous"

Virtue is a beauty of the mind.
—JONATHAN EDWARDS, *The Nature of True Virtue,* 1765

Jonathan Edwards

L AWRENCE FOUND HIMSELF UNUSUALLY EXHAUSTED WHEN HE arrived back in Brewer in August 1849 for a short holiday after his second year at Bowdoin. He wasn't up for riding his favorite mare, or taking out the family boat, or visiting old friends. In fact, by his twenty-first birthday on September 8, he was running a consistently high fever and confined to his bed. His birthday celebration was, in his words, "mournful."[1]

The nature of his illness perplexed the Chamberlains' family doctor. He advised bed rest and ordered cold compresses to try to bring down the fever. Day after day, Lawrence's mother and sister, Sae, tried to nurse him back to health. But the sickness persisted, and his family began to fear for his life.

In the first weeks of 1850, panicked about her eldest son's continued ailment, Sarah dismissed the doctor. She conferred with a homeopath, knowing full well that her decision left her open to ridicule from neighbors. Alternative medicine was rising in popularity in the early nineteenth century, and the homeopathic doctor, prescribing much smaller doses of medicine than the family doctor, instead emphasized a routine of rest, nourishment, and exercise.[2]

Whether from the new treatment or sheer chance, Lawrence recalled that "by some mysterious metempsychosis" his health began to return that winter. He became convinced his mother's "old Huguenot hilarity" played a large part in his healing. He wrote later, "the patient learned patience."[3]

FACING PAGE: *Joshua Lawrence Chamberlain as a student at Bowdoin College*

But with his recovery slow, Lawrence made the difficult decision to forego the entire 1849–1850 academic year. If enjoying reading and exercise, he worried about falling once again behind his Bowdoin classmates.

IN SEPTEMBER 1850, healthy at last, Lawrence returned to a very different college from the one he'd left twelve months before.

Bowdoin had become riveted by a debate taking place six hundred miles to the south, in the nation's capital. In January 1850,

Kentucky Senator Henry Clay had begun cobbling together a set of proposals intended to tamp down the increasing tensions between North and South. "Old Harry," as the senator was fondly dubbed, seventy-two years old and still standing a reedy six feet plus, introduced eight resolutions to achieve "an amiable arrangement of all questions in controversy between the free and slave states, growing out of slavery." Clay hoped his resolutions would encourage "a great national scheme of compromise and harmony."[4]

Senator Henry Clay, nicknamed "The Great Compromiser," was the architect of the Compromise of 1850.

Clay brokered the compromise in the Senate with Stephen A. Douglas, an up-and-coming Democratic senator from the frontier state of Illinois. At thirty-six, Douglas was half Clay's age and a full foot shorter, yet the young man communicated strength.

The seventh resolution, which aimed to interrupt the Underground Railroad, was one of the most contentious parts of the bill.[5] It fortified the 1793 Fugitive Slave Act by requiring that all escaped slaves be returned to their Southern owners upon capture. Furthermore, it mandated that both public officials and ordinary citizens in northern free states cooperate with the law. Anyone found to be helping slaves could be imprisoned for six months and fined one thousand dollars.

Southern legislators demanded the inclusion of the act if they were to sign on to the compromise; Northern legislators critiqued it as an overstepping of federal authority. Abolitionists quickly called it "the Bloodhound Act," for it would permit white slave owners to hunt down and recapture black runaway slaves in places as far away as Maine.[6]

Despite the debate, the Compromise of 1850 passed on September 18, 1850, just as Chamberlain was returning to college. Among the effects: it admitted California as a free state, set up the organization of Utah and New Mexico, where slavery would be decided by popular vote, abolished the slave trade in the District of Columbia, and passed the new Fugitive Slave Act.

FOR LAWRENCE AND his fellow students, the debates in Washington over the Compromise of 1850 were all-consuming. These were more important political and ethical questions than any they'd encountered before. Many passionate young voices on campus now joined Professor Smyth in speaking out against slavery.

Maine's conservative political climate and geographic isolation had kept the issue from igniting earlier. William Lloyd Garrison was the founder of *The Liberator*, a weekly abolitionist magazine. In its initial issue on January 1, 1831, Garrison blared, "I am aware that many object to the severity of my language, but is there not cause for severity? I *will* be as harsh as truth, and as uncompromising as justice."[7] Garrison came to Maine on a speaking tour in the summer and fall of 1832. Twenty-six years old, renouncing mainstream American politics, Garrison failed to attract sizeable audiences as he traveled from Portland to Bangor.[8]

William Lloyd Garrison

Many in Maine mistrusted abolitionists like Garrison as divisive radicals. The state tilted strongly Democratic, a party that stood in opposition to mounting antislavery advocacy. Mainers voted for Andrew Jackson in 1828 and 1832 and Martin Van Buren in 1836. While Whig candidate William Henry Harrison did eke out a win over Van Buren in 1840, Democrat James K. Polk in 1844 and Lewis Cass in 1848 carried Maine handily.[9]

Chamberlain's father voted Democratic. The senior Chamberlain had long admired South Carolina Senator John C. Calhoun and his states' rights viewpoint.[10] Young Lawrence's political views were not yet formed, but his third year at Bowdoin would start to mold them.

THE FEW MAINERS who did publicly call themselves abolitionists were mostly ministers. Yet these ministers struggled to enlist their churches in support of local and national antislavery societies. In 1847, and again in 1849, Congregationalist clergy asked their General Conference of Maine to take a stand against slavery and to stop any correspondence with slaveholders. The Conference answered in 1850, expressing their intention to remain in communion with slaveholders: "We must seek peace, not disunity. Let us not weaken our influence on this important subject by sending our discordant voices in relation to it."[11]

Into this atmosphere Bowdoin welcomed its newest member of the faculty in the fall of 1850. Calvin Ellis Stowe, who graduated first in Bowdoin's class of 1824, and known to his fellow students as "witty, brilliant, popular," was returning to his alma mater as the Collins Professor of Natural and Revealed Religion after seventeen years as professor of sacred literature at Lane Theological Seminary in Cincinnati.

"Everybody seemed to listen to him with eagerness and wonderment." Bowdoin student and future Civil War hero Oliver Otis Howard expressed his sentiment in a letter to his mother. "I couldn't comprehend how a man in the short space of thirty years could lay in such an immense store of knowledge."[12]

Stowe's wife, Harriet Beecher Stowe, arrived in Brunswick ahead of her husband to ready their new home at 63 Federal Street, which they rented for $125 a year. Calvin Stowe had shared this same house with Henry Wadsworth Longfellow during their student years.[13]

Mrs. Stowe, a small woman with gray-blue eyes, was six months pregnant with the couple's seventh child and still grieving the death of their infant son, Charley, from cholera a year earlier.

Seven years earlier, she had published *The May Flower, and Miscellaneous Writings,* a collection of stories she had published in magazines including *Lady's Book* and *The New-York Evangelist.*[14] Uneven in quality, in a field still dominated by male prose she was finding her female voice. Thus, in the essay "Frankness," in which she identified herself as simply "By a Lady." She told her audience, "Now, if you suppose that this is the beginning of a sermon or Fourth of July oration, you are very mistaken, though, I must confess, it hath rather an uncertain sound."[15]

Having just come from Cincinnati and the Ohio River—the dividing line between the free and slave states—where she had heard many wrenching stories from fugitives, she was searching for a more certain sound. She felt she had to write about this human tragedy and began to carve out an hour or two a day to do so at her kitchen table.

Alumnus Calvin Stowe returned to Bowdoin to teach Natural and Revealed Religion in 1850.

Harriet Beecher Stowe began writing Uncle Tom's Cabin *on the kitchen table of her home in Brunswick.*

That winter, the new Fugitive Slave Act had begun to turn even antislavery moderates across the North into radicals. They protested the "odious" law that saw "slave catchers" arriving in Northern cities, claiming the legal right of search, seizure, and return of fugitives to the South and slavery. While many New Englanders had not paid much attention to Southern slavery previously, as its effects pressed closer to home, they became incensed over what they saw as an attack upon the sanctity of the American home.[16]

One of Chamberlain's favorite teachers, Professor Upham, was one such moderate; he defended the fugitive law in an argument at Stowe's tea table, telling her he did not like the law, but that, in his eyes, a law is a law, and he could not disobey it.[17]

But Upham changed his mind when he came home the very next day to find a young slave at his door asking for help. Experience trumps ideas. The professor offered him food and provisions so that the fugitive could make his way north to Canada.[18]

WITH SUNDAY WORSHIP obligatory for Bowdoin students, Chamberlain would have been present at Brunswick's First Parish on March 2, 1851, when Stowe received an unexpected inspiration. She had just returned to pew twenty-three after receiving communion when she saw a vision "like the unrolling of a picture" of a black man being beaten to death by a white man. The vision was so vivid that she felt like crying aloud.[19]

She rushed home and scribbled down all its details.

In previous months, Stowe had received several letters from Gamaliel Bailey, a reporter soliciting articles for *The National Era,* the antislavery paper he had founded in Washington in 1847.[20]

"I feel now that the time has come when even a woman or a child who can speak a word for freedom and humanity is bound to speak," Stowe replied to Bailey one week after her vision.[21]

She titled her first article "Uncle Tom's Cabin." *The National Era* published it on June 5, 1851. It would be serialized in forty weekly installments.

As she continued writing, Stowe invited a small group of faculty and students into her home on Saturday evenings to discuss her chapters as she wrote them. She read excerpts and encouraged discussion and debate. Lawrence counted himself fortunate to be one of the students welcomed into her circle.[22] Of his time at Bowdoin, he recalled that the "chief of privileges was the 'Saturday Evenings' at Mrs. Stowe's witnessing the creation of 'Uncle Tom's Cabin,'" which caused Chamberlain to viscerally confront the attitudes and actions of the South toward slavery for the first time, and begin to imagine a moral problem beyond the boundaries of Maine.

UNCLE TOM'S CABIN;

OR,

LIFE AMONG THE LOWLY.

BY

HARRIET BEECHER STOWE.

VOL. I.

ONE HUNDRED AND FIFTH THOUSAND.

BOSTON:
JOHN P. JEWETT & COMPANY
CLEVELAND, OHIO:
JEWETT, PROCTOR & WORTHINGTON.
1852.

Title page of Harriet Beecher Stowe's bestselling
Uncle Tom's Cabin

Yet the story of young Lawrence's fascination with this newly arrived author, whose prose so vividly described the pain inflicted upon enslaved African Americans, could go only so far. In the winter of 1850–1851, President Woods's endorsement of the Compromise of 1850 would certainly have been the dominant sentiment on the Bowdoin campus. Harriet Stowe was a faculty wife and an unknown writer; neither she nor her appreciative Saturday evening guests could have imagined the enormous success that awaited the words she read in front of the fire. Published in book form ten months later by Boston's John P. Jewett & Company, *Uncle Tom's Cabin* sold ten thousand copies within the first week. Word of the book spread quickly; it would sell three hundred thousand copies by the conclusion of the first year.[23]

EVEN AS THE slavery debate consumed the campus, much of Lawrence's focus was academic, especially as he was now one year behind his original entering class.

Seeing himself as a man affiliated with two classes, Chamberlain, with a dry sense of humor, compared himself to the biblical Jacob who married both Leah and Rachel.[24]

JUNIOR CLASS

TERM. SATIRES OF JUVENAL.
German, (Follen's German Reader,)—or Greek.
(Demosthenes de Corona.)
Mechanics.

TERM. CALCULUS.
Electricity—Magnetism—Optics.
German (Schiller's William Tell, or Fouque's Undine).
Greek. (Demosthenes finished. The Antigone.)
Tacitus, (Germania and Agricola.)
Spanish Language.

TERM. GREEK, (GORGIAS).
German (Goethe's Faust.)
Moral Philosophy.
Vattel's Law of Nations—Spanish Language.
Review of the studies of the year.[25]

In his junior year, Chamberlain continued to follow Bowdoin's classical curriculum. In Latin, he read the Roman poet Juvenal, known for his satirical poems. In Greek, he recited the orations of the fourth century B.C. statesman Demosthenes. He found the essays of Tacitus, Roman historian and politician, about the lands, tribes, and leaders of Britannia most to his liking.

He also added several more languages to his repertoire. He studied German until he could read Goethe's *Faust* in the original. More and more confident with every growing year, he called his study of German "absolutely successful."[26]

If two modern languages were not enough, in the second term of his junior year he began the study of his fifth language: Spanish. In his very first reading lesson, he found himself absorbed by this sentence: *"Todo en este territorio clasico respira historia; todo requerda los tiempos de la caballeria, y las glorias pasadas de la Antigua Espania."* "Everything in this classic territory breathes history; all remember the times of the cavalry, and the past glories of Ancient Spain." He was mesmerized by "the remarkable quality of sonorousness in the Spanish language even in the plainest prose."[27]

As Chamberlain learned German, he appreciated the writings of Johann Wolfgang von Goethe.

In the first term of his senior year, Chamberlain also began to study Italian with Professor Goodwin (bringing his languages up to six). Under the "guidance" of Goodwin, Chamberlain read Dante, poet of the late Middle Ages, and Torquato Tasso, a sixteenth-century Italian poet.[28]

Chamberlain gave Professor Goodwin much credit for his linguistic achievements, particularly for teaching him "how to think into a thing, as well as to think it out."[29] By this he meant that, rather than simply focusing on memorization, he would from now on try to get inside the language's very spirit and culture.

His hard work paid off. Lawrence was honored with academic awards in French and German. He also won college prizes in both oratory and composition. In mathematics and astronomy, subjects that had unsettled him in his first two years, the faculty requested that he offer problems for the junior and senior exams.[30]

LAWRENCE WAS RECOGNIZED outside the classroom as well. The members of the Praying Society elected him president. He was invited to become organist for the Lockwood Musical Society, responsible for music in the college chapel. He had come a long way from his cornstalk bass viol. "Fingering the Chapel organ" in the beautiful new chapel expanded his octaves and became an important way for Lawrence to celebrate his Christian faith. Recognizing the young man's talent, President Woods sent him to Boston to study methods of conducting antiphonal chants based on the Psalms for the Sunday services.[31]

In his final year, Professor Cleaveland tapped him to become his special assistant in chemistry and physics. However, it meant "it would not do to be out late nights" for he had to arrive at 5 A.M. to see that all the elements Cleaveland would need would be ready for his 6 A.M. lecture. He called this selection a "dubious distinction" for he knew that Professor Cleaveland's temper meant that this "service was a somewhat anxious one."[32]

Yet Chamberlain's 1851 award for declamation may have been the most gratifying recognition of all. The thirty-dollar prize ($1,160 today), which he shared with another student, was a signpost of how far he had progressed in overcoming his stuttering.

CHAMBERLAIN CONTINUED TO expand the range of his reading both in and out of the classroom. To that end, he joined the Round

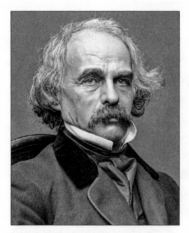

The novels of Bowdoin alumnus Nathaniel Hawthorne expanded the breadth of Chamberlain's reading.

Table, a circle of young men and women who met fortnightly in various Brunswick homes to discuss different readings.[33] Lawrence had read John Bunyan's *The Pilgrim's Progress,* a defining book when growing up, but now he discovered books a world apart from the Protestant moral classic. Among them was Nathaniel Hawthorne's recently published *The House of the Seven Gables.*[34] One of Bowdoin's own, a graduate in the famous class of 1825 that included Longfellow, Hawthorne deftly wove the story of a New England family with themes of guilt, reprisal, and atonement. Hawthorne's accusation that Puritanism was intolerant made it the kind of novel Chamberlain would have been forbidden to read by his family.

Chamberlain also fell in love with the poetry of Lord Byron, the most flamboyant of the English Romantic poets. In his poetry he encountered the paradox of romanticism: secret guilt, melancholy, and defiance, a champion of liberty in words and deeds, the poet finally giving his life in the Greek war for independence.

Chamberlain was attracted to the romantic poetry of Lord Byron.

> *Oh, God! It is a fearful thing*
> *To see the human soul take wing*
> *In any shape, in any mood.*[35]

Chamberlain's expanding literary horizons are reflected in his surviving assignments, which are marked by a highly imaginative prose style. These writings allow us to see the lively emotions that infused his writing.

In his essay "The Monomaniac," he wrote about the initial encounter between a physician and a potentially mad patient, offering a taste of his energetic and creative language:

> As I surveyed this strange scene dumb with astonishment, his eye caught mine in a look of unutterable agony. I could endure it no longer. Dropping at once my surgical instruments, and the dignity of a physician, I sunk to the floor in convulsions of laughter.[36]

Lawrence's often florid writing style was common to much of nineteenth-century writing. Byron's poetry may have influenced his sentimental tone. Yet it is also possible that Lawrence's prose allowed him to give voice to deep feelings from within. Still struggling with stammering, he began to write expressively what he found difficult to say orally.

In "Easter Morning," an undated essay likely written in Chamberlain's senior year, after he had begun the study of Hebrew, his seventh language, with Professor Stowe, he demonstrated that his thinking could be analytical as well as creative. He employed his language skills to explore the Hebrew roots of the word "Easter," as well as its roots in German mythology. This analysis is more radical than it might appear, growing up as Lawrence did within the circle of orthodox Christianity. It shows how far the young man had traveled intellectually in his four years at Bowdoin. "Let no one think slightingly of this Easter custom as 'drawn from' or allied to, old heathen customs; for these speak the cry of the great human soul."[37] In this essay, Chamberlain was able to balance the wider world of romantic thought with an affirmation of Christian belief.

SENIOR CLASS.

I. TERM
Paley's Evidences—Guizot's Hist. of Civilization
Upham's Mental Philosophy

II. TERM. CHEMISTRY
Butler's Analogy.—Guizot's Hist. of Civilization
Mental Philosophy, continued.
Hebrew and Italian Languages.

III. TERM
Wayland's Moral Science.
Upham's Treatise on the Will.
Hebrew and Italian, continued.
Review of the studies of the year.[38]

Lawrence's political mind was sharpening as well. In his senior year he wrote an essay on "Despotisms of Modern Europe." With refugees from the failed 1848 European revolutions streaming into the United States, the issue of the viability of democracies had become a vigorous topic of debate.

As the aggressive rhetoric between North and South grew louder, he understood that the dashed European hopes held up a frightening mirror to the fragility of American democracy. In his essay, Lawrence observed that "instead of being the representatives of the nation, entrusted with its obligations, and invested with its rights, the sovereign becomes the oppressor. The people have no voice."

Lawrence worried that a democratically elected American leader could become the oppressor that Europeans were fleeing.

"BE VIRTUOUS AND you will be happy" was the mandate at the top of Bowdoin's copybooks wherein Lawrence practiced his handwriting.[39]

The concept of "virtue," or being "virtuous," permeated philosophical and religious thought in eighteenth- and nineteenth-century America. For Chamberlain, and many young men of his New England generation, Jonathan Edwards, the eighteenth-century Calvinist theologian of the first Great Awakening, remained an important moral guide. A century earlier, at only twenty-three, the same age Chamberlain would be at graduation, the young Con-

gregational minister started a notebook he titled "The Mind." In this notebook, he reflected on the relationship of virtue to that which is excellent and good.[40]

Decades later, the brilliant Edwards was elected president of the College of New Jersey—what became Princeton. He died from smallpox only months after assuming office. After his death, found among his writings was *The Nature of True Virtue*. In it, the most philosophical of his writings, Edwards wrote, "Virtue is a beauty of the mind."[41]

Jonathan Edwards, theologian of the eighteenth-century Great Awakening, focused on the meaning of virtue.

Lawrence agreed with Edwards that however excellent academic achievements may be, they are never an end in themselves. At the conclusion of four years, Lawrence had begun to reach for something more. Through his own personal struggles with stammering, socialization, and expressions of faith, and through the intimate discussions about the evils of slavery at Harriet Beecher Stowe's home, his youthful naivete had begun to wear off.

As graduation approached, Lawrence received notification that he would be one of three students selected to deliver an oration at commencement.

When Chamberlain began his freshman year at Bowdoin, he suffered from what he called "a natural timidity of self-assertion."[42] After his upbringing in the small sphere of Brewer, Chamberlain welcomed the influence of Bowdoin's learned faculty and student friendships, which stretched him in many ways: his mental universe expanded, his intellectual curiosity quickened, his self-confidence mounted, and his emotional intelligence grew. At the end of his time at college, he had become an undisputed leader.

September 1, 1852, Bowdoin's graduation day, coincided with the fiftieth anniversary of the first classes offered at the college. A larger than usual crowd gathered for this special commemorative occasion, including three surviving members of the first class, and luminaries like Hawthorne, Longfellow, and Franklin Pierce, the Democratic presidential candidate, all members of the famous class of 1825.

Lawrence chose as his theme "The Last Gladiatorial Show at Rome." After four years at Bowdoin struggling to overcome his stammering, he had mastered the art of public speaking.

Still, as he rose to speak at the commencement in the First Parish Church, nerves took over. Whether it was the momentousness of the occasion or the faces of dignitaries before him, Lawrence had not gone far into his remarks when he suddenly stopped. He struggled to find the text, began pacing the stage, and almost fainted.[43] Finally, "grasping some evidently extemporaneous and strangely far-fetched phrases" he strove on. In what should have been the glorious conclusion of a successful student career at Bowdoin, the gladiator toppled in front of family, faculty, and classmates. Years later, he could still clearly recall his total embarrassment: he "delivered his conclusion straight from the shoulder like those who are determined to die early."[44]

. . .

ALL WAS NOT lost. Sometime before his stumbling at commencement, Lawrence had made a decision about the next chapter in his life. He respected the opinion of his father, who wanted him to attend West Point and pursue a military career, and his mother, who wished for him to pursue the vocation of minister or missionary and attend Bangor Theological Seminary. Pleased with what he had been able to achieve in four years at Bowdoin College, with high hopes he prepared to spend the next three years at Bangor Theological Seminary to prepare for some yet-to-be-determined form of Christian ministry.

FOUR

Fanny

It may seem foolish in me to tell you again that I love my darling
more and more every day—but that is becoming so much more true
every day that it is really new.

—JOSHUA LAWRENCE CHAMBERLAIN TO
FRANCES CAROLINE (FANNY) ADAMS, SPRING 1851

Joshua L Chamberlain

Yours is a true life . . . a thing of intensity and depth.

—FANNY ADAMS TO JOSHUA LAWRENCE CHAMBERLAIN, JULY 16, 1851

Miss Frances C. Adams,

EVERYONE CALLED HER FANNY. IN THE FALL OF 1850, UPON HIS
return to Bowdoin following his medical leave, Lawrence accepted an invitation to lead Brunswick's First Parish choir. His eyes

were supposed to be directed toward the singers, but they soon drifted toward the brown-haired young woman playing the organ.

FRANCES CAROLINE ADAMS was born to Ashur Adams and his third wife, Amelia Wyllys Adams, on August 12, 1825. At age fifty, Adams was old enough to be his seventh child's grandfather. The family lived in Jamaica Plain, then a rural area just outside Boston. Adams was proud to be a distant cousin of the current American president, John Quincy Adams. Despite such illustrious connections, Adams struggled with ill health, and his career as a banker was floundering.[1]

When Fanny reached the age of four, her father decided to send his small daughter to live with his much younger cousin, the Rev. George Adams, the minister at First Parish in Brunswick. In the nineteenth century, this kind of arrangement was not unusual for large families with many mouths to feed. George and Sarah Adams, in their twenties and childless, welcomed the girl into their home. Fanny soon called her adoptive parents Father and Mother.[2]

The Adamses also adopted another girl about Fanny's age: Anna Davis, granddaughter of Dr. John Delamater, a member of Bowdoin's medical school faculty. The girls would grow up as sisters.

The Adamses loved and indulged their adopted children. Fanny expressed early interest in literature, poetry, and art, and when her parents observed her special aptitude in music, George arranged organ lessons for her. But alongside her creativity and intelligence, she struggled with what was then called melancholy—bouts of depression. She spoke of longing to stay connected to her birth family. She also showed signs of an eye condition endemic in her family, an illness that caused irritation and swelling and contributed to her frequent headaches.[3]

Fanny's high school assignments revealed her spirited wit. For one, her teacher, Mr. Alfred Pike, asked the students to compose a paper using verbs ending in "fy." Knowing that Pike did not entirely approve of her humor, she wrote: "This is to certify, notify, exemplify, testify, and signify my obedient disposition; and I hope that it will gratify, satisfy, beautify, and edify my teacher, and pacify, modify, and nullify his feelings of dissatisfaction toward me . . . Please do not exclaim 'O fie!' when reading this paper."[4] Young Fanny was smart and she knew it.

A slender, pretty young woman with dark eyes, Fanny had an independent streak that sometimes clashed with the behavioral expectations set by her minister father. As she neared adulthood, in her independence she grew less willing to hear his counsel about female modesty—gravitating toward expensive, stylish clothing—and his opinions on a woman's place in society.[5]

This was further tested when Sarah Adams's younger unmarried sister, Deborah Folsom, arrived from Hoboken, New Jersey, to live with the Adamses. She became Fanny's most stinging critic, especially on the subject of modesty: "Your love of beads and furbelows, and finery, is a *weak* spot in your character and you ought to fight against it."[6]

Throughout all the years of Fanny growing up, Sarah sought to offer a consistent, nurturing presence. But on February 27, 1850, after a drawn-out illness, Sarah died, a heavy blow to Fanny. She lost the only parent who tried to understand her desire to chart an independent path as a young woman in the world. At the same time, George, her remaining adoptive parent, fell into despair over his wife's death.

AFTER ONLY A few months in the tense, grieving household, and after arguments about her future, Fanny struck out on her own, eager to try life without her father's or her aunt's interference—an unusual decision for a young woman at this time. She made the twenty-nine-mile trip from Brunswick to Portland on the new Kennebec and Portland Railroad line to live in Maine's largest city, with nearly twenty-one thousand residents, and the state's artistic hub.

At a time when it was rare for a woman to aspire to be an artist, Fanny determined to make her mark in Portland's burgeoning art scene. Artist's studios, or "painting rooms," as they were called in the nineteenth century, were proliferating in New York and Boston, and beginning to make their way north. She set up a painting room where she could also display her work.[7]

At the same time, she continued to pursue her interest in music. She studied with Frederick N. Crouch, a well-known composer and

cellist. Before immigrating to the United States in 1849, Crouch
had performed at St. Paul's Cathedral, as well as London's Drury
Lane and Covent Garden theatres in his native England.[8]

On some weekends, Fanny returned to Brunswick to play the
organ at her father's church.

At Brunswick's First Parish she
started to notice the new choir director: a tall Bowdoin student with a
baritone voice. Soon, Lawrence and
Fanny began conversing, perhaps
about their shared love of music.
The beautiful wooden Gothic church
became a safe place to get to know
each other without arousing undue
interest or gossip.

*Fanny studied music with English
composer Frederick N. Crouch, who
came to the United States in 1849.*

At first, Fanny felt self-conscious
about her interest in Lawrence be-
cause he was three years younger than her. In the middle of the
nineteenth century, husbands were typically three to six years older
than their wives.[9] But the choir director's intelligence and wit
quickly overcame Fanny's hesitancy.

They began attending Harriet Beecher Stowe's Saturday evening
readings together, and then a weekly literary circle that met in a
Brunswick home.

Their relationship quickened in early 1851—but at different
speeds. Lawrence's feelings leaped ahead as he fell deeply in love
with Fanny, while she struggled to discern whether her deep respect
and appreciation for Lawrence was the romance and love she desired.[10] It is not known if this was a first serious relationship for each
of them.

Keenly aware of this disjunct, Lawrence used letters to express
what he was too shy to say in person. Calling himself a "silly clown,"
he wondered, "Will I not be driven mad" in his love for Fanny? At
times, a sort of torment pulses through these early letters. Aware he
was overly sensitive to what she did or did not say, he referred to a
recent time together: "I turned away before you should see my
tears," and "I cling to the hope that at some time you will see but

one single glimpse of me and know me."[11] It may be that Lawrence felt secure in his familiar world of farm, forest, church, and school, but not in Fanny's sophisticated world of art and society.

Another potential hurdle to their relationship was their different attitudes about the church where they first met. To her adoptive father's profound disappointment, Fanny decided not to join First Parish. She did not feel able to give assent to the traditional Christian beliefs required for membership.[12]

The roots of Fanny's belief or unbelief are not easy to trace. She had been nurtured in her adoptive family's deep Christian faith. But, as in all things, Fanny had a mind of her own.

It is possible that during her periodic stays in Portland she might have worshipped at Portland's First Parish, one of Maine's first churches to become part of the Unitarian wing of Congregationalism. The congregation's minister, Rev. Ichabod Nichols, who graduated first in his class at Harvard, was known as a convener of Portland's intellectual elite. His sermons may have drawn her attendance and interest.

Unitarians disavowed the traditional Congregational teachings on the sinfulness of human nature in favor of an optimistic assessment of human possibility. Nichols avowed, "Christianity seems to me to have for its object not so much the introduction of a new belief as a new life in the world."[13] His liberal views may well have appealed to an artistic and independent young woman.

Whatever influenced her refusal to join the church, her decision did not deter the devout Lawrence. If he was disappointed, this topic was not discussed in their correspondence. He appears to have been comfortable with, or at least accepting of, Fanny's choice. Perhaps love conquers all.

In spring 1851, Lawrence happened to return home to Brewer at the same time Fanny was visiting friends across the river in Bangor. He invited her to meet his parents. It went well. She wrote later that being with his family was "a dream I will never forget."[14] She and Lawrence's mother got on well together, and his family already seemed to know quite a bit about the artistic young woman from Brunswick, lending credence to Fanny's worry that Lawrence let his family read her letters. In one letter, she wrote, "Lawrence don't you preserve this among the valuable and interesting documents in your portfolio, will you? But destroy it at once."[15]

IN THE SUMMER of 1851, Rev. Adams left Brunswick for nine weeks to attend a Foreign Missions conference in Chicago. During his absence, Fanny invited Lawrence into the Adams home, a two-story Federal-style parsonage on Maine Street. By that point, Fanny appeared less conflicted in her feelings. She sent him a coaxing note: "I am disappointed at not seeing you last eve. Why not give Mary J. her lesson early and give rehearsal the skip for I will be home alone."[16]

BUT FANNY AND Lawrence's burgeoning romance took a back seat when her father returned home in August.[17] He announced he was courting Helen Root, a woman he had met in Chicago, the sister of George Frederick Root, a well-known musician and songwriter.[18]

The rapid courtship took everyone by surprise. Fanny's father had been a widower for only a year and a half. An added surprise— Fanny learned that Helen was only six months older than herself.[19]

By October, George and Helen were engaged. Throughout the fall, the Maine Street house was brightened with fresh carpet and paint to prepare for the new Mrs. Adams. On December 30, Fanny traveled to Reading, Massachusetts, to attend the wedding.

On the wedding day, a restive Lawrence arrived at the Adams home where there was only Fan-

Rev. George Adams with his second wife, Helen Root, in 1851

ny's aunt Deborah to welcome him. He had missed his chance to see Fanny and fell into a deep pit of insecurity.

"I was perfectly and uncontrollably wretched," he wrote Fanny.

"Would to God that I might see you for one half hour, or that you had said a few words to me the other day, which would have lifted my soul out of such shadows forever."[20]

Ready to depart for Brewer for the holidays, he closed melodramatically, "Be happy—even if to be happy is to forget me a little . . . May God be over you and in you and keep you till we meet again or above."[21] He left the letter for her at the Adams home.

ON THE FIRST of the year, after reading Lawrence's sad letter, Fanny sought to reassure him: "How could you think that I would shrink from you ever! You who seem so holy, so pure, and noble to me—how could I even if you did not press my finger to your dear lips?" Remembering their times alone, she wrote, "Ah! Those nights! So full of terrible beauty."[22]

She now unburdened herself of her shortcomings. "I know that I am not natural, and I am not rational, and there are no words to say to you all that I feel and think—but I will tell you more, and you will forgive all that is wrong in me." Finally, she pleaded, "O! Lawrence take me as I am . . . I would nestle closely in your arms forever and love you."[23] At last, they were both ardent in their affections for each other.

FANNY NOW KNEW that she loved and admired Lawrence, but was it enough for marriage? She shared her concerns with Stephen Allen, a successful businessman and politician she had met in Boston. He counseled against the union: "You say you love him—yet do not feel that sort of love for him of which you have for years dreamed so wildly." Allen told her he wished Chamberlain were a few years older than Fanny and more advanced in his studies or vocation of ministry. Referring to "hints from you," he voiced further concern that Chamberlain sounded like someone "rather jealous" who "makes large demands and might be hard to please or satisfy."[24]

ALLEN WAS NOT the only one with concerns about the match of Lawrence and Fanny for marriage. Relatives and friends appreciated Lawrence as a serious, devout young man who had committed himself to becoming a minister or missionary after graduation. He heard the voices of apprehension: "She is accomplished and amiable, but then he can't think her suited to him."[25]

Fanny's adoptive father worried as well. He knew she enjoyed and needed attention. She was intelligent and talented, but she could sulk when she did not get her way. Her moodiness might make her a difficult wife. On March 29, 1852, Adams recorded in his diary, "Chamberlain called to talk about Fanny," but he does not reveal the content of their conversation.[26]

Adams also worried about Lawrence. He did not share everyone else's high estimation of the young man directing his congregation's choir.[27]

Lawrence, fully aware of her adoptive father's concerns, wrote, "Your Father has not much faith in our relation . . . he does not expect that much will ever come of it, or that it will last very long." But love gave Lawrence an iron will: "As to this, I simply say he has mistaken his man. I am not so easily managed."[28]

Sharing the home with the second Mrs. Adams proved difficult for Fanny, her sister Anna, and her aunt Deborah. Helen was so different from the mother and sister they had loved. Fanny complained that Helen, though only six months older, treated her like a child.

For his part, Adams believed the three women were prejudiced against Helen, never giving her the benefit of the doubt. He confided to his diary on February 13, 1852, "Helen not very well, & somewhat dispirited." He added, "I am troubled too about Fanny."[29]

IN APRIL 1852, having closed the door on her Portland painting experience, Fanny decided to pursue her interest in music by moving to New York, which had the added benefit of taking her out of the pressure cooker her family's Brunswick house had become. She would study with Professor Root, Helen's brother.

Root dreamed of establishing music in the curriculums of public schools. To that end he had set up an institute to train music teachers in New York. During the Civil War, he would become famous as the composer of the songs "The Battle Cry of Freedom" and "Tramp, Tramp, Tramp."[30]

Fanny studied music with George Frederick Root, who aspired to set up a music school in New York.

Fanny was startled when Rev. Adams let her know that he expected her to pay him back for the expenses of living and studying in New York. He had not asked her to do so when she had lived in Portland.

MONTHS PASSED WITH Fanny in New York and Lawrence in his final year at Bowdoin. Her infrequent letters reawakened Lawrence's self-doubt and anxiety. To one such letter in May, he replied, "Your letter only made me feel how far away from me you were." He pleaded with her, "Oh, Fanny, do not let anything estrange you from me."[31]

To his delight, the next day a letter arrived. Fanny answered his love with her love. She told him she would marry him.

Fanny's letter has not survived, but Lawrence responded jubilantly: "You do love me, as I love you—What more do I ask—what can I not do—what can I not be, if that only be true."[32]

This was probably not the first time Lawrence proposed to Fanny. In these months her appreciation turned to love.

THE COURTSHIP OF Lawrence and Fanny was never straightforward. There were Lawrence's anguished, often unreasonable demands; Fanny's hesitations and fears; their religious differences; the doubts of family and friends. Ultimately though, two quite different people chose to step over these many barriers to link their lives together in marriage.

But only after three years. Lawrence gave Fanny an engagement ring but told her their marriage would need to take place after he completed his studies at Bangor Theological Seminary.

Notwithstanding, from this moment forward, he would call Fanny his wife, and she would call Lawrence her husband.

FIVE

Bangor Theological Seminary

*By letters a lover can say a thousand extravagant things which he would
blush to utter in the presence of his fair charmer. He heaps up
mountains of epithets and hyperboles, expressing the inexpressible
heights, and depths, and lengths, and breadths of his affections.*
—The Dictionary of Love, 1858

WITH MIXED EMOTIONS LAWRENCE STARTED CLASSES AT
Bangor Theological Seminary in October 1852. He entered
eager to focus on his new studies, yet understood that Fanny felt
hesitant about his vocational choice, especially the thought of his
becoming a missionary.

His three years at Bangor Theological Seminary have received
no more than several sentences in all previous Chamberlain biographies. Yet his experiences at this Congregational seminary between
1852 and 1855 and between his ages twenty-four to twenty-seven are
crucial to understanding his life story. For here his three years as a
student would be key in the formation of his beliefs and values.

The charter establishing the first theological seminary in northern New England was signed on February 25, 1814, six years prior to
Maine becoming a state. Five years later, the seminary was permanently located in Bangor, thanks to the donation of a hayfield west
of town. By the time Chamberlain arrived, locals had dubbed the
seven-acre site "the holy hill," the school having a commanding
view of the town and the Penobscot River below.[1]

Bangor Theological Seminary was one of the first of a new kind
of institution. In the previous two centuries, young men who wished
to become ministers in New England received their academic education from Harvard or Yale and then apprenticed themselves to
seasoned pastors to learn the practices of ministry.[2] The Rev. Joseph

FACING PAGE: *Lawrence began his studies at Bangor Theological Seminary in 1852.*

Bellamy, Congregational minister in Bethlehem, Connecticut, trained one hundred students in his home between 1742 and 1790. The Rev. Nathaniel Emmons, Congregational minister at Franklin, Massachusetts, trained eighty-seven ministerial students starting in 1769.[3]

This long-held pattern of theological education underwent a decisive change—one repercussion of a dramatic battle that took place at Harvard at the beginning of the nineteenth century. The 1803 death of David Tappan, who had occupied the Hollis Chair of Divinity since 1792, precipitated a bitter clash at the nation's earliest college. The Hollis Chair, established in 1721, was the oldest endowed chair in the United States, and in 1803 considered the most prestigious endowed professorship. Tappan was a Calvinist and a Congregationalist. His death undid the delicate balance between conservative Christian orthodoxy and liberalism at Harvard.

After two years of conflict, Henry Ware, minister of the First Parish in Hingham, Massachusetts, and influential in the formation of Unitarianism, succeeded Tappan. Unitarianism, a liberal movement rising up within Congregationalism, objected to the doctrine of the Trinity and espoused human free will.[4]

"It is a day of alarm and danger. There is a flood of anti-Christian error and soul-destroying corruption coming in upon us and threatening to sweep away every remnant of primitive truth and goodness."[5] Congregational minister Leonard Woods, the father of Leonard Woods, Jr., who would be the president of Bowdoin College when Chamberlain studied there, shared his worries with a fellow Congregationalist minister, Charles Spring, in 1807. Capturing the shock that many Massachusetts Congregationalists felt, Woods wrote, "The state of things in Boston and Cambridge caused deep solicitude among Orthodox ministers and Christians." He believed "something must be done to check the prevalence of error."[6]

What was done was to establish a new model of theological education. Embittered toward the liberalism they saw developing at Harvard and Yale, Calvinists moved quickly to establish a new kind of institution to carry on their tradition. They founded Andover Theological Seminary in Newton, Massachusetts, just three years later in 1808. Located just seven miles west of Cambridge, the purpose of the new seminary, stated in its constitution, was to increase the "number of learned and able defenders of the Gospel of Christ, as well as orthodox, pious, and zealous ministers of the New Testament."[7]

Woods was invited to become one of the first members of the faculty. The faculty were asked to subscribe to what became known as the Andover Creed, a confessional document pledging their allegiance to traditional Christian beliefs. Andover set up a three-year post-college degree program that sought to combine high-quality academic education with the arts of preaching and pastoral care.[8]

Bangor Theological Seminary would follow the Andover model in its aspiration to offer a theological education that combined academic study with the practical arts of ministry, both rooted in the Calvinist tradition.

WHEN LAWRENCE ARRIVED in 1852, Bangor Seminary consisted of three professors and forty-three students. Although the "Terms of Admissions" stated that the seminary was open to "Evangelical Christians of every denomination," the overwhelming majority of students were Congregationalists.[9] By "Evangelical" the seminary meant a fidelity to the Bible as the Word of God, the centrality of the preaching of Jesus Christ, and, at the beginning of the new century, emphasis on a modern missionary movement beginning to spread the Gospel of Christ around the world.

Chamberlain's entering class, called the junior class in seminaries, comprised thirteen students: six from Maine, three from New York, two from Vermont, one from New Hampshire, and one from Scotland. He moved into room 2 in Commons House, for which he paid two dollars annually.[10]

Lawrence took advantage of the proximity of his family's home in Brewer, located just across the covered wooden bridge that spanned the Penobscot River, to strengthen his relationship in the next three years with his younger sister, Sae. At their home, he enjoyed playing German airs, especially those of Franz Schubert, on his bass viol, while Sae played the piano.[11]

Deciding not to accept aid from the seminary, he paid for his theological education by several means. He taught German language and literature to a group of women in Bangor, an unusual initiative at that time; accepted an appointment as superintendent of schools in Brewer; played the organ in his hometown Brewer church; and joined two friends in teaching a Sunday school class out on the Ellsworth Road—all of this on top of keeping a rigorous course of studies.

As LAWRENCE SETTLED in at the seminary in Bangor, a dispersion was taking place at the Adams home in Brunswick. One by one, three women—Anna, Deborah, and Fanny—departed the Adams home. "There is no Brunswick now," Fanny's older sister Charlotte wrote in September 1852. "Who could have thought that one death could have changed everything."[12]

The first to leave was Fanny's adopted sister, Anna Davis. She departed for Mississippi in October, participating in a New England tradition of young women going south to teach.

Next was "Cousin" Deborah, who long since had made amends with Fanny; the two were now quite close. Exasperated with her brother-in-law, Deborah presented him an inventory of items she wanted to secure for herself and his two adopted daughters. Then she left for Hoboken, New Jersey, in October.[13]

Finally, Fanny prepared to leave again. In October, she wrote Lawrence "how changed, terribly changed everything here was; it was hard indeed for me to bring myself to enter into the house." What was more, she discovered that her private letters from Lawrence "had been taken from their envelopes and put into new ones." She suspected that her father had done this under the urging of "Helen in her great anxiety." She complained that Helen, only a half year older than Fanny, insisted on treating her as if she were "aged twelve."[14]

Two weeks later, Fanny wrote again. "Things seem to be coming to some terrible crisis here at home now. Father and I have been having some very painful talks." Yet she told Lawrence, "I can endure now when I have your blessed heart, strong and noble, as it is, to lean upon what I never could have borne without you, never."[15]

In early December, Professor Root secured Fanny a position teaching music at Miss Lucia Bass's female academy in Milledgeville, Georgia.[16] Fanny would receive the sum of eight hundred dollars a year, a substantial salary for a young woman at that time. She could earn extra money by offering private piano lessons. With this money she wanted to begin to repay her father.[17]

On December 22, Rev. Adams poured out his concerns for his daughter in his diary: "My poor Fanny left for Georgia at noon." From this point on he would refer to her as "my poor Fanny." He believed "Her prospects are good, if her health is sufficient, & she has enough energy and punctuality." From his perspective, her inability to be on time reflected larger problems. "But I fear. Poor child! God protect her."[18]

Fanny traveled to Savannah from New York on the steamer *Florida*. She arrived in Milledgeville, Georgia's fourth state capital, in the last week of December 1852.

She stayed first in the home of Richard and Abby Orme. A civic leader in Milledgeville, Richard Orme had published *The Southern Recorder* since 1820. Abby Adams Orme, a friend of Fanny's father, was originally from New England, the daughter of Dr. John Adams, principal of the Phillips Academy of Andover, Massachusetts.

Fanny moved to Milledgeville, Georgia's fourth state capital, at the end of 1852 to teach music.

Fanny was astonished by a discovery she made in the Orme home. She wrote her sister Charlotte, "I just glanced up to the mantelpiece in this room and what book do you suppose I saw there? no other than 'Tom's cabin' in two volumes, well-thumbed and worn out too!" She was surprised because she had learned that *Uncle Tom's Cabin* was banned throughout the South. Her eyes were beginning to be opened to the diversity of opinion in America.[19]

Mrs. Orme took upon herself the responsibility of sponsoring Fanny in her new surroundings, including helping her find a place to board. Free from the criticism of her father, she nevertheless soon found herself under another burden: social pressure from women in the town to volunteer and participate in their numerous social activities.[20]

Fanny received an invitation to play the organ at the Milledgeville Presbyterian Church. Although Baptists far outnumbered Presbyterians in Georgia and the South, the Presbyterian Church, established on Statehouse Square in 1826 on land provided by the state legislature, included some of the town's leading citizens. Richard Orme served as a trustee of the congregation.[21]

Fanny was invited to play the organ at the Milledgeville Presbyterian Church.

As Lawrence wondered and worried about Fanny, now living 1,300 miles from Bangor in Georgia, he began his theological education based on a formal curriculum that consisted of:

1. Sacred Literature
2. Theology and Church Polity
3. Sacred Rhetoric
4. Ecclesiastical History
5. Pastoral Duties

Classes in sacred literature began in the first year of seminary and continued through all three years, whereas classes in pastoral duties all took place in the third year.[22]

The seminary's doctrinal goals resided in the capable hands of Professor Enoch Pond. A graduate of Brown and Andover Theological Seminary, Pond joined the Bangor faculty in 1832. By the time Chamberlain arrived twenty years later, the learned and winsome Pond had become the face of the seminary.

Cyrus Hamlin, an early graduate who became a missionary in the Ottoman Empire, where he founded Robert College in Constantinople, and whose older brother, Hannibal, would become Abraham Lincoln's first vice president, spoke of Pond's presence in the seminary, crediting Pond's "earnest enthusiasm" as responsible for the school's growth.[23]

Professor Enoch Pond, professor of Systematic Theology, was the central figure at Bangor Theological Seminary in Chamberlain's student days.

Because Maine was desperate for ministers, in the seminary's first decades, it had accepted students who were not college graduates. One of Pond's first initiatives was to travel to Bowdoin and Dartmouth on recruiting trips. By the time Chamberlain arrived, nearly all the seminary students were college graduates.

Chamberlain recalled that the faculty held "pretty stiffly to the 'Old School.'"[24] Indeed, one can see this in the introduction to Pond's 1844 publication *The Mather Family,* in which he wrote about three generations of the prominent Puritan family. Pond lamented the "reproaches and aspersions which, in our own times have been cast upon them." In this volume, Pond took upon himself "the task of *vindication* of these excellent men,"[25] which can be read as a defense of traditional Calvinist values.

ONE CAN PICTURE Lawrence sitting in a Pond class listening to the professor expound on these Puritan leaders not simply as important historical figures, but as examples for Bangor students aspiring to become ministers.

Lawrence enrolled in a seminary that took pride in a Congregationalism that embraced an intellectual tradition. In Pond's course in Systematic Theology, Lawrence took copious notes—one hundred twenty-three pages. Professor Pond structured the course:

I. Being and Attributes of God
II. The Scriptures
III. Person of Christ
IV. The Human Mind
V. Natural and Moral Ability
VI. Nature of Holiness

Although the study of the Bible sat at the core of the curriculum, "systematic" theology encouraged aspiring ministers to think logically about the Christian faith. Even as the newer denominations— Methodist and Baptist—were espousing a religion of the heart, and ordaining ministers who were neither college nor seminary graduates, Congregationalists advocated a religion of the mind and continued to insist on an educated clergy.

The influence of Pond's theology class can be measured by the fact that Chamberlain held on to these notes for the rest of his life.[26]

CHAMBERLAIN WAS ALSO drawn to the Rev. George Shepard, who led the Department of Sacred Rhetoric. Shepard was called to the seminary in 1836 after serving for eight years as minister of the South Church in Hallowell, Maine. Widely respected, in the 1840s, Auburn Theological Seminary offered Shepard the professorship of Christian theology, while the prestigious Pilgrim Congregational Church in Brooklyn invited him to become their pastor. In these same years, Amherst College twice invited Shepard to become their president.[27]

But Shepard loved teaching and preaching to seminary students. He offered courses on the history, principles, precepts, and uses of rhetoric and oratory, on homiletics, on the style of the pulpit, and on sacred eloquence. In these courses, Chamberlain heard Shepard offer reviews of the sermons of eminent preachers as examples for his students.[28]

In Lawrence's early months at the seminary, he wrote lengthy romantic letters to Fanny. Although not all of her letters from Georgia have survived, it is possible to discern some of what she wrote either by his own quotations from her letters, or his responses to her questions and ideas.

Because Lawrence and Fanny both understood that their marriage would need to take place after Chamberlain completed his three years at Bangor Seminary, he wrote with encouragement— "Only think, honey-bee, it is like a dream—three years will go like a flash," or gentle teasing—"What'll you bet I shan't be as old as you are, then."[29]

In the first months of their engagement, she posed the possibility of a platonic marriage, writing that "children are the result of tyrannical cruel abuse and prostitution of women." She also expressed her fear that childbirth could be both painful and dangerous.[30]

Choosing his words carefully, he countered, "I think you are not so foolish as to suppose either you or I are destitute of a fair degree of humanity." Then, in a shift of tone, he went on, "Be careful how you kiss my lips, or you will set me all on fire."[31] Lawrence, in his constant stream of love letters to Milledgeville, strove to encourage Fanny to be hopeful about their future life together.

AT THE SEMINARY, as at Bowdoin, Lawrence relished the study of languages. Believing he was "lame in Latin and fresh in German," he "resolved to read all his 'Theology' in these two languages." His professors were not too sure about his reading theology in German, for German scholarship was a significant source of newer, liberal thinking. Chamberlain, unworried, believed that reading in German "presented vital questions in widely variant lights."[32] At Bangor, far more than Bowdoin, Chamberlain became exposed to a wider range of theological literature and thinking.

EVEN MORE THAN in his initial study of Hebrew at Bowdoin, he found at Bangor that this Semitic language, "with its strong, old, three-letter verbal roots, its virile forces, its susceptibility to sense impressions," held more fascination for him now that he studied it within the context of his other theological subjects.[33] He had been introduced to the Hebrew language at Bowdoin, but now he studied it within the larger context of the theology of the Hebrew Bible, or the Old Testament.

Believing his field of service after graduation might be as a missionary in what was then called the Orient, Lawrence determined to learn two more Semitic languages, Arabic and Syriac, which shared features with Hebrew. In the study of these languages, he discovered "whole new concepts of thought, new images of life." He learned to appreciate that in Hebrew thinking, unlike in Greek thinking, language is doing, is an activity.

Educational institutions have both formal and informal curriculums. The formal consists of the academic courses; the informal consists of the extracurricular societies and groups whose participation by students is voluntary. During Chamberlain's time at Bangor, he participated in two voluntary societies that met in the evenings: the Society of Missionary Inquiry and the Rhetorical Society.

Chamberlain came to Bangor eager to explore what it might mean to be a missionary to a far-off country. He thought about being posted "to some country where the social conditions might give him a chance to 'keep school,' and show that Christianity is obedience to the law or right living as well as of right worship."[34]

While still at Bowdoin, Lawrence had corresponded with Benjamin Galen Snow, a Brewer resident, Bowdoin graduate, and then a student at the seminary. He encouraged Lawrence's interest in missions, and would, after graduation and ordination, set sail for distant Micronesia in 1851, under the auspices of the American Board of Commissioners for Foreign Missions.[35]

Upon arriving at the campus on the hill, Chamberlain learned that Snow was but one of a number of Bangor graduates who went on to serve in foreign missions in a number of countries. In recent years, graduates had also begun serving in the western United States on what were called "home missions." This missionary impulse undergirded both faculty teaching and student interest.

FUELING THIS INTEREST in mission was the growth of hundreds of evangelical voluntary societies in the early nineteenth century. Some of the characteristics of these societies included: the leadership was led by laypeople, not ministers; they were organized around a task to be done, not a creed to be believed; their participation was ecumenical rather than denominational; and women stepped forward to take on important roles at a time when they could not serve as ministers in the churches.[36]

Some of the leading societies included the American Board of Commissioners for Foreign Missions, founded in 1810, American Education Society (1815), American Bible Society (1816), American Home Missionary Society (1816), American Tract Society (1825), American Peace Society (1828), American Antislavery Society (1833), and American Sunday School Union (1834).

Although the First Amendment of the Bill of Rights forbade the establishment of a national church, the formation of these societies created an alternative Protestant Christian establishment. The energy and momentum from these societies helped to grow church membership dramatically for the first time since the American Revolution.

Lawrence came to seminary already knowing a good deal about these societies. Rev. Adams had regularly invited their representatives, especially those of the American Board of Commissioners for Foreign Missions, or ABCFM, to participate in Sunday worship. He regularly urged his congregation to support the societies with special offerings and "took up an 'extra collection' for ABCFM."[37]

To advance their common interests, the societies created a convention circuit called Anniversary Week that met annually in New York, Philadelphia, and Boston to showcase various societies and their respective missions.

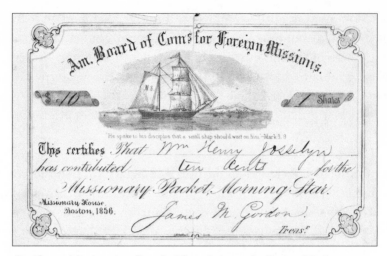

Certificate of the American Board of Commissioners for Foreign Missions.
Founded in 1810, it was the largest American missionary organization.

"Off to Boston to attend meeting of American Board of Commissioners for Foreign Missions." Adams recorded in his diary that he traveled regularly to Boston for both the May Anniversary Week that highlighted the work of the ABCFM, and, in this case, a special September meeting. He enjoyed serving as song leader at these gatherings.[38] Adams also served as president of the Maine Missionary Society.

It is quite possible that Lawrence, given his growing interest in missions and with Rev. Adams's encouragement, attended an anniversary week in Boston when a student at Bowdoin or Bangor.

AT THE SEMINARY, Lawrence participated in the Society of Missionary Inquiry. The Society met monthly in the chapel. The purpose of the meetings was to discuss the various options and opportunities in mission. On June 27, 1853, the members debated the question "Ought the present condition of the Home Field of Missionary Labor prevent Theol. Students from deciding to enter the For [Foreign] Field?" Behind this question stood the new reality of the opening up of the western United States for "home missions" precipitated especially by the beginning of traveling the Oregon Trail west in 1843.[39] Attending this society challenged Lawrence's thinking about his own missionary intentions.

The Society of Missionary Inquiry possessed its own library, separate from the seminary library. They ordered publications from the American Tract Society, a voluntary society that served as a resource for many other societies. The tracts of the Society of Missionary Inquiry that have survived in the Bangor Theological Seminary records include:

I Have a Message from God Unto Thee
Friendly Hints to the Young
The Worth of the Soul
The Act of Faith
On Repentance

A typical tract of the hundreds published by the American Tract Society—Great Christian Library

The tract *Friendly Hints to the Young* encouraged its young readers, "Suffer us to beseech you to pause whilst yet you stand on the threshold of life and consider the course you are resolved to pursue." This tract may have been read by young Lawrence as he considered his own course for the future.[40]

KEEN ON CONTINUING to develop his public speaking skills, Lawrence also participated in the Rhetorical Society. Students participating in this society wished to develop their speaking and debating skills. Each student was given the opportunity to offer a speech to fellow members, to be followed by questions and evaluations—done by students, not a professor.

One year into his seminary education, on August 29, 1853, in an evening of "Exercises," Lawrence spoke to the Rhetorical Society on "The Melancholy of Genius."[41] Such an intriguing title. Who was the genius or geniuses? Was the talk in any way autobiographical? We would like to know more.

STARTING IN HIS first year in seminary, Lawrence wrote Fanny at least once a week. To his consternation, she corresponded less frequently. For her part, she thought he did not appreciate that her days in Milledgeville were busy, filled not only with teaching classes and private lessons, but with many social engagements she felt required to attend.

Also, Fanny's eyes began causing her increasing discomfort. After long days, her eyes would become swollen, sometimes becoming nearly shut with pain.

In Fanny's years in Georgia, her adoptive father was often the best barometer of how she was doing. Two months after her arrival in Milledgeville, he wrote in his diary on February 21, "Received letter from Fanny, encouraging except as to her health, which I fear is very poor."[42]

Adams cared deeply for Fanny, and he continued to be worried about her: "In my anxiety and distress about Fanny, I laid [sic] awake part of the night."[43]

TOWARD THE END of their first year of separation, Lawrence and Fanny began to write about various plans to bring them together sooner than the three years. Perhaps he could do three years of seminary classes in two. Maybe he could join her in the South, or they could both teach in the West, perhaps in California. In June 1853, he wrote, "The 'Western project' (or Southern) is full before me."[44]

He thought about writing Professor Stowe to ask for his aid in finding a teaching position. He offered to help pay Fanny's debts, which might shorten her time teaching in Georgia. Fanny wrote that Mrs. Orme thought he might be able to get a teaching position at Athens College in Georgia. "How would you like that, darling?"[45]

Despite Lawrence's struggles to discern where he would serve, during his years at Bangor Theological Seminary, he began to believe God was preparing him for a place of leadership. In June 1853, he shared this conviction in a heartfelt letter to Fanny: "I feel capable of something—with your dear help, of much." Conscious of his youth, "I would indeed be willing to begin very small & trust to my own diligence & your blessed love, under God's favor, to rise to the place to which I hope to attain."[46]

As for the present, "I don't know whether to teach school somewhere, or to remain about my old premises here." He shared with Fanny thoughts of his wanderlust. His grandfather wanted him to accompany him to Indiana. "If I do, I shall make an effort to slip into such a place there in some of the western colleges as we were talking of." Perhaps looking over his letter, he concluded, "I feel pretty sure that the Providence which has hitherto led me by so pleasant a way will order all things so that I shall at last be in the right place." He encouraged her, "We should pray. I think that God will not suffer us to have our own way but will lead us in his."[47] Chamberlain's deference to "Providence," the idea that God acts in history, and directs the lives of men and women, was central in the Calvinist beliefs of Bangor Seminary students.

EVEN AS LAWRENCE had faith in Providence, Fanny expressed her lack of confidence in the future the young couple was moving toward. On February 22, 1854, she unburdened herself: "I have never felt so strongly before, my peculiar unfitness for being a minister's wife." She attempted to explain why: "It is not that my trials and troubles are so great, believe me it is not so selfish a feeling, but it is my whole mind, character and temperament are entirely inappropriate for that position and I never could be useful in it." She worried "It would grieve me to death to feel that I was necessarily a draw-back to your influence as a minister, and I know how important it would be to your success that I should be happy and free from such crushing anxiety."[48]

In response, Lawrence protested that he would not try to persuade her "of the sweet office of ministering to poor weary souls & pointing them to the marvelous tenderness of that love that cared for them & would save them"—but yet he did try to persuade her.[49]

He asked, echoing her words, "for *what* position she thinks 'her mind, character & temperament *are* appropriate.'" He urged her to come to Brewer that summer, concluding the letter with "Kiss me."[50]

In a continuing internal tension, his love for Fanny pushed against his ministerial dreams.

FEW LETTERS HAVE endured from the correspondence between Lawrence and Fanny in 1855, his last year at seminary. This period seems to have been one of uncertainty, frustration, and concern for both of them. It may well be that some of these letters were relegated to the fire.

Spring was the time when congregations looking for ministers turned their attention to Bangor's upcoming graduates. In their senior year, Professor Shepard required each student to prepare four sermons. Rather than having the students deliver the sermons at the seminary campus, he arranged invitations from congregations where the students could preach on spring Sundays.[51]

Years later, when Chamberlain filled out a form for Bangor Seminary's *Historical Catalogue,* he wrote that he received "calls to pastorates" from two of the churches where he preached. First Parish in Belfast, Maine, with its beautiful Federal-style church sanctuary, invited Lawrence to become their pastor. He also received a "call" from the First Parish of Wolfeboro, New Hampshire.[52]

. . .

WHILE PREPARING FOR graduation exercises at the seminary, Lawrence received an unexpected invitation. Bowdoin College wrote
that he had been chosen to offer the master's oration at the college's 1855 commencement. By offering an address, Bowdoin would
confer upon him the degree of master of arts.[53]

Having already been chosen to be a student speaker at his seminary graduation, Lawrence worried he would not have time to prepare two separate addresses. The college agreed that he could offer
the address he was already slated to deliver at the seminary.

Adding to the excitement of this period, Fanny wrote that she
would arrive in Brunswick on August 1.

No records of their reunion have survived, but they must have
had a rush of feelings as they fell into each other's arms.[54]

One can imagine Lawrence's emotions as he prepared to step to
the lectern at First Parish for Bowdoin's commencement. This was
the same setting where he had faltered so badly as an orator at his
college graduation. This would be a different day and experience.
Years later he wrote in the third person in his memoirs, "the flush
on his face was far different from that with which he had left it three
years before."[55]

He took as his subject "Law and Liberty." He argued that law
and liberty, contrary to popular opinion in both religion and politics, were not in opposition to each other. "The superabounding
life lavished in the universe was proof that the play of infinite freedom was to work out the will of infinite law." He declared, "the
whole universe showed that freedom was part of law."[56] His address,
originally to be offered only at the commencement of Bangor
Theological Seminary, was typical of the many addresses Chamberlain would offer in the future. He enjoyed taking intellectual concepts, in this case law and liberty, and creatively reimagining their
relationship to each other.

This time, the effect of his address upon the audience surprised
the speaker. Older and wiser, freed from nervousness and stammering, his address was an overwhelming success. "The effect of this
[address] among those who heard it was an utter and overwhelming surprise to its author."[57]

In the audience that day was Joseph P. Thompson, a founder of
the New York *Independent,* which from its beginning in 1848 repre-

sented the energetic antislavery wing of the Congregational church. Thompson was impressed by Chamberlain's understanding of liberty. Antislavery advocates, criticized for their alleged willingness to break the law in the cause of abolition, argued that they were following a higher law in their campaign to free the enslaved.[58]

Bowdoin president Woods was also impressed. The very next day, he offered Lawrence a teaching position. Professor Stowe had accepted a faculty position at Andover Seminary, and the college hired Lawrence to teach Stowe's classes in logic and natural theology. In addition, he was asked to assume responsibility for freshman Greek.

WHAT WOULD CHAMBERLAIN do? It has always been assumed that this was an easy decision. But was it? On one hand, he loved his four years as a student at Bowdoin, yet the position he was offered would be as a "provisional instructor"—not a permanent position. Yet even this temporary teaching position would allay Fanny's worries about his becoming a missionary. On the other hand, Lawrence had enjoyed his three years of theological education, and it would mean giving up his dreams of becoming a minister, accepting one of the invitations he received to serve a Congregational congregation.

In the end, Lawrence accepted the invitation to teach at Bowdoin.

ALTHOUGH HIS TIME at Bangor Theological Seminary has been omitted from the Chamberlain story, he never felt those three years were wasted. At Bangor he deepened his Christian faith, expanded his command of languages, and increased his rhetorical abilities. Through his theological education he enhanced the resources through which he wished to fulfill his oft-expressed desire to serve both God and his fellow human beings. The fruits of his theological education will be seen again and again in the next chapters of his life.

Now, with an invitation to teach at his alma mater, and marriage to Fanny, the love of his life, on the near horizon, Lawrence looked forward with hope.

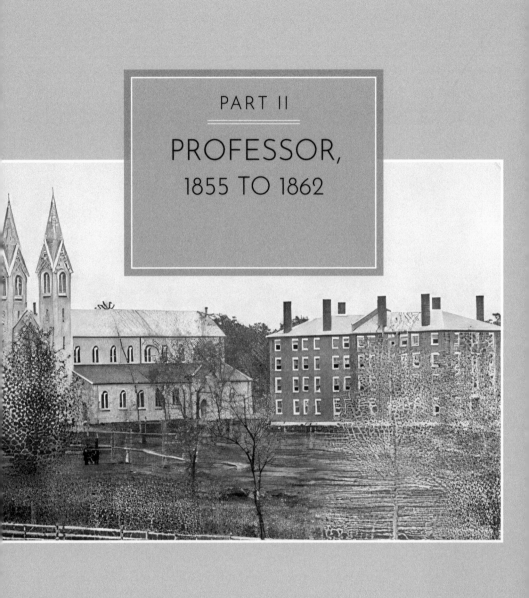

PART II

PROFESSOR,
1855 TO 1862

SIX

" 'Getting at' the Student's Mind (& Heart) "

Awakening an enthusiasm in my pupils and keeping my own style free
and mind fresh and whole.

—JOSHUA LAWRENCE CHAMBERLAIN'S PRIMARY GOALS IN TEACHING,
REPORT TO BOWDOIN COLLEGE VISITING COMMITTEE, 1858

[signature: Joshua L. Chamberlain]

I F LAWRENCE BELIEVED IN GOD, HE ALSO BELIEVED IN EDUCA-
tion.

On August 24, 1855, barely twenty-six years old, he returned to
the college he revered, excited and surely nervous. His salary as a
junior "provisional instructor" in "logic and natural theology" was
only for one term and at a modest fifty dollars a month. The college
also asked him to tutor freshman Greek; ironically, Greek was the
language he had struggled to learn in his Brewer attic seven years
earlier, causing him to delay his entrance as a freshman.[1]

Chamberlain faced the future with a measure of optimism, but
his prospective father-in-law, Rev. Adams, long an overseer at Bowdoin, cautioned him not to expect to receive a permanent position
at the college. His warning stemmed not from a lack of confidence
in Lawrence, but rather his knowledge of the tight finances of the
college, and that perhaps they would once again look externally to
secure a more senior person, as they did with Professor Stowe.[2]

IN THE WEEKS leading up to the fall term, Lawrence had offered a
number of emotional farewells to people and places that had become important to him: First Parish Brewer; Bangor Theological

OVERLEAF: *A photo of Bowdoin College campus, c. 1860*
FACING PAGE: *As a young professor, Chamberlain dressed with a high collar and silk tie
on a starched white linen shirt.*

Seminary; the Brewer schools where he served as supervisor; a group of young Bangor women to whom he taught German language and literature; and the Whiting Hill Sunday school, where he had tested his skills as a teacher. The grateful students of Whiting Hill gave him a New Testament in the summer of 1855, which he would keep into the 1860s.[3]

HIS COMPLEX, ROMANTIC relationship with Fanny must also have sat front of mind that August. After a courtship of five years, including a difficult separation of three years when she was teaching in Georgia, the two were finally to marry.

But when? Fanny had returned to Maine expecting a late summer or early fall wedding. She was living again, uncomfortably, under the same roof with her adoptive father and Helen. Fanny's female friends bombarded her with questions about the exact date. She could not give them an answer.

Lawrence, after three long years apart, was eager to marry Fanny but felt insecure because of his provisional faculty position. Worried about his ability to support a wife on his meager Bowdoin salary—very possibly temporary—he could not bring himself to agree on a day for the wedding. Their joyous reunion quickly clouded over as Fanny felt let down by her fiancé's indecision.

Feeling gloomy over this turn of events, Lawrence turned, as he often did, to his mother. He wrote her that he was seeking God's direction in his life. Wanting to support her oldest child, Sarah replied that God "will find work for you, just where it will be best for you and for his glory . . . therefore be cheerful and not let your heart be troubled." Aware of his financial situation and knowing the college's fall term would close at the end of November, she invited him and Fanny to "come home" to Brewer for Bowdoin's long winter break, giving them an opportunity to clear their minds.[4]

DESPITE CHAMBERLAIN'S EMOTIONAL state, the teaching in his fall term evidently went well. Although a new instructor at Bowdoin, Chamberlain was not new to teaching, having taught a wide range of students, from the toughs at Milford to the ladies of Bangor to various Sunday school classes.[5]

At the conclusion of the fall term, a dozen of his students signed a letter of appreciation. They wrote of their sorrow that he might be leaving Bowdoin and expressed their "sincere thanks for your . . . faithful manner in which you have sought to point out to us the path of life, but also your love and esteem for the kind and continual interest which you have shown in our temporal and eternal welfare." Wherever Chamberlain taught, his students recognized he was not only teaching the subject at hand, but also offering guidance for their character and faith development. These Bowdoin students signed their letter "Your affectionate Pupils." They wanted him to know they hoped the college would bring him back to teach in the winter term.[6]

ALTHOUGH STILL UNCERTAIN whether Bowdoin would extend his contract, Lawrence finally made plans with Fanny to be married at the end of the fall term.

Weddings at this time were nearly always held in homes, but Lawrence and Fanny wanted their wedding to be in First Parish, a place central in their courtship. They would become one of the first couples to be married in the splendid nine-year-old First Parish sanctuary. On December 7, 1855, at 4:30 P.M., five years after they began dating, four months after Fanny returned from the South, Lawrence, twenty-seven, and Fanny, thirty, exchanged vows in a Congregational marriage service. Rev. Adams officiated at the wedding.[7]

Lawrence and Fanny had surmounted many obstacles to arrive at this moment, not the least their three-year separation. In their wedding vows they pledged to join their love and lives and build their futures together.

On that same day, Rev. Adams expressed in his diary his concern about Fanny: "At 4½ at Church, married Fanny & Mr. Chamberlain." He continued, "I feel sadly about poor Fanny, greatly fearing she will not make herself happy."[8] In his various diary entries, Rev. Adams is never specific about the content of his worries for Fanny.

He underlined his words in this last sentence to express his deep concern about Fanny's capacity to be happy as a person, and therefore happy in her marriage to Lawrence.

The day after the wedding, the newly married couple traveled to Brewer to be with Lawrence's family. The Chamberlain family, father, mother, and sister Sae, would again and again be a haven of comfort and encouragement for the married couple.

After Bowdoin's long winter break, seven weeks, Lawrence and Fanny returned to Brunswick and moved into rented rooms at the Stanwood House. He had been offered another provisional appointment at Bowdoin, this time as instructor in rhetoric and oratory for the winter term beginning in early February. Lawrence also accepted the assignment of working with students in German language and literature for an additional one hundred dollars. With hope about their future, and his characteristic humor about their circumstances, Lawrence referred to their diminutive bedroom as "Mrs. Stanwood's closet."[9]

FOR THE FIRST time for Lawrence, being at Bowdoin also meant being near family. Two of Chamberlain's younger brothers were now students at Bowdoin: Horace, who went by the nickname Hod, was a junior and John a freshman. Chamberlain's mother worried about her youngest son's welfare and was delighted that Lawrence would be close at hand; she encouraged Johnny, barely seventeen, to "mind Lawrence, be a scholar, be a man, be a Christian."[10]

A warm family life sprang up in Lawrence and Fanny's rented lodging. The young couple invited Hod and John to join them on winter evenings in their small sitting room, where the two played duets, Fanny on the piano and Lawrence on the bass viol.[11]

DESPITE ALL THAT seemed to be going well at Bowdoin, Lawrence felt like his life was at a crossroads; he was still unsure of which direction to take. Even as he accepted the provisional appointment at Bowdoin, Lawrence was still entertaining the idea of serving as a minister of a Congregational church. His fond memories of his time at the seminary continued to pull at him. At the end of March,

Charles Chesley, a Bowdoin classmate, informed Lawrence of a likely vacancy in Wolfeboro, New Hampshire, at a church where Chamberlain had preached one of his four senior sermons as a student at Bangor Theological Seminary. Chesley asked Chamberlain to "Reply immediately," but no reply has survived.[12]

Six weeks later, Chamberlain entered into discussions with the Congregational church in the coastal community of Belfast, Maine, which was in search of a new pastor. He had also preached one of his four senior sermons in this congregation. Belfast's deacon, Edwin Beamon, wrote Chamberlain on May 13, "I think I express the true sentiment and desire of our people when I say that they are disposed to wait upon your own time if you will consent to give an affirmative answer to a call."[13]

The conversation did not progress far before a letter to Chamberlain from the current pastor expressed certain troubles in the congregation.[14] It is not possible to know exactly what those troubles may have been. But perhaps they put Lawrence off, because he did not continue conversations with the Belfast congregation. What is clear is that just a half year after beginning to teach at Bowdoin, seminary graduate Chamberlain still considered becoming a pastor. Was Chamberlain still discerning whether his vocation led toward teaching or the ministry? Was he discouraged by the tenuousness of his teaching position at Bowdoin? At this crucial moment, we do not know what Fanny encouraged him to do.

DESPITE HIS UNCERTAINTY, Chamberlain again threw himself into teaching, this time as a professor of rhetoric.

In the middle of the nineteenth century, the discipline still occupied a central place in curriculums of American colleges. It was considered a critical part of what it meant to be an educated person.

Chamberlain probably began his basic class in rhetoric by having his students read Aristotle's *Treatise on Rhetoric,* which laid the groundwork for all ensuing conversations on the subject. The Greek philosopher defined rhetoric as "a faculty of considering all the possible means of persuasion on every subject."[15]

As for modern understandings of rhetoric, it is likely Chamberlain selected one or more of the standard pre–Civil War textbooks

Richard Whately, English professor and minister, had a profound influence on rhetorical theory with his Elements of Rhetoric.

written by English and Scottish rhetoricians. He may have used one or more of the big three: George Campbell, *The Philosophy of Rhetoric* (1776), Hugh Blair, *Lectures on Rhetoric and Belles-Lettres* (1783), and Richard Whately, *Elements of Rhetoric* (1828). He had read Whately as a student.[16]

All three rhetoricians were both university professors and Protestant or Catholic ministers who brought a strong moral dimension to their writing.[17]

It is unlikely that Chamberlain would have used the books of any Americans writing on rhetoric. John Quincy Adams, the first Boylston Professor of Rhetoric and Oratory at Harvard, holding the chair from 1806 to 1809, published *Lectures on Rhetoric and Oratory* in 1810. Adams's treatment of rhetoric was mostly a restatement of prevailing ideas.[18] The romantic rhetoric growing out of the writings of Ralph Waldo Emerson and Henry David Thoreau would not make its way into the curriculums of American colleges until after the Civil War.[19]

UNDER THE PEDAGOGICAL system Lawrence had inherited at Bowdoin, the young professor found the responsibilities of his new position taxing. Students would write themes, or essays, the professor would correct and return them, and the students would promptly consign them to the nearest fire. In this first year, 1855–1856, by his count Chamberlain reported he examined 1,200 themes.[20]

As Chamberlain endeavored to encourage his students to be more creative in their writing, he may have remembered a discouraging remark he received on one of his papers when he was a student. Professor Henry Boody commented, "If the writer of this will hold his imaginative powers well in hand, he will be heard from in due time."[21] But Chamberlain, contrary to Professor Boody's advice, could not then, and did not now, want to limit either his or his students' imaginative powers.

He was determined to put in place a more creative and productive method. "I have virtually superseded that course by adopting a regular system of *rewriting;* for the sake of 'getting at' the student's mind (& heart too, for he has one)."[22] In this new process, he encouraged his students not to be "cramped" in their original drafts, assuring them that "attention to the rules" of grammar could come afterward. Very careful with his own prose, he told his students there was no such thing as good writing, only good rewriting. Therefore, he required each student to revise his theme until it was brought to "tolerable accuracy."[23] Lawrence's vigorous teaching method reflected his practice of continually editing and rewriting his college lectures and public speeches.

Later, Chamberlain added a third-year course in which he took an even more active role. He commented on draft versions of student themes and then worked with them closely as they rewrote their original drafts. His goal: watch over the rewriting until they "actually carried a point once and for all."[24]

Student appreciation of the young professor was high, and by the college commencement in August 1856, President Woods found the money to offer Lawrence a permanent full-time position as professor of rhetoric and oratory at an annual salary of eight hundred dollars. Bolstered by his students' enthusiasm and the monetary recognition, Lawrence seemed to have hit his stride in the academic sphere. At this point in his life he felt committed to a path of teaching. With his raise in salary, he felt more comfortable in supporting himself and Fanny.

IN THEIR FIRST year of marriage, Fanny seemed content to be the wife of a young professor. On October 16, 1856, Fanny gave birth to a first child. Rev. Adams rejoiced in his diary, "Lawrence and Fannie [as her name was sometimes spelled] have a daughter!"[25] He expressed his happiness in a letter to Lawrence: "My heart was gladdened."[26]

Chamberlain would write poetically of this momentous event, "In the golden days of the Indian summer of that year, there came to his house an angel of God, who left his living smile—for the loving earth part of the infinite heaven! There was a daughter of the house."[27]

New married life seemed to be going well for Lawrence and Fanny. Despite Rev. Adams's wedding-day worries about Fanny, nothing in the correspondence between husband and wife, or in Rev. Adams's diary, pointed to the contrary. More than Lawrence could have imagined at her birth, he would bond so closely with his and Fanny's first child.

As was the custom at the time, the couple did not name their child at birth. Lawrence, Fanny, and their infant daughter spent the seven-week winter break in Brewer with Lawrence's parents and younger sister. Sae, now twenty years old, joyful in personality, began what would become a deep-rooted friendship with her older brother's wife. Fanny, slow to regain her physical strength, unable to hold the baby when she went downstairs, was grateful for the care and support of Lawrence's family.

Lawrence's parents encouraged Fanny to stay in Brewer when Lawrence returned to Bowdoin. The couple reluctantly agreed.

They continued to be short on money and worried they could not afford the assistance Fanny would need when she returned to Brunswick.[28]

Without the company of Fanny and their baby, Lawrence wrote his wife, "Our rooms are cold & cheerless. I think I shall live altogether at the College." He concluded, "I miss something which was light & life to me."[29]

Soon, he was asking for her return—"How can I let you stay away from me for another long, dreary week."[30] But Fanny hesitated, citing her continued fragile health.

Daughter Grace Dupee Chamberlain, called Daisy

In the spring, Fanny finally made plans to return to Brunswick. But she still had not decided on a name for the child. So Lawrence wrote his wife, "I shall name her Grace Wyllys Chamberlain." In acknowledgment of her grandmother's Huguenot heritage, Grace was later given another middle name: Dupee. As their daughter grew, they called her Daisy. With her brown hair and hazel eyes, everyone said she resembled her father.[31]

Although Fanny and Daisy were settled again in Brunswick, Fanny soon left on a lengthy trip to visit her birth parents and shop in Boston for furniture for their rooms, leaving her baby daughter with Lawrence in Brunswick. Knowing he was concerned about their modest finances, she told him she decided to buy what she could at auctions. While away she wrote loving letters to him. In May a lonely husband wrote her, "Perhaps I am too much a lover for a husband, as the world goes."[32]

In November 1857, the young family had saved enough money to move to a larger home on Lincoln Street. Lawrence's brother Johnny began to board with them, with Joshua Chamberlain paying his eldest son the standard Bowdoin College rent, a help to the young family's finances.[33]

WITH A NOW-PERMANENT position, and an increasingly stable family and financial life, Chamberlain began to settle into teaching at Bowdoin. But the college was at something of a crossroads. On one hand, the institution continued to be oriented toward orthodox Congregationalism. Professors Upham and Smyth had long been the school's religious gatekeepers, finding an enemy in the liberal Unitarianism that was splitting many of the Congregational churches in Maine, and more recently, romantic transcendentalism, which criticized nineteenth-century Congregationalism's continuing ties to earlier Puritan thought.[34]

On the other hand, not all students accepted the boundaries of Bowdoin's orthodoxy. Even Professor Smyth's son, Newman, recalled that, as a freshman in 1859, "I found myself lost in a maze of questionings which my professor seemed to shun as forbidden ground."[35] Newman did not elaborate on the questions, but he may have pushed his professors on the tension between the Calvinist teaching on the depravity of humanity and the new Unitarian emphasis on the perfectibility of humanity.

Chamberlain blended in agreeably with the college's traditional religious orientation. He returned to his participation in the life of First Parish, but with the theological education gained from three years at Bangor Theological Seminary he took a more active leadership role. He led prayer meetings during the week, and often led the prayers in the Sunday morning worship.[36]

IF CHAMBERLAIN FELT comfortable with Bowdoin's religious orthodoxy, he approached the college's educational orthodoxy with a different attitude. He did not go so far as to challenge the classics-steeped curriculum, but he did begin to push back against the old-fashioned teaching methods practiced by most of the faculty. His initial years of teaching would be consumed by seeking a more creative way forward for himself and his students.

Many professors saw their students as boys who needed to be constantly supervised; he saw them as young men who could assume responsibility for their own learning.

Chamberlain quickly came to believe that the standard method of daily recitations was counterproductive to good learning. Rather than simply reciting Virgil, often from memory, he wanted to encourage his students to seek out the meaning of the essays or poetry whose words they were declaiming.

To his dismay, he found the senior faculty opposed to the alterations he was making in his pedagogy. Recitation was the default teaching method. In Bowdoin's recitation rooms, young students typically handed their books to their professors and then recited what they had memorized.

However, after several long and likely heated discussions, he received approval to make some additions to this established method of teaching. Lawrence was not against memorization, for he loved memorizing the Bible, the Westminster Catechism, and poetry, and recalled its positive effects from his time as a student at Bowdoin. Yet he was eager to expand the methods of his teaching to embrace a more dynamic method of questioning received ideas and texts, with an ultimate goal of encouraging critical thinking in his students. He also wanted to devote more time to mentoring his students.

He quickly discovered that his new methods ended up increasing his teaching workload. Chamberlain did not shy away from hard work, but did not want his brain "to be dulled" by simply becoming a corrector of themes.[37] One way he kept his mind fresh was the creation of new courses. In his second year, he created an "optional" class in the Old Norse language as well as a class in Early English language and literature, rare listings in a curriculum in which there were few electives; he also offered "optional instruction in the Spanish language."[38]

WHILE CHAMBERLAIN, NOW a third-year member of the faculty, slowly established his distinctive teaching practices, fast-moving national politics, especially growing tensions between North and South, suddenly swept up Bowdoin with the August 1858 commencement.

The correspondent for the *Portland Transcript* initially described an ordinary annual commencement: "The same old hat on the same dignified Presidential head entered the church at the usual hour surrounded by the dignitaries of the day and the young aspirants for baccalaureate honors."[39] Yet one of the honorees was Mississippi Senator Jefferson Davis, invited by the college to receive an honorary LLD, or doctor of laws degree. After the death of South Carolina Senator John C. Calhoun in 1850, Davis was considered a chief spokesman for the South.

Why was Davis honored? The conferring of honorary degrees in the nineteenth century often did not go through the vetting practices that would become standard in later years. The motivation and chronology behind Davis's invitation remain murky.

President Woods probably learned that Davis, recovering from illness, and at the encouragement of his doctor, was spending three months that summer in the cooler climes of New England, most of it in Portland. Bowdoin's president also knew Davis to be a close friend of Bowdoin alumnus Franklin Pierce, the nation's fourteenth president; Davis served in the Pierce administration as secretary of war from 1853 to 1857.[40] Woods may have also heard of the warm reception the Mississippi senator received when he spoke at several public meetings in Portland where he voiced his hope that in the midst of increasing tensions between North and South peace could prevail.

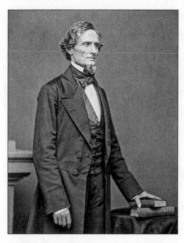

Mississippi senator Jefferson Davis received an honorary doctorate at the 1858 Bowdoin College commencement.

Davis, who some Southern contemporaries described as haughty and cold, knew how to appeal to northern audiences.[41] At one Portland event that summer, the blue-eyed, wavy-haired senator toasted his hosts, "Surely no place could be more inviting to an invalid who sought refuge from the heat of a southern summer." But then he declared his firm belief in the distinct role of the states compared to the federal government: "The general government strictly confined to its delegated functions, and the States left in the undisturbed exercise of all else."[42]

Woods may have expected a parallel set of remarks and a similarly friendly reception at Bowdoin's commencement to what Davis had received in Portland.

At the same commencement Woods and the Bowdoin trustees and overseers awarded an honorary degree to Maine's antislavery senator, William Fessenden. This degree may have been meant to balance the one awarded to Davis, but probably was decided before the idea of awarding a similar degree to Davis was brought forward.[43]

What most in the commencement audience did not know was that only six months earlier, Fessenden, a tall, angular man with a severe manner, got into a shouting melee with Davis, the two hurling insults at each other on the floor of the U.S. Senate.[44]

Davis, in his brief acceptance remarks, did indeed speak in the same tone of the other speeches he'd made in Maine. He emphasized an American identity rooted in the shared legacy of the American Revolution. He attacked those who wanted to divide the country as "trifling politicians," and he emphasized that "local matters"—obviously referring to slavery—should remain local concerns.[45]

Chamberlain, as a member of the college's faculty, would have met Davis at the reception that followed commencement, but he left no account of his reaction to the awarding of the degree to Davis. His focus in 1858 was not on the South and not on the issue of slavery.

The Bowdoin commencement and the awarding of the honorary degree to Davis initially received favorable reporting in the press. The *Portland Advertiser* wrote, "everything seemed to pass off in a manner satisfactory to all concerned."[46]

Two weeks later, however, the same Republican newspaper believed everything had not been so "satisfactory." An editorial portrayed the presentation of the degree to Davis as "a prostitution of the honors and degrees of one of our first literary institutions." The paper asserted that Davis was "destitute of those peculiar acquisitions" that deserve an LLD degree. Because of Davis's zealous sectionalism, it deemed him an "enemy to the Union."[47]

By contrast, *The Argus,* a Portland Democratic newspaper, slammed the attack on Davis, pointing out that the *Portland Advertiser* was stridently Republican. *The Argus* affirmed Bowdoin's decision to grant the degree, declaring there was "universal gratification" over the "justly bestowed" honor given to Davis, who the newspaper portrayed as "not only a distinguished statesman and soldier, but a thorough scholar."[48]

An irony of the debate over Davis's speeches in Maine was that the strongest criticism came not in the Northern but in the Southern press. The *Charleston Mercury* criticized both Davis's speeches and the reception they received from Northern audiences. The leading Southern newspapers considered his speeches much too moderate and thus pro-Union. The *Charleston Mercury* declared, "The Jefferson Davis that we loved is no more!"[49] The New Orleans *Delta* was "distressed at the gallant man's defection."[50]

In 1858, as national politics heated up, and as the honorary degree conferred on Davis sparked controversy among Maine newspapers, Chamberlain focused on his teaching, not politics.

CHAMBERLAIN DID BEGIN to take a more active role in campus politics. He believed there was a growing leadership problem at Bowdoin.

The college's system was governed by two ruling bodies, the

overseers and the trustees, a bicameral system common to many nineteenth-century colleges. The overseers desired that Bowdoin remain an orthodox Congregational college, deeming this identity crucial for continuing financial support. The more independently minded trustees, comprising some members who were not Congregationalists, advocated for more openness to changing ideas, such as the importance of the study of science and a broadened religious identity for the college.

The overseers and the trustees were at frequent loggerheads over professorial candidates. The overseers wanted to consider a professor's faith as well as his educational résumé, while the trustees wanted to place more emphasis on a candidate's academic credentials. In 1856, the college had failed to reelect the professor of modern languages because the candidate had become a Unitarian.

Two years later, Professor Thomas Upham, known for his political maneuverings within the college, approached Chamberlain about accepting the chair of modern languages. Upham believed that Chamberlain, known for both his traditional Congregational faith and his championing of newer methods of teaching, would be acceptable to both governing bodies.[51]

Chamberlain was no doubt flattered by the offer, but in 1858 he was not willing to accept the position. He did not want to give up teaching rhetoric. He was also aware that some faculty still resisted the study of modern languages.

Lawrence's brother Horace applauded the decision to reject the offer. "I am aware of all those pleasant features in the Mod. Lang. Dpt. but still there's nothing so dignified, nothing so ennobling to a man after all, as straining through his mind the noblest thoughts & the finest dictions of his own native Language & pointing them out to others."[52] Hod's mention of "pleasant features" referred to Bowdoin's policy of providing a full salary while the incumbent of this chair spent his first two years in the position in Europe studying modern languages.

But Upham would not give up. He understood that his former student, now the youngest member of the faculty, was one of the keys to Bowdoin flourishing in the years ahead. In 1858, Chamberlain continued to resist the offer, even for a position with a better salary and more influence.

. . .

CHAMBERLAIN'S FAMILY LIFE continued to grow in multiple ways. He had the gratification of seeing Horace graduate with honors from Bowdoin, be admitted to the bar, begin to practice law in Bangor, and marry a young woman named Mary Wheeler.

Lawrence was now deprived of a chief male companion. In good times and bad, Hod had been a conversation partner and a comforting presence. Hod felt the same about his older brother. He wrote Lawrence, "You don't know how much I miss running in to see you once in a while to have a social talk—to congratulate, condole."[53]

In November 1857, Fanny gave birth to a second child, a son. But three months premature, he lived only a few hours.[54] Few records of the child's birth remain. Infant mortality was still quite high in 1857, with approximately three hundred deaths for every one thousand births.[55] Despite this well-known statistic, his death must have taken an emotional toll on Fanny and Lawrence.

Horace "Hod" Chamberlain, younger brother of Lawrence, also graduated from Bowdoin College.

One year later, on October 10, 1858, Fanny gave birth to another son, Harold Wyllys. Fanny outfitted curly-haired Wyllys in dresses, a custom for small boys in that time, enjoying how everyone commented on how much the son resembled his mother.[56]

With a growing family, Chamberlain began to look for a larger home. In 1859, he set his heart on the brown one-and-a-half story Cape Cod house where he and Fanny had earlier rented rooms. Built by a sea captain, Jesse Pierce, the house was situated on Potter Street, close to the Bowdoin campus. Chamberlain knew that the poet Longfellow, now a national celebrity, had once lived in rooms there. The house was also appealing to Lawrence because of its large, beautiful garden—something he had always coveted since enjoying it in his more rural life in Brewer. But the price was $2,100,

Son Harold Wyllys Chamberlain, called Wyllys

far beyond what a young Bowdoin professor could afford to pay.[57]

Joseph Badger, longtime president of the Pejepscot Bank, stepped forward to help. While driving in his carriage about town, he had observed the young Chamberlain hard at work in his garden on Lincoln Street. In a small town, the banker no doubt also knew of Lawrence's growing reputation at Bowdoin. Badger, known for his generosity, with a reputation as "charitable in his feelings," especially toward the young, offered Chamberlain not only a loan from the bank to pay for the house, but a personal note for any expenses he would need to furnish it. What's more, there was no timeline on the notes—they were to be paid back whenever the young professor was able to do so.[58]

With immense gratitude, Lawrence and Fanny were thrilled to reach the milestone of homeownership—one that their financial situation would not have otherwise allowed for a long while. Lawrence took the opportunity to begin to buy and collect books and build a personal library. Always an early riser, he enjoyed being at work in his garden by 5 A.M. in summer months.

But everything was not so easily tended to inside the house. In these early years of their marriage, Fanny suffered from various physical ailments. In 1857, she had become sick with erysipelas, an infection of the skin and tissues that is accompanied by high fever. The illness was so acute that her face became blackened from the disease. Lawrence sat by her bed, reading poetry to her, as he sought to comfort her.[59]

LAWRENCE CONTINUED TO find purpose in his work. By now he was growing into a position of greater leadership within the college. Chamberlain believed Bowdoin needed to change. In conversations with faculty colleagues, he argued that too often the college was offering training for work rather than education for life. His pedagogical interests expanded beyond the teaching of his own courses to the entire college's curriculum.[60]

Chamberlain suggested a number of changes to the teaching-learning dynamics he had pioneered in his classroom. Instead of lectures, which traditionally took up almost the entire class time, he encouraged more student participation. Chamberlain went beyond recitations, believing that students needed more free play in their minds. He wanted to encourage students, not discourage them with criticism of their efforts that was too often in effect in the college. He believed that this more dynamic method of teaching-learning, in which students were encouraged to discover their own agency, could be applied across the college.

As for the teaching of rhetoric, he was convinced the focus should not be simply on the techniques of public speaking, but rather on "what every man most cherishes & most sensitively regards, that is *expression of himself*—the outward manifestation of the thoughts and feelings which are most characteristic, most sacred to him."[61]

For student readings, he sought to balance a heavy reliance on the classics with works of modern language and literature, such as those in French and German. Recognizing that the memorization and recitation of "dead" languages like Greek and Latin bored many students, he wanted to find more effective ways to teach a classical culture he remained convinced would benefit the future leaders of their young republic.[62] Chamberlain's students, encouraged to find and use their own voices, repaid his efforts with their appreciation.

BEYOND THE CLASSROOM, 1860 ushered in a presidential election year. The year would see times of both rejoicing and heartache for Lawrence and Fanny. In the early months, the dreary brown fogs of a Brunswick winter were accompanied by an epidemic of scarlet fever that swept through the town. In these same months, Fanny fell ill again, this time with the burning pain of neuralgia, intermittent pain along the course of a nerve, especially in the head or face, which became a recurring illness. To add to Lawrence's worries, word came from Bangor that his brother Horace was sick with tuberculosis.

In May, Fanny gave birth to a daughter, whom they named Emily, but the baby girl lived only until September. Again, one can imagine the vast grief that Fanny and Lawrence would have experienced over another such loss.

In the following months, Lawrence became concerned that Fanny was spending a significant amount of time away from him and their children. She was either with his parents in Brewer, or with her birth parents in Boston. When in Boston, Fanny heard lectures by transcendentalist Ralph Waldo Emerson and by Thomas Starr King, Unitarian minister of the Hollis Street Church, two of the most sought-after speakers on the lecture circuit. If the ideas of Emerson and King were not Chamberlain's cup of tea, there was no sign that he tried to persuade Fanny against these thoughts.[63]

Lawrence was worried Fanny was spending too much money in Boston, money they did not have with his meager earnings as a young college professor, despite an 1860 raise that brought his salary to one thousand dollars, a recognition of his accomplishments as a teacher.

Too, he was lonely: "The house seems desolate without you—my heart not otherwise."[64] Not wanting to limit his wife's freedom, he wrote a second letter days later, "really painful as it is to me to limit in any way your few, brief seasons of relaxation & enjoyment."[65]

MEANWHILE, TENSIONS WERE building throughout the nation. In the U.S. Senate, Jefferson Davis's speeches veered strongly away from the moderate tone he had struck at Bowdoin's commencement two years earlier. Speculation abounded about who the old Democratic Party and the new Republican Party would nominate as their candidates for president in 1860.

The presidential election in Maine took place on Friday, November 2, 1860.

Abraham Lincoln, the Republican candidate, received 62,811 votes; Stephen Douglas, the Democratic candidate, 29,693; John Breckenridge, the Southern Democratic candidate, 6,368 votes; and John Bell, the Constitutional Union candidate, 2,046 votes.

With 62.24 percent of the popular vote, Maine would prove to be Lincoln's fourth-strongest state, after Vermont, Minnesota, and Massachusetts.[66] But nationally, Lincoln won only 39.8 percent of the national vote, the lowest for a winning presidential candidate in the nation's history—a warning sign.

Chamberlain's father-in-law, Rev. Adams, wrote in his diary the day after Lincoln's election, "Went out before breakfast to learn of the great (probable) triumph of the Republican Party." He voiced his hope: "God grant that it be a triumph, rather of truth and justice."[67]

The next month, Adams confided in his diary the growing sentiments of many in the North: "In these days we are much concerned about Southern secession etc."[68] Nine days later, on December 20, South Carolina seceded. Subsequent secession conventions quickly led to the withdrawal of Mississippi, Florida, Alabama, Georgia, Louisiana, and Texas from the Union, making seven states in all.

At the end of 1860, at age thirty-one, Lawrence had already achieved a well-respected career as a professor at a fine New England college. He, Fanny, and their two children were settled in their new home in Brunswick.

If Rev. Adams was deeply engaged in national politics, there is no record of Chamberlain's response to the election of Lincoln, or to the crisis that the nation faced. But at the end of 1860, the national events that were unfolding rapidly would soon change Chamberlain's life forever.

SEVEN

"Duty Called Me"

This issue embraces more than the fate of these United States.
It presents to the whole family of man, the question, whether a
constitutional republic, or a democracy—a government of the people,
by the same people can or cannot, maintain its territorial integrity,
against its own domestic foes.

—ABRAHAM LINCOLN, MESSAGE TO CONGRESS
IN SPECIAL SESSION, JULY 4, 1861

Abraham Lincoln

L AWRENCE WAS IN BOSTON WHEN CONFEDERATE GUNS AT-
tacked the Union Garrison at Fort Sumter, South Carolina, before dawn on April 12, 1861. He wrote Fanny, describing "this city of
flags and bayonets" now alive with young New England men eager
to enlist to fight this civil war.[1]

When Chamberlain returned to Brunswick, he found the town
transformed.

"War! War! Civil War!" Young John Furbish, at work at Furbish's
Hardware, his father's store on Maine Street, had begun a journal
in February. On April 13 he wrote in his journal "A shudder passes
over us when we think of such a thing, but it has already begun." In
the coming months, Furbish's journal, unknown to Chamberlain
and his fellow townspeople, would provide story after story of the
shifting emotions of Brunswick's citizens as the Civil War began in
1861. On April 17 Furbish wrote, "The people are fast becoming as
one man at the North and the 'Union' is the cry from all mouths."[2]

"The excitement is intense." Two weeks after the attack on Fort
Sumter, Furbish captured the mood of the town. He wrote in his
journal that forty men from the town had already enlisted to serve
in the Union army. "Flags are flying from every prominent building."[3]

In 1861, Bowdoin College counted 269 students gone to serve, including fifty in the medical school, the vast majority of whom had favored Lincoln in the 1860 presidential election.[4]

IN THE FIRST days of the Civil War, a group of students formed the Bowdoin Guard. They were instructed by twenty-four-year-old Charles A. Curtis, who was receiving training at the Military College of Vermont (later Norwich University), and who happened to be in Brunswick visiting friends. He called the Bowdoin students "an unsized mass of green, but intelligent and enthusiastic young men."[5]

Curtis held military drills on the open space in front of the chapel. Clean-faced boys would then march proudly four abreast on Maine Street. Chamberlain, who as a young man had briefly considered a military career at the urging of his father, took an interest in these activities. According to Curtis, the professor "attended drills, listening to commands and observing the responsive movements."[6]

One afternoon, a cart arrived with eight boxes containing twenty muskets each. Their appearance elicited great excitement among the student soldiers. Too much excitement. Curtis had failed to think through what the arrival of muskets might mean to energetic young men.

When Curtis returned to the typically quiet Bowdoin campus that evening, he was met with a shocking sight: "Suddenly, from every window and every doorway of every dormitory blazed volleys of musketry filling the air with the rattle of irregular discharge" of bullets.[7]

In the midst of this "grand fusillade," five figures suddenly appeared: President Woods, a lone professor, and three tutors. The professor, Chamberlain, offered his opinion that the best thing to do was to wait out the students. He advised President Woods, "The young scamps will have to carry their fun to the end."[8]

Curtis remembered that one "irreverent" sophomore spotted Chamberlain from his window and called out, "O Professor! First time under fire! How do you like it?" Taking it all in stride, Chamberlain advised Woods, "Doctor, I think the boys will have to fire their last cartridges before they stop. We had better adjourn."[9]

The episode of the muskets would take its place in Bowdoin lore, with the exact dialogue changing with each retelling of the story over the years. It's a story that is humorous at first glance, but ironic on subsequent reflection: these college boys were not yet aware of the real life-and-death stakes of the coming war.

IN EARLY JUNE, real soldiers, volunteers in the Third Maine Regiment, arrived at Brunswick's large train depot, commanded by Oliver Otis Howard, a Bowdoin graduate in the class of 1850, two years ahead of Chamberlain. Born on November 8, 1830, in the Maine village of Leeds, Howard had enrolled at West Point after Bowdoin. He graduated fourth in the West Point class of 1854 (first place was won by Custis Lee, son of the West Point Commandant, Robert E. Lee). Full-bearded and standing five feet nine inches tall, Howard had dark blue eyes, and abundant brown hair, curled at the side and back.[10]

Howard remembered that patriotic day in Brunswick: "Professors and students, forgetting their wonted respectful distance and distinction, mingled together in the same eager crowd." Tears and cheers and "God speed you, my son," greeted former Bowdoin students, now soldiers, as they marched down Brunswick's Maine Street.[11]

AS THE FALL semester began in 1861, Chamberlain became acutely aware of the empty chairs and familiar faces now missing from his classroom. More and more Bowdoin students were enlisting in the war. Of the sixty-one students in the just-graduated class of 1861, twelve would enlist in the Union army. Two students from North Carolina enlisted on the Confederate side. One student, Charles S. McCobb, enlisted in the Union army on June 15, 1861, and was captured and imprisoned a month later at the Battle of Bull Run on July 21, 1861. Because Bowdoin had almost no electives, Chamberlain would have known all these students.[12]

Union passions were high on campus. The *Bowdoin Orient,* the student newspaper, bantered that if Bowdoin men in the army "hear of a stray LL.D. in their Southern rambles," they ought to "speedily secure him, and send him to Maine—Bowdoin has a little account to settle with him," referring to a desire to withdraw the 1858 honorary degree awarded to Jefferson Davis.[13]

In the early months of the war, most Northerners did not believe this conflict would last long—three to six months at most, people said. Everyone was aware that the North had a much larger army and a greater industrial base. Surely the South could not hold out for long.

FOUR MONTHS INTO the war, Chamberlain made a major professional decision. After three years of soul-searching about his future position at the college, he accepted the position of professor of modern languages. His acceptance brought with it a five-hundred-dollar bonus. With his love of teaching rhetoric, he does not say what caused him to change his mind. It may well be that he accepted the position for the larger good of the college.[14]

Traditionalists in the college applauded his decision. After the previous rejection of a Unitarian candidate for the position, they were pleased with the appointment of Chamberlain. He knew he was following in the footsteps of distinguished predecessors, Henry Wadsworth Longfellow and Daniel Raynes Goodwin. As a huge perk of taking on this role, he was granted a two-year leave to study languages and literature in several European countries. Bowdoin expected Chamberlain to begin his leave early in the fall of the academic year 1861–1862, but because of a number of family issues, especially his brother Hod's ongoing struggle with tuberculosis, he requested to delay it to the following year, 1862–1863.

DEEPLY INTERESTED IN the well-being of his students now serving in the Union army, Chamberlain made a point of corresponding with them. Walter S. Poor, serving in the New York Mounted Rifles, wrote his former professor of his discouragement with the lack of leadership he witnessed every day: "If you see the soldiers drill, hear the confused murmur of voices in the ranks drowning the commands of the officers and distracting the attention of the men, could see the beardless boys, and lifeless and characterless men who command them, you would not be surprised at the panic at Bull Run or our reverses elsewhere."[15] Poor was referring to the early Civil War battle of Bull Run, which took place less than thirty-five miles south of Washington. What was expected to be a great Union victory turned into a stunning defeat, with soldiers straggling back into the capital to the surprise and disgust of citizen spectators. Poor went on to describe the kind of officers they lacked: "We want cool, self-reliant, *self-controlling* officers."[16] Chamberlain must have read Poor's report with dismay. Did this letter spark any initial consideration for his own possible involvement in the war?

In late November, Lawrence traveled with five-year-old Daisy to Bangor to be with his brother. After some initial improvements, Horace relapsed and died of tuberculosis on December 7, 1861. The two brothers had talked often of doing the Grand Tour in Europe together one day.[17] With his brother's death, Lawrence lost a chief source of support in his life, sending him into a winter melancholy.

IN THE NEW year, Chamberlain's grief continued to overshadow his typically positive spirit: "I feel very sad this winter." In February 1862, he wrote his sister Sae, "That [Hod] should be cut down at the very opening of his career, & when he had so much reason to anticipate a prosperous course, seems almost against the course of nature." Perhaps reflecting on what he had just written, he added, "I have no doubt, the change is not a sad one. I do not think for a moment that it is not infinitely better for him, & that having once passed the great boundary he has no wish to be here again."[18]

Two weeks after Lawrence wrote Sae, Brunswick's church bells rang with the announcement that a hitherto unknown western Union general, Ulysses S. Grant, had won a stunning victory at Fort Donelson in Tennessee. As the war lurched on, the college on this day was lit up to join in the celebration.

DURING THE WINTER and spring of 1862, Chamberlain made a number of speeches exhorting young men to respond to President Lincoln's call to arms. He spoke from notes that he subsequently gathered in a folder labeled "Notes of my little speeches & doings which led to my going into the army in 1862." With Chamberlain now a talented speaker, it's easy to imagine the powerful effect of these addresses: "I feel that we are fighting for our country—for our flag—not as so many stars & stripes, but as the emblem of a great & good & powerful nation—fighting to settle the question of whether we are a nation, or only a basket of chips." He concluded, "Come out for your country—answer the call."[19]

Despite widespread patriotism, a great sense of discouragement began to spread across the North. Since the beginning of the war, the cry had been "On to Richmond," but progress to Richmond, the capital of the Confederacy, was agonizingly slow. General McClellan, nicknamed "the little Napoleon," had finally launched the Army of the Potomac in Virginia in what was being called the Peninsula Campaign, and by the middle of May, his army of 105,000 men finally glimpsed the church spires of Richmond. Yet McClellan stopped there and called for reinforcements.[20]

On May 31, Confederate general Joseph Johnston attacked McClellan in the battle of Seven Pines or Fair Oaks. Johnston was severely wounded and replaced by Robert E. Lee.

At fifty-five, the respected and resourceful Lee had made a name for himself in the Mexican War, served for three years as superintendent of West Point, and accepted the assignment to stop the abolitionist John Brown at the U.S. Arsenal at Harper's Ferry, Virginia, in 1859. Now he led a counteroffensive in the Seven Days Battles, a series of battles fought over seven days. McClellan was compelled to retreat, and his peninsular campaign came to an inglorious end at the end of June.[21]

ON JULY 1, President Lincoln issued an impassioned call for three hundred thousand more men willing to commit to three years' service.

Thirteen days later Chamberlain wrote Maine governor Israel Washburn offering his services to Maine and to the Union. Instead of his usual hurried scribble, it seemed he slowed down to write more decisively on heavy white paper, "I have always been interested in military matters." He qualified his declaration, "what I do not know in that line," and underlined "I know how to learn."[22]

Chamberlain knew that his age, thirty-three—ten years older than the average age of enlistment for Union soldiers, twenty-three and a half—and with a wife and two young children meant that he could not be condemned for staying home.[23] What's more, Bowdoin had just elected him to a prestigious faculty position that came with a generous sabbatical in Europe. Yet thinking of all these mitigating factors, Chamberlain told the governor, "But, I fear this war, so costly of blood and treasure, will not cease until the men of the north are willing to leave good positions, and sacrifice the dearest personal interests."[24]

He informed the governor that by the first week of August he would complete his obligations to the college for the 1861–1862 academic year. He added that he would not need to resign his faculty position because he would be on salary during his two-year leave of absence. He was confident he could help raise the one thousand men needed for a regiment that he could help lead.

The governor replied at once, inviting Chamberlain to come to Augusta. At the state capital, Chamberlain met the forty-nine-year-old Washburn. The governor, short and stout, who wore glasses because of his nearsightedness, had won his way in politics with a quick mind and cordial, engaging personality.[25]

Maine governor Israel Washburn, Jr.

Washburn offered Chamberlain a colonelcy and command of one of five new Maine regiments being formed in response to Lincoln's call for three hundred thousand men. Washburn's offer to Chamberlain was typical of what governors in the other twenty-two Union states were offering. The governors understood that the best way to raise military units was to tap men of well-known position, often elected politicians, who could encourage volunteers to enlist.

Chamberlain accepted Governor Washburn's offer but replied that because he was short on military experience, preferred to start at a lower rank and hoped that in time he would prove worthy of being colonel. "Give the colonelcy of the regiment to some regular officer now in the field. I will take the subordinate position and learn and earn my way to the command."[26]

TWO DAYS LATER, Chamberlain introduced fellow Bowdoin alumnus General Howard when he spoke at a rally at the Brunswick train depot on July 19. The general had returned to Brunswick in June to convalesce after the amputation of his right arm in the battle at Seven Pines in Virginia.

Known as "the Christian general," Howard had experienced a conversion at a Methodist prayer meeting while stationed in Florida in 1857. In the ensuing years, whether first teaching mathematics at West Point, or serving in the Civil War, he aimed to make his decisions based on Christian values. Wherever he served, he set up Bible and Sunday school classes. The well-known moniker "Christian general" brought Howard admiration but also derision.

The *Portland Daily Advertiser* reported that in Howard's speech, he offered a strong endorsement of Chamberlain, with whom he believed he shared much in common: "The Professor said that it had been his lot to deal in words for some time past but believed now was the time for deeds. He was willing to go to serve his country at once, if he could do more good elsewhere than by staying at home."[27]

General Oliver O. Howard, the "Christian general," graduated from Bowdoin College in 1850, two years ahead of Chamberlain.

Howard additionally stated, "He was the only man in the State who dared to address an audience upon the negro question and tell them what he thinks." He declared African Americans should be looked to as another pool of soldiers.[28]

Finally, Howard directed some of his remarks to the women in the audience. He said many men were ready to volunteer but were being discouraged by mothers or wives. "It will not do for them to be detaining their husbands, brothers and sons at home, when they are needed by their country."[29]

Fanny left no record of her response to Lawrence's enlistment. It is natural to imagine she was at the very least apprehensive about his absence from her and their children, let alone that he might be wounded or lose his life in the war.

Alice Rains Trulock, Chamberlain's early biographer, wrote that Fanny opposed his decision: "He was risking not only his life, but

Frances Adams Chamberlain, Fanny, with a pensive look, in a photograph in 1862

the entire support of her and their two young children." Trulock based her conclusion on a newspaper interview given by Catherine T. Smith (née Zell) in 1976, who served as Chamberlain's secretary after Fanny's death and thus never met his wife.[30] Although Fanny's "opposition" has been repeated again and again by Chamberlain biographers, and historians of Bowdoin College, it is long past time to question the credibility of this objection, absent any words at any time from either of the parties directly involved.

WORD OF CHAMBERLAIN'S appointment was reported in newspapers from Bangor to Portland before it had been made official. After reporting, incorrectly, that Chamberlain had accepted the colonelcy of the Twentieth Maine Regiment, the *Bangor Daily Whig*, recognizing the unusual nature of Chamberlain's decision, offered its opinion that "This is a significant and gratifying index to the State . . . When such men relinquish high positions of comparative ease and safety to enter the service of their country, it is evidence that the danger is pressing, and the patriotism of the men of '76 still burns brightly in their descendants."[31] The *Portland Daily Press* commended Chamberlain, "who patriotically proposes to exchange the recitation room for the camp."[32] It is likely that Howard, enthusiastic about Chamberlain's decision and hopeful that it might influence others, had spoken with newspapers eager for news about Maine's participation in the war.

An embarrassed Chamberlain wrote Governor Washburn, "I beg your Excellency will understand that these mortifying reports in regard to my appointment, did not come from me." He explained that he had spoken to no one except General Howard "in a private conversation."[33]

CHAMBERLAIN, ENCOURAGED BY the support he received from the governor and General Howard, did not anticipate the response from some of Bowdoin's faculty. They were surprised to read about his decision in the press, and for some of them their astonishment quickly turned to anger.[34] Chamberlain had not thought to consult his colleagues before deciding to leave his Bowdoin post.

Ironically, William "Chalkboard" Smyth, the antislavery faculty member whose home had provided refuge for runaway formerly enslaved persons, led the resistance to Chamberlain's enlistment.[35] Smyth worried that if Chamberlain were to lose his life and therefore not return to his faculty position, his very strategic chair of modern languages might be filled by someone who did not share their adherence to orthodox Congregational faith. Smyth's concern was first and foremost for the identity of the college.

Professor Smyth found a supporter in Maine attorney general Josiah Drummond. The attorney general wrote Governor Washburn on July 22, "Have you appointed Chamberlain Col. of the Twentieth? His old classmates etc. here say you have been deceived: that C. is *nothing* at all; that is the universal expression of those who know him."[36] Not a Bowdoin graduate, rather an alumnus of rival Colby College, Drummond somehow believed he could speak for all Bowdoin alumni.

Years later, Chamberlain would feel greater appreciation for the faculty's opposition, rooted in their concern about the religious identity of the college: "The Professors were men of military experience in the religious contests for the control of the College."[37]

Despite their opposition, the Bowdoin faculty didn't want to lose him altogether. In accepting his appointment, they did not insist he resign from the college, but rather agreed that his two-year sabbatical would become an unpaid leave of absence.

BUT CHAMBERLAIN HAD many defenders as well. Brunswick physician John D. Lincoln, the Chamberlain family physician, who had

delivered their babies, offered a strongly contrasting opinion. He described Chamberlain as a man of "energy and sense," one "as capable of commanding a Regt. as any man out of . . . West Point." He wrote Governor Washburn that many young men "would rally around his standard as they would around a hero."[38]

John D. Lincoln, the Chamberlain family physician

GOVERNOR WASHBURN AGREED. On August 8, he wrote Chamberlain, "I hearby tender you the office of Lt. Col., 20th Regt. ME Vol."[39] On August 14, Furbish wrote in his journal, "Prof Chamberlan [*sic*] goes Lieut Col of 20th Regt."

The governor also appointed twenty-six-year-old Adelbert Ames, the son of a shipmaster from Rockland and an 1861 graduate of West Point, as colonel of the Twentieth.

Chamberlain had declared to Governor Washburn, "I know how to learn."[40] But that would remain to be seen. On the military road ahead, he would encounter challenges nearly unimaginable for a small-town professor accustomed only to commanding a classroom.

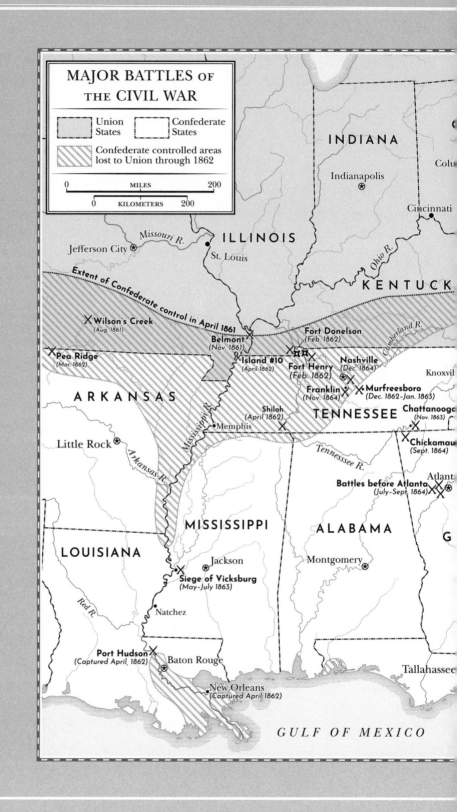

MAJOR BATTLES OF
THE CIVIL WAR

Union States

Confederate States

Confederate controlled areas lost to Union through 1862

0   MILES   200

0   KILOMETERS   200

INDIANA

Indianapolis ✪

Colu

Cincinnati ●

ILLINOIS

Missouri R.

Jefferson City ✪

St. Louis ●

Ohio R.

KENTUCK

Extent of Confederate control in April 1861

✕ Wilson's Creek
(Aug. 1861)

Belmont
(Nov. 1861)

Fort Donelson
(Feb. 1862)

Cumberland R.

✕ Pea Ridge
(Mar. 1862)

Island #10
(April 1862)

Fort Henry
(Feb. 1862)

Nashville
(Dec. 1864) ✪

Knoxvil

Franklin ✕
(Nov. 1864)

✕ Murfreesboro
(Dec. 1862-Jan. 1863)

ARKANSAS

Mississippi R.

Shiloh
(April 1862)

● Memphis

TENNESSEE

Chattanoog
(Nov. 1863)

Little Rock ✪

Arkansas R.

Tennessee R.

✕ Chickamau
(Sept. 1864)

Atlant

Battles before Atlanta ✕✕
(July-Sept. 1864)

MISSISSIPPI

ALABAMA

G

LOUISIANA

Jackson ✪

Montgomery ✪

Siege of Vicksburg
(May-July 1863)

Red R.

● Natchez

Port Hudson ✕
(Captured April, 1862)

Baton Rouge

New Orleans
(Captured April 1862)

Tallahassee

GULF OF MEXICO

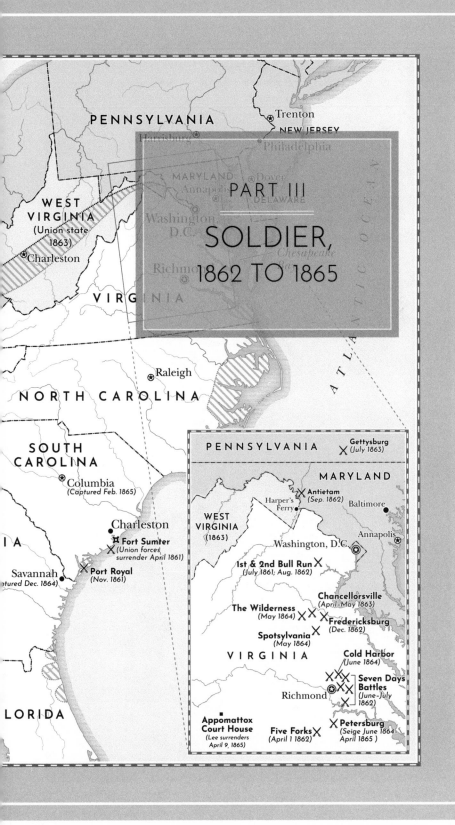

PENNSYLVANIA

Trenton
NEW JERSEY

Harrisburg

Philadelphia

MARYLAND

Annapolis

Dover

DELAWARE

PART III

SOLDIER,
1862 TO 1865

WEST
VIRGINIA
(Union state
1863)

Charleston

Washington,
D.C.

Richmond

Chesapeake

ATLANTIC OCEAN

VIRGINIA

Raleigh

NORTH CAROLINA

SOUTH
CAROLINA

Columbia
(Captured Feb. 1865)

Charleston

Fort Sumter
(Union forces
surrender April 1861)

Savannah
(Captured Dec. 1864)

Port Royal
(Nov. 1861)

PENNSYLVANIA

Gettysburg
(July 1863)

MARYLAND

Antietam
(Sep. 1862)

Harper's
Ferry

Baltimore

WEST
VIRGINIA
(1863)

Washington, D.C.

Annapolis

1st & 2nd Bull Run
(July 1861; Aug. 1862)

Chancellorsville
(April–May 1863)

The Wilderness
(May 1864)

Fredericksburg
(Dec. 1862)

Spotsylvania
(May 1864)

VIRGINIA

Cold Harbor
(June 1864)

Seven Days
Battles
(June–July
1862)

Richmond

Appomattox
Court House
(Lee surrenders
April 9, 1865)

Five Forks
(April 1 1862)

Petersburg
(Seige June 1864–
April 1865)

FLORIDA

EIGHT

The Twentieth Maine

The man of the highest physical courage and the soldier of highest discipline may find that he has something of himself yet to learn.
—JOSHUA LAWRENCE CHAMBERLAIN, AFTER BATTLE OF FREDERICKSBURG,
LETTER TO FANNY, DECEMBER 17, 1862

Joshua L Chamberlain

NEARLY THIRTY YEARS BEFORE THE CIVIL WAR, HARRIET Beecher Stowe mused that certain men would always long to do something more than teaching:

> Men of tact, versatility, talent and piety will not devote their lives to teaching. They must be ministers and missionaries, and all that, and while there is such a thrilling call for action in this way, every man who is merely teaching feels as if he were a Hercules with a distaff, ready to spring to the first trumpet that calls him away.[1]

The trumpet called Chamberlain.

THE CIVIL WAR would be fought mainly by amateurs. These men, called "volunteers," enlisted to meet a crisis. They were not regular army. They joined for a specific amount of time and then expected to go home. America's great tradition of volunteers or citizen soldiers was forever embodied by George Washington. Volunteers like Chamberlain gave their military service to a republic that in turn gave them a voice in their government. The generals in the "regu-

FACING PAGE: *Lt. Col. Joshua Lawrence Chamberlain, Twentieth Maine Regiment, 1862*

lar" army, mostly West Pointers, might grab the headlines, but the "volunteers" did much of the work.

"I found it far more difficult to make officers than soldiers," wrote Edward E. Cross, a colorful colonel of neighboring New Hampshire's Fifth volunteer regiment.[2]

Like Chamberlain, Cross volunteered for the Union army with almost no military experience. A native of New Hampshire, he had established the first newspaper in the Arizona territory, *The Weekly Arizonian,* in 1859. In his only military experience before the Civil War, he commanded an army unit crossing the border into Mexico in support of the revolution for Mexico's independence.[3]

Cross came to believe that the enormous casualties in the Civil War were not the result of new rifle technology, but rather the ineffectiveness of volunteer officers.[4] His observation is a reminder that the transformation of Chamberlain from college professor to military officer was an unlikely story. Despite the recently remembered Chamberlain of historical novel, documentary series, and movie, it was never simple or easy. Nevertheless, from the start, he was determined to make himself into a good officer.

The decision to enlist for war is an individual decision; fighting a war is a collective endeavor. Chamberlain had made his personal choice, but a greater challenge now lay ahead: could he help bring together the 979 men of the Twentieth Maine into a cohesive fighting group?

The Twentieth was the last of the Maine regiments raised to comply with President Lincoln's July 1862 call for three hundred thousand volunteers.[5] Recruits for the Twentieth Maine—farmers, lumbermen, seamen, and merchants—came from ten counties from across the state: Houlton in the north, Portland in the south, and Bangor, Calais, Cornville, Augusta, Brunswick, and Bristol in between.

The Union army was organized by a structure dating to before the Civil War. It divided soldiers into regiments, brigades, divisions, and corps. The basic unit was the regiment, composed of approximately one thousand men, typically commanded by a colonel. A brigade was usually made up of four regiments, led by a colonel or brigadier general. Three brigades typically made up a division in the Army of the Potomac. Two to five divisions made up a corps. In 1862, the Twentieth Maine was part of the Third Brigade, First Division, Fifth Corps of the Army of the Potomac.[6]

Union recruitment rules stated that volunteers were to be between eighteen and forty-five, but many lied about their age: some were as young as sixteen and a few shaded fifty. Chamberlain's youngest brother, Tom, age twenty-one and weighing only 120 pounds, signed on as one of the 979 men in the Twentieth Maine.

ON AUGUST 18, 1862, Chamberlain arrived at Camp Mason, south of Portland, a Civil War training camp established earlier that year. There, new recruits in crisp blue uniforms drilled without Col. Adelbert Ames, who had been severely wounded at the Battle of Bull Run in July and was not due to return to duty until the end of the month. His delay meant brand-new Lt. Col. Chamberlain would have to temporarily assume command.

Chamberlain was painfully aware of his lack of experience. He was immediately grateful for the help of Charles Gilmore, a Bangor native and tough former sheriff who had served in the army since 1861. Gilmore, well-connected politically, arranged a transfer from the Seventh Maine to serve as captain to the Twentieth. The regiment lacked muskets, so Gilmore armed the green recruits with pieces of stove wood and took charge of leading them in their drills.[7]

Chamberlain recognized one man who had been his student at Bowdoin. Ellis Spear, twenty-seven, of slight build, with curly brown hair, was a schoolteacher from Wiscasset. Spear would write later, "I had known him as a student [at Bowdoin]. He was (and is) a gentleman and a scholar and although he was also without military knowledge or experience, he was a man of such intelligence and urbanity and kindliness of feeling that he exerted a useful influence even in the organization of the regiment."[8] Student Spear, who had admired Professor Chamberlain at Bowdoin, was pleased to serve under him in the Twentieth Maine.

·   ·   ·

AFTER A FEW days a delegation from Brunswick arrived to make a presentation to their fellow townsman: a magnificent dapple-gray horse. William Field spoke on behalf of the group. "We beg you to accept this gift . . . appreciating the sacrifice you have made . . . that you may be borne on it only to victory . . . till the spirit of rebellion is crushed and you return, laden with honors."[9]

The new lieutenant colonel expressed his gratitude: "No sacrifice or service of mine merits any other reward than that which conscience gives to every man who does his duty." Conscious of his new position: "I accept it, if I may so speak, not to regard it fairly as my own, until I have earned a title to it by conduct equal to your generosity."[10]

Duty was a word that would be on Chamberlain's lips frequently in the weeks and years to come. This value grew from both his Christian and classical formation. If Chamberlain hoped to win his title by deeds, he already began winning his men with words that pointed beyond himself.

But tension would enter the camp in the person of Col. Ames, who arrived in late August. The regular army officer was just fourteen months past his 1861 graduation from West Point, where he finished fifth in a class of forty-five. He stood six feet tall, broad-shouldered, with a round face and wide forehead, dark brown hair, and hazel-brown eyes. Now the thirty-three-year-old Chamberlain, who had asked to start at a lower rank, was to serve under Ames.

Young Col. Adelbert Ames, a West Point graduate, led the Twentieth Maine Regiment at its formation in 1862.

Spear spoke for many in the regiment when he observed that Ames "very little understood volunteers." Tom Chamberlain voiced even stronger sentiments in a letter to his sister Sae. "I'm sure they will shoot him the first battle we are in." Tom's wish: "Ames would be either put in state's prison or promoted to brigadier general."[11] Lawrence Chamberlain, the new lieutenant colonel, did not complain.

Sometime around this period, Chamberlain's father penned a letter to his eldest son:

> Lawrence, You are in for it. So distinguish yourself as soon as possible and be out if tis long & sanguinary if we lead, short and bloody if they lead. It has got to be settled in 3 mo[nths] for them or three years for us—Shape yourself accordingly. And come home with honor as I know you will if that lucky star of yours will serve you in this war. We hope to be spared as tis not our war. Take care of Tom, as well as you can by way of easy work until he gets seasoned to the Trenches. Good luck to you.[12]

This letter was a fatherly benediction from a man who did not support the war, and who, having already lost one son to illness, did not want to lose another. Yet the man who long ago had told his young son, "Do it! That's How!" also believed a "lucky star" would protect and lead his first born.

Young men of Chamberlain's generation went to war steeped in both patriotic and religious values that they expected to carry with them into battle. In ways none of them could imagine, these values would be tested, frustrated, rejected, changed, and transformed in the crucible of camp, battlefield, and hospital.

On September 1, 1862, Chamberlain's final day at Fort Mason, Fanny and Rev. Adams came from Brunswick to be with him.[13] On a cold, rainy evening, Fanny's feelings must have been heavy as she said goodbye to her husband, surely wondering when and if she would see him again. The Civil War was quickly becoming two wars, the first fought by soldiers, the second experienced by civilians in their homes and towns.[14]

At 6 A.M. the next day, the Twentieth Maine embarked from Portland by train, bound for Virginia. Chamberlain carried with him the New Testament the Whiting Sunday school class had presented to him nine years earlier, surely to keep close to the values first instilled in him.

. . .

IN BOSTON, LATER that day, the Mainers marched through the streets from the railroad station to the steamer *Merrimac* to the sound of sporadic cheers.

"Where are you from?" inquired an old gentleman.

"From the land of spruce gum and buckwheat cakes," responded a burly lumberman, to which the adjoining crowd laughed.

Another gentleman waved his hat and shouted, "Three cheers for the old Pine Tree State."

A tumultuous scene in Boston in the beginning months of the Civil War

"Hip, hip, hip," chanted the Mainers energetically as they made their way toward the port.[15]

On this day, Boston's newspapers were full of reports of yet another Union defeat. At a second Battle of Bull Run, Robert E. Lee's Army of Northern Virginia defeated John Pope's much larger Union army, driving the federal forces back once more toward Washington.

The first sixteen months of the Civil War had not gone according to Northern expectations. With a much larger military, and a huge advantage in industrial capacity, the North expected to win the war in a matter of months. But by September 1862, a sobering reality was settling in: there was no real end in sight.

On the five-day voyage to Washington, student Chamberlain spent much of his time studying drill books, memorizing military practices, and receiving instruction from Ames. Many of the men took umbrage at Ames's stern manner, but Chamberlain was eager to learn what he could from this West Point graduate.

The *Merrimac* docked at Alexandria, Virginia, seven miles south of Washington, on September 7. With church bells ringing for Sunday worship services, Chamberlain and the Twentieth Maine marched into the nation's capital. Everywhere these farm boys and lumbermen looked, they saw signs of the war, including American flags adorning government buildings and private homes.[16]

Twentieth Maine private Theodore Gerrish captured the turbulent scene: "Regiments of soldiers filled the squares, squadrons of cavalry were dashing along the streets, batteries of artillery, long lines of baggage wagons and ambulances were seen in every direction."[17] Chamberlain dispersed English-made Enfield rifled muskets from the Washington arsenal to the men, along with cartridge boxes, bayonets, and scabbards. The regiment spent several days training to fire the muzzle-loading rifles as swiftly as three times a minute—no easy feat.[18]

On the morning of September 12, the Twentieth Maine started marching south. Soldiers in the Civil War typically marched between eight and thirteen miles per day, with the upper limit being around twenty miles. Each man carried more than fifty pounds of equipment: ammunition, knapsack, haversack, blankets, and tin-plated canteens covered with cloth. These Mainers, nearly all of whom had never been out of their state, and outfitted in woolen uniforms, struggled in the intense Virginia heat. As a field officer, Chamberlain rode at Ames's side, or rode up and down the increasingly disorganized line, offering encouragement.[19]

TWO WEEKS AFTER departing Maine, Chamberlain and the Twentieth Maine set up camp near the village of Keedysville, Maryland. Confederate victories in Virginia had emboldened Lee to advance into Maryland. Just miles away, McClellan, young leader of the Army of the Potomac, maneuvered between Antietam Creek and the village of Sharpsburg.

Early on the morning of September 17, General Joe Hooker's First Corps attacked Lee's left line, defended by General Thomas "Stonewall" Jackson. Chamberlain clambered up a hill to watch the ensuing battle, which took place in orchards and farmer David Miller's cornfield. Men in blue and gray fell as casualties mounted.[20]

At 8 A.M., Union general Ambrose E. Burnside was ordered to take his Ninth Corps across the creek and attack Lee on the right. Although Burnside would be criticized for dallying in crossing the stone bridge over Antietam Creek, it was not easy to get across with artillery and wagons.[21]

At midmorning, McClellan ordered General Edwin Sumner's Second Corps to cross Antietam Creek and head for the Dunker Church. The Dunkers were a congregation of German Baptist brethren for whom a central feature of their faith was commitment to pacifism—of which there was none that day.

Confederate soldiers killed at Dunker Church at battle at Antietam

At sixty-five, Sumner, called "Bull," pushed forward bravely. But soon his lead division, commanded by General "Uncle John" Sedgwick, marched into an ambush. Lee, operating with a smaller army, was becoming adept at shifting his forces to meet the point of pressure, and had moved two divisions to meet Sumner's advance.[22]

At 1:25 P.M. McClellan telegraphed Lincoln, "We are in the midst of the most terrible battle of the war, perhaps of history."[23]

Burnside's Ninth Corps, still delayed at the other side of Antietam Creek, bought time for Confederate general A. P. Hill's Light Division to join the battle. Hill commanded 5,824 men on the eve of the battle, of which 3,014 made it to Antietam after a seventeen-mile march from Harpers Ferry to smash into Burnside's flank.[24]

At about 4 P.M., Chamberlain's Twentieth Maine, as part of the Third Brigade, received orders to move up to support General Sumner. They maneuvered roughly a half mile to the right, where they were commanded to wait for further orders.

"We had never seen a battle before," Private Gerrish, who had lied about his age to enlist as a young teenager, later remembered. Chamberlain would have watched the deadly scene Gerrish described: "whole lines melted away."[25]

Late that evening, with the battle paused, but anticipating it would continue the next day, Lawrence tried to prepare Fanny for what he might experience: "Tomorrow we expect to be in the thickest of it all day & as for me I do not at all expect to escape injury. I hope I shall not fall; but if it be God's will I believe I can say amen."[26]

But in fact, neither side chose to resume the battle. Both armies, exhausted, chose to instead treat the wounded and refit.

On that single day, 2,108 Union and somewhere between 1,546 and 2,700 Confederate soldiers lay dead on the battlefield; 9,549 Union and between 7,752 and 9,024 Confederates were wounded.[27]

These were statistics. As a Pennsylvania soldier wrote in his diary, "No tongue can tell, no mind can conceive, no pen portrays the horrible sight I witnessed."[28]

It was the bloodiest battle in American history up to that time; the casualties were four times larger than American casualties on D-Day, and two times larger than the losses from the terrorist attacks on the World Trade Center in New York and the Pentagon in Washington on September 11, 2001.[29] The Twentieth Maine, if not participating, witnessed some of the carnage.

McClellan had the larger army. Of the many indictments against him after the battle, there was the fact that he let the Fifth Corps, within it the Twentieth Maine, remain idle in reserve, when employing them might have shifted the momentum of the battle.

But it wouldn't take long for the Twentieth Maine to take part in the fighting. Two days later, Chamberlain experienced his first skirmish. On September 18, Lee's forces began returning to Virginia. The next morning, Union general Charles Griffin sent two regiments across the Potomac River at Shepherdstown Ford to pursue Lee's rear guard. They encountered Confederate general Hill's Light Division about a mile from the river, but Hill's forces quickly turned and became the pursuers instead of the pursued.

Simultaneously, Col. Ames took some men of the Twentieth Maine across the river and up some steep bluffs, while Chamberlain positioned himself on horseback in the middle of the river to monitor the action. That day, he was riding a black horse lent to him by Major Charles Gilmore in order to spare the magnificent dapple-gray horse given to him at Camp Mason, which he had named Prince, from exposure to gunfire.

As the Twentieth men returned from the bluffs, struggling to navigate the deep, fast-flowing river on foot, minie balls, a type of hollow-based bullet invented in 1847, splattered everywhere. Chamberlain calmly secured his mount and offered encouragement until a bullet wounded his borrowed horse near the bridle, the first of his horses to be shot under him in the war. Inexperienced Confederate soldiers often shot the horse and not the rider, their intended target.[30]

The next day, Lawrence would describe his first action to Fanny. "I was ordered to stand in the middle of the river & urge on the men who halted for fear of fire."[31] In his description to her, he chose matter-of-fact language, not dramatizing his role.

TWO WEEKS LATER, in the first days of October, Chamberlain had his first opportunity to get a glimpse of Abraham Lincoln. President Lincoln had traveled to Sharpsburg to meet with McClellan and review the troops. He visited the Fifth Corps headquarters, where he posed in his tall silk hat, even without it a head taller than his generals, for what would become a famous photo.[32] Lincoln's tall, angular frame attracted notice wherever he went, even before he was nationally known. People of the nineteenth century were smaller than people in the twenty-first century, so that six feet four inches would be the equivalent of someone six feet nine or ten inches today.

Famous Mathew Brady photograph of President Lincoln with his generals at Sharpsburg after the battle of Antietam

Chamberlain and the Twentieth Maine settled into their white tents to wait for new orders. Their assignment: guard the river fords, looking out for "plenty of spies around us." On some days Chamberlain would spend "12 or 15 hours in the saddle." He had always loved horses and had ridden for hours in Maine, but he had never experienced anything as grueling as these long rides, day after day, to guard the fords. On other days, he devoted his time to learning more from Ames. In candlelit evening sessions, they talked about both tactics and military administration, perhaps how to find and attack an enemy's weakest point, or the need to strike the enemy's communications. Lawrence told Fanny, "I study, I tell you, every military work I can find."[33]

Young Tom Chamberlain, writing his sister Sae, spoke for many of his fellow soldiers when he negatively compared Col. Ames to his older brother. According to Tom, Ames drilled and trained and pushed and prodded, and then drilled some more: "I tell you he is about as savage a man as you ever saw." As for the second-in-command, Tom wrote proudly, "I wish you could hear Lawrence give off a command & see him ride along the battalion on his white horse."[34]

. . .

IT IS IMPOSSIBLE to predict how a soldier will fare in the privations that are part of war. Although letters home from Union soldiers are filled with the grim details of camp life, Lawrence seems to have chosen to make the best of a rough environment. When the weather turned cold in November, he wrote Fanny,

> I take my saddle for a pillow—rubber talma for a bed—shawl for a covering & a big chestnut tree for a canopy & let it blow. A dashing rain & furious gale in the night make me put on a skull-cap . . . & pull the talma over me—head & all—curl up so as to bring myself into a bunch—and enjoy it hugely. I would confess to anybody but you, that I was cold—feet especially. However, I enjoy it I say, & get up (I don't say wake up) bright as a squirrel & hardy as a bear.[35]

In another letter, Lawrence described what it meant to be camped in the midst of Confederate territory: "It is difficult to get anything here, because the Rebels who live here will not sell or give. One amiable lady of whom we meekly requested some milk, said she would like to kill the whole of us."[36]

TWO MONTHS INTO the war and their separation, both Lawrence and Fanny were already thinking about when they could next be together. Chamberlain knew American armies did not fight in winter weather—Washington crossing the Delaware on Christmas Day 1776 being an exception: "I don't know where we shall go into winter quarters. Maybe near Washington, we hope Richmond, but possibly near here."[37] He hoped she could make her way south to be closer to him.

In November, Lawrence worried about Fanny's mood, especially as she was prone to depression. He knew she had her hands full with their two energetic children, Daisy, now six, and Wyllys, age four. "You mustn't think of me much. I am in earnest,"[38] he wrote her, adding encouragingly, "I want you to be cheerful & occupy your mind with pleasant things, so as not to have time to grow melancholy."

But she did think of him. On Thanksgiving Day 1862, she wrote

Lawrence from her father's home, "It is about time to go to our lonely home, you cannot imagine *how* lonely to *me,* this Thanksgiving night, when you ought to be at your own home, with all those who long to see you so."[39]

Fanny Chamberlain in a very different photograph, 1862

ON THE MORNING of December 11, Chamberlain's regiment marched from their camp to General Burnside's headquarters at the Gothic Revival–style Phillips House, located at the outskirts of Fredericksburg, Virginia. Chamberlain learned the Fifth Corps would be held in reserve for an impending battle. Fredericksburg, founded in 1727, lay midway between Washington and Richmond. This picturesque Virginia town had grown to five thousand people, but by December 1862, most of its citizens had fled.

With the January 1 signing of his Emancipation Proclamation rapidly approaching and sensing a dispirited northern public in need of a battlefield victory, President Lincoln had authorized a rare winter assault. Frustrated with slow-moving McClellan, Lincoln had relieved him from duty and appointed McClellan's friend, Ambrose Burnside, as the

General Ambrose Burnside, "Old Burn," new commander of the Army of the Potomac

new leader of the Army of the Potomac. Even in a heavily bewhiskered army, Burnside's facial hair set a new standard. In fact, the later term "sideburns" was a corruption of the original "burnsides."

Burnside had planned to defeat Lee at Fredericksburg in mid-November, and then race on to Richmond before Lee could stop him. The army Burnside took over, however, churned with upheaval, many key officers loyal to McClellan having resigned when the president fired "the little Napoleon." Burnside decided to reorganize the Army of the Potomac into three grand divisions, led by Hooker, Edwin Sumner, and William Franklin.[40]

The new leader of the Army of the Potomac believed he would be successful through the pure power of numbers; he commanded 115,000 men while Lee only had 80,000. This led him to move with a deliberate slowness that, when combined with some bureaucratic bungling not his fault, delayed the arrival of necessary pontoon bridges, which he wanted to place both in front of and below Fredericksburg. Their slow arrival gave Lee time to adapt his plans.[41]

On December 11 at 3 A.M., with the section of the frigid waters of the Rappahannock in front of Fredericksburg too deep to ford, engineers began putting the pontoon bridges in place. As more than one hundred Union big guns fired on the town, Chamberlain moved his men forward to observe the bombardment that quickly set fire to building after building.[42] In the evening, the Twentieth Maine moved back a mile to bivouac and wait for orders for the following day.

On December 12, with the temperature due to rise to a balmy fifty-six degrees, Lee, from his headquarters atop a northern group of hills, watched Burnside's movements from his ubiquitous field glasses. The Confederate general wanted time for "Stonewall" Jackson's division to arrive, which would stretch out his defensive line to an impressive three miles. Lee would spend the day improving his positions, waiting for Burnside to attack across an open field of a thousand yards where they would be easy targets for Confederate artillery and guns.[43]

"The whole scene and surroundings on all hand wear an air very romantic and theatrical," noted a New Hampshire soldier in his diary, as he watched thousands and thousands of Union troops clatter across the pontoon bridges.[44] A brass band played "Yankee Doodle." When Sumner, William H. French, and Winfield S. Hancock's men entered Fredericksburg, Lee seemed to offer little resistance. What was the Confederate general up to?

If the New Hampshire soldier thought the scene looked "romantic" from his side of the river, inside the town, the order of the Army of the Potomac broke down. Once-disciplined soldiers became unruly looters. They broke into stores and homes with wanton disregard for civilized norms of behavior. Some justified their pillaging as their due from a city fairly won. But others wrote home of their disgust. A Pennsylvania soldier told his local newspaper that his fellow soldiers pillaged "in a manner worthy of the most Gothic of Goths or hungriest of Huns."[45]

Still on the other side of the river, Chamberlain and the Twentieth Maine relocated across from the lower part of Fredericksburg. And waited. That evening they spent another nearly sleepless night wrapped in blankets on the frigid ground.

On December 13, Burnside ordered his left division, led by Franklin, to attack Lee's right, commanded by Jackson. After initially piercing the Confederate line, Franklin's forces were hurled back. Meanwhile, Burnside ordered the right and center divisions, commanded by Sumner and Hooker, to start frontal assaults on Confederate James Longstreet's First Corps, entrenched behind a sunken road at the base of Marye's Heights. It would long be debated whether Franklin, a staunch ally of McClennan, disobeyed Burnside's orders, or, lacking boldness, simply moved too slowly. A division led by George Meade did break through part of Jackson's line, but "Stonewall" counterattacked and drove the Union forces back.

Louis Kurz and Alexander Allison, Battle of Fredericksburg, *December 13, 1862, lithograph, 1888*

Late in the afternoon, as Union forces continued to storm Marye's Heights, the Twentieth Maine, as part of the Fifth Corps, was
ordered into the town. Chamberlain and his men crossed over one
of the swaying pontoon bridges. He remembered, "The air was
thick with flying, bursting shells; whooping solid shot swept length-
wise on our narrow bridge."[46] At some point in that initial advance,
a musket ball nicked his right ear and neck, but did little injury.

As part of the Third Brigade, the Twentieth Maine formed near
the edge of town. Chamberlain and Ames dispatched their horses
to the rear of their line. Shortly before sundown, the order came to
move out into battle. Confederate guns thundered above them.
Ames called out to Chamberlain, "God help us now! Colonel, take
care the right wing! Forward the Twentieth!"[47]

As the Twentieth Maine was advancing over dangerous open
ground, several of Chamberlain's men fell—wounded or dead. A
soldier up ahead in the Massachusetts Twenty-second Regiment,
Robert G. Carter, looked over his shoulder and described what he
saw in a letter written after the end of the battle: "I saw the Twentieth Maine, which was in our division, coming across the field in line
of battle as upon parade, easily recognizable by their new state colors, the great gaps plainly visible as the shot and shell tore through
the now tremulous line. It was a grand sight, and a striking example
of what discipline will do for *such* material in *such* a battle."[48] Ames
and Chamberlain's drills, day after day, had borne fruit in this moment when needed most.

With darkness descending, Chamberlain's regiment moved
quickly "over fences and through hedges—over bodies of dead
men and living ones" until they reached a ridge that they hoped
would give them shelter and protection for the night.[49]

The men were hungry and thirsty, with the smell of death all
around them, on a very cold and wet night. Colder still because the
men had left their blankets behind in order to move more quickly.
It would be another nearly sleepless night, in part because "we
could hear the voices of the Rebels in their lines, so near were they."
Chamberlain wrote Fanny, "My ears were filled with the cries and
groans of the wounded." He made a grim bed between two dead
men, the dead hopefully protecting him well enough to leave him
among the living by morning's arrival.[50] After seven years of daily

life on a tranquil college campus Chamberlain suddenly found himself in this horrific and deadly warscape.

The Twentieth Maine, frustrated that they were not really in the fight, ended up having to stay "in that hell for thirty-six hours," with the Confederates constantly trying to dislodge them, until the order finally came for Chamberlain's regiment to be relieved. Picking their way through dead bodies, they joined the rest of Burnside's retreating army, crossing back across the pontoon bridges. The regiment lost four men; thirty-two were wounded. In their first real taste of battle, the regiment had fought as a disciplined, organized unit, thanks to the leadership of Ames and Chamberlain.[51]

But the picture was grimmer for the larger Union army: there were more than 13,000 Union casualties to less than 5,000 casualties for the Confederates.

The Twentieth Maine wearily marched back to their camp near Falmouth. As Chamberlain rested for a few minutes, leaning against a tree, Hooker rode through astride Colonel, his large white horse. Seeing Chamberlain, he said, "You've had a hard chance, Colonel, I am glad you are out of it."

Chamberlain replied in frustration, "That was the trouble, General. You should have put us in." Even in those early days, Chamberlain did not shy away from straight talk to a division commander.[52]

Hooker did not reply, but the excitable general was himself furious with Burnside for directing a piecemeal assault at Fredericksburg; his own center division had been divided. He believed that if Burnside had directed a coordinated attack, the outcome of the battle would have been quite different, so he may have agreed with Chamberlain.

AFTER THE ARMY'S crushing defeat at Fredericksburg, Burnside traveled to Washington to present his resignation.[53] Lincoln, who had developed a fondness for Burnside, and who admired a general willing to accept accountability for a defeat, did not accept the resignation. Instead, he chose to give Burnside another opportunity to succeed. "Old Burn," as his men called him with affection, was buoyed by Lincoln's support and determined to win a triumph in January that had prevented him in December.[54]

. . .

ON JANUARY 1, 1863, President Lincoln, visibly fatigued, signed the Emancipation Proclamation, which would change the nation forever: "All persons held as slaves" within the rebellious states "are, and henceforward shall be free."[55] Uncommonly, he signed his name, *Abraham Lincoln.*

The Proclamation's ramifications for the military were not fully understood by Chamberlain and most American soldiers on that historic day. Chamberlain had signed up for a war with the understanding that its sole intent was to preserve the Union. With a stroke of his pen, Lincoln had enlarged the conflict's purpose.

BURNSIDE DID NOT wish to keep his troops shut up in their winter quarters as would have been traditional practice. Wanting to reap the benefit of this rare dry January, he mounted his walleyed gray horse, Major, to do a personal inspection of the fords of the Rappahannock, seeking the best location for a crossing, this time above Fredericksburg.[56]

On January 20, a beautifully dry Tuesday, Burnside's blue-clad troops, including the Twentieth Maine, began to march. The troops traveled rapidly on the dry roads. Burnside hoped this would be the opening of a huge Union victory.[57]

His hopes were quickly shattered. At 7 P.M., after three weeks of clear weather, rain began to fall. There was no Weather Channel to provide a forecast in 1863. Chamberlain and the Twentieth had made it only three miles from camp. Rain fell all through the night, occasionally mixed with sleet, and accompanied by winds that blew away some of the tents.[58]

The next morning, the soldiers awoke to a sea of mud and relentless rain cascading down. Horses struggled to pull the heavy artillery through the quagmire the roads had become. Wagons became stuck in the viscous reddish Virginia mud. On the other side of the Rappahannock, Confederate soldiers set up large mocking signboards, one of which read BURNSIDE STUCK IN THE MUD.[59]

One piece of poetry that circulated among Union troops at the time:

Now I lay me down to sleep
In mud that's many fathoms deep;
If I'm not here when you awake,
Just hunt me up with an oyster rake.[60]

On January 23, Burnside ordered the troops back to winter camp, only to see the sun reemerge on January 24.

What would the Northern public think of this latest debacle? By 1863, a large body of embedded war correspondents and illustrators were reporting on every battle of the war for eager readers across the nation. Photography was invented in 1839, but photographic equipment was too unwieldy and exposure speeds too lengthy to be of use on battlefields. Besides, there was no means to transmit a photograph to a printing plate for publication.

Thus, illustrators like Alfred R. Waud, a full-time "special artist" for *Harper's Weekly,* traveled with the Army of the Potomac. His illustration of Burnside's march brought the disaster immediately to the public's attention. This latest failure for the Army of the Potomac became christened, contemptuously, the "Mud March."[61]

British-born Alfred R. Waud depicts Union forces coping with the challenge of winter weather in 1863 in what would be called Burnside's "Mud March."

Chamberlain understood that Burnside could no longer keep his command. But who would Lincoln choose to replace him at this time of sinking morale? Whoever he chose, the president's selection would be the fourth commander of the Army of the Potomac in less than two years.

On January 26, 1863, Lincoln replaced Burnside with Hooker, though the president let Hooker know that he did not like his loose talk, especially his criticisms of Burnside after Fredericksburg.

Handsome, with brown hair, blue eyes, and an outgoing person-

ality, Hooker received the nickname "Fighting Joe" for his bravery in the spring 1862 Virginia Peninsula campaign. He did not like the nickname because he believed it led the public to think "I am a hot headed, furious young fellow" not given to calm and thoughtful military leadership.[62]

Still, Hooker had gained a reputation for caring about his soldiers. Upon assuming command, he built new hospitals, gave instructions to let his troops observe the Sabbath— soldiers now had time to do much of their letter writing on Sundays—and improved the quality of foods: vegetables arrived, and bakeries were set up to provide the men with fresh

President Lincoln selected "Fighting Joe Hooker" to replace Ambrose Burnside as commander of the Army of the Potomac.

bread instead of hardtack. Hooker stated, "My men shall be fed before I am fed, and before any of my officers are fed."[63] Chamberlain welcomed the appointment of Hooker, having made it the first principle of his own leadership to care for his men in every way possible.

AFTER FIVE MONTHS of war, Professor Chamberlain had learned many lessons that were altogether new to him. The unique bond between soldiers was a relationship he had never encountered, very different from his bond with the young Bowdoin students. As a teacher, he took pride in being a good judge of students; as a lieutenant colonel, he was still trying to discern the difference between a courageous soldier and a skulker—a soldier who shirked his duty. Finally, he was gaining the skill to make instantaneous decisions on the battlefield, so different from the periods of calm reflection he had had to make choices about the curriculum at Bowdoin.

He loved the drama and the danger of the soldier's life, but he was about to learn much more about the courage it demanded.

NINE

"As Good a Col as in the Army of the Potomac"

A gentleman of the highest moral, intellectual and literary worth.
—COLONEL ADELBERT AMES, REPORT ON LT. COL. JOSHUA LAWRENCE
CHAMBERLAIN, ANNUAL REPORT OF THE ADJUTANT GENERAL,
STATE OF MAINE, 1862

Adelbert Ames

I N THE DIFFICULT MILITARY WINTER OF 1863, CHAMBERLAIN
was about to receive an unexpected opportunity.

Hooker, the new commander of the Army of the Potomac, recognized the need to raise morale after Burnside's "Mud March"
and subsequent resignation. One of the first things Hooker did
upon assuming command at the end of January was to tell his officers they could apply for ten-day winter leaves. Chamberlain wasted
no time in putting in his request.

Officially, Chamberlain wished to return to Maine to meet with
the new governor, Abner Coburn, in Augusta, for the purpose of

Maine governor Abner Coburn

recruiting soldiers, especially officers, for the Twentieth Maine. Unof-
ficially, his heart leaped at the
prospect of being with Fanny and
the children in Brunswick.

His first stop on his return to
Maine was the house on Potter Street.
Rev. Adams penned a flurry of entries in his diary over the next several
days about the warm welcome Lawrence received—a dinner in Adams's
home, a reception at First Parish on

Sunday, visits with faculty and students at Bowdoin, and other joyous reunions.[1]

Chamberlain had missed the birthdays of Wyllys and Grace when he turned four and she turned six the previous October. With many husbands, fathers, and sons away in the war, the brief return of one soldier to his family was treated as a communal event in the small town.

Chamberlain then turned his attention to his recruitment assignment. Casualties, both from battles and disease, tended to greatly reduce the strength of regiments within the first months of their formation. Maine, like most of the states, had no standard method in place to replace members of regiments, except to dispatch someone from the field to recruit new men.[2] Eleven officer positions needed to be filled. Lawrence wanted to avoid nepotism, but later in the month Col. Ames would elevate young Tom Chamberlain to lieutenant.[3]

Military mission accomplished, Lawrence stopped once more in Brunswick to pick up Fanny to accompany him south. Cousin Deborah would care for the children in her absence. Lawrence and Fanny traveled together to Washington where she applied for a pass—not easy to get—to visit him in his winter camp. Lawrence then returned to Virginia, while Fanny would have to wait in the capital to receive permission to join her husband.

AT WINTER CAMP Lawrence once more took on the role of student. This time the teacher was Strong Vincent, a colonel of the Eighty-third Pennsylvania. An 1859 Harvard graduate, former schoolmaster, and lawyer from Erie, Pennsylvania, the colonel's appearance matched his name. He commanded respect with

Twenty-five-year-old Col. Strong Vincent of the Eighty-third Pennsylvania became a mentor to Chamberlain.

his powerful voice and purposeful face as much as his rank. The twenty-five-year-old Vincent had earned a reputation as a master teacher of volunteers. His roster of lessons was constantly evolving, and he had already added the lessons learned from the difficult battles of Antietam and Fredericksburg to his curriculum.[4]

And Ames continued to drill—monotonous, draining, exhausting sessions. But now Chamberlain understood all this drill was necessary to be ready for the next battle—whenever and wherever that might come.

In March, Hooker instituted another change intended to add to the esprit de corps of each unit. Every man would wear an insignia badge. They would be different-colored two-inch squares, and they would be worn on the center of the top of the cap. The badges would be a means of identification, but more importantly, they became a source of pride.

The eight-pointed Maltese cross was adopted by the Fifth Corps as their symbol.

The badge of Chamberlain's Fifth Corps was a Maltese cross. The Maltese cross was an ancient symbol of protection. Its origin dated back to Crusaders ready to sacrifice their lives for their fellow soldiers. Measuring one and seven-eighth inches across, it consisted of four V- or arrowhead-shaped concave quadrilaterals converging at right angles.[5]

BACK IN WASHINGTON, Fanny waited impatiently to join her husband. Everywhere she walked, she saw soldiers: boisterous soldiers on leave, wounded soldiers on ambulances being delivered to one of the growing number of hospitals. She also witnessed the sadness of distressed wives, mothers, and fathers who arrived daily in search of loved ones in hospitals.[6]

When her pass finally arrived, she traveled fifty-two miles south to Lawrence's camp near Falmouth, Virginia. Her arrival brought her into a very different space—deeply male and military in nature. All around her, mostly young men played cards around campfires, bathed and urinated publicly, hollered profanities at one another, and saturated their conversations with cheeky stories about women.

Lawrence and Fanny rejoiced in being together. In camp, she delighted in listening to the regimental bands, while outside of camp, the two enjoyed horseback riding in the Virginia countryside. Solemnly, they observed military processions that placed fallen soldiers in their final resting places. After her allotted time was up, Fanny returned to Washington, eager to apply for another pass.[7]

THE DAYS AND weeks immediately following Fanny's departure were difficult for Chamberlain. But an early April visit by President Lincoln provided a huge boost of morale to him and the Twentieth Maine.

Lincoln joined General Hooker in a formal review and inspection of the Fifth Corps. Each man in the Twentieth Maine proudly wore his new cap with the new red Maltese cross badge on it.

Lawrence viewed a president dressed in a black suit, which to many made him look like an undertaker. The soldiers had to hold back their laughter when the tall Lincoln was placed upon a small horse.

Chamberlain's Twentieth Maine participated in an April 1863 review by President Lincoln.

At the same time, the men could not miss the brooding, sorrowful face of their commander in chief.[8] The war was going badly, and critics had begun to call it "Mr. Lincoln's War."

Hooker, determined to change the momentum of the war, was in the midst of preparing his large army for what he hoped would be a decisive 1863 spring campaign. He planned to cross the Rappahannock and Rapidan upriver from Fredericksburg and attack Lee's left flank at Chancellorsville.

But first, there was a more urgent matter to attend to. With smallpox on the rise, the medical department wanted to be sure every man in the army was vaccinated. Most federal soldiers had received the vaccination before they were sent from their home staging areas, but the Twentieth Maine had not. Smallpox, over the span of the Civil War, would kill almost 40 percent of the Union soldiers who contracted it.[9]

On April 9, the men of the Twentieth Maine were given the vaccine, which had been developed by Edward Jenner in 1798. Preventive inoculation produced a mild form of the disease that would then provide immunity against the actual disease. But knowledge of bacteriology was limited, and things could go amiss.[10]

Horrifically, the vaccine the Twentieth Maine received was defective, causing the dreaded disease to sweep through Chamberlain's men.

In a little over a week, there were eighty-four cases of smallpox within the Twentieth Maine, thirty-two of them serious, with three men dead. Surgeon Nahum P. Monroe worried the men would spread the disease to other regiments. So rather than preparing to

As the Twentieth Maine looked forward to the beginning of the 1863 spring campaign, to their great disappointment they were confined to "Camp Small Pox."

join Hooker in the spring campaign, on April 22 the Twentieth Maine was ordered to be sequestered at Quarantine Hill, or, as some soldiers called it, "Camp Small Pox."[11]

Chamberlain, frustrated by this unexpected turn of events, did not allow his disappointment to be reflected in an April 24 letter to Fanny, which he titled not "Camp Small Pox," but "New Camp." He did not even write about the disastrous outbreak of smallpox.

Instead, he spent much of the letter telling her of his conflicted feelings over news he had just received from Brunswick. Captain Joseph Badger, who had helped them to purchase their Potter Street home, had died and named Chamberlain executor of his estate. Lawrence knew he would receive a sizeable compensation to act as executor, but also understood he would need to be in Brunswick on May 4 when the will would be read. However much he wanted to fulfill Badger's request, "Nothing will induce me to be absent from my Regt when they went into battle."[12]

JUST AS LAWRENCE completed the letter, his life was about to change again. Col. Ames, seeking a higher opportunity, had obtained a position on the staff of the Fifth Corps Commander, General George G. Meade. Ames's appointment meant Chamberlain was now elevated to command the Twentieth Maine.[13]

When he learned of Ames's promotion, he may have thought of all he had learned from the West Point officer. They were so different in temperament, but Chamberlain would always be grateful that Ames had taught him that there was no substitute for tough-minded preparation.

Ames departed the Twentieth Maine for what would become an outstanding military career in the Civil War. In the years that followed, he would remain in touch with Chamberlain, whom he admired greatly.

ON APRIL 27, when Hooker broke camp from winter quarters to begin his spring campaign, and Ames rode off to join in the fight, Chamberlain was left behind in charge of the "pest house," his new quarantine command.[14]

Hearing the guns beginning the Battle of Chancellorsville, the usually mild-mannered Chamberlain went so far as to ride to Hooker's headquarters at Falmouth, where he pleaded with Hooker's chief of staff, General Daniel Butterfield, to be given some role in the battle. When his request was turned down, he protested, "If we couldn't do anything else, we could give the enemy the small-pox."[15]

In the end, Chamberlain and the Twentieth Maine were given an assignment, if only a small one: guarding the federal telegraph lines from the Confederates who sought continuously to break them.[16] "I was in my saddle *all* the nights inspecting every inch of the line," he wrote Governor Coburn. On May 4, while riding on nighttime duty, Lawrence's prized horse Prince was wounded by part of a shell. It is unknown whether Prince ultimately survived.[17]

Chancellorsville, like Fredericksburg five months earlier, ended in an ignominious defeat for federal forces. William Swinton, war correspondent for *The New York Times,* captured the contradictions of Hooker's leadership best.

> Till he met the enemy, Hooker showed a master-grasp of the elements of war, but the moment he confronted the antago-nist, he seemed to suffer collapse of all his powers, and after this his conduct, with the exception of one or two momentary flashes of talent, was marked by an incomprehensible feeble-ness and faultiness; for in each crisis, his action was not only bad—it was, with a fatal infelicity, the worst that could have been adopted.[18]

When word reached Lincoln that Hooker's troops were retreat-ing across the Rappahannock River, the president was crestfallen. Noah Brooks, correspondent of the *Sacramento Daily Union,* was with the president when he received the news; he reported that he had never seen the president "so broken, so dispirited." Lincoln, clasping his hands behind his back, walked up and down his office exclaiming, "My God! My God! What will the country say! What will the country say!"[19]

Chamberlain was disappointed that he did not participate in the Battle of Chancellorsville, successful or not. Still in quarantine, he used this time to catch up on his correspondence, including to his six-year-old daughter, "My dear little Daisy." He wrote of "a big battle, and we had a great many men killed or wounded," and told her, "We shall try it again soon, and see if we cannot make those Rebels behave better, and stop their wicked works in trying to spoil our Country, and making us all so unhappy."[20] It would not be until late May that the quarantine was lifted, and Col. Chamberlain could move his men from Camp Small Pox.

SOON AFTER, THE new colonel found himself dealing with an unexpected problem. As Spear recorded in his diary, forty men from the Second Maine who refused to fight any longer were brought into Chamberlain's camp under guard.[21]

The Second Maine was the second regiment recruited at the outbreak of the war in 1861, and the first to depart Maine to fight. Mustered in Bangor, its men had signed up when everyone thought the war would be over within a few months. By 1863, the Second Maine had fought bravely in eleven battles. Their two-year commitments were up in May 1863, and they looked forward to joyous reunions with family and friends.

Or so they thought. It turned out that some of the men had signed three-year enlistments, but the paperwork had not been easy to comprehend. They believed they had the right to accompany their comrades in arms home to Maine. The remaining men, deemed mutineers, arrived in Chamberlain's camp under guard of the 118th Pennsylvania. They were accompanied by orders from General Meade to "make them do duty or shoot them down the moment they refused."[22] Now, shortly after Ames left, the new colonel found himself dealing with a dilemma.

What was Chamberlain to do? He knew that Ames probably would have followed Meade's orders—but he was cut from different cloth. He sympathized with the men, judging that they may have been deceived by zealous recruiters; they had certainly demonstrated their willingness to fight over the last two years.

Chamberlain rode to Meade's headquarters. He requested and received permission to deal with the forty men of the Second Maine in his own way. Upon his return, discovering the men had not been fed the previous three days, he immediately provided them with rations and fresh clothing.[23]

He then called the forty men together and told them he would deal with them "as soldiers should be treated." He promised he would examine their cases and that, in the meantime, "they would lose no rights by obeying orders."[24] In the succeeding weeks, nearly all did fight. Chamberlain wisely placed the forty in different companies, thereby reducing any opportunity for resistance to serve out their three years. Another positive effect? The ranks of the Twentieth Maine, having been thinned by smallpox, were replenished.

Meanwhile, Chamberlain wrote Governor Coburn, "I sincerely wish these men were fairly dealt with by those who made them their promise."[25] In one of his first tests as the new colonel of the Twentieth Maine, Chamberlain exercised firm but empathetic leadership.

Fanny, unable to get a second pass to visit Lawrence, and realizing he could not come to be with her, decided to leave Washington, travel to New York, and wait to see what might happen next. When she arrived at the St. Germain Hotel, she wrote Lawrence of her new location, and notified Cousin Deborah in Brunswick.[26] Why Fanny decided to travel to New York rather than staying in Washington or returning to Brunswick and her children is a never-answered riddle.

To make the distance between them even more challenging, mail service in these years was often erratic, especially during wartime. It would be weeks before Lawrence received her first letters, so not knowing Fanny's whereabouts he wrote letters to her in Brunswick.[27]

"Did you ever *hear* of such a thing?"[28] Sae, at the Chamberlain family home in Brewer, voiced dismay in a letter to Tom that Fanny would be gone from home for such a long time.

Cousin Deborah, finally receiving a letter from Fanny in New York in early June, responded tartly: "Oh Fanny if I am not vexed with you awfully, to think you should let your indolence so far overcome your sense of propriety as to be all this time at the St. Germaine & not write to any living being to let them know where you are."[29]

. . .

As for Chamberlain's Brewer family, John Chamberlain finally had the opportunity to visit his brothers Lawrence and Tom after his second year at Bangor Theological Seminary. He accepted an assignment as a representative for the U.S. Christian Commission, an organization founded in November 1861 for the purpose of serving the spiritual and physical needs of Union troops—furnishing supplies, medical services, and Christian literature.

John Chamberlain visited brothers Lawrence and Tom in Virginia while a representative of the U.S. Christian Commission.

Once in Virginia, John learned that Lawrence was away from camp, guarding the fords of the Rappahannock. While he waited for his older brother's return, John participated in religious services, distributed Bibles and Christian literature, and wrote letters home for sick soldiers. One day, while visiting the Fifth Corps headquarters, he wrote later in his diary:

> I spoke with 20 + every man had the same story to tell of their Col. To a man they said, "We have as good a Col as in the Army of the Potomac." When they learned that John was the brother of their colonel, they were eager to voice their feelings. "He is full of military brass but considerate & treats the men like men not dogs as Ames did." They told John, "Would you believe it he had some breastworks [temporary fortifications] to throw up and what does he do but off the coat and into it himself." John wrote, "Every man had the same story to tell of their Col."[30]

John stayed on so that he could see Lawrence, the popular "Col," and his brother Tom.

Meanwhile, all along the picket lines on the Rappahannock, rumors spread that the army was about to move—but when and where?

While Hooker struggled to decide on his next action, Lee was certain of his. On June 3, the Confederate general started a march north, but federal intelligence services labored to detect his intentions.[31] What was his objective? Baltimore? Philadelphia? Harrisburg?

In the following days, Hooker struggled with a response to Lee's initiative, finally sending a telegram to Lincoln recommending that, as Lee moved north, he wanted "to pitch into his rear." Lincoln, by this point comfortable in his role as commander in chief, saw more clearly than Hooker that Lee was "tempting" the Union commander, confident he could elude him as his Confederate army made its way north. The president employed one of his colorful analogies to make his point: "I would not take any risk of being entangled upon the river, like an ox jumped half over a fence, and liable to be torn by dogs, front and rear, without a fair chance to gore one way or kick the other." With his increasing understanding of military strategy, Lincoln was out-generaling his leading general. We now know that Lee had decided he could not stay below the Rappahannock River and await the Army of the Potomac to attack him a third time. Buoyed by triumphs at Fredericksburg and Chancellorsville, he had become convinced that the way to contest a larger and better-equipped adversary was to move north in a bold military advance, which might persuade the North they could not win a prolonged war. He also was hopeful that Confederate battlefield success could lead to greater strength at the ballot box for anti-Lincoln politicians in 1863 and 1864.[32] Lee was looking for both military and political routes to win the war.

FOR THE FIRST time since their quarantine, on June 13, Chamberlain and the Twentieth Maine broke camp and began hurrying north. That evening, at Morrisville, Virginia, Strong Vincent, recently promoted to lead the Third Brigade, invited two men to dine with him: Colonel Joshua Lawrence Chamberlain and General Adelbert Ames—a reunion meal of sorts.[33] How we would like to know what they discussed.

The men of the Twentieth Maine were in good spirits and well rested. The next day they arrived at Catlett's Station, a busy telegraph station and mail stop, where they took their place in Meade's Fifth Corps.[34]

Chamberlain had only been commanding the Twentieth Maine for less than two months. His leadership had not yet been truly tested under battle. Many a promising officer, including West Pointers with elite military education and training, had succeeded in drills but faltered in the turmoil of war. Yes, Chamberlain had exhibited courage at Fredericksburg, but how might the college professor perform when commanding nearly five hundred men remaining in his regiment through protracted fighting?

Even through his many successes, Chamberlain always held himself with humility and an eagerness to learn. When Maine governor Washburn first appointed him a volunteer officer, Chamberlain had readily admitted his lack of military knowledge and training, but stated, *"I know how to learn."* As the new colonel of the Twentieth Maine, anticipating the greatest battles the war had seen yet, one question was surely at the forefront of his mind: had he learned enough?

Little Round Top

I place you here! This is the left of the Union line. You understand!
You are to hold this ground at all costs!
—GENERAL STRONG VINCENT TO JOSHUA LAWRENCE CHAMBERLAIN,
GETTYSBURG, JULY 2, 1863

I N JUNE 1863, TWO HUGE ARMIES BEGAN MARCHING NORTH FROM Virginia toward what many believed would be a crucial battle—although ordinary soldiers in both armies, including Chamberlain, did not know exactly where or when it would take place. The Army of Northern Virginia, 75,000 men, their morale soaring, victorious in the battles of Fredericksburg and Chancellorsville, moved with confidence in their leader, Lee, and themselves. Hooker's Army of the Potomac, 112,000 strong, uncertain of Lee's intentions, and worse, unsure of their commanding general, nonetheless marched with belief in their fighting ability.

IN WASHINGTON, PRESIDENT Lincoln was often working eighteen hours a day to end the war. Every few hours, he would pick up his hat and cross the street from the White House to the War Department at the corner of Seventeenth Street and Pennsylvania Avenue. There, he would read through a stack of telegrams from Virginia, determined to keep well-informed of military strategies and developments.[1]

The commander in chief habitually downplayed his influence in the war. He closed a June 16 letter to Hooker by recalling the story of Jesus's commendation of the poor widow who willingly gave away two of her small coins, called mites, saying that he would continue to contribute "his poor mite."[2]

EMBEDDED WITHIN THE opposing armies were two regiment leaders whose names would soon become known beyond their native states. Two days after Chamberlain and the Twentieth Maine left their camp on the Rappahannock River to march north, William Oates and his Fifteenth Alabama Regiment departed their encampment at Culpeper Court House in central Virginia. Like Chamberlain, Oates received command only in April, but the Alabamians were already veterans of seven battles, including Stonewall Jackson's Shenandoah Valley Campaign, the Virginia Peninsula battles, Antietam, and Fredericksburg; they marched as part of Evander M. Law's Brigade, John Bell Hood's Division, and James Longstreet's First Corps, one of three corps in the army Lee had reorganized after the recent death of Stonewall Jackson in May 1863.[3]

But while Oates and Chamberlain assumed their roles at the same time, their personalities and values could not have been formed in more different families and circumstances.

Five years younger than Chamberlain, Oates was born in rural Pike County, Alabama, on November 30, 1833. His parents, William and Sarah, had recently migrated from South Carolina to start a farm in the largely uncultivated land of southeastern Alabama. Unlike Lawrence's father, who worked hard to instill his Christian values in his close-knit family, William grew up with an alcoholic

William Calvin Oates, leader of the Fifteenth Alabama Regiment

and abusive father.[4] Unlike Lawrence's parents, who valued education for their children, when William asked his father for the opportunity to go to school, he was told that there was no time for school—his oldest son's labor was needed on the farm.[5] In contrast to the intellectual New England Congregationalism that formed young Lawrence's religious values, the emotional Second Great Awakening that shaped the Baptist churches of Oates's youth had little influence on William, for whom faith was not a part of his formation as a child. As opposed to Lawrence's steady advancement from student to professor, at age eighteen William embarked on three wild years during which he roamed from Florida to Texas, gambling, fighting, cavorting with criminals, having run-ins with the law, and pursuing romantic dalliances.[6]

Yet the two leaders did share some similarities. Determined to make a fresh start upon returning to Alabama at age twenty-one, Oates discovered both Christian faith and education. He pursued his schooling at Lawrenceville Academy, graduating with the equivalent of a high school education. Like Chamberlain, Oates came to love books and became an insatiable reader. After just four months' study in a law office in Eufaula, Alabama, Oates was admitted to the bar in October 1858. He set up a law office in Abbeville and became a respected lawyer. He also purchased a Democratic newspaper, *The Abbeville Banner,* and as its editor exercised a prominent voice in his community. Oates initially opposed secession but joined the Confederate army when war erupted.[7] Like Chamberlain, his newly embraced faith, education, and professional ambition helped form a set of values—integrity, truthfulness, and a compassionate spirit toward others—that would mark his leadership in the Civil War.

In June 1863, the two men's courses were set on a collision course.

OATES'S REGIMENT MARCHED west and north up the eastern edge of the Blue Ridge mountains. On June 17, the Fifteenth Alabama, with rifles held high, forded the swift-running waters of the Potomac into Maryland.

That same day, Chamberlain's regiment experienced one of their hardest marches to this point in the war. They walked eighteen miles in the kind of heat and humidity that his soldiers had never experienced in Maine, their trek aggravated by lack of water. Dust, which coated their faces and clothes, marched with the men. Four men died of sunstroke; more fell out along the roadside.[8]

Chamberlain was one of the men who fell ill: "Col Chamberlain quite sick & sent to a neighboring house," Captain Spear wrote in his diary.[9] "Our beloved Col Chamberlain is not able to command us owing to sickness, but he is on the recovery, and we all hail the day he is able to resume his command of the regiment," Lt. Holman Melcher wrote to his brother. Chamberlain would rest and recover in Gum Springs, Virginia, as the Twentieth Maine marched on, crossing the Potomac at Edwards Ferry on 1,400-foot pontoon bridges nine days after Oates's Alabamians had done so.[10]

On Sunday, June 28, the Twentieth Maine rested outside Frederick, Maryland, in observance of the Sabbath. Stopping on Sunday gave the men the opportunity to attend religious services, write letters home, and boil their clothes—the only protection against the ever-present lice.[11] William Livermore, a farmer from central Maine, confided to his diary, "I had a restless night, for the lice were aware of my designs and they seemed to rally their whole force, and they were drilling a skirmish drill except when they were falling in for rations."[12]

Lice was a constant companion of Civil War soldiers.

The men had received no mail for sixteen days when a bugler sounded the welcome news to an army on the move: mail call! Newspapers brought two pieces of major news: Lee had crossed into Pennsylvania, and, having accepted Hooker's resignation, Lincoln had appointed Meade to command the Army of the Potomac.[13]

Meade would be the fourth commander in a little over two years, taking on the role previously held by McClellan, Burnside, and Hooker.

George Gordon Meade was competent if colorless. An 1835 West Point graduate, he fought in the war with Mexico and led Pennsylvania reserves at the outbreak of the Civil War. In 1862, he served

under McClellan in the Virginia Peninsula campaign, where he was wounded seriously when a musket ball struck him above his hip, just missing his spine. When recovered, Meade directed his troops with courage and skill as a corps commander at Chancellorsville. In the aftershock of the battle, with confidence in Hooker shaken, some of Hooker's generals wanted Meade to take over as commander, but he dutifully refused to be part of any uprising.[14]

General George Gordon Meade, "Old Snapping Turtle," assumed command of the Army of the Potomac.

Beak-nosed, and older looking than his forty-seven years, Meade did not possess the good looks or charisma of McClellan and Hooker. He had also acquired the moniker "the Old Snapping Turtle" because he was short-tempered. Yet, Chamberlain had already sized up Meade when he led the Fifth Corps; he respected him as an able and courageous commander.[15]

IN THE LAST days of June, Oates's Fifteenth Alabama crossed from Maryland into South Central Pennsylvania and marched fifteen miles to Chambersburg, a town of 5,600 in the Cumberland Valley. Chambersburg would serve as a rendezvous location for Longstreet's First Corps and A. P. Hill's Third Corps. On June 30, the Fifteenth Alabama assumed picket duty—the formation on a forward defensive line to provide warning against a Union advance—at New Guilford, seven miles southeast of Chambersburg.[16]

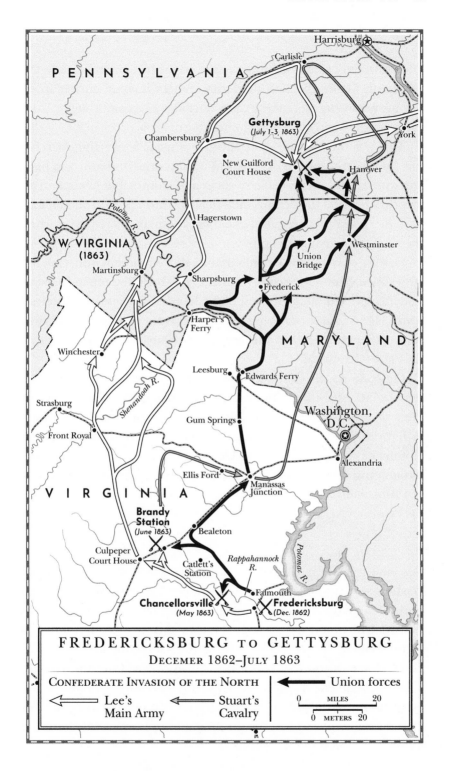

PENNSYLVANIA

Harrisburg

Carlisle

Gettysburg
(July 1-3, 1863)

Chambersburg

York

New Guilford
Court House

Hanover

W. VIRGINIA
(1863)

Potomac R.

Hagerstown

Westminster

Martinsburg

Sharpsburg

Union
Bridge

Frederick

Harper's
Ferry

MARYLAND

Winchester

Shenandoah R.

Leesburg

Edwards Ferry

Strasburg

Gum Springs

Washington,
D.C.

Front Royal

Ellis Ford

Alexandria

VIRGINIA

Manassas
Junction

Brandy
Station
(June 1863)

Bealeton

Culpeper
Court House

Catlett's
Station

Rappahannock
R.

Potomac R.

Chancellorsville
(May 1863)

Falmouth

Fredericksburg
(Dec. 1862)

FREDERICKSBURG TO GETTYSBURG
DECEMBER 1862–JULY 1863

CONFEDERATE INVASION OF THE NORTH

Union forces

Lee's
Main Army

Stuart's
Cavalry

0   MILES   20

0   METERS   20

. . .

ON JUNE 29, Chamberlain, recovered from sunstroke, led the Twentieth Maine through Frederick. John Chamberlain recorded the town's warm welcome in his journal: "Flags were flying from every window and everybody honored our troops."[17]

This was the beginning of another physically exerting march—this time twenty-two miles. The sun was blazing, humidity was high, and dust encrusted his soldiers' faces and clothes, but Chamberlain had now learned to keep his men healthy through heat and exhaustion: he rested them regularly, keeping them always ready for when the time would come to fight.[18]

On the way north, Chamberlain enjoyed riding with Colonel James Rice, leader of the Forty-fourth New York Regiment. Rice was much respected by his troops, and Chamberlain sensed a kindred spirit. He looked forward to deepening his friendship with this winsome officer as together they approached an unknown battle that they knew lay ahead.

On June 30, the Twentieth Maine marched twenty-three miles, starting at 4:30 A.M., some men now walking in stocking feet or even barefoot. Chamberlain knew Maryland to be a border state with divided loyalties, but in western Maryland they passed through Unionville, Union Bridge, and Uniontown, the names of the towns designating their Union sympathies, finally stopping late in the day at Union Mills.[19]

THAT SAME DAY, June 30, Union general John Buford rode into Gettysburg, a town of 2,400 residents seventy-five miles north of Washington, 115 miles west of Philadelphia, and eight miles north of the Maryland border. In consulting his maps, the battle-shrewd Buford had noted the tactical value of this crossroads town, the county seat, where ten roads converged. Leading the Eighth Illinois Cavalry, one of the regiments in his division, he found the town's citizens in an excitable mood, with rumors swirling about Confederate troops in the adjoining countryside. To prepare for whatever may come, he positioned his two brigades of horse soldiers on the high ground west of Gettysburg.[20]

The next morning, July 1, Confederate general A. P. Hill dispatched Henry Heth's division down the Chambersburg Pike. As Heth neared the town, Union and Confederate soldiers glimpsed each other in the distance at nearly the same instant. It was 7:30 A.M. Marcellus E. Jones of the Eighth Illinois Cavalry borrowed a rifle, steadied it on a fence rail, and fired an initial shot at murky figures in gray.[21] Realizing he was outnumbered, Buford called for support from First Corps commander John Reynolds, who soon arrived at a gallop, leading two brigades.

The two armies had stumbled into the biggest battle ever to be fought in the western hemisphere. Lee, who entered Pennsylvania before Meade, approached Gettysburg from the west and north, while Meade came up from the south.[22] Lee, who had invaded the North in part to reduce the burden on war-devastated Virginia, would have liked to go into battle in Pennsylvania at a time and a place of his choosing. That was not Gettysburg. Meade, in the very first days of his command, perched on his horse Old Baldy, with his hat pulled low over his face, would have preferred to do the same. Neither planned for their clash to be at Gettysburg. But here they were: nearly 160,000 soldiers converged on a small market town.

CHAMBERLAIN DID NOT yet know what was taking place at Gettysburg. Tired cheers went up when the Twentieth Maine finally crossed into Pennsylvania at noon on July 1. The men were happy to be back on "Northern soil." Vincent, Chamberlain's teacher of battlefield tactics who was recently elevated to command the Third Brigade, ordered fife and drums from his old regiment, the Eighty-third Pennsylvania, to play "Yankee Doodle." As the Union flag unfurled, Strong turned to John Clark, his adjutant general, and Oliver Norton, his bugler, and exclaimed, "What death more glorious can any man desire than to die on the soil of old Pennsylvania fighting for that flag."[23]

The Union soldiers were greeted warmly by residents who had set up roadside stands. Private Theodore Gerrish expressed annoyance that the locals "endeavored to make money by selling us water, fruit, and provisions at most exorbitant prices."[24] He learned a lesson: patriotism doesn't always trump economics.

. . .

JOHN CHAMBERLAIN, WHO had stayed with his older brother's command, recorded the evidence of war as they heard the boom of artillery coming from the west: "Here were scattered along the road cartwheels and half-buried teams and soon dead horses." The death and destruction were the remains of a cavalry battle between Jeb Stuart's fabled Confederate cavalry and Union horsemen. Weary soldiers trudging in the opposite direction spoke of the "disaster" now just sixteen miles ahead.[25]

Exhausted, the Twentieth Maine stopped at 4 P.M. near the town of Hanover. As they stacked their arms, started fires, and boiled coffee, a fast-riding courier brought news: First Corps Commander Reynolds was killed, and the Eleventh Corps, led by Howard, had been mauled, pushed back through Gettysburg, and lost several thousand, dead, wounded, and captured. For Chamberlain, this news was personal: he had long admired Howard, his fellow Bowdoin alumnus.[26]

At 6 P.M., over blaring bugles and shouts of "To the march!" the Fifth Corps resumed its forward motion. Rumors were circulating everywhere; men began whispering that George McClellan had once again assumed command of the Army of the Potomac. This rumor brought a lifting of spirits as "Little Mac" remained popular with soldiers; Gerrish observed, "our old love for him broke out afresh."[27] Soon, another story circulated: the noble form of George Washington, long dead, was seen riding in the hills near Gettysburg. As to the Washington sighting, John Chamberlain confided, "I have believed it myself."[28] Soldiers facing the prospect of battle reached out for assurance wherever it could be found.

Under a moonlit sky, civilians emerged from their homes to bear witness to this nighttime march. Women brought food and much-needed water—no high prices this time. Groups of young girls greeted the soldiers, bearing flowers and singing patriotic songs. More than one young soldier leaned down from his horse for a kiss from a young woman.[29]

The Fifth Corps stopped at around 1 A.M., now within four miles of Gettysburg. Chamberlain's men had marched nearly thirty miles since the early morning, the final fourteen in darkness.

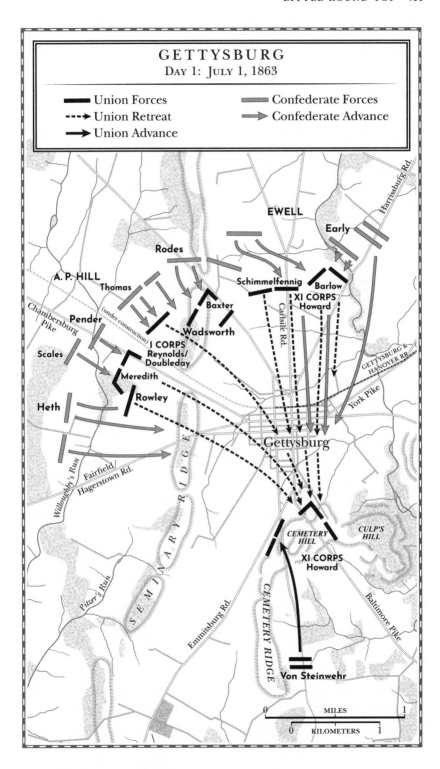

GETTYSBURG
DAY 1: JULY 1, 1863

— Union Forces   — Confederate Forces
---▶ Union Retreat   ⟹ Confederate Advance
—▶ Union Advance

EWELL

Early

Harrisburg Rd.

Rodes

A. P. HILL

Thomas

Schimmelfennig

Barlow

XI CORPS
Howard

Baxter

Carlisle Rd.

Pender

(under construction)

Chambersburg
Pike

Wadsworth

I CORPS
Reynolds/
Doubleday

GETTYSBURG &
HANOVER RR

Scales

York Pike

Meredith

Rowley

Heth

Gettysburg

Willoughby's Run

Fairfield/
Hagerstown Rd.

S E M I N A R Y   R I D G E

CEMETERY
HILL

CULP'S
HILL

Pitzer's Run

XI CORPS
Howard

C E M E T E R Y   R I D G E

Emmitsburg Rd.

Baltimore Pike

Von Steinwehr

0   MILES   1

0   KILOMETERS   1

As the sun rose, Vincent assembled the four regiments of his Third Brigade—the Sixteenth Michigan, Forty-fourth New York, Eighty-third Pennsylvania, and Twentieth Maine—to complete the march to Gettysburg.

At 11 A.M., Chamberlain and his men reached the outskirts of Gettysburg, stopping near Culp's Hill and Wolf's Hill, just off the Baltimore Pike, which angled into the town from the southeast. Knowing that Meade had ordered the Fifth Corps held in reserve, after nearly twenty-four hours of unbroken marching, Chamberlain snatched a moment to rest his tired feet.

Dispiriting news of the previous day's battles began to pour in. Union troops—with only 20,500 men present—were overwhelmed by a Confederate force of 27,500. The Union army suffered 5,500 killed and wounded, with another 3,500 captured.[30]

But hopes were high that the tide of battle could change now that the Fifth Corps had arrived, with the Sixth Corps, led by "Uncle John" Sedgwick, expected by 2 P.M. Officers read Meade's order of the day to their troops. The directive concluded, "Corps and other commanders are authorized to order the instant death of any soldier who fails to do his duty at this hour."[31]

ON THE CONFEDERATE side, Oates's Fifteenth Alabama had spent the previous day bivouacking west of the New Guilford Courthouse; that evening, a courier arrived with orders for Law's brigade to rejoin Longstreet's First Corps at Gettysburg the next morning. On July 2, Oates's men set off on the Chambersburg Pike. This day's march, twenty-five miles under the same scorching sun and suffocating dust that Chamberlain and his men faced, would be their most difficult.

These brutal marches were costly. The Fifteenth Alabama marched from Virginia with nearly six hundred men; 487 left New Guilford Courthouse; only 450 would arrive at Gettysburg. Two nineteen-year-old soldiers, exhausted, asked permission to replenish their canteens, but never returned. Were they killed by bushwhackers, or did they desert?[32] Their fate would never be known. At 2 P.M., after ten long hours, Oates's regiment arrived within sight of

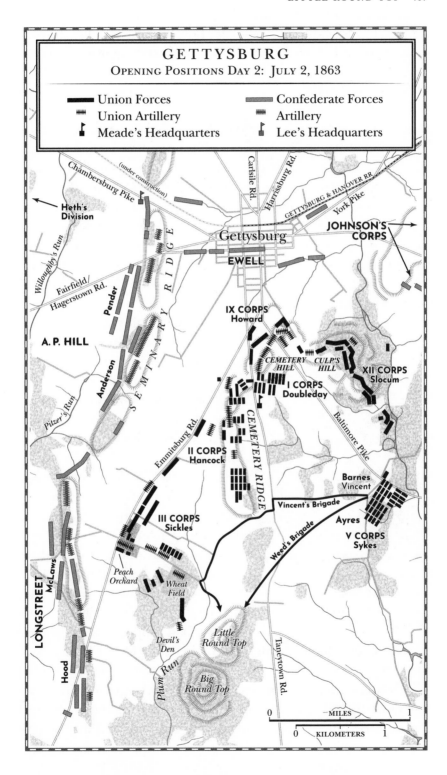

GETTYSBURG
OPENING POSITIONS DAY 2: JULY 2, 1863

▬▬▬ Union Forces	▬▬▬ Confederate Forces	
₪ Union Artillery	₪ Artillery	
⚑ Meade's Headquarters	⚑ Lee's Headquarters	

Chambersburg Pike

(under construction)

Carlisle Rd.

Harrisburg Rd.

GETTYSBURG & HANOVER RR

York Pike

Heth's
Division

JOHNSON'S
CORPS

Willoughby's Run

Gettysburg

EWELL

Fairfield/
Hagerstown Rd.

Pender

IX CORPS
Howard

CEMETERY
HILL

CULP'S
HILL

XII CORPS
Slocum

A. P. HILL

Anderson

I CORPS
Doubleday

Pitzer's Run

S E M I N A R Y   R I D G E

C E M E T E R Y   R I D G E

Emmitsburg Rd.

II CORPS
Hancock

Baltimore Pike

Barnes
Vincent

Vincent's Brigade

III CORPS
Sickles

Weed's Brigade

Ayres

V CORPS
Sykes

LONGSTREET

McLaws

Peach
Orchard

Wheat
Field

Little
Round Top

Taneytown Rd.

Hood

Devil's
Den

Plum Run

Big
Round Top

| 0 | MILES | 1 |
| 0 | KILOMETERS | 1 |

Gettysburg.[33] Longstreet would later praise the Fifteenth Alabama's long footslog that day, calling it "the best marching in either army, to reach the field of Gettysburg."[34]

THE TWENTIETH MAINE rested in the rear of a troop configuration that resembled a large upside-down fishhook. The barb of the fishhook began southeast of Culp's Hill and turned north, running past Cemetery Hill, before veering south along Cemetery Ridge, finally ending two miles south of town at a rocky prominence called Little Round Top. Meade believed he had the advantage: Union troops occupied the higher ground and the interior lines of the fishhook, whereas Lee's Confederate forces occupied the lower ground and the exterior lines, making communication and movement more difficult.

General Gouverneur Warren, formerly a professor at West Point, was chief engineer of the Army of the Potomac.

As Chamberlain waited, he had his men draw twenty more rounds of ammunition. He believed an attack could come at any moment. Corporal William Livermore wrote on the back of the last page of his diary, "There will probably be a great battle tomorrow."[35]

At 3:30 P.M., Union general Gouverneur Kemble Warren glimpsed something through his binoculars that alarmed him. A slender New Yorker who had finished second in his 1850 West Point class, he had gained a reputation as one of the smartest men in the Union army. Hooker had tapped him to be the chief engineer of the Army of the Potomac, and Meade kept him in that role.[36]

Peering through his binoculars again, Warren saw several signal men with their flags at the top of Little Round Top, but it was otherwise unoccupied by Union troops. He worried that if the Confederates seized it and brought their artillery to its top, they could direct gunfire at the whole Union line up to Cemetery Ridge.[37]

As Warren surveyed the situation further, he spotted the glint from the guns from one of Confederate John Bell Hood's divisions. He realized that a second day assault, intended to turn the Union left flank, was about to begin.[38]

Illustration of the moment General Warren looked up in alarm at an almost empty Little Round Top

Indeed, Hood began a massive attack at 4 P.M., a mere half hour after Warren sounded the alarm. Hood had a reputation for bravery and aggressiveness; he always rode his horse up front. But shortly after the attack began, an artillery shell explosion injured his left arm, incapacitating him. His ranking brigade commander, young Evander Law, now assumed command.[39]

Meanwhile, the Union army scrambled to react to this unexpected attack. Meade ordered General Dan Sickles to defend the Union left line from the southmost part of Cemetery Ridge all the way south to the round top.

A soap opera would have trouble conjuring up all the scandals associated with the controversial Sickles. Most notable: the killing

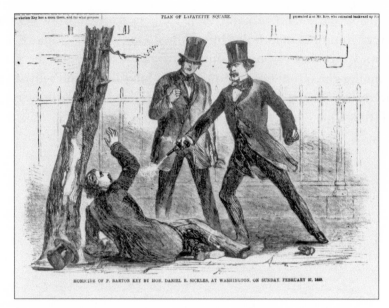

Daniel Sickles's killing of wife's love Philip Barton Key II in Lafayette Square

of his wife's lover, Philip Barton Key II, in broad daylight in Lafayette Square directly across from the White House. Key, U.S. attorney for the District of Columbia, was the son of Francis Scott Key who wrote the lyrics for the "Star-Spangled Banner."

Sickles was acquitted after a plea of "temporary insanity" for what his defense lawyer called "a crime of passion"—the first time such a plea was entered in the U.S. legal system.[40]

A top non–West Point general in the Army of the Potomac, Sickles was known derogatorily as a "political general," meaning he received his appointment because of his political office but without military experience. He walked to the beat of his own drum. Long believing in "flexibility" in interpreting orders, when he received Meade's command to defend the Union left line from the southmost part of Cemetery Ridge, he took it upon himself to decide to position his Third Corps in Joseph and Mary Sherify's Peach Orchard, arguing that this alternate location presented higher ground than the order for his original position. The problem: Sickles now was 1,500 yards west of his initial location, thus further removed from Little Round Top. Through his binoculars, Warren saw that Hood's division already extended well past Sickles's line, making coordination of their forces all the more difficult.[41]

Sensing the urgency of the situation, Warren sent two aides scurrying down the hill to request help for this developing crisis at Little Round Top. Sickles, now heavily engaged from his position in the Peach Orchard, refused to help. One aide, Lt. Ranald Mackenzie, encountered General George Sykes, who had assumed command of the Fifth Corps following Meade's promotion to command the entire Army of the Potomac. In response to Warren's urgent request, Sykes, in only the fifth day of his new command, responded. A small man, who had received the nickname "Slow Trot" as a student at West Point, on this day hurried forward. He gave orders to one of his division leaders, James Barnes, to dispatch one of his brigades to Little Round Top.[42]

But before Barnes could act, Mackenzie encountered Vincent, who asked, "What are your orders?" When Warren's aide attempted to explain he was seeking Barnes, Vincent persisted, "Give me your orders." Learning the order was to proceed immediately to occupy Little Round Top, Vincent, not delaying waiting for an order from a superior, responded, "I will take the responsibility of taking my brigade there."[43] The young Pennsylvanian understood every minute was crucial.

As bugles reverberated throughout the Fifth Corps, Vincent, an intuitive soldier despite lacking military training, summoned his four regiments: "To the left." Turning toward the sound of guns, at a double-quick march, Chamberlain's Twentieth Maine traveled south for three-quarters of a mile on the Taneytown Road, then west on a farm road, across a log bridge over Plum Creek, through tilled fields, and over a stone wall. The three Chamberlain brothers rode together. As they drew closer to their destination, Chamberlain saw that the west side of Little Round Top was cleared of trees—oak and hickory trees had been removed the fall prior by landowner George Weikert, for firewood for his farmhouse. Taking the measure of the place they were called upon to defend, Chamberlain wrote later, "It had a rough forbidding face, wrinkled with jagged ledges, bearded with mighty boulders, even the smooth spots were strewn with fragments of rock like the playground or battle-ground of giants."[44]

Seeking a place where their horses could climb, Chamberlain circumvented the steep north side and instead took a lumber trail on the south side. The three Chamberlain brothers were still together when a shell burst above them. Lawrence immediately dispatched Tom to the back and John forward to help with the wounded, saying, "Another such shot might make it hard for mother."[45]

At about 4:30 P.M., on a spur below the crest of Little Round Top, Vincent reconnoitered the ground to determine where best to place his four regiments, eleven hundred men total. Deciding on a quarter circle, he deployed from right to left: Sixteenth Michigan, Forty-fourth New York, Eighty-third Pennsylvania, and the Twentieth Maine on the left flank of the brigade. Vincent, riding crop in hand, told Chamberlain: "I place you here! This is the left of the Union line. You understand! You are to hold this ground at all costs!"[46] Chamberlain adjusted his regiment—358 men, barely more than a third of the nearly one thousand men who had assembled at Portland in August 1862—accordingly, placing Walter G. Morrill and the nearly fifty men of Company B at an angle facing Big Round Top to protect against any fire that might come from that direction. Chamberlain's Twentieth Maine now anchored not only the left of the brigade, but the left of the entire Union line.[47]

MEANWHILE, LAW HAD given orders to his 1,933-man brigade, consisting of the Fourth, Fifteenth, Forty-fourth, Forty-seventh, and Forty-eighth Alabama regiments, plus two regiments from a neighboring Texas brigade. The seven regiments advanced directly east toward the two Round Tops. The elevation of Big Round Top, called by some locals Sugar Loaf, was 785 feet; Little Round Top, sometimes called Granite Spur, topped out at 650 feet. Trees and rocks obstructed the way to the top of both hills.

Photo of Little Round Top and Big Round Top on July 3, 1863

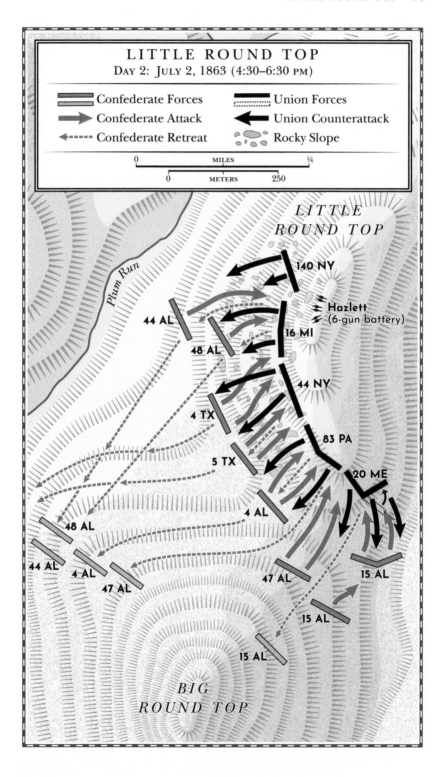

LITTLE ROUND TOP
DAY 2: JULY 2, 1863 (4:30–6:30 PM)

Confederate Forces   Union Forces
Confederate Attack   Union Counterattack
Confederate Retreat   Rocky Slope

0   MILES   ¼
0   METERS   250

LITTLE ROUND TOP

140 NY

Hazlett
(6-gun battery)

44 AL

48 AL

16 MI

44 NY

4 TX

83 PA

5 TX

20 ME

4 AL

48 AL

44 AL   4 AL

15 AL

47 AL

47 AL

15 AL

15 AL

BIG ROUND TOP

Plum Run

July 2 turned into one of the warmest days of 1863. Oates's Fifteenth Alabama arrived at Gettysburg with parched throats and swollen lips. Seeking to relieve their dehydration, he sent twenty-two men, each one carrying a dozen canteens, to find a well.[48]

As the Fifteenth Alabama continued to advance, they were slowed by Hiram Berdan's Second U.S. Sharpshooters. Dressed in green, the sharpshooters fired .52 caliber Sharps rifles with deadly accuracy. Even though Oates's men carried new .577 Enfield rifles, they could not match the Second's firepower, and they suffered numerous dead and wounded, but still they pushed ahead as the sharpshooters retreated toward Big Round Top. One often-forgotten detail of the advance of Law's brigade is that the resistance by the Union sharpshooters caused the brigade to splinter, never to fully come together again; this could very well have changed the outcome of the battle.[49]

Oates's men made the difficult climb up the southern slope of Big Round Top (an arduous climb even today, on the path built by the Park Service). Lee had not given much thought to occupying Big Round Top because he believed it nearly inaccessible for both armies. At the hill's crest, recognizing his men's thirst and exhaustion after the twenty-eight miles they had already walked that day, Oates paused for a well-earned ten-minute rest.[50] At this point, he still hoped for the arrival of the regiment's canteens—he did not know that the water carriers had been captured by the sharpshooters and would not be bringing the desperately needed water.

From his current position, Oates believed he could "convert" Big Round Top "into a Gibraltar that I could hold against ten times the number of men."[51] But within minutes, he was surprised by the arrival of a staff officer, Leigh Terrell, who came with the news that Hood had been wounded, Law had assumed command, and Oates's new orders were to assault unoccupied Little Round Top. In a vigorous exchange, Oates argued for the importance of occupying Big Round Top in Lee's overall strategy. He was undoubtedly correct, but after the wounding of Hood, and under command of the less experienced Law, a breakdown of communication had caused the division to lose some of its unity and dexterity. Oates finally acceded.[52]

Descending back down the north slope, Oates crossed the lightly timbered swale between the two hills. Now situated to the right of the seven other Confederate regiments, advancing without map, guide, or any skirmishers in front, Oates was "blind," in military terms. He had occupied Big Round Top with no resistance. What and who might he encounter at Little Round Top he did not know.

Atop Little Round Top, Chamberlain understood this fight would be his regiment's first full-fledged battle. They had participated in a brief skirmish at Shepherdstown, been held in reserve at Antietam, and made a courageous advance at Fredericksburg. But after ten months of war, their combat experiences were slight and their casualties light.

As Colonel Chamberlain stood thinking about the impending battle, Colonel Rice, leader of the Forty-fourth New York, appeared. He suggested "it would be profitable for us to utilize these few minutes" to walk to a clear space to get a clearer view of the maelstrom happening below in the Devil's Den, the Plum Rim gorge, and the Wheatfield—"the direction of the advance on our front."[53] Chamberlain and Rice looked and then separated—without speaking a word.

Howard Prince, a twenty-three-year-old teacher from Cumberland, Maine, would later depict Chamberlain's leadership in the moments before the fight began: "Up and down the line, with a last word of encouragement or caution, walks the quiet man" with the "calm exterior."[54] Chamberlain had earlier admired Adelbert Ames's coolness under fire; perhaps he held that example in mind, now that it was his turn.[55]

Chamberlain noticed a sudden silence. The thunder of Confederate artillery, which had been firing since the beginning of Hood's assault, had stopped.[56] All around them, there was only a frightful hush. Chamberlain knew this could only mean one thing: Confederate troops were poised to attack Little Round Top, and their artillerymen did not want to risk hitting their own troops.

"Look, look," shouted his men as soldiers in gray uniforms suddenly began appearing below them. The Fourth, Forty-fourth, and Forty-eighth Alabama, plus the Fourth and Fifth Texas, attacked the center of the Union line. The Fifteenth and Forty-seventh Alabama came in behind, focusing their charge at the Twentieth Maine, positioned on the extreme left of Vincent's brigade line.

Jim Nichols of Brunswick, who commanded Company K, alerted

Chamberlain that Confederates were attempting to get around the Twentieth's left side. Spear would later say he was the one who alerted Chamberlain.[57] With his troops now under fire, and his mind surely racing, Chamberlain climbed on top of a large rock to gain a clearer look. He called his company commanders together. To keep the right of his regiment in contact with the retreating Eighty-third Pennsylvania, he could order his whole line backward. But believing the Alabamians meant to flank the left of his line, Chamberlain decided to instead adjust the left wing of his line to the left and to the rear, forming a right angle, thus extending his line farther to the east to prevent an attack of both his exposed flank and rear.[58]

Major Ellis Spear, a former Chamberlain student at Bowdoin, commanded the left side of the Twentieth Maine's defensive line at Little Round Top.

"I saw their legs first," recalled Spear.[59] Oates's Fifteenth Alabama and Michael Jefferson Bulger's Forty-seventh Alabama came up from the south and then southeast with the two Texas regiments attacking from farther west. Tree by tree, boulder by boulder, they came. Oates was in overall command of the two regiments, a combined 650 men. A big responsibility fell to Spear, who managed the left half of the regiment's line.

Could Chamberlain resist the envelopment of his entire line by this larger force, nearly twice the size of the Twentieth Maine?[60] The Maine men met the initial assault with concentrated firepower that stunned the attackers. "My men . . . advanced about halfway to the enemy's position, but the fire was so destructive that my line wavered like a man trying to walk against a strong wind," Oates would write later.[61] Yet the Fifteenth and Forty-seventh kept coming.

In the ensuing minutes, two determined armies fought. The lines of offense and defense quickly lost any semblance of order. The outcome of the ferocious battle was uncertain.

Vincent, moving back and forth among his four regiments, seemed to be everywhere at once. He sought to rally the Sixteenth Michigan, on the brink of collapse under ferocious attack by the Fourth and Fifth Texas. He mounted a huge rock in order to see better, but this action made him a target, and suddenly a bullet smashed into him. He fell, severely wounded.[62] Rice, leader of the Forty-fourth New York, now assumed command of the brigade.

In every battle, there are unexpected heroes. Chamberlain elevated Andrew J. Tozier to the position of color sergeant, responsible for holding high the regiment's colors in battle. From Plymouth, Maine, the son of an alcoholic and abusive father, Tozier manned a dangerous position; when the Twentieth Maine's center started to give ground, he stood resolute. With the regimental flag held under the elbow of his arm so he could keep it upright, he grabbed the rifle of wounded comrade Charlie Reed and returned fire as bullets whizzed around him. His bravery in upholding the Twentieth Maine's colors became an inspiration as Companies D, E, and F recovered to take back the center.[63]

"Ammunition!" The cry went out as the regiment's ammunition began to run low. Each of Chamberlain's men had started off with sixty rounds of ammunition, but by the end of an hour, they were running out. Men furiously restocked bullets from the boxes of fallen friends, or even enemies. But those sources could not supply their need for long.

In this moment of extreme peril, Chamberlain made the critical decision to go from defense to offense. Having brought his regiment together into mostly one line, he shouted: "Bayonet."

The Civil War bayonet (from the French *baïonnette*) was a sharpened steel shaft with a ring that fit over the end of a rifle. Soldiers seldom utilized their bayonets in fighting in the Civil War; they were generally deployed only in dire situations lacking any other possibilities.

This moment was dire. Chamberlain's one word, "Bayonet!," was sufficient. With this simple command, his line moved forward, pushing the Fifteenth and Forty-seventh Alabama back and down the hill.

Holman Melcher, twenty-two-year-old first lieutenant of Company F, became the first to spring forward—to no one's surprise. He was known for his bravery.[64]

Twenty-two-year-old Lt. Holman Melcher was one of the first to advance at Little Round Top.

Spear would say later that because of the roar of the guns, he did not hear Chamberlain's command, but he observed Melcher and "all rushed promptly" in the counterattack.[65]

The Twentieth Maine line, which Chamberlain had shaped into a right angle, moved decisively forward. Writing later, he captured the dynamism of the battle whose outcome was never certain: "The two lines met and broke and mingled in the shock. The cuts of musketry gave way to cuts and thrusts, grapplings and wrestlings. The edges of conflict swayed to and fro, with wild whirlpools and eddies. At times I saw around me more of the enemy than of my own men; gaps opening, swallowing, closing again with sharp convulsive energy."[66]

Coming down the hillside, Chamberlain suddenly came face-to-face with twenty-one-year-old Robert Wicker, a Fifteenth Alabama soldier, who had a sword in one hand and a navy revolver in the other hand. With the saber directed at Chamberlain's throat, the gray-clad soldier would write later that a "queer notion" came over him such that he could not fire the gun, but rather handed it and the sword to Chamberlain and surrendered himself as the Union colonel's prisoner.[67]

Responding to the Twentieth Maine's charge, the Fifteenth and Forty-seventh Alabama attempted to make a stand. It appeared for a moment that Oates might be successful in arresting Chamberlain's assault, but they were quickly overcome by a long-standing weapon of war: surprise. At the same time, Morrill's Company B fired into their rear, shattering their defensive position. The Alabamians fled toward the woods or in the direction of Big Round Top, although Oates would insist in the following years that he ordered a retreat. Most of his men ended up surrendering.[68]

. . .

Edwin Forbes, landscape painter, with his etching of Little Round Top,
7:30 P.M., July 3, 1863

THE BATTLE OF Little Round Top was over. Any moment of cheer
was short-lived. The dead and the wounded lay scattered everywhere Chamberlain looked. The Twentieth Maine suffered 130 casualties, about one-third of the regiment, including forty killed or
mortally wounded. Tom Chamberlain came through the battle un-
hurt.

John Chamberlain captured the chaotic scene in a letter to a
friend.

> From every quarter, the ambulances were hurrying with the
> dying, I say dying for those who were not in the most critical
> condition did not receive the comfort of a ride. The paths and
> woods were filled with groups of men who were wandering
> around in the sun searching for their respective hospital that
> they might get their wounds dressed.

He concluded: "Poor fellows!"[69]

Oates would write later, "The dead literally covered the
ground."[70] The battle of Little Round Top would quickly assume an
important place in American memory, seen through different sets
of eyes in the haze of memory in the years to come. Union and
Confederate veterans would unceasingly debate what happened in
the sound and fury of that battle, and it will never be possible to
resolve the specific recollections of all the blue and gray actors that
day.

But even the simplest version of the story is undeniably powerful: the small Twentieth Maine regiment, down to 386 men—358 guns—tired and footsore, was asked to defend a 650-foot hilltop. A good number of these men had been at Antietam, Fredericksburg, and Chancellorsville. In the late afternoon of day two at Gettysburg, they were commanded to defend something much larger: the far-left line of the entire Union army. The battle went back and forth until Chamberlain called for a bayonet charge. These citizen soldiers—lumbermen, fishermen, farmers, and shopkeepers—with a discipline instilled in them over many months by their colonel, answered his order, and bravely charged down the hill to victory.

ELEVEN

Petersburg

We know that all things work together for good for those who love God,
who are called according to his purpose.

—ROMANS 8:28

Nᴇᴡs ᴏꜰ Cʜᴀᴍʙᴇʀʟᴀɪɴ'ꜱ ᴄᴏᴜʀᴀɢᴇᴏᴜꜱ ʟᴇᴀᴅᴇʀꜱʜɪᴘ ᴀᴛ Lɪᴛ-
tle Round Top traveled swiftly. The next day, July 3, Ames, now
a brigadier general commanding a division in Howard's Eleventh
Corps, scribbled a note to Chamberlain: "I am very proud of the
20th and its present Colonel."[1]

Bᴜᴛ ᴛʜᴇ ᴀꜰᴛᴇʀɢʟᴏᴡ of victory was quickly dulled by the task of
burying the dead. Over the past ten months, Chamberlain had
come to care deeply for the men under his command; a deep bond
develops between men who live and die for each other day after day.

On July 4, as a heavy rain began to soak their camp, Chamberlain sat down to write Fanny, full of the recent victory: "The 20th
has immortalized itself." Using his knee as his desk, he wrote, "I am
receiving all sorts of praise." Perhaps then looking at what he had
written, he added, "but bear it meekly."[2] He may have wanted to
share his triumph with his wife, yet meekness was a value that had
long shaped his behavior.

As he addressed the envelope, Chamberlain did not realize
Fanny was not at Brunswick but rather at the St. Germain Hotel in
New York where she had been living for many weeks. In turn, Fanny
did not know Lawrence had not been receiving her letters. As reports of Gettysburg began to fill the New York newspapers, she worried: was her husband all right?[3]

· · ·

A PAUSE ON July 6 allowed Chamberlain and the other commanders to write their official reports. In it he wrote, "As a last desperate
resort, I ordered a <u>charge</u>"—underlining the word to stress its importance.[4] Rice, as brigade commander, wrote in his report, "I ordered Colonel Chamberlain, of the 20th Maine, to advance and
take possession of the mountain. The order was promptly and gallantly executed by this brave and accomplished officer, who rapidly
drove the enemy over the mountain, capturing many prisoners."[5]
By "mountain," Rice referred to Chamberlain's push to drive the
Confederates also from Big Round Top.

Chamberlain learned that Strong Vincent died on July 7. He
would always appreciate the central role Vincent had played in defending Little Round Top. "I grieve him much," he wrote Fanny. "I
am going to write Mrs. V. and I wish you would."[6]

IF FANNY THOUGHT of leaving New York after Gettysburg, draft
riots that broke out the morning of July 13—some within blocks of
her hotel in the city's Eighteenth Ward—would have deterred her
plan. By then, the Union army was in great need of more men.
Working-class New Yorkers rioted for four days over a new federal
draft law that made all single male citizens between twenty and
thirty-five, and all married men between twenty-five and thirty-five,
eligible for military service by lottery. The order also stated that any
man could buy his way out of conscription by hiring a substitute or
paying the government three hundred dollars—the average annual
salary for a working man in 1863. Angry rioters attacked well-dressed
men on the street, shouting "There goes a $300 man." The riot's
official death total was 105, but some estimates placed the actual
toll in the multiple hundreds.[7]

Finally, a letter from Deborah to Fanny included one of Lawrence's letters. At the same time, Lawrence received a letter from
Fanny.

As the Army of the Potomac trekked back to Virginia in pursuit
of Lee, Lawrence replied to Fanny: "I was much surprised to have a
letter from you dated New-York. I have been writing you at Brunswick." He told her more about the battle of Little Round Top, how
"we exhausted our ammunition" before charging the Alabamians.

Not wanting to frighten her, he sidestepped telling her about his near-death experience with a Confederate soldier with a sword and pistol. Rather: "I took several officers in the fight prisoners—& one of them insisted on presenting me a free pistol."[8]

Now that he was back in communication with his wife, Lawrence wrote Fanny frequently, telling her of the activity of these days, like one spent trudging down the eastern side of the Blue Ridge Mountains in Virginia in a day-and-night pursuit of Rebel soldiers. Pausing near Front Royal, Virginia, he penned a rare complaint: "I tell it wears men out to encounter all these [pursuits] for twelve or twenty-four hours." Responding to Fanny's quandary of finding herself in the midst of draft riots: "But New York! I am sorry you are there. It is not safe to try to get away is it?" He then voiced his deeper reaction: "I wish you were at home. You should have been there before."[9]

John Chamberlain did return home. After serving with the Christian Commission, he took up his studies again at Bangor Theological Seminary in 1863, graduating the following year.

TOWARD THE CONCLUSION of Chamberlain's July 17 letter to Fanny, he wrote, "You know I am not well," but did not say more.[10]

The next evening, Spear recorded in his diary that while riding to check on pickets he and Chamberlain had encountered a "heavy thunder shower."[11] At a distance from their camp, the two were forced to sleep in the drenching rain.

Two days later Chamberlain requested a leave. He wrote an army physician, "I am convinced that I can no longer continue these duties without the most serious consequences."[12] The physician who examined Chamberlain determined he was experiencing "nervous exhaustion." The words "nervous exhaustion" became a catchall phrase in the Civil War to mean extreme physical fatigue. Military and medical officials in the 1860s had little understanding of how war could affect minds as well as bodies. On July 30, Chamberlain traveled to Washington, D.C., for care, the same day Fanny finally returned to Brunswick.[13]

On August 3, granted a fifteen-day leave, Chamberlain left Washington for home, traveling the last miles on the new Maine Central Railroad that started service the previous year.[14]

He arrived in Brunswick on August 6 to a joyous welcome from Fanny. For six-year-old Daisy and four-year-old Wyllys this meant pony rides and games with their father.[15]

In a war being fought on two fronts—battlefields and hometowns—news of a soldier home on leave, for whatever reason, quickly traveled beyond the immediate family. That evening, First Parish held a service of thanksgiving to celebrate Union victories at Gettysburg and Vicksburg. Rev. Adams invited the returning hero to speak to the congregation. In his diary, Adams declared his son-in-law's speech "capital."[16]

At home, rest and the cooler Maine air began to bring Chamberlain some recovery. On August 12, he traveled with Fanny and Daisy to Brewer to visit his parents and sister.

If the leave to return home was an occasion for joy and relief, it could also become an instance of tension as family members, while saluting the courage of their loved ones, often sought to persuade their husband, son, or brother that he had given enough service to the Union cause; now his duty was to remain home to care for his family.

As the end of Chamberlain's leave drew near, not feeling fully restored, he applied for another fifteen-day leave. His family physician, Dr. Lincoln, believed he should not return to the field for at least another week.[17] While waiting for a reply to his request, Chamberlain received a letter from Rice asking if he would return and relieve him as temporary brigade commander so he could visit his wife.[18] Chamberlain wouldn't have taken long to make up his mind: he would return immediately.

In the weeks after Gettysburg, Chamberlain had formed a deepening friendship with Rice. Friendship is like a mirror that reflects back the values of the subject. Lawrence shared much in common with Rice. Both were born in 1828.[19] Both

James Clay Rice, a Yale graduate, became a close friend and admirer of Chamberlain.

graduated from excellent New England colleges—Rice from Yale. Rice, in the words of a contemporary, was "nurtured in the sunlight of Christian environments"—as was Chamberlain. Both were "imbued by a lofty patriotism" and were strong believers in the preservation of the Union. Both were volunteers. Both, without military training, had risen to positions of command.[20]

CHAMBERLAIN ARRIVED BACK at brigade headquarters at Beverly Ford, on the Rappahannock River in Virginia, on August 25. Upon his return, he learned that Rice had been promoted to brigadier general and that he was tapped to replace Rice as commander of the Third Brigade.

Chamberlain shared with Maine governor Coburn his mixed emotions about his promotion. Pleased with his appointment, he expressed regret that he had to depart the Twentieth Maine, "the noble Regiment with which I have had so many hardships & perils, & not a few honors too." He was not about to forego his attachment. "I shall have it still under my eye, & in my care, & shall spare no effort to maintain its high & deserved reputation."[21]

"THIS WAR, I supposed you can see, is rapidly coming to a close, & the heavy fighting is nearly over," Lawrence predicted to Fanny at the end of August 1863. "We may see one or two battles more like Gettysburg, though many doubt that."[22] His belief was shared by many Union soldiers.

In a summer of relative calm, Robert Goldthwaite Carter, a Fourth U.S. Cavalry officer, provided a portrait of free time in the Army of the Potomac: soldiers gathered to watch officers race their warhorses, with friendly wagering enlivening the proceedings; men formed a "Lyceum," devoted to "declamation, reading, singing, and a paper" about current issues of the day; and many participated in worship services, with "preaching every Sunday," and well-attended prayer meetings.[23]

For Chamberlain, this lull in fighting gave him extra time to write Fanny. When he received a letter from her, he would respond that very evening. Every one of his letters conveyed how deeply he loved her: "I am happy to think of you at home again—now my little dear ones are all nestled together—'all'—I paused over that word—the tears filled my eyes—a dull, heavy pain flowed over my heart." Passion and faith mingled in his words: "Come & let me kiss your dear lips precious wife—sad mother—let our hearts worship together God's love & wisdom & mercy."[24]

IN THE FALL, Chamberlain's superiors recommended him for advancement to brigadier general. Rice wrote Maine senator Fessenden, "My personal knowledge of this gallant officer's skill and bravery upon the battlefield, his ability in drill and discipline, and his fidelity to duty in camp, added to a just admiration for his scholarship, and respect for his Christian character, induces me to ask your influence on his behalf." Writing about Little Round Top, he added, "History will give credit to the bravery and unflinching fortitude of the Twentieth Maine Volunteers more than to any other equal body of men upon the field." Rice concluded that the regiment "had its inspiration and great success from the moral power and personal heroism of Col. Chamberlain."[25]

Division Commander Charles Griffin, a West Pointer, did something he had never done previously: endorse one of his colonels for a brigadier general's star. His October 7 recommendation went up the chain of command—endorsed by Corps Commander Sykes, and by Meade, who sent it to the War Department.[26]

Supporting recommendations also came from Ames and Howard. Lincoln's vice president, Hannibal Hamlin, a Mainer himself, wrote the president, "[Chamberlain] is a superior man and has proved himself an efficient, brave and gallant officer."[27]

Lincoln did not accept the recommendation. No explanation was ever offered, but military appointments were part of a political process. Perhaps Senator Fessenden did not follow through energetically enough with Secretary of War Edwin Stanton. Stanton was known for his prickly personality, Fessenden for his thorny temperament. Did their strained relationship influence Stanton's decision not to recommend the appointment to the president?

There is no indication that the adverse decision affected Chamberlain. He delighted in his new responsibility as brigade commander. He now would have a self-contained headquarters and a staff.

AROUND THE SAME time, soldiers brought a sad spectacle into camp: a small horse captured from the Confederates. The horse arrived with sores all over his body, indicating his previous employment as a pack animal. When Chamberlain saw him, however, it was love at first sight. He knew horses and understood that this horse was a Morgan, one of the original breeds established in the United States; compact in size, Morgans were noted for their stamina. They were used by the cavalry in both Union and Confederate armies. He purchased the horse from the government for $150.[28]

He gave the horse a royal name: Charlemagne. The Bowdoin professor knew that Charlemagne united much of Europe three centuries after the fall of the Western Roman Empire.

Morgan horses, if relatively small in size, were appreciated in the Civil War for their endurance.

Chamberlain spent hours caring for Charlemagne. Slowly, the horse's bruises healed and his chestnut-colored coat began to shine again. Rider and horse developed a deep affinity for each other.[29]

. . .

IN THE FALL, still recovering his health, on October 1, Chamberlain was assigned to sit on a court-martial board in Washington, D.C. Court-martial duty was often given to men with health issues. Cases brought before these boards were varied: desertion, murder, rape, spying, treason, embezzlement, theft, conduct unbecoming an officer and a gentleman, disobedience of orders, disloyal statements, and drunkenness.[30]

After sitting through court-martial duties, the marches caught up with Chamberlain, who had never fully recovered from his summer illness. He slept outside on the ground more than once, sometimes in wind and snow, under a "no fire" order so that light wouldn't attract Rebel batteries across the river.[31]

On November 15, Chamberlain, feeling completely exhausted, signed an order requesting sick leave. Sent to Washington in a cattle car, he arrived unconscious.[32]

The next day, an officer at the Third Brigade headquarters wrote Fanny:[33] "Madam—I am much pained to be obliged to inform you that your husband, our Colonel, is quite ill." This time the illness was identified: "He is attacked with malarial fever." Characteristically, Chamberlain was never one to blame others. The officer added, "The Colonel insists that his illness has been brought on by his own carelessness."[34] Fanny would learn that, before his collapse, Lawrence had spent the night unsheltered in the snow. A physician, worried for Chamberlain's life, placed him in the Seminary General Hospital in Georgetown.[35]

Malaria was a new experience for soldiers from far northern climates like Maine. People who develop malaria are typically very sick with high fevers, chills, and flu-like maladies—but in 1863 these symptoms were also associated with the ubiquitous "physical exhaustion."[36] *Scientific American,* less than twenty years old at the time, wrote, "Any soldier is in five times more danger of dying from malarious disease than of being killed in battle. . . . What malaria is nobody knows."[37]

We now know that malaria is a disease caused by a parasite. The parasite is spread to humans through the bites of infected mosquitoes. During the Civil War, malaria would account for 1.3 million cases and 10,000 deaths.[38]

The news of Chamberlain's serious illness provoked alarm in Brunswick and Brewer. Fanny had recently lost her housekeeper, and, realizing that Deborah was too old to take care of the children, she would need to stay home. Sae volunteered to go to Washington to take care of her brother.[39]

In Washington, Chamberlain was fortunate to fall under the nursing care of Sarah H. Sampson, an energetic woman from Bath, Maine, who first came to Washington with her husband, Charles A. W. Sampson, of the Third Maine Regiment. Initially, she occupied her time by visiting Maine soldiers in Washington hospitals. In July 1862, her husband resigned due to ill health, and Sarah went with him back to Bath. But not for long. Two months later, she returned to Washington, now as a salaried worker for the Maine Soldiers' Relief Agency. By the time she met Chamberlain, she had earned the nickname "Angel of Mercy."[40]

As part of her ministrations to families, Sampson wrote Fanny, telling her that in his first days in the hospital her husband showed little improvement.[41]

Sarah H. Sampson, who became known as the "Angel of Mercy," nursed Chamberlain in Washington.

On October 3, 1863, President Lincoln, voicing thankfulness for the momentous Union victory at Gettysburg, announced the nation would celebrate a national Thanksgiving holiday on the last Thursday of November. Prior to the addition of Thanksgiving, the only national holidays celebrated in the United States were George Washington's birthday and Independence Day. Yet in New England, remembering the first thanksgiving of the Pilgrims, this special day had long been celebrated.

While Rev. Adams and Helen gathered at Fanny's home on November 26, word from Washington caused them to offer the greatest thanks of all: Chamberlain was beginning to show some improvement.[42]

Less than one month later, on December 18, the hospital released Chamberlain to his family's care. Initially, his father-in-law confided to his diary, "Chamberlain very feeble."[43]

At home for Christmas and New Year's for the first time since 1861, reunited with Fanny and his children, Chamberlain's health soon began to return. By the middle of the month Chamberlain was able to venture out to church.[44]

CHAMBERLAIN RETURNED TO Washington in February 1864. Still not fully recovered, he was assigned again to court-martial duty.

He was well enough to enjoy the nation's capital. Chamberlain returned to a city very different from the one he passed through two and a half years ago in September 1862. At the beginning of the Civil War, Washington was a small city, the fourteenth largest in the nation, with a population of 61,122.[45] Now it had swelled to more than a hundred thousand, with the arrival of soldiers, medical persons, and workers in an expanding federal government. The workman's hammer was heard everywhere as a separate army constructed temporary and permanent buildings.

The nation's capital during the Civil War had become a city of contrasts. Washington society gathered in theaters, balls, levees—special social events—and dinners, in a daily pursuit of enjoyment. At the same time, pigs and cows ambled on muddy streets, dead horses lay rotting under the winter sun, and wounded and dying soldiers lay in beds in the myriad hospitals that dotted the city. At all hours of the day and night, infantry, cavalry, and army wagons could be seen—and heard—on Washington's busy streets.[46]

Lawrence's life brightened when Fanny traveled to Washington. Although he might have liked staying at one of Washington's large hotels—Willard's on Fourteenth Street, the Kirkwood at Twelfth, or the Metropolitan and National at Sixth—on his budget he rented a home at 402 Thirteenth Street.

During the day, as Lawrence and Fanny walked the streets of Washington, army blue predominated everywhere. A popular daytime activity had become visiting the galleries of the House and Senate. In hotels and bars, placards read NO LIQUORS SOLD TO SOLDIERS—not a problem for Chamberlain, who drank only occasionally.[47]

In the evenings, the couple probably enjoyed plays in the city's theaters. They may have attended older theaters, like the flag-draped Varieties Theatre on Ninth Street, which ended performances with the audience singing a patriotic song.[48]

Or they could have attended newer theaters, like the National Theatre on Pennsylvania Avenue. Owner Leonard Grover called his theater the capital's only "Union playhouse," deriding nearby Ford's Theatre's Democratic "secesh" leanings.[49]

Ford's Theatre opened in August 1863 in a former Baptist Church. President Lincoln would attend Ford's Theatre ten times during his presidency, including *King Lear* on April 8, 1864.[50] Perhaps Lawrence and Fanny saw *King Lear* there as well.

King Lear was one of countless productions across the nation that was celebrating the tercentenary of Shakespeare's birth that year. Lawrence and Fanny saw Edwin Booth, America's most celebrated actor and John Wilkes Booth's older brother, play Shylock in Shakespeare's *The Merchant of Venice*.[51]

In April, Lawrence took Fanny to Gettysburg. He wanted to visit the new National Cemetery, which had been dedicated the previous November when Lincoln offered his Gettysburg Address. By the time Chamberlain had left Gettysburg on July 5, 1863, the majority of the dead from both sides had been quickly buried in shallow graves, without consistent concern for their identities. About two months after the battle, plans began for a national soldiers' cemetery at Gettysburg. Pennsylvania governor Andrew Curtin made David Wills, thirty-two-year-old Gettysburg lawyer, his agent in developing the cemetery. Wills put out bids to rebury the bodies; the winning bid was $1.59.[52] Month by month the bodies of Union soldiers, including men of the Twentieth Maine, were disinterred from their temporary graves to sites more permanent and appropriate to their sacrifice.

Visiting Little Round Top proved to be a very emotional moment for the couple. Fanny, who had experienced the battle at Little Round Top through Lawrence's letters and newspaper reports, now stood on the hallowed ground. Her husband took his time to explain to her in great detail what took place on that momentous day.[53]

WHILE CHAMBERLAIN CONTINUED to serve on court-martial duty, in March, Lincoln welcomed General Ulysses S. Grant to Washington and appointed him general-in-chief of all the Union armies, replacing Henry W. Halleck, who now became his chief of staff.[54]

Grant's reputation had grown as the victor of battles in the west: at Fort Donelson and Shiloh in Tennessee in 1862, and at Vicksburg and Chattanooga in 1863. The president admired this fellow westerner who, unlike previous eastern generals, did not complain about men he did not have, did not overestimate the size of the enemy's forces, and did not boast about what he would do before doing it.

But soldiers in the Army of the Potomac were not yet ready to give Grant their trust. Yes, he had won victories in the west, but he had never faced "Bobby" Lee. Charles Francis Adams, Jr., great-grandson of President John Adams, summed up these sentiments in a letter to his father, Charles Francis Adams, Sr., Lincoln's minister to Great Britain, "The feeling about Grant is peculiar—a little jealousy, a little dislike, a little envy, a little want of confidence . . . All, however, are willing to give him a chance . . . if he succeeds, the war is over."[55]

WHILE GRANT MADE plans to start the Union army's spring campaign, Chamberlain fretted about his ongoing court-martial duty, which he described as "very tedious." With his duty now relocated to a court in Trenton, New Jersey, he complained to Cousin Deborah, "My health is pretty good [and] will be better when I get to the field which I have been trying to do for a month."[56]

UNLIKE MCCLELLAN, WHO had established his headquarters at an expensive house in Washington, Grant made his headquarters in a simple brick house in Culpeper, Virginia, near the Army of the Potomac. Meade, under investigation by Congress's Joint Committee on the Conduct of the War for his failure to follow Lee after Gettysburg, felt certain Grant would replace him with one of his generals from the west. He was surprised when the new general-in-chief invited him to stay on, writing his wife that Grant "showed much more capacity and character than I had expected."[57]

Grant planned a strategy of relentless attack. Prior to 1864, the focus of Union generals had been on capturing places—key Confederate cities, and ultimately Richmond, the Confederate capital. Grant's objective? Attack Lee's army. He told Meade, "Lee's Army will be your objective point. Wherever Lee goes there you will go also."[58]

Coordination would be key. Grant intended to advance with five armies concurrently. The two largest armies, led by Meade in the east and William Tecumseh Sherman in the west, would be supported by three smaller armies: Franz Sigel would go up the Shenandoah Valley; Benjamin Butler would come from the Virginia Peninsula toward Richmond; and Nathaniel Banks would attack Mobile, Alabama, then drive north to unite with Sherman.[59]

WITH CHAMBERLAIN STILL on court-martial duty, Grant began the spring campaign in Virginia on the morning of May 4. Riding his huge bay horse, Cincinnati, he crossed the Rapidan River at Germanna Ford as other parts of the huge army crossed at Ely's Ford. *The New York Herald's* war correspondent Sylvanus Cadwallader wrote, "Never since its organization had the Army of the Potomac been in better spirits, or more eager to meet the enemy."[60]

Newspapers in Washington initially struggled for information about Grant's advance against Lee. Grant hoped to move his army of 125,000 men—a two-to-one advantage over Lee—quickly through the second-growth scrub forest known as the Wilderness. But the dense underbrush and Lee's aggressive counterstrategy slowed the Union advance and caused numerous casualties. With telegraph lines down, a Connecticut cub reporter, Henry Wing, finally got through to Washington with Grant's succinct message to Lincoln: "There will be no turning back."[61] When this bold message reached the public, it made Chamberlain all the more eager to rejoin the Army of the Potomac.

On May 9, Chamberlain wrote again to the office of the adjutant general in the War Department, asking to be relieved of court-martial duty.[62] This time he received an immediate affirmative reply. Overjoyed, he hurried to return to the army in Virginia. Because of structural reorganizations Grant had made to the army, Chamberlain rejoined not as commander of a brigade but once again leader of his old regiment, the Twentieth Maine. He offered no complaint.[63]

Chamberlain traveled sixty-five miles from Washington to arrive in the midst of the battle for Spotsylvania Court House, the second major battle in Grant's Overland Campaign. The earlier battle in the Wilderness had triggered changes in strategy for both Grant and Lee. The Confederate general developed defensive barriers of wood and earth, predecessors of the trench warfare of World War I. In response, Grant had to learn how to assault this new defensive strategy.

Upon his return, Chamberlain learned there had been enormous casualties in the first ten days of fighting. He was saddened to hear that his friend Rice was mortally wounded on May 10.[64] He also learned that within the Twentieth Maine, more than one hundred men—one-quarter of the regiment—had been killed or wounded. William Morrell was dead and Herman Melcher severely wounded. Tom Chamberlain continued to serve with the Twentieth Maine. As despair mounted among the troops, the Twentieth Maine's Theodore Gerrish spoke for many: "We had expected so much from General Grant, and now he was to be defeated as our other generals before him had been."[65]

Gerrish's judgment was premature. In the days ahead, Grant delivered on his promise to conduct an unrelenting campaign. He understood that Lee's strategy, with his smaller army, was to shift his interior lines to meet Union attacks. Prior to 1864, when faced with Lee's aggression, Union generals typically often withdrew, and paused to refit and treat the wounded. Under Grant, there would be no pause; there would be no turning back.

Also part of Grant's restructuring, Gouverneur Warren had become the new commander of the Fifth Corps. Chamberlain's admiration for Warren, the chief engineer who had been instrumental in sounding the alarm before the battle for Little Round Top, would grow in the months ahead.

The feeling was mutual. On June 6, Warren appointed Chamberlain to command the new First Brigade of Griffin's First Division. The brigade would comprise five Pennsylvania regiments, each of which had by now dwindled to around 250 men each, plus the new, larger 187th Pennsylvania.[66]

Chamberlain found himself participating in a campaign unlike any seen in the first three years of the war. Lee proved resourceful and capable, but Grant unceasingly kept the pressure on Lee's army, even if it meant incurring high casualties. During the first four weeks of the spring campaign, Grant's army suffered forty-four thousand casualties, while the Confederates suffered about twenty-five thousand. Grant's aggressive tactics, however, began to incur criticism from politicians and the press.[67]

In May neither Grant nor Lee expected the scale of the battle that erupted at Cold Harbor, a crossroads village located just eight miles northeast of Richmond. Grant finally reached a location ahead of Lee when Philip Sheridan's Union cavalry arrived at the crossroads. Grant believed this might be his last opportunity to take advantage of his greater numbers by fighting Lee in open countryside. He attacked on the evening of June 1.[68]

That first charge achieved some ground, and Grant planned to attack again early on the morning of June 3. But his army, advancing on Cold Harbor from various directions, was spread out and late in arriving. Lee's army, which now had nearly forty-eight hours to get ready, unleashed a deadly counterattack.

By the afternoon Grant called off the attack. In all, the Federals sustained 7,000 casualties, many in the first half hour, while the Confederates sustained 1,500 casualties. Chamberlain's First Brigade, part of the Fifth Corps, suffered light casualties. In the evening, Grant conceded defeat. He would write later, "I regret this assault more than any I have ever ordered."[69]

For three years, the cry in the North had been "On to Richmond." But Grant now decided to attack Petersburg first. Located twenty-five miles south of Richmond, Petersburg was a transportation and supply center, with five railroads that supplied the capital of the Confederacy.

As Lee struggled to discern Grant's intentions, the Union army began to move one hundred thousand men across the James

River—a mile wide with a dangerous tidal current. On June 12, never-ending lines of troops, wagons, and artillery began to cross one of the longest pontoon bridges ever built, 2,100 feet, a tremendous engineering accomplishment.[70]

William Waud's illustration of the Union army crossing the James River in Grant's 1864 spring campaign

At daybreak on June 16, Chamberlain's First Brigade boarded the transport *Exchange* at Wilcox's Landing on the "Mighty James's" north bank. Disembarking at Windmill Point, they collected two days' rations, then marched under a sweltering sun, stopping when they approached Petersburg sometime between midnight and one A.M. on June 17.[71]

GRANT KNEW HE had to strike Petersburg quickly before Lee could arrive. He ordered William "Baldy" Smith to attack from the northeast. But the usually aggressive Smith turned unexpectedly cautious, declaring he needed time for reconnaissance.[72]

Time became an ally of the defending army. Confederate general Pierre G. T. Beauregard, second in his 1838 West Point class, "the little Creole" from Louisiana, with only 2,500 troops, outnumbered seven to one by the Union's Second and Eighteenth Corps, put in place a multipronged defense. He knew that every hour that passed gave more time for Confederate reinforcements to arrive. Still, Smith continued to delay.[73]

Grant had had enough. He ordered a coordinated assault.

On the next morning, June 18, Chamberlain's brigade advanced on the left of Griffin's division and in the middle of Warren's Fifth Corps. He had not gone far before encountering dead bodies that "strewed the field." He later recalled, "The sights we beheld were sickening."[74]

He ordered his brigade to attack in two lines. In the first line, he placed his four veteran regiments, about 250 men each. The alignment, from left to right: the 142nd, 150th, 149th, and 143rd Pennsylvania regiments. The new, larger 187th Pennsylvania, about one thousand men, lacking any combat experience, manned the rear line.[75]

Chamberlain's first brigade crossed ravines and open fields before confronting a railroad "cut" eighteen feet deep, through which the Norfolk and Petersburg Railroad ran. Once there, Confederate shelling and federal confusion stalled the Union advance.[76]

Historian John J. Pullen aptly called the Bowdoin-professor-turned-soldier a "scientific worrier." When preparing for a battle, Chamberlain would play over all its possibilities and problems in his mind. A master of maps, just like the man he admired, Grant, he wanted to understand the terrain in which the battle would be fought. The critical question Chamberlain may have asked himself: what would he do if attacked?[77] He would soon find out.

Meade, more angry than usual on this morning, not certain of the size and status of Confederate reinforcements, ordered a renewed advance at noon. In this uncertain situation, he ordered his commanders to keep in touch with him by field wire.

Chamberlain led his men across the railroad cut and then up into an open field, knowing there now would be little cover for his troops. They were immediately met by a fusillade of Confederate bullets; a twelve-pound solid shell burst above them, killing three men, including the color-bearer, pitching men from their horses, and wounding Charlemagne.[78] Chamberlain picked up the flag, with its bold red Maltese cross, wanting to rally his men.[79]

Union skirmishers approached the Confederate rifle pits, only to discover that during the night Beauregard had withdrawn his

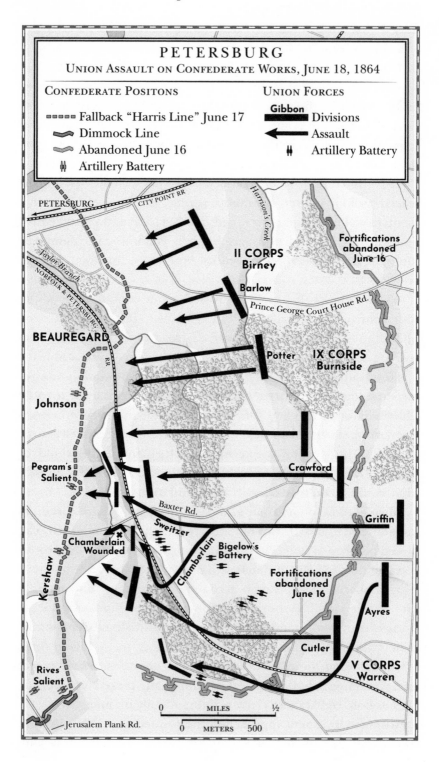

PETERSBURG

UNION ASSAULT ON CONFEDERATE WORKS, JUNE 18, 1864

CONFEDERATE POSITONS

===== Fallback "Harris Line" June 17
Dimmock Line
Abandoned June 16
Artillery Battery

UNION FORCES

Gibbon Divisions
Assault
Artillery Battery

troops to a more secure line. They now occupied a chain of redoubts—temporary fortifications that were typically square or polygonal to protect from more than one side. Through his field glasses, Chamberlain could see more and more soldiers filling in Confederate defensive positions. Sensing the surging firepower he was about to face, Chamberlain called for the support of artillery.[80]

Suddenly, a staff officer arrived. Chamberlain did not recognize the officer, but he wore the silver oak leaves of a lieutenant colonel and brought with him an oral order from "the general commanding"—the officer did not name the general—"to attack and carry the works in front"—the Confederate fortifications.[81]

Believing an advance by his brigade to be unreasonable based on what he was observing ahead, Chamberlain took out his notebook and replied to the commanding officer: "I have just received a verbal order not through the usual channels, but by a staff officer unknown to me . . . directing me to assault the main works of the enemy in my front. Circumstances lead me to believe the General cannot be aware of my situation, which has greatly changed within the last hour."[82]

Was Chamberlain's response insubordination, or was it leadership? His reply went on: "Fully aware of the responsibility I assume, my duty to my veteran soldiers compels me to postpone this charge until the General can be informed of the circumstances." At that moment, Chamberlain understood that to obey such an order would lead to almost certain death. He would need to lead his men a long distance with precious little cover. He and his men were courageous, but he was unwilling to needlessly sacrifice men's lives.[83]

It has been argued that Chamberlain could not have taken the time to write such a response in the heat of battle, and to write directly to Meade, who was levels above Chamberlain at this point.[84] But Meade, agitated about the Union's missteps in attacking Petersburg, frequently asked his commanders to write him from the front lines of the battle.

About a half hour later, the same staff officer reappeared. This time a new order came: the army would attack at 3 P.M. Chamberlain was ordered to attack the well-fortified earthworks and cannon despite his premonition of looming failure.

Chamberlain called his regimental commanders together to discuss how they would make the assault. He then stepped to the front of his two lines. Walking slowly, he delivered a speech to his troops, a practice common by commanders in the Civil War before soldiers were asked to go into battle.

Sgt. Patrick DeLacy and Capt. M. L. Blair of the 143rd Pennsylvania would remember the basic content of Chamberlain's speech: "Comrades, we have now before us a great duty for our country to perform, and who knows but the way in which we acquit ourselves of our grand republic." DeLacy, older than most of his comrades at twenty-eight, with a wife and two little girls back in Pennsylvania, was struck by the kindness in Chamberlain's voice. "We know that some must fall, it may be any of you or I; but I feel that you will all go in manfully and make such a record as will make all our loyal American people grateful."[85] The short speech lifted the spirits and strengthened the resolve of Chamberlain's brigade.

Chamberlain stared at his watch. When the minute hand reached 3 P.M., he ordered the bugler to sound the "charge." Now on foot, he took up a position in the brigadier's customary place, at the center point between the two lines. Thrusting his saber in the air, he barked out the familiar commands: "Attention! Trail arms! Double-quick march."[86]

Chamberlain's account of Petersburg, written decades later, has him leading his men against the Rives' Salient in close proximity to the Jerusalem Plank Road, along a place where Union forces would locate "Fort Hell, a redan or rectangular shaped fort." The exact location of his advance, repeated by generations of historians and biographers, has been corrected recently by the meticulous research of Dennis A. Rasbach, who offers a more accurate rendering of the exact site of these events.[87]

As Chamberlain and his men moved forward and downhill, they quickly came into the plain view of thousands of guns firing at them from the defensive Confederate lines. Union soldiers were running forward into a maelstrom of death. Sensing the dire situation ahead, Chamberlain ordered his brigade to take momentary shelter atop a small ridge.

Once regrouped, in an attempt to avoid a bog or marsh that he knew his men could pass through only with difficulty, Chamberlain gave the command "Incline to the left. To the left." Half turned

QA 33

JOSHUA L. CHAMBERLAIN
PROMOTED "ON THE SPOT"

In this vicinity on 18 June 1864 Col. Joshua L.
Chamberlain received a near-fatal wound while
leading a Union brigade in a charge against Confederate works defending Petersburg. Lt. Gen.
Ulysses S. Grant promoted him to Brig. Gen. of
Vols. "on the spot" for "gallant conduct."
Chamberlain returned to duty in November and
was wounded again in March 1865. On 12 April
at Appomattox he commanded the ceremony at
which the Army of Northern Virginia formally
surrendered its arms. He was governor of Maine
from 1867 to 1871 and received the Medal of
Honor in 1893.

DEPARTMENT OF HISTORIC RESOURCES, 2014

The sign repositioning where Chamberlain fought at Petersburg

backward to his advancing men, he was hit by a minie ball. The conical bullet penetrated just below Chamberlain's right hip and ripped through his body, severing blood vessels, scraping his bladder and urethra, and smashing bone before stopping at the edge of his left hip. Staggering, he looked down to see blood spurting from his right hip and pooling around his feet. In that split second, worried that his men might waver if they saw him go down, he thrust his sword into the ground in an attempt to steady himself. But before long, the loss of blood forced him to one knee, and then to the ground.[88]

Two staff officers, Lieutenants West Funk of the 121st Pennsylvania and Benjamin F. Walters of the 143rd Pennsylvania, rushed to him and pulled him back from the Confederate line of fire. Chamberlain told the two to get word to Lt. Col. John Irwin of the 149th Pennsylvania that he might assume command.[89]

Capt. John Bigelow of the Ninth Massachusetts Battery, which was trying to suppress the Confederate artillery, received a report that a brigade commander lay gravely wounded in front of him. He sent an ambulance, a four-wheel cart drawn by two horses. Chamberlain told the four men who arrived at his side to leave him be, for he believed himself to be mortally wounded. Help others, he insisted, who were less seriously hurt.[90]

"Begging pardon, but you are not in command now," one of Bigelow's artillerymen replied. "Captain Bigelow's order to us was to bring you back, and that is what we must do."[91]

The men lifted Chamberlain, who was in shock, onto a stretcher and into the ambulance. By 1864 the Union's ambulance corps had transformed battlefield medical treatment, allowing the majority of soldiers to receive care much more quickly and efficiently. Ambulances typically had room for four patients on stretchers. The ambulance moving through the chaos that afternoon of men fighting and dying transported him to a field hospital in woods three miles behind the Union lines.

Surgeon R. A. Everett probed the wound and, unable to find the bullet, was not hopeful. The minie ball had ripped through Chamberlain's entire body. At this time this kind of wound would be deemed mortal because it involved the bladder and the loss of blood from several severed arteries. The field surgeon told Chamberlain he would die.[92]

Tom Chamberlain, hearing about his older brother, hurried to find two surgeons from the Third Brigade, Dr. Abner O. Shaw of the Twentieth Maine and Dr. Morris W. Townsend of the Forty-fourth New York. Shaw, only twenty-seven, had interrupted his medical studies in New York to enlist. He had earlier won Chamberlain's admiration, with Chamberlain recommending that despite his young age Shaw be advanced from Assistant Surgeon to Surgeon of the Twentieth Maine. Townsend, who had joined the regiment in December 1862, had quickly established a reputation as among "the ablest and most distinguished surgeons of the 5th Corps." In the Civil War the term for a physician was not doctor but surgeon. The Forty-fourth New York regimental historian would write of Townsend, "No wounded soldier whose life and death hung in equal balance was ever laid upon the operating table without a feeling of confidence that the wisest and best thing would be done."[93] Chamberlain was now that soldier.

Working through the night, in the difficult conditions of an operating tent full of disease and infection because of lack of sterilization and hampered by a limited knowledge of germs, Shaw and

Townsend understood the severity of the wounds but refused to give up on the life of their friend. At last, they were able to find and extract the bullet.

During these long hours Generals Warren and Griffin, who had both previously recommended Chamberlain be promoted to general, visited him in his time of anguish and pain.[94]

IN 1864, IF physicians were practicing without a knowledge of germ theory and sterile technique, Civil War surgery was not the Middle Ages of medicine that is often portrayed. Shaw and Townsend were skilled physicians, and in the end they found the bullet and removed it. They eliminated dead tissue and tied off blood vessels. They even inserted a urinary catheter, which allowed them to try to repair the urethra.[95]

When, against all odds, Chamberlain opened his eyes around midnight, there stood brother Tom and "true-hearted" Spear, offering support. He had survived the battlefield.[96] But he was not out of the woods yet.

Early the next day, still believing himself to be dying, he wrote a letter to Fanny on a page of his order book:

> My darling wife, I am lying mortally wounded the doctors think, but my mind & heart are at peace. Jesus Christ is my all-sufficient savior. I go to him. God Bless & keep & comfort you, precious one, you have been a precious wife to me. To know & love you makes life & death beautiful. Cherish the darlings & give my love to all the dear ones. Do not grieve too much for me. We shall all soon meet. Live for the children. Give my dearest love to Father & mother, Sallie & John. Oh how happy to feel yourself forgiven. God bless you ever-more precious one.
>
>   Ever yours, Lawrence.[97]

But even while Chamberlain recognized his dire medical state, he persisted in his fight to live.

As Chamberlain hovered between life and death, eight soldiers transported him in a horse-drawn ambulance sixteen bumpy, painful miles to City Point, a huge complex at the confluence of the James and Appomattox rivers where Grant had established his headquarters. Soon, Chamberlain was placed on the main deck of the *Connecticut,* a hospital steamer. The four-hundred-bed ship was already overcrowded, with sixty officers and 462 enlisted soldiers, all suffering serious wounds. Chamberlain was transferred to the U.S. general hospital at the Naval School at Annapolis, Maryland.[98]

WHEN COMMANDER WARREN received a report that Chamberlain was mortally wounded, he immediately wrote Grant that Chamberlain "expresses the wish that he may receive the recognition of his service by promotion before he dies for the gratification of his family and friends, and I beg that if possible, it may be done."[99]

Grant responded by issuing Special Order No. 39 on June 20: "Colonel Joshua L. Chamberlain . . . is, for meritorious services on the field of battle, and especially for gallant conduct in leading his Brigade against the enemy at Petersburg, Virginia, appointed Brigadier General of Volunteers, in rank as such from the 18th of June, 1864."[100] In the Civil War a brigadier general, a one-star general, ranked above a colonel and below a major general.

Two decades later, in his *Personal Memoirs,* Grant would write, Chamberlain "was gallantly leading his brigade at the time, as he had been in the habit of doing in all the engagements in which he had previously been engaged." He continued, "He had several times been recommended for brigadier-generalcy for gallant and meritorious conduct. On this occasion I promoted him on the spot."[101]

THIS SPOT WAS now a hospital tent with men dying all around him. Nearly two years earlier, in 1862, he had signed up to preserve the Union. One year before, in 1863, he had led the Twentieth Maine in their heroic defense of Little Round Top. Now he lay hovering between life and death, not knowing what tomorrow would bring.

TWELVE

Appomattox

They were not afraid to follow you or go wherever you ordered them to
go, having implicit confidence in your judgment as a commander.

—THOMAS CHAMBERLIN, 150TH PENNSYLVANIA REGIMENT

Thomas Chamberlin

"INTELLIGENCE HAS REACHED US OF THE DEATH OF GEN.
Chamberlain—very painful—for as a commander I had learned
to love him." As newspaper reports about Chamberlain's injury
reached Maine, an undated letter arrived at the Chamberlain home
in Brewer from the Twentieth Maine's Holman Melcher.[1]

By 1864, many knew that reports of deaths in the Civil War were
not always accurate. What was to be believed?

REV. ADAMS, PARTICIPATING in a church convention in Bangor,
immediately crossed the Penobscot River to join the Chamberlain
family in anxious vigil. Was Lawrence alive or dead? If the former,
what was the extent of his wounds, and his prospects for recovery?

Sae wrote her brother a worry-filled letter: "We could almost an-
nihilate distance and fly to you." She went on to tell him that the
family prayed for his recovery but expressed their prayer for the
"grace to endure if it should be otherwise."[2]

Desperate for reliable information, Fanny traveled right away to
the United States Naval Hospital at Annapolis to find out for herself
the extent of her husband's wounds. Once arrived, she found him
struggling to recover. He suffered from both his wounds and their
infections, high fever and chills. More than a half century before
the discovery of antibiotics, it was a wonder that Chamberlain survived.[3]

The U.S. Naval Hospital at Annapolis, Maryland, where Chamberlain
recovered after his near-mortal wounding at Petersburg

At the naval hospital he received skilled care from Mary Clark, a nurse from Boston. Observing Chamberlain's pain, she expressed "wonder why God allowed it." Fanny, pregnant again, proved a helping presence, for nurse Clark wrote later to her former patient and offered her appreciation of "the dear, suffering wife."[4]

One day before the 1864 Fourth of July celebration, Lt. Col. Charles Gilmore of the Twentieth Maine, on court-martial duty in Washington, traveled to the hospital in Annapolis to present Chamberlain his commission as brigadier general, signed by Secretary of War Edwin Stanton. Gilmore wrote Maine's adjutant general that Chamberlain "had earned this promotion long ago. He has been a most gallant and worthy Officer and the state of Maine should be proud to own him as one of her sons."[5]

But the pace of Chamberlain's recovery remained slow. Yet on the last day of August, over two months after his injury, with Fanny still with him, he wrote Maine governor Cony, "I long to be in the field again doing my part to keep the old flag up, with all its stars."[6]

DURING CHAMBERLAIN'S ABSENCE from Petersburg, Confederates had resisted the Union attack in July and turned the battlefield into trench warfare. Although often called the Siege of Petersburg, it was not actually a classic military siege, in which a city is surrounded and all supply lines cut off. Confederate and federal troops battled to keep open or shut down supply routes to the city.

As SUMMER TURNED to fall, the hospital was abuzz with speculation about the 1864 presidential election. The Democrats chose General George McClellan. Even though he'd been removed by Lincoln as commander of the Army of the Potomac, he remained popular among soldiers. The Republicans, calling themselves the National Union Party in 1864, renominated Lincoln as their candidate.

With Grant stalled at Petersburg, in August the prospects for Lincoln's reelection looked bleak. But the spirits of Chamberlain and his fellow hospital veterans soared when word arrived that Sherman had captured Atlanta on September 2, completely changing Lincoln's prospects to be elected for a second term.

Four days later, Rev. Adams expressed his political sentiments in a letter to his son-in-law: "I will not whine or grumble. Stand by, stick to it, hold on, trust in the Lord. That's my politics, & that's my religion. And so I vote for Cony & Lincoln."[7] Chamberlain could not have said it better himself.

In early September, Bowdoin College president Woods sent word through Rev. Adams that, although Chamberlain's two-year leave of absence had elapsed, his teaching position was still available to him.[8]

But did Chamberlain wish to return to teaching? His long confinement at Annapolis left him with time for a mixture of thoughts and emotions as he contemplated his future. His two and a half years in the army had brought a vibrant meaning to his life, but did he want to serve in the army in peacetime? What might Fanny want him to do when he finally returned to Brunswick?

On SEPTEMBER 20, the army furloughed Chamberlain, still in a weakened condition, from the Annapolis hospital. He and Fanny, who had stayed the entire two months, started for Maine.

After thinking he was going to die, he welcomed the opportunity to be home.

Friends and admirers, both at Bowdoin and at First Parish, were eager to greet him. During his recuperation, Chamberlain stayed mostly in his house. He did accept an invitation to speak at a fund-raising event for the Christian Commission in Bangor, the organization his brother John represented in Virginia. Received by "hearty cheers," he told the audience, "I know the character of the men whom this organization sends to minister in the name of Christ to the soldiers of our country—how kind, and faithful, and fearless they are."[9] He was also pleased to hear from fellow Mainer Ames, who sent his best wishes for a full recovery, signing his letter "With love, your friend, A. Ames."[10]

Still undecided about what to do next, he tried to enjoy time with family and friends, who without a doubt wanted him to stay home for good. They told him he had done his duty. Now was the time to let others finish the fight.

But by the end of October, Chamberlain had decided otherwise. He wrote a difficult letter to his mother in which he tried to answer her concerns: "I confess, not a selfish ambition: for I assure you not all the honors & titles that be given or won, would tempt me to haz-ard the happiness and welfare of my dear ones at home, nor would they be an equivalent whatever for these terrible wounds as must cast a shadow over the remainder of my days, even though I should apparently recover." Instead, he wrote, "I believe in a destiny—one, I mean, divinely appointed, & to which we are carried forward by a perfect trust in God."[11]

At critical moments in his life, we hear Chamberlain express his faith in a purposeful God. He was not referring to nineteenth-century fatalism—whatever will be will be—but rather to a Calvinist conviction about a God who acts in history.

On the evening of November 8, Chamberlain joined Rev. Adams in celebrating the reelection of President Lincoln over Democrat General George McClellan, whose party's strategy to win with the soldiers' vote had failed. The final result showed a decisive victory. Lincoln received 2,203,831 votes to McClellan's 1,797,019. He won the electoral vote even more definitively, 221 to 21, winning every state except Delaware, New Jersey, and Kentucky. Nationally, Lincoln won 55 percent of the vote, while in Maine he overwhelmed McClellan, winning 59.07 percent of the vote.[12]

.   .   .

TEN DAYS LATER, still not able to mount a horse or walk one hundred yards, Chamberlain returned to Petersburg. Since his departure five months earlier, the Richmond-Petersburg campaign had
settled into a series of battles. Petersburg's location was critical to
the supply of Lee's army in Richmond. Grant intended to suffocate
Petersburg by severing rail and wagon lines to the south and west.
Numerous raids were conducted and battles fought, which ended
up lengthening Union trench lines around the city.

Chamberlain arrived at corps and division headquarters to find
his First Brigade completely changed. His five Pennsylvania regiments had been assigned to the Third Division of the Fifth Corps.[13]

Even though he had led these men for only a brief time, he had
so bonded with them that this felt like a loss. Military units quickly
become like families, and Chamberlain and his men had made lasting impressions on one another. A member of the 150th Pennsylvania wrote that he and his fellow soldiers loved Chamberlain "as a
father and you in return loved them like your children and treated
them as equals."[14]

To replace the departed regiments, two new regiments were
moved over to Chamberlain's First Brigade: the oversize 198th
Pennsylvania, with its fourteen companies, and the 185th New York.
Together the two regiments totaled about 1,700 men, making
Chamberlain's brigade the smallest in the Fifth Corps.

In the months during which Chamberlain was recuperating,
Confederates had reinforced their defenses around Petersburg. On
December 7, Chamberlain's First Brigade started south. Its objective? Destroy railroads and bridges forty miles south of Petersburg,
near the North Carolina state line, in what would become known as
the Weldon Railroad Raid. Soldiers wrenched rails from their
wooden ties, then heated them and bent them into new shapes; this
process rendered them useless and impeded Confederate railroad
transport.[15]

Exuberant with their accomplishment, men filled their canteens
with applejack, a form of brandy, before starting the march back to
Petersburg. At first, their drunkenness produced only harmless hilarity, but when they found stragglers killed by bushwhackers, some

soldiers turned violent. In their retribution, they burned buildings and attacked civilians. Chamberlain, bringing up the rear of the march, wrote Sae: "I [had] some sad work in protecting helpless women and children from outrage, when the Rebels had been firing from their houses on us, and the men were bent on revenge."[16] Their violent actions did not align with Chamberlain's military values. He saw from this experience that even with a just cause war can bring out individuals' dark sides.

WITH CHAMBERLAIN'S PHYSICAL health still weak in mid-January 1865, Fifth Corps Commander Warren ordered sick leave for him once more. Chamberlain traveled north to Philadelphia for a second surgery. Men wept at his departure, believing they would never see him again in the army. Captain Francis B. Jones wrote Chamberlain a farewell letter, commending him as not only "a protector, but a confidant."[17]

Chamberlain's surgery was performed in Philadelphia by Dr. Pancoast.[18]

From Philadelphia, Chamberlain traveled north to Brunswick, arriving home on January 20, 1865, to find a baby girl, Gertrude Loraine, had been born four days earlier.

In the deep freeze of a Maine winter, Chamberlain mostly stayed in his house, not even visiting his parents and sister in Brewer. Bowdoin reached out again, assuring him his old professorship waited for him.

Chamberlain's friends also helped secure him an offer to become collector of customs at the port at Bath, a town only eight miles east of Brunswick. His friends told him it would be a cushy job with a good salary.[19]

But these positions no longer held the appeal they would have in the past. He wrote his father on February 12: "I am anxious to get back with my command."[20]

He elaborated: "I shall probably resign my professorship here this summer and be ready to throw myself on the current of affairs, & either remain in the military service (as is most congenial to my temperament) or strike into some other enterprise of a more bold & stirring character than a College chair affords."[21]

He was not surprised when his father and mother replied expressing their disappointment.

But duty, which first called him in 1862, still called in 1865. He replied to his parents: "I owe the Country three years' service. And I am not scared or hurt enough yet to be willing to face to the rear, when other men are marching to the front."[22]

Chamberlain promised Fanny and his Brewer family that, with his physical constraints, he would be wise about what he could and could not do: "I shall not feel obliged to lead any more charges . . . and hope to escape any further injuries." But he added—"unless it becomes necessary."[23]

AT THE END of February, unwilling to overstay yet another sick leave, Chamberlain started back to Virginia, only to be delayed in Philadelphia by his wounds. These wounds caused him constant pain in both hips and the lower portion of his abdomen.[24]

Finally arriving in Virginia, Chamberlain found that during his absence, the First Brigade had been led by General Horatio G. Sickel of the 198th Pennsylvania, who, while outranking Chamberlain, willingly returned to being a regiment commander. With Virginia already warming in March, Chamberlain worked quickly to ready the First Brigade for the beginning of Grant's spring campaign, which many believed would end the war.

In this same month, coming up from the South toward Richmond, Sherman's army departed Savannah, Georgia, on February 1, preparing to march north through the Carolinas. Union forces captured Columbia, South Carolina, on February 17, and Wilmington, North Carolina, on February 22. Sherman's steady march north seized the attention of the Northern public, discouraged by the continuing battles at Petersburg.

ON MARCH 4, Lincoln gave his second inaugural address in Washington. Already looking to the end of the war, to his audience's surprise, instead of calling for vengeance on the South as many in the North wanted, he instead called for reconciliation, concluding his brief address, "With malice toward none; with charity for all."[25]

If Lincoln's address signaled his hopes for what was being called Reconstruction when the long war would finally be over, the Confederates were not yet willing to surrender. By March 1865, Confederate and Union trenches around Petersburg extended thirty-seven miles. At the same time, Grant and Meade continued pressing west, aiming to sever the South Side Railroad, the last line supplying Petersburg.

On March 25, Confederate commander General John B. Gordon launched a predawn attack on Fort Stedman, east of Petersburg, in an attempt to break the Union encirclement. Pretending to be deserting Confederate soldiers, they deceived Federal pickets and captured one thousand Union prisoners. But a counterattack led by General John G. Parke's division of the Ninth Corps soon recaptured the fort.[26] Grant, believing the attack on Fort Stedman a last desperate gambit by Lee, determined to move swiftly to conclude the war.

Two days later, Grant organized a meeting to discuss the end of the war and the coming peace. Gathered on the River Queen at City Point were Grant; President Lincoln; General Sherman, who came up to Virginia by boat from North Carolina; and Admiral

The Peacemakers *by George P. A. Healy: William T. Sherman, Ulysses S. Grant, President Abraham Lincoln, David D. Porter*

David Porter, chief of naval operations. Sherman asked Lincoln, "What [is] to be done with the rebel armies when defeated?" In response, the president emphasized again his wish for reconciliation. He would like to "get the men comprising the Confederate armies back to their homes, at work on their farms and in their shops."[27]

Grant began his spring campaign in Virginia on March 29, 1865. Within his command, General Philip Sheridan, who Grant brought from the west, reported directly to Grant, a special status that offended many eastern generals.

Grant directed Sheridan to link up with Warren's Fifth Corps. Grant's objective was to turn the right flank of Lee's Petersburg defenses, cut Confederate supply lines, and force Lee's dwindling Army of Northern Virginia into a final open-field battle.

Chamberlain's First Brigade started at the front of the Fifth Corps. Each man carried four days' rations—coffee, sugar, hard bread, and salt meat—on their persons, and another eight days' rations in accompanying wagons.[28]

Chamberlain rode chestnut-colored Charlemagne, recovered from the near-fatal wound he'd suffered the previous June at Petersburg. Division commander Griffin ordered Chamberlain to cross Rowanty Creek, swelled by March rains, then advance north up the Quaker Road, where he was to position his two regiments among the buildings of the Lewis farm. Soon after the First Brigade arrived, a courier reported that the right flank of Lee's defenses lay just ahead.[29]

On a spring afternoon made humid by rain, Griffin ordered Chamberlain's brigade to lead the attack. Chamberlain placed the 198th Pennsylvania on the right and the 185th New York on the left. Then, neglecting his promise to his family to lead no more charges, he spurred Charlemagne forward at the front of his brigade, the men dashing across the flooded Gravelly Run, ordinarily only a small tributary of Hatcher's Run. The First Brigade quickly encountered Confederate skirmishers; in the ensuing firefight, and under his courageous leadership, Chamberlain's men pushed a larger group of Confederate general Richard H. Anderson's Fourth Corps up the road beyond the Lewis farm. There, Chamberlain encountered General Henry A. Wise, former governor of Virginia, leading

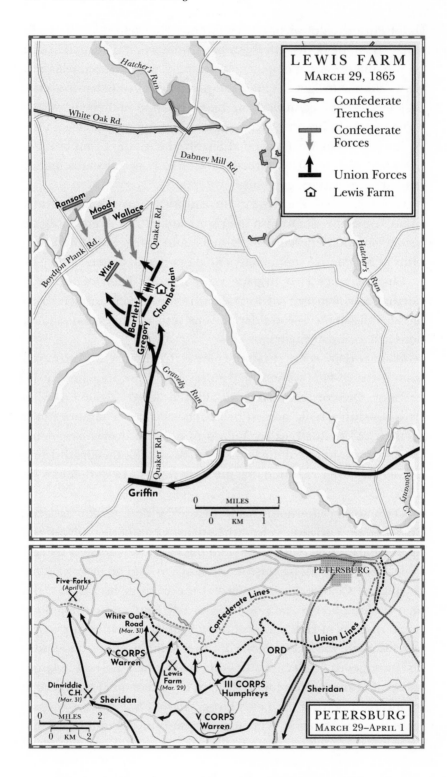

LEWIS FARM
MARCH 29, 1865

Confederate Trenches

Confederate Forces

Union Forces

Lewis Farm

Hatcher's Run

White Oak Rd.

Dabney Mill Rd.

Hatcher's Run

Ransom

Moody

Wallace

Quaker Rd.

Boydton Plank Rd.

Wise

Bartlett

Chamberlain

Gregory

Gravelly Run

Quaker Rd.

Rowanty Cr.

Griffin

0   MILES   1

0   KM   1

PETERSBURG

Five Forks
(April 1)

White Oak
Road
(Mar. 31)

Confederate Lines

Union Lines

V CORPS
Warren

Lewis
Farm
(Mar. 29)

ORD

Dinwiddie
C.H.
(Mar. 31)

Sheridan

III CORPS
Humphreys

Sheridan

V CORPS
Warren

0   MILES   2

0   KM   2

PETERSBURG
MARCH 29–APRIL 1

four Virginia regiments; the First Brigade successfully pushed them back toward the junction of Quaker Road and Boydton Plank.[30]

But not for long. William Wallace's South Carolina brigade joined Wise's Virginians in a counterattack, forcing Chamberlain to stop at the edge of a dense wood where Confederates had positioned themselves behind fieldworks of logs and earth.[31]

The First Brigade regrouped at the Lewis farm. There, Griffin, confident in Chamberlain, asked his brigade commander to lead his two regiments forward again. Chamberlain rode out front once more, but when he attempted to check his excited horse, Charlemagne reared. At just that moment, a minie ball ripped through the large muscle of the horse's raised neck, exiting the other side to hit Chamberlain just below the heart. The twin blows stunned horse and rider. Chamberlain fell forward, covered with blood, intuitively hugging Charlemagne's neck.[32]

Griffin, observing Chamberlain slumped on his horse, raced forward. He put a supporting arm around his brigade commander's waist, believing at that moment Chamberlain, his head and hair coated with blood, was "gone."[33]

Yet a moment later, Chamberlain raised his head unsteadily—his life had been miraculously spared; the minie ball had hit the brass frame of a hand mirror and a leather case of field orders, both in the breast pocket of his old, faded jacket. The bullet had only bruised his left bridle arm before exiting through the back of his jacket. Once again, he'd come within inches of dying. Chamberlain, recovering his equanimity, instructed an aide to take the wounded Charlemagne back to the Lewis farm. Soon, mounting a borrowed, mud-spattered white horse, he set off into the fray again.[34]

Griffin, recognizing the need for extra firepower, having started his military service with the artillery, ordered Charles S. Wainwright, respected chief of artillery of the Fifth Corps, to bring up his "long-arms." As Chamberlain's men found themselves caught up in a difficult fight, he welcomed the "Napoleons." The French had revolutionized artillery in 1853 when they introduced this twelve-pound cannon—Canon obusier de 12. Named after Napoleon III of France, nephew of Napoleon Bonaparte, these cannons were light enough to be pulled rapidly by a team of horses but heavy enough to destroy defenses a half mile away.

Wainwright's four cannons began to belch out shells at Confederate foot soldiers, and also at snipers in the trees.[35] The battle waged back and forth for two more hours, but the extra artillery caused the tide to change. Wainwright reported later, "Chamberlain told me that he should have been gone had not the battery came when it did."[36] Finally, the arrival of additional federal reinforcements brought the bloody battle to an end.

The twelve-pound "Napoleon" became decisive for the Union in the battle of Quaker Road.

Chamberlain rode back to the Lewis farm over the body-strewn field. He lost over four hundred casualties on this one day, including several fine officers. In the conflicting emotions of war, he must have been elated with the day's victory but at the same time deeply saddened by the large losses his lead brigade had suffered.

Major Spear, who had arrived as part of the reinforcements, approached his friend. Drawing a flask from his breast pocket, Spear offered Chamberlain some "choice wine." It was one of the few occasions in his life that he accepted.[37]

. . .

IN HIS OFFICIAL report, Griffin credited Chamberlain with pushing the "enemies' infantry and cavalry" into their entrenchments on White Oak Road.[38] Warren told Chamberlain he was telegraphing President Lincoln about his courageous leadership.[39] His official report called Chamberlain "the brave General Chamberlain of Maine."[40] Ultimately, Chamberlain would receive a promotion to the brevet rank of major general "for conspicuous gallantry in action on the Quaker Road, March 29, 1865."[41]

That evening, Chamberlain, hardly able to walk because of his new wounds, looked after Charlemagne, who had survived another wound. He visited wounded soldiers, kneeling beside dying major Charles MacEuen of the 198th Pennsylvania.

General Sickel, who had received a serious wound to his left arm, observed Chamberlain's caring ways and whispered, "General, you have the courage of the lion, and the gentleness of a woman."[42] Chamberlain has been criticized for recalling—or inventing—these words years later in his *Passing of the Armies,* but the same words were cited decades earlier in 1884 by Major E. M. Woodward in his *History of the One Hundred and Ninety-Eighth Pennsylvania Volunteers.*[43]

WITH RAIN TURNING the Virginia roads into ever more treacherous mud, Grant ordered Sheridan and his cavalry to remain in place rather than pursue Lee's retreating army. Ever eager, Sheridan rode over to Grant's headquarters and urged, "I'm ready to strike tomorrow and go to smashing things."[44] It did not take much to convince Grant.

On April 1, rain gave way to a sparkling spring day. At Five Forks, a junction seventeen miles southwest of Petersburg, whose only building was a blacksmith shop, Sheridan deployed his cavalry on foot against the Confederate defensive line manned by George Pickett's infantry division, as well as cavalry led by Lee's newly appointed cavalry chief, his nephew, General Fitzhugh Lee.[45]

Sheridan had a well-devised plan and far greater numbers, but defective intelligence, miscommunications, and muddy roads would threaten to unravel the federal advantage.

Initially, Sheridan, astride his huge black horse Rienzi, took the fight to the Confederates. Pushing forward, he discovered that Pickett's two-mile-long line was not well-formed. He would have been delighted to know that Pickett, last in his 1846 West Point class, believing all was quiet, was currently enjoying a fish bake of Nottaway River shad, and a nap, two miles behind his line.[46]

Although his cavalry were doing well, Sheridan knew he needed Warren's infantry to complete the victory. But where was Warren?

Chamberlain's brigade had begun the day held in reserve, by the Benjamin Boisseau farm on the road from Dinwiddie Court House to Five Forks.[47] But early that afternoon Chamberlain came face-to-face with Sheridan: "I report to you at the head of Griffin's Division."

Sheridan replied gruffly, "Why did you not come before? Where is Warren?"

"He is at the rear of the column, sir."

In an insulting tone, Sheridan replied, "That is where I expected to find him."[48]

Chamberlain explained that Warren was withdrawing from the battle at White Oak Road, where his men had fought courageously all day. Later, Warren responded to a courier sent by Sheridan that he would not be ready to attack again until 4 P.M.

General Philip H. Sheridan, "Little Phil," became a controversial leader in Grant's 1865 spring campaign.

That day, the tension between Sheridan and Warren became a battle within the battle. The hot-tempered cavalry commander had lost confidence in Warren, believing he lacked an aggressive military determination. For his part, Chamberlain respected the man responsible for alerting Union forces of the potential disaster at Little Round Top. He understood that Warren, a former professor like himself, could sometimes appear to be irresolute, but that this came from his desire to consider all options before plunging into battle. Chamberlain knew that

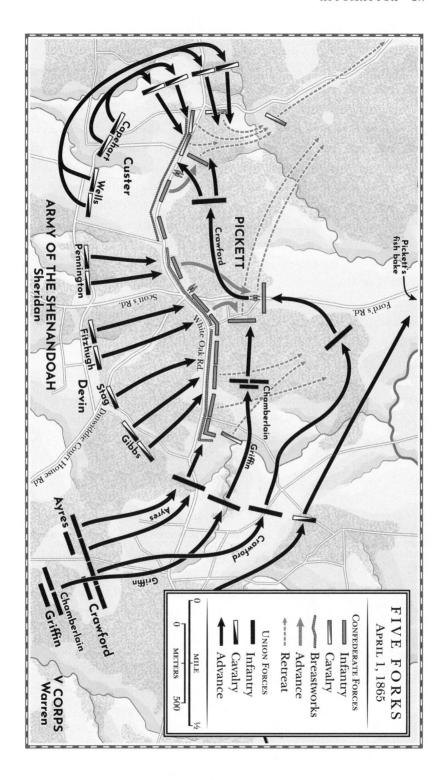

FIVE FORKS
APRIL 1, 1865

CONFEDERATE FORCES
Infantry
Cavalry
Breastworks
Advance
Retreat

UNION FORCES
Infantry
Cavalry
Advance

MILE
0 ½
METERS
0 500

ARMY OF THE SHENANDOAH
Sheridan

Capehart

Wells

Custer

Pennington

Fitzhugh

Devin

Stag

Gibbs

Dinwiddie Court House Rd.

Scott's Rd.

White Oak Rd.

Crawford

PICKETT

Pickett's
fish hoke

Ford's Rd.

Chamberlain

Griffin

Ayres

Ayres

Crawford

Griffin

Chamberlain

Crawford

Griffin

V CORPS
Warren

Warren specifically questioned the frontal attacks ordered by Grant and Sheridan, believing that they resulted in needless loss of lives.[49]

At Five Forks, Sheridan, convinced Warren's corps was moving too slowly, took charge of portions of the Fifth Corps, determined to cut off Lee's last lifeline.

Two of Warren's three divisions, led by General Romeyn B. Ayres and General Samuel W. Crawford, assembled at the Gravelly Run Methodist Church at 4:15 P.M., but the two division commanders struggled in their attacks, only Ayres hitting the Confederate defensive line.[50]

At this moment, as the Confederates tried to organize a new line, Griffin signaled Chamberlain to attack the Rebel left flank. Astride Charlemagne once again, with the bugler sounding brigade calls, his Pennsylvania and New York regiments drove the Confederates back toward their defensive works. Up and over the temporary fortifications of logs and earth, Chamberlain and his men engaged in hand-to-hand fighting, the final part of a battle, which resulted in capturing many of the men of the Fifty-sixth Virginia.[51]

Union troops won a decisive victory at Five Forks. They took some 4,500 prisoners, over 3,200 of which were captured by the Fifth Corps.[52] The triumph finally severed Lee's lifeline, his last supply line, the South Side Railroad. The Battle of Five Forks would come to be called the Waterloo of the Confederacy.

George Alfred Townsend, with the pen name "Gath," was a war correspondent for the New York World.

One loss at Five Forks would be debated for years to come. Grant accepted Sheridan's demand to replace Warren. This controversial decision would affect many people in future years, including Chamberlain.

On the evening of April 1, congratulations went all around as Fifth Corps officers gathered at Five Forks. When Sheridan arrived, George Alfred Townsend, Washington correspondent for the *New York World,* asked if he would describe the tactics of the battle. Sheridan eagerly accepted the invitation.

Townsend, at twenty-four, one of the youngest correspondents in the war, wrote under the pen name "Gath," which he derived by adding an "H" to his initials; the nom de plume was inspired by the biblical passage 2 Samuel 1:20, "Tell it not in Gath, proclaim it not in the streets of Askalon."

He also interviewed Chamberlain. In the story he published three days later, he wrote, "And what shall I say for Chamberlaine [misspelling his name]—who, beyond question, is first of all our brigade commanders . . . the hero of both Quaker Road and Gravelly Run, and in this action at Five Forks making the air ring with the applauding huzzas of his soldiers, who love him." The young correspondent then made this forecast: "His is one of the names that will survive the common wreck of the shoulder straps after the war."[53] The war correspondent's observation and prediction reflected the fact that Chamberlain's reputation as a hero in the Union army was growing.

THE NEXT DAY, April 2, was a Sunday. As Jefferson Davis listened to the Rev. Charles Minnigerode's sermon at St. Paul's Episcopal Church in Richmond, a messenger walked down the aisle and gave Davis a telegram from Lee.[54] Now that Petersburg had fallen in a campaign that had lasted 292 days, Lee made the decision it was time to evacuate the Confederate capital as well in order to preserve his army. Without controlling Petersburg, Richmond could no longer be defended.

With Richmond and Petersburg now both under federal control, Grant had Lee's army on the run. The chase after Lee picked up speed. General Griffin, now in command of the Fifth Corps, took a prominent part in the pursuit. With Chamberlain's brigade in the lead, they captured the last train, the Southside Railroad, to leave Petersburg.[55]

Now began a race westward, closely following the Appomattox River. Exhausted after two days of nearly continuous fighting, Chamberlain's brigade joined Sheridan's cavalry. On April 4, his men marched thirty miles, finally stopping at Jetersville, blocking

Lee's escape route south, the Confederate leader's exhausted and hungry army now reduced to forty thousand men. On April 5, Union forces cut the Richmond and Danville Railroad. Lee had hoped to adhere to the railroad line down to Danville, and there link up with Johnston coming up from North Carolina.[56] Although Chamberlain's brigade were the pursuers, they had to be alert at every moment for a potential rear guard of Confederates, who might suddenly peel back to fire and fight.

Even amid the constant tension, humor managed to break in. While Chamberlain was crossing the Buffalo River on the morning of April 8, he paused to take a drink of water; in a lapse of attention, he allowed Charlemagne to take an additional step into the main channel of the river. Suddenly, both horse and rider plunged head-first into this deeper water.

Chamberlain managed to climb out of the river, but it took three men to rescue Charlemagne. Both man and horse, covered with mud, provoked peals of laughter from the men of his brigade. Chamberlain laughed too, acknowledging that the joke was on him.[57]

As Chamberlain prepared his brigade to march and fight Lee's retreating army, the Civil War was racing to an end. On April 7, sitting on the porch of the brick hotel in Farmville, Grant wrote out a note asking for Lee's surrender: "The result of the last week must convince you of the hopelessness of further resistance on the part of the Army of Northern Virginia in this struggle."[58]

When Grant wrote a second note on April 8, Lee parried Grant's note by suggesting a discussion about a "restoration of peace."[59]

Finally, early on the morning of April 9, Lee sent a note through the lines offering to surrender.

Palm Sunday, Chamberlain watched in awe as first Lee and then Grant entered Appomattox Court House, the small village ninety miles from Petersburg, from different roads.

Later, Chamberlain would recall with appreciation the appearance of the Union commanding general.

Slouched hat without cord; common soldier's blouse, unbuttoned, on which, however, the four stars; high boots, mud-splashed to the top; trousers tucked inside; no sword, but the sword-handle deep in the pocket; sitting in his saddle with the ease of a born master, taking no notice of anything, all his facuities gathered into intense thought and mighty calm.[60]

Chamberlain described not only Grant's outer physical appearance but what he believed to be his inner power.

GRANT WALKED UP the white wooden steps of Wilmer McLean's two-story brick house. Lee, wearing his full dress gray uniform trimmed in gold braid, complete with red sash and sword, waited for Grant in the parlor.[61]

In a brief 185 words that he wrote on the spot, Grant offered a magnanimous peace. The concluding sentence reflected his desire for the surrender: "This done, each officer and man will be allowed to return to his home, not to be disturbed by U.S. authority as long as they observe their paroles and the laws in force where they may reside."[62] A parole gave Confederate veterans legal protection, allowed them to draw rations from the federal government, and receive free passage on any railroad or ship, thus making transport home faster and safer. The Confederate soldiers, unlike Union soldiers, owned their horses. Responding to a suggestion from Lee, Grant decreed that the Confederate soldiers could keep their horses, which they would need when they returned home to work their farms. Lee responded, "That will have the best possible effect upon the men."[63]

As news of the surrender and peace spread, impulsive firing into the air spread throughout the troops. Grant quickly issued an order to his men: cease all demonstrations. He exclaimed, "The war is over; the rebels are our countrymen once again."[64]

AS TELEGRAPH WIRES sang north with the news of Appomattox, residents in Brunswick awakened on Monday morning, April 10, to newspaper headlines that blared the good news.

VICTORY

GLORY TO GOD

FINAL TRIUMPH OF FREEDOM

SURRENDER OF LEE

UNION AND FREEDOM TRIUMPHING[65]

Rev. Adams recorded in his diary, "Early this morning. Shouting, bells crackers [firecrackers], etc. which was easily understood to indicate the surrender of Lee."[66] Church bells rang. American flags were hung in windows. Citizens shouted the good news up and down Maine Street and across the Bowdoin College campus.

John Furbish wrote in his journal, "A general illumination was observed throughout the village, nearly every building on Maine Street, together with the college & private dwellings on nearly every street."[67] The long-held English tradition of using candles as a signal of welcome to strangers, a sign of hope, or the celebration of an important community event, crossed the Atlantic and took hold in the colonies and continued in the new nation.[68]

People in Brunswick placed candles in the street-facing windows of their homes, a communal illumination to celebrate the preservation of the Union. Helen Adams lit up the entire Adams parsonage with candles.

Furbish noted in his journal that one soldier was particularly celebrated: "Our fellow citizen Professor or General Chamberlain distinguished himself, and in one of the battles received fresh wounds, Honorable wounds!"[69]

In Brewer, the Chamberlain family watched in awe as someone in the town made a big kite, about twelve feet long, attached an American flag, and let it float two thousand feet in the air. On this day at the end of a bloody war, one newspaper reporter called the flag "doubly dear."[70]

NEITHER GRANT NOR Lee would attend the formal surrender, which was to take place on April 12. On the afternoon of April 10, Grant set out for Washington. Much of the Union army, including Sheridan's cavalry, departed on April 10 and 11.[71]

Grant appointed Generals Griffin, Wesley Merritt, second-in-command to Sheridan, and John Gibbon of the Army of the James as commissioners to organize the surrender. Either late on April 9 or early on April 10, Griffin and Gibbon informed Chamberlain he had been designated to command the surrender ceremonies.

Why Chamberlain? He was not a West Pointer, nor regular army, not in command of the cavalry or artillery, nor an officer who had worked to ingratiate himself to senior leadership. The selection probably came from Grant through Griffin, commander of the Fifth Corps, who had long thought highly of his brigade commander. No written order appointing Chamberlain or anyone else has been found, but in the rush of these final days it needs to be remembered that oral orders were not unusual.

The appointment surprised Chamberlain. He believed that the honor really fell to all the men of the Army of the Potomac, an army that had experienced many defeats on the road to final victory, and especially its Fifth Corps. He felt particular gratitude for the Twentieth Maine, with whom he had begun in the Third Brigade in 1862 and whom he had led after Gettysburg. To include them, Chamberlain asked that he be transferred temporarily to lead the Third Brigade; he commanded the division in Bartlett's absence. He wanted to give the veterans of that brigade the honor of participating in the ceremony. Although his selection to lead the surrender ceremonies was a personal honor, Chamberlain instinctively wanted to be sure it was also a communal honor. Recognizing that his single brigade would not be adequate to receive the surrender of so many Confederates, he also invited the rest of the division to witness this epoch-making event.[72]

PREPARATIONS GOT UNDERWAY at 5 A.M. on April 12. Saddling the resilient Charlemagne, Chamberlain formed his men on both sides of the Stage Road at the lower, or east, end of Appomattox. The flag of the Third Brigade, the red Maltese cross shown on a white field fringed in blue, flew in the morning breeze. Union soldiers stood at "order arms"—butt plate of rifle on the ground, rifle resting on right side—the main position for all stationary, facing, and marching movements—as they awaited the soldiers in gray.

Lee assigned thirty-two-year-old Georgian general John B. Gordon to be in charge of the Confederate surrender. Born on a farm in Georgia, despite having no military training, Gordon had risen through the ranks from captain to major general, earning Lee's trust by his skill and courage at Antietam—where he was wounded

General John B. Gordon led the Confederate surrender at Appomattox.

five times—and in the Wilderness. Thin, yet stately in bearing, his men called him "the gallant."[73]

From across the valley where they were camped, Gordon started his troops toward the village at 9 A.M. The various flags of the Stars and Bars flag of the Confederacy flew at the front of their marching columns, three horizontal stripes, two red and one white, and a blue box containing white stars in the upper left-hand corner. As they marched, their minds had to be on the brutal past years of fighting; others surely thought of the uncertain future ahead.[74]

Chamberlain, sensitive to the significance of the moment, determined to mark the surrender in the spirit of the magnanimity Grant had expressed to Lee three days before. As Gordon approached Chamberlain, only three or four yards now separated the blue and gray lines. In this moment, Chamberlain sought to replace the wide chasm that had divided these soldiers for four long years with what he believed bound them together at this moment. He wanted to offer some recognition, not to the Confederacy or the cause for which they fought, but rather to the bravery and courage of the soldiers in ragged uniforms marching toward him.[75]

When Gordon arrived directly opposite him, Chamberlain, to the sound of a bugle, ordered his command to bring their muskets from "order arms" to "shoulder arms"—the marching salute, with the musket held in the right hand, perpendicular to the shoulder—and saluted his former enemies.

Gordon, surprised by Chamberlain's salute, wheeled his black horse and touched his sword to his toe. He then signaled his men, rank upon rank, to respond to what he would later call "a token of respect."[76]

As Chamberlain was about to depart, his act of generosity to Confederate soldiers was suddenly interrupted: a Confederate general was scolding some of his men with harsh words.

*Illustrator John R. Chapin, in a pencil drawing, portrayed the
surrender at Appomattox for* Harper's Magazine.

Chamberlain approached the general; he did not know he was
encountering Henry A. Wise, a former governor of Virginia. With a
white beard and wrinkled face, Wise looked older than his fifty-
eight years. Chamberlain attempted
to offer words of hope to the unknown general, wishing future good
relations between North and South.[77]

Wise would have none of it. He
shot back at Chamberlain, "You may
forgive us, but we won't be forgiven.
There is a rancor in our hearts which
you little dream of. We hate you,
sir."[78]

Wise's stinging words, so unlike
the demeanor of Gordon, would not
be forgotten.

THE NEXT DAY, Chamberlain wrote a
letter to his sister Sae about the surrender. He did not boast about his

*Confederate general Henry A. Wise,
former governor of Virginia,
confronted Chamberlain at
Appomattox.*

role, simply telling her that his old brigade "was drawn up to receive the surrender of the Rebel arms." He described the Confederates as "men we had faced a score of times & almost recognized by face," adding, "Poor fellows. I pitied them from the bottom of my heart."[79]

Six days later, still in Virginia, he completed a long letter to Fanny that he had begun weeks before. In a matter-of-fact manner, he told her, "I happened to be designated to receive the surrender of the arms of that great Army of Northern Virginia." He didn't say more but promised "I shall have something to tell you of this, as of other matters never to be forgotten."[80]

THIRTEEN

The Grand Review

A youthful subordinate when I first took command of this division, now through so many deep experiences risen to be tested, trusted, and beloved commander.

—GENERAL CHARLES GRIFFIN, FIFTH CORPS COMMANDER, COMMENDING CHAMBERLAIN ON THE EVE OF THE GRAND REVIEW, MAY 22, 1865

FOLLOWING THE SURRENDER AT APPOMATTOX, CHAMBERLAIN began to think about what it would mean to return to Maine. After three years of war, what would it be like to return to Fanny? And to his children? He had missed so much of their young lives.

Most men living in the nineteenth century experienced their lives as a single chapter: They would be born, married, and buried in the same town. Men would begin and end their lives in the same occupation and on the same farm or in the same town as their fathers. They would be farmers, lumbermen, shipbuilders, or shopkeepers. The world that would emerge after the Civil War would change the lives for so many soldiers returning to Maine.

Chamberlain knew he was not the same person who had reported to Portland's Fort Mason in August 1862. He had traveled far beyond the small towns where he lived for the first thirty-three years of his life. He had engaged with a larger, more diverse world than had been available to him at Bowdoin College and Bangor Theological Seminary. He had met a much wider variety of people in the army.

CHAMBERLAIN HAD SET incredibly high standards for himself since he was a youth. As a student at Bowdoin, he excelled in all his classes and won multiple academic prizes. As a professor, he was not content with the established curriculum or the traditional teaching methods but determined to pursue new ways.

But the Civil War had given him the opportunity to face challenges and exercise leadership not possible in the classroom. He had entered an army where West Pointers formed the peak of a military caste system. Yet even in this system, volunteer Chamberlain rose steadily through the ranks, so that by the end of the war, his accomplishments were recognized by all, including General-in-Chief Grant.

Now, he would measure all future challenges by what he had managed to accomplish in the Civil War.

ON SATURDAY, APRIL 15, Chamberlain and the men under him left Appomattox in the rain. The next day, Easter Sunday, news of the assassination of President Lincoln reached Chamberlain. "Words will not tell you the feeling with which this Army received this news," he wrote Fanny. On April 19, at the same hour of the funeral for Lincoln in Washington, Chamberlain led his troops in holding their own funeral service honoring their fallen leader. In his letter to his wife he described "the drooping flags—the dirges of the bands—the faces of the men."[1] Chamberlain was not able to leave for home right away. In the final weeks of April, as the million-man Union army began to disband, conditions in Virginia roiled with fresh turmoil. Gangs, both white bushwhackers and black freedmen, roamed the countryside harrying local citizens. Without a court system in place, and with a direction from the army to maintain order, Chamberlain took it upon himself to set up a temporary court to adjudicate disputes.

During this period, Chamberlain exhibited feelings toward formerly enslaved African Americans that are troubling from a contemporary standpoint. He found them "unruly," but he also believed that "without accustomed support, without food, or opportunity to work, they not unnaturally banded together." That said, he believed his primary task was to keep the peace, not to assist the freedmen as they sought to find their way in a completely new world. From his perspective, "without much deliberate plotting of evil, they still spread terror over the country."[2]

. . .

On May 2, Chamberlain started north to Washington for what he heard was to be a review of the eastern and western Union armies. Four days later he crossed into Richmond on a temporary pontoon bridge over the James River. He had spent years reading newspaper headlines blaring "On to Richmond," but had never entered the former Confederate capital. He witnessed a city in ruins. Formerly enslaved persons greeted the Union soldiers' arrival with excitement, while white residents, standing cautiously behind curtains shrouding the windows of their homes, were not sure what to make of this new reality. Ten days later Chamberlain and his men went into camp at Arlington Heights, located just across the Potomac River from Washington. He learned that, before the mustering out of most of the army, a review was to take place on May 23 and 24 in the nation's capital.

The encampment evoked memories of his initial arrival at Camp Mason, south of Portland, as a new lieutenant colonel of the Twentieth Maine in September 1862. So much had happened in the three years since. He would call this final encampment "the graduation day of our Alma Mater."[3]

On May 20, Sherman's western army began to arrive at Washington, camping on the same side of the Potomac, but farther south near Alexandria. Both eastern and western armies used the next days to prepare for the review. The Army of the Potomac, senior in date of formation, having suffered many inglorious defeats in the first years of the war, long the defender of the nation's capital, would enjoy the pride of marching on the first day of the review.

CHAMBERLAIN WELCOMED REV. Adams to Washington on May 17. He had traveled from Brunswick to witness the review and celebrate his son-in-law's successes. Fanny was home caring for their new baby, Gertrude Lorraine.

In ensuing days Adams would fill his diary with descriptions of all he saw and heard as he accompanied his son-in-law through his busy schedule. He wrote of "men coming for passes, all sorts of papers, all sorts of complaints, dissatisfactions, crooks, quirks."

Adams was also impressed by Charlemagne: "Chamberlain's horse has 5 wounds, rode him in every battle since Fredericksburg."[4]

On Saturday, May 20, Chamberlain rode into Washington to call upon Sheridan, who was about to depart for the Texas border and would miss the Grand Review. Grant had appointed Sheridan commander of the Military District of the Southwest with a double mission: he had orders to defeat E. Kirby Smith's Trans-Mississippi troops in Texas, the last remaining Confederate holdouts, and provide a show of force against France's Napoleon III, who had set up Austria's Maximillian I as a puppet ruler in Mexico.

The purpose of Chamberlain's visit was to offer a good word about Griffin, who had landed on Sheridan's bad side by being what Sheridan perceived to be too critical of others. Griffin had long affirmed Chamberlain, and in turn, Chamberlain wanted to affirm his corps commander. It was a successful mission. Upon his return, he told Rev. Adams, "Sheridan seemed delighted to see a Fifth Corps man," and that "Griffin would not be disturbed."[5] Though the war was over, the coming days and years would witness continuing competition and criticism among its leading generals.

On Sunday, Adams attended church with Chamberlain and his son-in-law's friend Spear. The old minister, now in his thirty-sixth year as pastor of First Parish in Brunswick, expressed his delight upon finding the military chapel filled with soldiers even while all the preparations were going forward for what was being called the Grant Review.[6]

The next day, Adams fell into conversation with Dr. W. R. DeWitt, chief surgeon of the First Division. The physician told Adams he had never observed a man work as hard as Chamberlain, especially considering he could barely move because of the severity of the wounds suffered at Petersburg.[7] Adams confided to his diary, "The Gen. pretty miserable but constantly working."[8]

That evening, the Fifth Corps and their guests assembled for a farewell party in honor of their leader, Charles Griffin.

Chamberlain, chosen to give the tribute speech, offered his admiration: "Our hearts stir as I speak the name,—so familiar, so revered; so interwoven with experiences deep as life and death."[9] He had also been entrusted to design a gold pin with a red Maltese cross against a white background surrounded by diamonds created by Tiffany of New York. He placed the pin on an emotional Griffin.

He responded by praising Chamberlain: "You are an example of what experiences of loyalty and fortitude, of change and constancy, have marked the career of this honored division."[10]

Rev. Adams, by now a familiar face, was also invited to address the soldiers. He told them he "would have enlisted myself, but 1st was too great a coward & 2nd was too old. Had no sons to send unfortunately,

General Charles Griffin, leader of the Fifth Corps

so sent my boys from Bowdoin College (I call 'em 'my boys' & not content with that sent my son-in-law Gen. Chamberlain) Applause— 'Cd not have done better.' "[11] To Adams's delight, several officers pinned first one and then three more Fifth Corps badges on him.

At the close of the evening, soldiers clasped hands and sang "Auld Lang Syne," as some among them wept. The bugle sounded the now-familiar retreat, which later would become known as "taps," as the men dispersed.[12]

IT WOULD BE a short night. Reveille sounded again at 2 A.M. on May 23. By 4 A.M., Chamberlain, leading the First Division at the front of the Fifth Corps, began crossing the Long Bridge over the Potomac River into the nation's capital. He passed Maryland Avenue and halted near First Street for breakfast.[13] It was a bright, clear morning.

The city of Washington, after more than a month of grieving for the dead president, had replaced the black mourning crepe with red, white, and blue decorations as it prepared for the celebration. For the first time since the assassination, flags were raised to full staff, signifying the end of the official mourning period. The American flag flew atop the White House once more.

The Army of the Potomac had successfully protected the nation's capital from breach by Confederate armies, but a different invasion took place in the days leading up to the Grand Review. Citizens flocked to Washington from across the North, wanting to cheer for the soldiers from their home states. Special trains were put into service. Fathers and mothers brought their children for what they believed would be a once-in-a-lifetime experience: 150,000 soldiers marching up Pennsylvania Avenue. Police were kept busy arresting thieves, pickpockets, and prostitutes. As hotels filled up, churches opened their doors so that people could sleep on pews. Many more slept outdoors in parks. A *New York Herald* reporter estimated that the crowd numbered seventy-five thousand.[14]

On the first day of the review, onlookers dressed in their Sunday best: men wore hats, everything from straw to stovepipe, while women wore bonnets. Temporary stands had been erected between Fifteenth and Seventeenth streets. Some homeowners rented window positions for five dollars. People lined sidewalks eight to ten deep, gathered on front porches, or peered down from rooftops. Boys climbed trees. Dr. Adams, bearing a ticket from his son-in-law, sat in a select location on Pennsylvania Avenue in a Fifth Corps stand.[15]

Patriotic mottos were visible everywhere. A huge banner hung on the west portico of the Capitol, declaring THE ONLY DEBT WE CAN NEVER REPAY; WHAT WE OWE TO OUR GALLANT DEFENDERS. On the east portico, another banner announced "The public schools of Washington welcome the heroes of the Republic." Early that morning, two thousand five hundred children marched to the Capitol from public schools in the area. The girls wore white dresses while the boys sported blue jackets.[16]

Situated directly before the White House stood the main reviewing stand, a roofed structure bedecked with banners naming the great battles from the past four years: GETTYSBURG, VICKSBURG, SHILOH, RICHMOND. Soon the stand would be filled with dignitaries led by President Andrew Johnson, the self-educated blacksmith from Tennessee who, as vice president, succeeded Lincoln, and General Grant. A few seats would be left empty, to be filled by commanders like Chamberlain who would dismount from their horses and take their places temporarily on the reviewing stand.[17]

. . .

AT 9 A.M., a gun sounded, signaling the beginning of the parade. General Meade, on his show horse, Blackie, led the eighty thousand men of the eastern armies. "Old Snapping Turtle" had ridden only a few blocks when a Pennsylvanian in the crowd began shouting "Gettysburg." Others quickly joined in, chanting, as Meade tipped his hat.[18]

A tumultuous, joyful greeting welcomed the soldiers as they marched up Pennsylvania Avenue, twelve abreast, rank upon rank, in immaculate precision, led by bands playing "When Johnny Comes Marching Home," "When This Cruel War Is Over," and "Tramp, Tramp, Tramp! The Boys Are Marching." Schoolchildren and spectators joined in the singing.

Nothing excited the onlookers more than the sight of the battle flags, many frayed by bullet holes. From time to time, someone from the crowd would rush past guards for an opportunity to touch, even press their lips to these flags.[19]

The Grand Review of May 23 and 24 in Washington as depicted in Harper's Weekly

At one point, General George Custer, a golden-haired twenty-five-year-old general, approached the reviewing stand on his powerful stallion, Don Juan. At just that moment, a young girl tossed a garland of flowers at him; he snared it with his free hand, but the horse, ridden by Custer for only one month, was frightened, reared, and raced off past the presidential reviewing stand. Custer's hat fell off, and his sword dropped to the street, but with his left hand, the expert horseman brought his mount under control. To the cheers of the crowd, Custer and Don Juan retraced their steps and passed a second time in front of the reviewing stand.[20]

The Fifth Corps now came into view. Slender General Griffin led the way, erect in his saddle. Chamberlain followed, accompanied by his staff, including his younger brother Tom, and Spear. The crowd, familiar with the feats of Chamberlain at Five Forks and in the surrender at Appomattox, greeted him and his men with loud cheers.

Suddenly, another feat of horsemanship occurred. Charlemagne had been in many battles, but never in a huge parade. As with Custer, a young girl approached Chamberlain to hand him a garland of flowers; as she lifted the flowers to Chamberlain's free hand, Charlemagne reared. Chamberlain's first instinct was to protect the young girl standing perilously near the hooves of the rearing horse, and he managed to bring Charlemagne's hooves down safely. Unlike Don Juan, Charlemagne, long accustomed to Chamberlain, did not race away. Chamberlain steadied his old friend, and together they marched on.[21]

Just past the reviewing stand, Chamberlain dismounted and joined President Johnson and General Grant in the seats. Voices in the crowd called out: "This is the Fifth Corps" and "These are straight from Five Forks and Appomattox."[22]

Rev. Adams, sitting proudly in a spectator's reviewing stand, wrote on that day, "None showed to better advantage than Chamberlain and his command."[23]

Leading newspapers across the nation would devote many pages to covering the Grand Review. *Harper's Weekly* told its readers that the larger story was the survival of the Union, connecting these citizen-soldier heroes on review to the earlier heroes of the American Revolution. James Gordon Bennett's *New York Herald,* the American newspaper with the greatest European audience, depicted the salvation of the Union against a world of European monarchs and aristocrats as the true meaning of the review. The marchers "secured the perpetuity of that Union which the hopes of

The Reviewing Stand at the Grand Review

the oppressed of all climes and countries depend." The *Herald* opined that the cheers of the crowds in Washington were also taking place "across the Atlantic, echoed alike from the Alps and the Andes."[24]

The first day's parade over, Chamberlain stayed to witness the second day and the review of the western armies under Sherman.

THE GRAND REVIEW became a line of demarcation for Chamberlain: on one side, his vigorous army life, marching and fighting across great expanses of hitherto unknown geography; on the other, his upcoming return to Fanny and his children, and to a peaceful, familiar college town in Maine, but facing an unknown future.

Two weeks later he attempted to express his mixed emotions in a letter to his sister Sae: "My own affairs are in an exceedingly uncertain state. My wounds trouble me still."[25]

Then, in his now-familiar reflex toward optimism, he pivoted: "But I am by no means disturbed by them.... I have plenty of 'strings to my bow,' or in better words, Providence will both open and guide my way."[26]

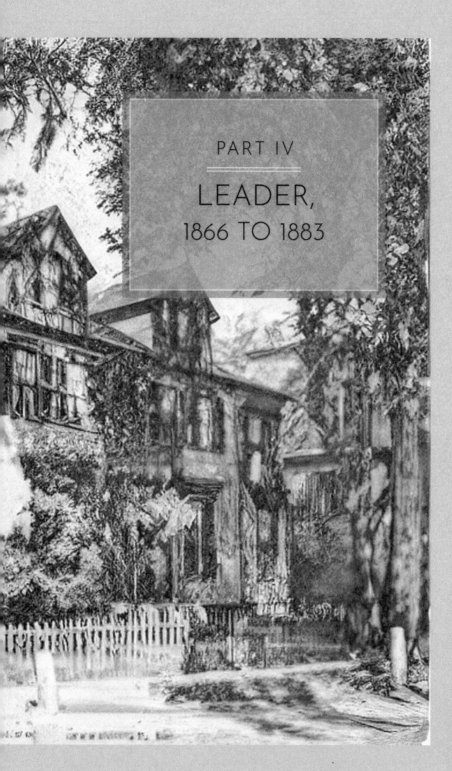

PART IV

LEADER,
1866 TO 1883

FOURTEEN

Decisions

Would it be prudent, in view of our dear bought experience,
to take a man for Governor of the State, who is not known
even to have voted or acted with our party, and has never had
a day's experience in political affairs?
—*Portland Press* APRIL 27, 1866

C HAMBERLAIN, HOWARD, AND AMES, THE THREE MOST PROMI-
nent Maine Civil War heroes, were now faced with important
decisions when it came to their postwar plans. The choices they
made and the places they served would determine the quite different ways they would ultimately participate in Reconstruction.

Otis O. Howard contemplated stepping away from the army and
returning to Maine to purchase a farm. But President Lincoln had
other ideas for him. Knowing the former general cared deeply
about the well-being of formerly enslaved African Americans, the
president had intended to tap Howard to lead the new Freedmen's
Bureau.

After Lincoln's death, President Johnson, at the encouragement
of Secretary of War Stanton, appointed Howard to lead the new
bureau in May 1865. Howard led an organization charged with providing a plethora of services—shelter, food, clothing, and medical
services to newly freed African Americans. Controversy would soon
erupt over the bureau's attempts to settle formerly enslaved persons on land that had been abandoned or confiscated during the
war. The bureau also established schools, including a school in
Washington that was finally called Howard University.[1]

Adelbert Ames agonized whether to remain in the army. After
the war, while on occupation duty in South Carolina, he expressed
skepticism about granting suffrage for the freed African Ameri-

OVERLEAF: *Chamberlain returned to his home on Potter Street at the end of the Civil
War.*

cans.[2] After a year's leave of absence, which he spent in Europe, he returned to the army in 1867. Soon after, Ames was appointed commander of the Fourth Military District, consisting of Mississippi and Arkansas. There he underwent a transformation in his views on the rights of African Americans: "I found when I was Military Governor there that there was a black code existing, and that the Negroes had no rights at all."[3] He watched as families were ejected from their lodgings with no money or food, only to then be frequently arrested as vagrants.

Ames believed that the path to change was the participation of African Americans in self-government. In his words, he wanted to give them "the protection they were entitled under the Government of the United States." Ames terminated all ex-Confederate officers from state and local offices and hired in many of their places African Americans.[4]

During the next years Ames would serve as senator and governor of Mississippi, harried by Democrats as a scalawag, and hailed by black voters for his courageous support of their rights.

When the war ended, Chamberlain returned to Maine, where he encountered a different set of challenges than those facing Howard and Ames. Rather than confronting Reconstruction fights in Washington and the South over expanding the rights of African Americans, he came home to a far northern state dealing with the economic problem of rapidly diminishing lumbering and shipbuilding industries and a college thinking hesitantly about its educational mission in a post–Civil War America.

Chamberlain came home to a Maine that had been greatly changed by the Civil War. His home state was now less isolated than it had been prior to the war. Moving forward, its citizens would be more heavily influenced by the crosscurrents of opinion emanating from the rest of the nation.

Chamberlain, too, was changed. Concealed beneath his civilian clothing were the terrible wounds he had incurred at Petersburg. When one imagines the staggering non-mortal casualties of the Civil War, one usually pictures the visible wound of amputation. But of the 281,881 Union soldiers who were wounded and lived beyond the war, only 20,892 were amputees.[5] Many of the wounded, like Chamberlain, bore less immediately visible scars from the battle, and seldom talked about their wounds, though they would shape the rest of their lives.[6] Chamberlain was changed in other ways too. Back in Brunswick, the ambitious thirty-six-year-old found himself restless with an internal tension. He yearned for a more active life but was not certain what that might look like. He had liked his time at Bowdoin but was not sure he wanted to be a teacher again. And while he enjoyed being in the army, he was not convinced he wanted to make a career in the military. He had discovered himself to be an able leader but wondered about where his leadership could be most effective. Yet, with no other clear path to support his family, and with Bowdoin eagerly claiming him as one of their own, Chamberlain reluctantly accepted Bowdoin's offer to become a professor once more, returning to his earlier position as professor of rhetoric and oratory.

At the same time, the professor had a new status as a returning Civil War hero. A local paper reported, "The General looks brown and hardy despite rebel bullets, grayer than four years ago, but hardier and grafted into fame. And none have better won their laurels." The article went on to mention the "fearful wounds" he suffered at Petersburg, but assured its readers, "another surgical operation will be demanded before those wounds will turn to honorable scars."[7]

Another newspaper reported Chamberlain "quietly ensconced here in his pleasant home" with Fanny and the children. In reality, however, these first days were anything but quiet.[8] He arrived home only days before Bowdoin's August commencement events, which this year would honor all the college's sons who had fought in the war.

LEARNING THAT GENERAL Grant, as part of his extensive postwar travels, had accepted an invitation to come to Portland, Chamberlain wrote his former commander, inviting him to come also to Bowdoin's August commencement.[9] Grant accepted, to the huge excitement of the college and Brunswick community.

Undergraduates met Grant at the train station on August 2 and escorted the general and his wife, Julia, to Lawrence and Fanny's home.

The two Civil War heroes conversed, then Chamberlain escorted the Grants to First Parish, site of the Bowdoin commencement.[10] Rev. Adams, brimming with pride, welcomed Grant. The *Brunswick Telegraph* observed, "The Congregational church was never so elegantly and tastefully decorated." Red, white, and blue bunting decorated the majestic oak sanctuary. The number 65 hung over the pulpit, while the names of three Bowdoin students of the class of 1865 who died in the war were listed over the clock. The commencement program included a printed list of 248 graduates who served in the army and navy.[11]

President Woods announced that the college's two boards would confer an honorary LLD degree—doctor of laws—on Grant. Woods gave Chamberlain the honor of presenting the degree.

That evening, the church held a soldiers' reception, which Brunswick resident Furbish described as "the greatest jam I ever saw in this place."[12] In characteristic behavior, Grant, the man of the moment, happily ceded the stage to Chamberlain. Chamberlain said "he missed the faces of many who were there once, many who had been his pupils." Yet, he told the assemblage, "He could see them with the eyes of his soul."

Concluding his remarks, Chamberlain stated, "I have tried to get Gen. Grant to speak, but he says 'No,' and when he says that word, he means it. Lee knows it means something." Faced with the cheering crowd, the self-effacing Grant surprised everyone by paraphrasing his famous single-sentence report to Lincoln, sent in the midst of the battle of the Wilderness: "I continue to fight it out on that line."

At the reception, prominent Boston lawyer and Bowdoin alumnus Peleg W. Chandler chided President Woods to "wipe off Jeff Davis and his LL.D. from the college record." He told Woods that the Davis LLD should signify "Long Let Him Dangle." A local newspaper, reporting on the commencement, declared Grant's honorary degree made up for the "great mistake" of giving the same degree to Davis in 1858.[13]

As PUBLIC FESTIVITIES receded, Chamberlain settled into the house on Potter Street. Daisy, eight, and Wyllys, six, were delighted to have "Papa" home for good. After the war, with husbands returning home after years away, many couples found that their marriages and family lives had forever changed. During the war, many wives took up responsibilities that had formerly belonged to their husbands. How would Lawrence and Fanny adjust?

Fanny and Lawrence were thrilled to be reunited. Within weeks, however, sadness intervened when baby Gertrude Lorraine, just seven months old, died on August 14 after a short illness. If the deaths of infants remained high in the middle of the nineteenth century—181.3 deaths per one thousand births in 1860—this did not take away the grief of the parents.[14]

Despite his joy at being home with his family, the Civil War was never far from Chamberlain's mind, and he endeavored to honor the milestones of the war in his house. He embellished his home with artifacts from the war: he affixed the Fifth Corps flag on one wall, alongside several Confederate flags captured by his units. Over the fireplace mantel, he placed the sword and scabbard he used at Gettysburg. Elsewhere, he exhibited the revolver he took from the Confederate soldier who attempted to shoot him at Little Round Top, and displayed the bullet removed from his body at Petersburg.[15]

But his most treasured wartime memento arrived late in the summer. Charlemagne, who had survived almost as many wounds as his master, came to Brunswick to be welcomed by Daisy and Wyllys as the family pet.

In these first weeks back home, Chamberlain received multiple requests to speak about his war experiences. He worked long hours on these lectures, just as he had always done for his lectures at Bowdoin. He developed two main presentations: "Gettysburg" and "The Surrender of General Lee." He also set his sights on writing a history of the Fifth Corps. He sent letters requesting materials to all the regimental commanders who had served throughout the war.

Fanny and the children would often vacate their home so that he could work in uninterrupted peace. They even boarded the family cat, Collatinus (called Coladnus by the children, who struggled with unfamiliar pronunciation), with another family. Collatinus was named for one of the first Roman consuls, an odd name for a cat perhaps, but in naming his horse Charlemagne, he'd shown he loved historic names.

Chamberlain enjoyed the renown he received from his lectures. Many other veterans took speaking engagements in the months and years after the end of the war, but Chamberlain quickly stood apart; as a professor of rhetoric, he was uniquely able to speak about his battle experiences in a compelling way.

In one such instance, Chamberlain, in full military dress uniform, traveled north to Augusta, where he spoke about the recent secession and conflict: "We must have guarantees good and sufficient against any future attempt to destroy this government."[16] With his regular speaking engagements, Chamberlain was beginning to find his post–Civil War footing.

BUT EVEN AS Chamberlain enjoyed being with Fanny and the children, and the validation of the lectures he offered, he struggled with depression. His despair came from the realization that he would need more surgery, and to add to his worries, he received word he would be mustered out of the army on August 24. He had counted on the army to pay for the surgery.[17]

In October, his spirits brightened briefly when he welcomed General Charles Griffin and his wife, Sarah, for a visit to Brunswick. As leader of the Fifth Corps, Griffin had been assigned command of the district of Maine; his headquarters were in Portland. After sev-

eral wonderful days together, reminiscing about this battle and that military decision, Griffin had to depart to continue his challenging career in the army, while Chamberlain returned to the sameness of teaching at Bowdoin.[18] As they said their goodbyes, Chamberlain's mind must have lingered on paths not taken.

For their tenth anniversary, Lawrence gave Fanny this gold-and-diamond bracelet depicting the twenty-four battles in which he fought in the Civil War.

AS THEIR TENTH wedding anniversary approached, Lawrence designed a gold-and-diamond bracelet inscribed with Fanny's name and the date of their anniversary: December 7. He decorated the bracelet with the names of the twenty-four battles in which he engaged. He placed a red Maltese cross enveloped by small diamonds at the center. The underside held a general's dark-blue shoulder strap with two stars, both with a diamond. Tiffany of New York made his extravagant gift for $250.[19]

If the bracelet was meant to be a memento of love for his wife, its design was all about him and his accomplishments. The bracelet is about war rather than anything specific about their love shared over ten years. With his reverence for the chivalry of earlier centuries, perhaps for Chamberlain it symbolized what a knight would give to his lady.

Once it had become clear that his wounds would not turn into "honorable scars" without further medical intervention, a number of friends petitioned the government to restore Chamberlain to his army rank so he could receive another surgery. As early as September, unbeknownst to Chamberlain, Maine governor Cony had written Maine senator Lot Morrill asking if the government could step up to help Chamberlain. Morrill rallied other state leaders, and a petition went to Secretary of War Edwin Stanton. Stanton needed General Grant's approval to revoke Chamberlain's muster-out date; Grant gladly signed it and passed it on to President Johnson for his final approval. Chamberlain was mustered out effective January 16, 1866, allowing him to have the necessary surgery with the support of army pay.[20]

Chamberlain underwent yet another surgery, but he received a bitter truth: his wounds could never completely heal. For the rest of his life, he would need to deal with urine seeping from his injured urethra. The route the bullet took through his body meant that he would be subject to repeated infections.

Chamberlain returned home from the hospital to recuperate at the beginning of 1866. In a cold Maine winter that exacerbated the physical pain of his wounds, he now carried the emotional pain of knowing that he would never fully recover from the wounds suffered at Petersburg. The effect of his wounds indisputably constrained Lawrence and Fanny's sexual relations.

.   .   .

James G. Blaine, leader of the Maine Republican Party, took an early interest in Chamberlain as a potential candidate for governor.

WHILE RETURNING TO teaching, one path Chamberlain found for his future was proffered by Maine congressman James G. Blaine and other Maine Republican leaders who came calling at the start of 1866.

A year and a half younger than Chamberlain, Blaine was born in western Pennsylvania, but moved to Augusta after marrying Harriet Stanwood, a Maine native. In 1853, he purchased Augusta's *Kennebec Journal* and became editor of this staunchly Whig newspaper. As the Whig Party transitioned into the new Republican Party, Blaine, known for his magnetic personality, caught the political bug and ran for office. Elected to the Maine House of Representatives in 1858, he became chairman of the Republican state committee in 1859. He made the move to national politics with his election to the U.S. House of Representatives in 1863 but continued to act as the czar of Maine politics.[21] It was from this position that he had a strong say about Chamberlain as a potential political candidate in 1866.

The Democratic Party in Maine had, for the most part, opposed the war, and had since fractured into combative factions. The Republican Party, on the other hand, came out of the Civil War a solid and united party. For a small state, Maine could boast of several Republican leaders in addition to the charismatic Blaine making their mark on the national stage. Hannibal Hamlin, a former Democrat and one of Lincoln's earliest supporters, had served as vice president in Lincoln's first term. Senator William Pitt Fessenden served for two years as secretary of the treasury under Lincoln before returning to the Senate.

As Republicans observed Civil War hero Chamberlain at speaking engagements around the state, they saw in him the potential for another great Maine leader. They wanted him to be their candidate for governor.

. . .

ALTHOUGH CHAMBERLAIN WASN'T finding fulfillment as a professor, he was unsure if politics would be his best step forward.

He did his due diligence. He knew the term of service for Maine's governors to be unusual: one year. There were no term limits, but the previous thirty-one governors had served an average of only one and a half terms.[22] Not exactly a recipe for a long-term career.

Maine Republicans also did their due diligence about Chamberlain. They wanted to know what he thought about what was being called Reconstruction. Historian Richard White aptly states: "The touchstone for American politics at the end of 1865 was a question: what would Lincoln have done?"[23] But without Lincoln, what heated up in the winter of 1865 were increasingly hostile battles between President Andrew Johnson and the Republican-dominated Congress over the direction and content of Reconstruction. Some Republicans worried Chamberlain might be supporting Johnson.

A self-educated tailor from Tennessee, Johnson was the only Southern senator who had remained with the Union during the Civil War. He was chosen for vice president on the Republican ticket in 1864 as a symbol of national unity.

In his vision for Reconstruction, Johnson wanted to shatter the dominance of the South's slave-holding aristocracy and supplant it with the elevation of small farm owners and village shopkeepers. This vision explicitly did not include political rights for freed slaves. During Johnson's presidency, the Mississippi's *Jackson News* quoted Johnson in its masthead: "This is a white man's country —President Johnson."[24]

Throughout the spring and summer of 1865, increasing numbers of Republicans had expressed exasperation with the new president. With no Congress in session, Johnson

President Andrew Johnson, succeeding Abraham Lincoln, became the target of Republican anger over his Reconstruction policies.

began to put his Reconstruction plans in place. He issued hundreds of pardons to Confederates who had been barred in initial amnesty proclamations.

When the thirty-ninth Congress convened on the balmy first Monday in December, Republicans were determined to retake the initiative. They enjoyed massive majorities—42 to 10 in the Senate and 149 to 42 in the House of Representatives. The Thirteenth Amendment, which formally abolished slavery, was passed by Congress in January, and was officially ratified on December 6.

Congress's first major fight with Johnson exploded over the legal standing of the Southern states. The issue: should representatives of the former Confederate states be seated in the new Congress? Johnson argued that the eleven Confederate states had never left the Union. Republicans countered that these were defeated states, and as such, should be required to meet certain qualifications before being readmitted to Congress. When sixteen recently elected Southern congressmen, including four Confederate generals, submitted their credentials, their requests were rejected.

These issues were on the minds of everyone, politician or not. In early January 1866, Chamberlain received a surprising letter from his mother. "Since the war I have been quite a *politician*," Sarah wrote. "I think this is a very perplexing time politically." He had not known her to be interested in politics, but she told him that since the war began, she had been "studying all the political speeches." Her conclusion: "I find myself with Congress rather than Johnson." She reasoned, "Better have left the Slaves in bondage than set them at liberty & withhold protection from them. Now they must suffer unless they are protected from the rage and violence of their former masters and put in the right way of taking care of themselves."[25] Chamberlain's mother's interest in politics reflected how many American citizens, not paying attention to politics before the war, suddenly became engaged.

IN THE EARLY months of 1866, Chamberlain was trying to make up his mind about what to do about the growing interest in his running for governor. In a March letter to Fanny: "I am summoned to Augusta today by dispatch—to see some of the gentlemen interested in having me nominated."²⁶ Though he clearly kept his wife abreast of these conversations, there is no record of what Fanny thought about the idea of her husband running for political office.

BY THE SPRING of 1866, the state's newspapers were openly discussing the potential of Chamberlain's candidacy for governor. Maine Republicans believed a Union war hero would be the best candidate against Democrats, who could be framed as unpatriotic because of their criticisms of Lincoln and the war effort.

The *Portland Press,* a leading Republican newspaper, cautioned, "Let us not be deluded by brilliant military service, into the folly of placing the vital political issues of the day in the hands of untried and uncertain men."²⁷

In response, Maine's Republican leaders discovered that Chamberlain had voted for Republican Hannibal Hamlin for governor in 1856.²⁸

The Bangor *Whig,* one of the leading newspapers in the state, had remained neutral in the first months of 1866, but once Chamberlain aligned himself with the Republicans in Congress, it declared its support for him on April 22, thirteen days after Congress decisively overrode President Johnson's veto of the Civil Rights Act of 1866, presaging a lasting divide between Johnson and Congress. The act was the first federal law to define American citizenship. It stated that "all persons born in the United States, with the exception of American Indians," were to be considered citizens and receive "equal protection by the law." The intent was to protect the civil rights of African Americans. Chamberlain supported the Civil Rights Act. The newspaper applauded Chamberlain's stance as "squarely upon the most advanced grounds occupied by Union men of the North."²⁹

AROUND THIS TIME, Lawrence surprised Fanny by informing her that he had made an offer to buy Professor Thomas Upham's house at 159 Park Row, believing their family had outgrown their Potter Street home.³⁰

Fanny, perhaps stung by not being consulted, replied, "I rather hope Prof. Upham will not take your offer for the house." Why? "I don't think you want it. . . . You will not probably stay in Brunswick long, and if you do anything with the old house it would only be a great expense to you, and no particular advantage when you wished to sell." Fanny's reply indicates two things about their relationship. First, she seemed willing to accede to his wishes about their home. Second, she often knew his mind better than he did his own, including his underlying political desires and abilities. Deftly, she concluded her letter: "Is it not so."[31]

ON JUNE 21, the Maine Republican Party, calling itself in 1866 the Union Party, met in Bangor to discuss nominations for governor. Chamberlain did not attend, but had agreed to be a candidate. His opponent was Samuel Spring, a prosperous Portland businessman. Spring tried to make an issue of whether Chamberlain supported Republicans in Congress and their Reconstruction initiatives, but to no avail. On a single ballot, Chamberlain received 599 votes to Spring's 438.[32]

The Democratic Party nominated Eben F. Pillsbury, editor of the Farmington *Patriot,* as their candidate at their meeting in Portland. The wealthy Pillsbury was part of the extreme wing of his party that had opposed the war. He stood in stark opposition to Chamberlain, which Chamberlain's supporters used to their advantage. During the summer, a pamphlet charged that Pillsbury expressed "disloyal sentiments during the very crisis of his country's fate," compared to Chamberlain, "a patriot who fought in the most critical battles of the War."[33]

In the campaign, the *Portland Star* stated that what distinguished Chamberlain from other Republicans, and now from Pillsbury, was his unmatched war record: "It is not extravagant to say that General Chamberlain will get ten thousand more votes in Maine than almost any man who could have been nominated." Echoing the martyred Lincoln: "That mystic chords of memory, stretching from a hundred battlefields of the war, will draw thousands to the polls that they may deposit for Joshua L. Chamberlain."[34]

.   .   .

NOT LONG AFTER Chamberlain's nomination, Bowdoin president Woods decided to retire. The college quickly turned to Chamberlain, asking him to serve as acting president. He agreed to serve as temporary president but made it clear that as a candidate for governor, he could not succeed Woods as a permanent president.[35]

At the end of August, just two weeks before the gubernatorial election, Chamberlain received another offer. General Warren, his former commander, had been asked by General Grant to submit a list of names of potential field officers in the reconstituted peacetime regular army. Warren told Chamberlain that he'd put his name at the head of the list. But Chamberlain, quite apart from his candidacy for governor, believed he could not accept the offer because of his health.[36]

It had been just a little over a year that Chamberlain had been home, and in that time he'd been offered the role of collector of customs for the port at Bath, professor and potentially president of Bowdoin, and a general in the reconstituted regular army. And then, on September 10, Chamberlain was elected governor, easily defeating Pillsbury. He polled 69,637 votes to Pillsbury's 41,917.[37] Rev. Adams rejoiced: "Great news as to the election. C elected no doubt by a great majority."[38] Indeed, it was the largest margin of victory in the history of the state.

SHORTLY AFTER THE election, Alfred C. Godfrey, former chaplain of the Twentieth Maine, wrote Chamberlain, "Well, Gen., honors have come down on you gloriously and I am glad of it." He went on, offering both affirmation and warning at a transitional moment in Chamberlain's life: "Don't get dizzy-headed. Be as true in Me. as you were in Va. and no man can take you down."[39]

FIFTEEN

Governor of Maine

In a government like ours one of the most delicate things which a
State could be told to do is to invade the ancient rights and dignitaries
of towns which the historian and statesman know, are the
foundations of our liberties.

—GOVERNOR JOSHUA LAWRENCE CHAMBERLAIN, JANUARY 1870

Joshua L Chamberlain

CHAMBERLAIN WAS INAUGURATED GOVERNOR OF MAINE ON
January 4, 1867, in a day of great celebration. The ceremony
took place in the state capitol on Weston's Hill in Augusta. Designed
by prominent New England architect Charles Bulfinch, the Greek
Revival building had been completed in 1832, twelve years after
Maine became a state. Chamberlain's inauguration made him
Maine's thirty-second governor.

Maine State capitol

. . .

CHAMBERLAIN INVITED GENERAL Grant to be present at his inauguration and was disappointed when he could not attend. Rev. Adams hoped to "witness Chamberlain inauguration," but wrote in his diary that he was "not quite well enough."[1] Chamberlain's parents did travel from Brewer to Augusta to attend. Years earlier, each had their hopes for their son: the father a military career, the mother a minister of missionary. Neither dreamed of a politician, but now they came to support their son's next chapter in his life.

YET DOUBTS HOVERED over the happy day. A question lingered on many lips. Despite his acclaim as a Civil War hero, was Chamberlain ready to be governor? Yes, he had

Sarah Dupee Brastow Chamberlain in the dress she wore for her son's inauguration

ably led soldiers into battle, but did that translate to leadership in matters of state, where he would face powerful lobbying groups instead of Confederate regiments; where the weapons would be arm-twisting and patronage, not rifles and cannons; where resistance to his leadership came not only from the stated enemy, the opposition Democratic Party, but from within his own Republican Party?

CHAMBERLAIN HAD SPENT the past eighteen months impressing Maine audiences with captivating lectures on the Civil War, but he knew his inaugural address had to be very different. No one, including Chamberlain, knew what to expect in post–Civil War America, but his audience expected him to have a vision for a postwar Maine.

In the hour-and-a-half-long address, Chamberlain began by recognizing the "many anxieties" Maine's citizens experienced in the war. The state of only six hundred thousand people had provided

72,945 men to the war, of whom 8,792 died and 11,309 suffered wounds.[2] That meant 12 percent of Maine's total population went to war. Of them, over one in four came back wounded—or didn't come back at all. Speaking to himself as well as his audience, Chamberlain said, "We have looked our sorrows fairly in the face and found that we could bear them."[3]

If, during the campaign, some had worried about where he stood in the conflict between President Johnson and Congress, Chamberlain's first address as governor made his position clear. He offered strong words about the recent posture of the South:

> We are struck with amazement and thrown upon our guard when we see those who with scorn and contumely spurned the Constitution, and defied the Government, and sought with violence and cruelty to destroy the Union, now demanding, with equal effrontery and the same spirit of violence, without apology for the past, without a guarantee for the future, the unconditional restoration of their rights under the Constitution, their place in the Union and their prestige in the Government.[4]

At the time, ten Confederate states were still knocking at the door of Congress asking to be readmitted. The key to opening the door was ratification of the Fourteenth Amendment, which advanced the rights of African Americans. Only Tennessee had done so. The other states delayed doing so with the knowledge that President Johnson stood on their side.[5]

In contrast, Chamberlain strongly endorsed the Fourteenth Amendment. In its first section it declared, "All persons born or naturalized in the United States . . . are citizens of the United States." Quoting the Bill of Rights, the amendment went on to say, "No state shall make or enforce any law which shall abridge the privileges or immunities of citizens . . . nor shall any state deprive any person of life, liberty, or property, without due process of law" or "deny equal protection of the laws."[6]

Although Chamberlain had initially enlisted in an army whose sole purpose was to save the Union, Lincoln had enlarged the war's objective to embrace freedom for enslaved African Americans and Chamberlain continued to support that expanded purpose.

The new governor then devoted a large portion of his address to the economic issues facing Maine. Recognizing that lumbering and shipbuilding were decreasing, he focused on government support for broader economic advancement, a mainstay of national Republican politics since the days when Henry Clay first advocated an "American System" of internal improvements in the 1820s. To strengthen both agriculture and industry, he encouraged river surveys and the extension of the railroads. Arguing for a positive role for government, he would be the first Maine governor to propose public loans to finance improvements to the railroads.[7] In the national talk of Reconstruction, Chamberlain insisted that "there must be Industrial and Financial as well as political reconstruction."[8]

He endorsed a new approach to education. A beneficiary of a classical education at Bowdoin, he offered his support for an agricultural college being established at Orono that would emphasize "practical science and mechanic arts." He declared the college would "not educate people out of their sphere but into it."[9]

In addressing the need to enlarge the state prison, he touched upon the hotly debated topic of capital punishment. He told the legislature it had a choice: "Either abolish capital punishment altogether, or fix upon a day after the year of grace on which the sentence shall be executed." Behind this sentence lay the long-held practice of previous governors to not follow through on court orders to execute convicted criminals. Chamberlain would soon discover that this vexing issue would not prove easy to resolve.[10]

Maine's newspapers applauded the new governor's address. The Lewiston *Evening Journal* wrote that it "will be read not only with interest but with pride."[11] The *Portland Transcript* praised his views as "broad, liberal, and comprehensive."[12]

Maine congressman Blaine, a rising star in the national Republican firmament, wrote from Washington that the address "does you great honor." He believed the address "bold, clear, comprehensive and statesmanlike."[13]

. . .

As CHAMBERLAIN SETTLED into his new position in Augusta, Fanny's feelings about her husband being elected governor are difficult to discern. Some have depicted Fanny refusing to uproot herself from Brunswick and live in Augusta, suggesting a tension between her and Lawrence over his new public role.

Nearly all correspondence between Lawrence and Fanny that might confirm or deny her point of view is missing from 1867, the year he began as governor.

For Fanny, the culture of the day, and her upbringing, had educated her to be a "good" wife. "Good" meant dutiful. The primary role expected of her was that of the general in charge of domestic life—the nurturing of children and the command of the kitchen. Yet for the many women who stepped forward during the Civil War into roles traditionally held by their husbands, the expectation that they were now supposed to return to their former domestic sphere would not be easy to fulfill.

There were other reasons Fanny may have chosen to stay in Brunswick. At this time there was not yet a governor's mansion in Augusta. Governors stayed in a boardinghouse. While it is clear that Fanny wanted Lawrence to succeed as governor, she had never been interested in the sort of networking and social climbing that was part and parcel of the political world. Ultimately, Lawrence would live part of the year alone in Augusta.

As LAWRENCE'S POLITICAL star rose, he received troubling news about his brother John. After graduating from Bangor Theological Seminary in 1864, John was offered the chaplaincy of the Eleventh Maine Infantry, but demurred, choosing instead to work as an inspector for the Internal Revenue Service in New York. In April 1865, he suffered a hemorrhaging of his lungs, but the family became convinced that he probably contracted the dreaded tuberculosis while serving with the Christian Commission. Ironically, he was behind the lines at Gettysburg, but served in the squalor of the unsanitary field hospitals.[14]

Sae, engaged to be married to Brewer merchant Charles O. Farrington, traveled from Brewer to help care for her brother. Lawrence also went to John's home in Brooklyn.[15]

But on August 10, 1867, Sarah Chamberlain's "good boy Johnny" died at the age of twenty-nine, from the same lung disease that had taken his brother Horace six years before. Even as things were going well for Lawrence professionally, on a personal level he endured increasing losses.

IN THE MAINE pattern of one-year terms for governor, Republicans nominated Chamberlain for a second term. He was only halfway through his first term when receiving the nomination. The Democrats renominated Pillsbury.

When the ballots were counted in September 1867, Chamberlain prevailed again. He received 57,332 votes to Pillsbury's 45,590 votes, winning by a slightly smaller margin.[16] In this off-year election, Democrats, pushing back nationally against what they called the radical Reconstruction measures of Republicans, scored gains almost everywhere.

THE WINTER OF 1868 would become a time of testing for the second-term governor.

The testing began with the temperance movement. In 1810 the American male drank nearly five and one-half gallons of liquor a year—more than twice what people drink today. If by 1850 the consumption of liquor had declined to four gallons a year, drunken-

True Temperance cartoon

ness was still common. Drunkenness among children was not unusual. It was a typical ritual for workingmen to pause in the afternoon for an alcoholic drink, often rum. Many spent an inordinate amount of their wages on alcohol. The abuse of alcohol was inflicting havoc not simply upon the lives of men, but upon women and families, reliant on men for financial support.[17]

Heavy drinking by women was not acceptable in society. But in actuality, many women had small bottles of liquor with their kitchen supplies, perfect for a quick swig.[18]

In Maine, the temperance movement was led by Neal Dow, a businessman who helped found the Maine Temperance Society, and who would become known across the nation as the Father of Prohibition. After being elected mayor of Portland in 1851, he had

a habit of riding around the city pointing out drunkenness and crime to anyone who would listen: "Rum did that." Believing personal moral suasion to be ineffective in changing attitudes toward alcohol, and that local options were not working, he pushed for a statewide legislative approach. In 1851, the legislature passed the "Maine Law," in so doing becoming the first "dry" state in the nation.[19]

The Maine Temperance Society held their annual convention following the conclusion of the legislative session each fall. By custom, they invited the governor to preside. Chamberlain had done so in 1867; they assumed he would do so again.

Portland mayor and temperance crusader Neal Dow in 1851

He declined. Chamberlain told them he believed it inappropriate to meet with them while temperance legislation was pending upon which he might be asked to act.[20]

Chamberlain began pushing back against the increasing influence of the temperance movement. He appreciated that some of Maine's immigrant population were Irish American Catholics in a largely Protestant state, and opposed such laws.

At the beginning of his second term, Chamberlain asked the Maine legislature to repeal laws that would imprison any person selling liquor. He believed these tactics interfered with the rights of the state's citizens. He also asked that the special constabulary police force created to enforce the law be suspended. He called both laws unconstitutional and stated that the temperance movement had gained too much power in Maine. Chamberlain, aware of the problem of alcohol abuse in society, believed strongly that the right to privacy in one's home outweighed the aggressive push of the temperance crusaders.[21]

The governor's stand provoked a number of angry responses. The *Bangor Whig and Courier,* usually a supporter of Chamberlain, warned, "If politicians see fit to thrust [the temperance cause] into politics, they must take the consequences."[22]

The battle over temperance would help shape Chamberlain's larger political convictions. If sympathetic to the idea of temperance, he came to the conclusion that the principle of individual rights was more important than any moral or political movement, however popular it might be.

This initial conflict in Chamberlain's governorship also revealed a trait beginning to emerge in his leadership: he would not back down when confronted with opposition.

Another stressor for the governor was the fact that young people were leaving Maine, and immigrants were declining to come to the state. He believed a primary reason for both was the lack of economic opportunity.

Chamberlain in his second term as governor of Maine

The inherited "snug policy of letting well-enough alone" would not do.[23] He believed the governing Republican Party needed to change its mindset. In the new post–Civil War landscape, with industrialism on the rise, government needed to play a more active role and offer public assistance, not only to the railroads, but also to new industries.

To address the problem of immigration, he announced a plan to hire an agent to travel to Sweden to publicize the possibility of establishing a colony within the state: "Maine is as good a State to migrate to as Minnesota."[24]

IN 1868 CHAMBERLAIN'S concerns as governor stretched beyond Maine's borders. At the beginning of his second term, national politics intersected with Maine politics.

On February 24, 1868, Republicans in the House of Representatives resolved to impeach President Johnson. They voted on eleven articles of impeachment. The major charge was that he had flouted the Tenure of Office Act enacted by Congress in March 1867 over the president's veto. The act stated that cabinet officers were to "hold their offices respectively for and during the terms of the President by whom they may have been appointed." Thus, Republicans argued that Johnson had illegally removed his foe, Secretary of War Edwin Stanton, appointed by Lincoln, from office.[25]

There had never before been an impeachment of an American president. As the impeachment trial moved toward its culmination in May, the demand for tickets surged as people sought to be present for this once-in-a-lifetime event.

Most Republicans in Maine joined Republicans across the nation in urging conviction. Republicans in Portland called a meeting on the evening of May 15 to discuss the impeachment. The meeting "strongly denounced the President as guilty of the blackest crimes." The Bangor *Whig and Courier* added its voice in favor of impeachment.[26] On Saturday, May 16, Chief Justice Salmon Chase, attired in his long black robe, directed the clerk to call, in alphabetical order, the roll of fifty-four senators representing twenty-seven states (ten former Confederate states had still not been readmitted) voting on each article of impeachment. Impeachment would require a two-thirds majority, or thirty-six votes, to convict. Everyone knew all nine Democratic senators would vote for acquittal. Therefore, it would take the votes of seven Republican senators to deny conviction.

Many eyes in the chamber and galleries fastened on Maine senator William Pitt Fessenden. Everyone knew Fessenden was antislav-

Packed gallery at impeachment trial of Andrew Johnson in May 1868

ery; his four sons had fought in the Civil War, and he chaired the Senate Committee on Reconstruction. Fessenden often sided with Republican Radicals in Congress. The Republican Radicals—Charles Sumner, Benjamin Wade, and Zachariah Chandler in the Senate, and Thaddeus Stevens, Henry Winter Davis, and Benjamin Butler in the House—pushed for the rights of African Americans and believed Confederate leaders should be reproved for their roles in the Civil War. The Radicals assumed Fessenden would vote with them to convict Johnson.[27]

While the Maine senator despised Johnson and his policies, he questioned whether the president's actions rose to "high crimes and misdemeanors," thus warranting conviction. As much as he abhorred Johnson, he worried that conviction could set a terrible precedent for future presidents.

The huge majority of Republican senators voted guilty. When Fessenden's name was called, he responded, "Not guilty." The final vote was 35–19, just one vote short of the two-thirds vote needed for conviction.[28]

Many Republicans in Maine believed Fessenden's vote made the difference. Furious, they turned on him. In one cartoon, radical congressman Butler, in the guise of a teacher, takes Fessenden to task for his vote, ordering him to spell "guilty."

Dame Butler - Head boy! - Spell guilty. In this cartoon, Congressman Benjamin Butler, one of the backers of impeachment, is taking to task Senator William Fessenden for his vote against impeachment.

Fessenden's vote ruined his political career. His son later re-membered, "He was told that if he voted against conviction, he might as well leave Maine." A leading Maine Republican at the time wrote that he "never believed [Fessenden] could betray his party, and begged him not to crush the people of Maine with shame and misery."[29]

Chamberlain respected Fessenden and supported his vote for acquittal. He was also critical of Johnson, but believed with Fessenden that his sins did not rise to "high crimes and misdemeanors." When Chamberlain's position became publicly known, he shared with Fessenden criticism from some members of the Republican establishment in Maine.[30]

IN 1868, CHAMBERLAIN contemplated running for a third term, but the toils of the office had begun to wear on him. He was aware that of his thirty-one predecessors, only six had successfully run for more than two terms. Believing he could accomplish more in sup-porting economic growth, encouraging education, and promoting immigration to Maine, he decided to seek a third term. But he was sure it would be his last.

On September 14, despite disapproval from some Republicans over his stance on impeachment, and criticism from the temperance lobby of his opposition to prohibition laws, Chamberlain won reelection easily. In a post–Civil War climate, continued appreciation for General Chamberlain drowned out criticisms of Governor Chamberlain.[31]

In November, Chamberlain rejoiced when Grant, running as a Republican, won an overwhelming victory over the Democratic candidate, former New York governor Horace Seymour, to become the nation's eighteenth president.

IN HIS THIRD term, Chamberlain faced a critical decision about Maine's death penalty law. Clifton Harris, a young black man, son of formerly enslaved parents, was arrested for the brutal murders of two Auburn women, Susannah Kinsley, sixty-four, and Polly Caswell, sixty-seven. Harris quickly confessed to the crimes, but sometime after his arrest he incriminated Luther Verrill, a white man. Verrill pleaded innocent, and the court discharged the case against him. The court found Harris guilty and sentenced him to be hanged.[32]

Many of America's early colonists came from England, where death was the penalty for a long list of crimes: arson, burglary, counterfeiting, manslaughter, murder, rape,

Clifton Harris, a young African American man, was arrested for the murders of two Maine women.

robbery, and treason. At first all were also capital crimes in the colonies. Adherents of capital punishment often argued that it served three purposes: first, deterrence; second, retribution; and third, penance—repentance before the death sentence was carried out.[33]

After the American Revolution, opponents of the death penalty argued it was outmoded, perhaps fitting for monarchies and aristocracies but not for a more egalitarian liberal democracy.[34]

Maine became a leader in this opposition. Although a bill abolishing the death penalty was rejected by the state legislature, a bill passed in 1837 would prove to have the same effect. It required the condemned criminal be held at Thomaston State Prison for one year from the date of the court order. The logic behind the waiting period was that it would give time for the passions surrounding the crime to subside. It seemed to work. Maine's governors did not sign papers for an execution from 1837 to 1863, on the grounds that the law required them to act as judicial rather than executive officer. The practical effect: the death penalty all but disappeared in Maine. Furthermore, the pattern of the Maine law was followed in Vermont, New Hampshire, Massachusetts, and New York.[35]

CHAMBERLAIN'S STANCE ON the death penalty, as tested by the Clifton Harris case, now became an unexpected fulcrum in his governorship.

When the year elapsed from Harris's sentencing, Chamberlain

Maine attorney general William P. Frye challenged Chamberlain's decision on the use of the death penalty in the case of Clifton Harris.

signed the death warrant on January 8, 1869. At the same time, he commuted the death sentences of two others.

Mainers were shocked by the crime Harris committed, but some were also outraged that the governor signed the death warrant. The editor of Augusta's *Maine Farmer* wrote, "For more than thirty years [this] barbarous punishment has slumbered on our statue book."[36] The Portland *Eastern Argus* questioned why the governor had commuted the death sentence for George Knight following twelve years in prison, while he signed the order to hang Harris.[37]

Maine attorney general William P. Frye emerged as Chamberlain's most able opponent on the subject of the death penalty. Frye graduated from Bowdoin in 1850, two years ahead of Chamberlain. Handsome and well-spoken, Frye became attorney general in 1867, after serving in the Maine House of Representatives and as mayor of Lewiston.

He challenged Chamberlain's decision in his official report: "I do not think that justice requires the execution of Harris." After pointing out that a white man who had murdered his wife had avoided the death penalty, he continued, "it seems to me that some consideration, in determining this question, should be given to the birth, the early life and training, and the circumstances of this man." He went on to describe his understanding of Harris: "born on a Southern plantation, educated only as to his brutal instincts, compelled into ignorance and degradation, and a subserviency to a white man by force of the law itself."[38] The attorney general, a successful Maine lawyer, based his opposition on the story of Harris's difficult early life as an African American growing up in the South.

In his third inaugural address, Chamberlain spent considerable time giving his reasons for his decision and answering Attorney General Frye. In response to Frye's description of Harris's difficult early years, he replied, " 'Previous good character' is a plea in mitigation—but to plead a 'previous bad character' is a novelty of jurisprudence." He asserted that convicted wife-murderer Knight, whose death sentence he commuted, "still protests his innocence while Harris boasts of his guilt." Finally, he pointed out that the state legislature had more than once rejected a bill to do away with the death penalty entirely, and he concluded that personal or public opinion about the death penalty did not contravene his duty to carry out the law.[39]

Duty. It had summoned him to enlist in the Civil War, became even more central to his service in the war, and now became the core value behind his controversial decision to uphold the death penalty. Yet in their debate, Frye understood what Chamberlain did not: the toll that being a son of enslaved parents may have taken on young Harris growing up.

. . .

IF RESOLUTE IN public, at the end of January, Chamberlain unburdened himself in a letter to his mother: "Many are bitter on me about capital punishment, but it does not disturb me in the least." He told her he was receiving hostile letters, including one from a man who knew him long ago in Brewer when Lawrence was "a little good boy." He told her, "I go on the strength of conscious rectitude & you can't scare me."[40] Once again, Chamberlain was determined not to give in to opposition.

Three days later, Lawrence's no-nonsense father weighed in on the "Cavil of Clowns" who were criticizing his son, expressing his disdain for Frye, whom he labeled "over reformed attorney generals odious."[41]

The death penalty controversy affected Chamberlain deeply. The whole episode seemed to him an example of how politics so differed from the military. There had been a long-standing law on the death penalty, but civilian administrators had refused to follow it. More so, the attorney general, responsible for carrying out the laws of the state, stood against the governor who wanted to carry out those very laws. And then the governor who decided to carry out the established law was now subject to criticism.

IN THE MIDST of the public controversy over the death penalty, Lawrence and Fanny struggled in their marriage. On November 20, 1868, Lawrence wrote a long, emotional letter to Fanny: "In the midst of all the uproar of obloquy now hurled at me by the friends of Harris & the rampant temperance men I find myself assailed by only one thing which distresses me." He expressed his dismay that she was "making a confidant of unworthy persons," which he believed to be private conversations. "You were complaining to everyone who came into the house of my conduct & treatment of you." He now became specific: "Miss Courlaender, it seems is freely telling people that 'you told her (& Mrs. Dunning also as well as everybody else) that I abused you beyond endurance—pulling your hair, striking, beating & otherwise personally maltreating you, & that you were gathering up everything you could find against me to sue for a divorce.' " Turning the personal political, Chamberlain added that a political friend "says this is doing immense harm, whether the fact is so or not, & the bitter enemies who now assail me on public grounds, will soon get hold of this & will ruin me."[42]

What was the solution, according to Lawrence? "I think we had skill enough to adjust the terms of a separation without the wretchedness to all our family which these low people to whom it would seem you confide your grievance & plans, will certainly bring about." But he followed this suggestion with "You never take my advice, I am aware. But if you do not stop this at once it will end in hell."[43]

After the menacing tone of most of the letter, his concluding sentence is filled with pain: "It is a very great trial to me—more than all things else put together—wounds, pains, toils, wrongs & hatreds of eager enemies."[44]

This is a striking letter. It is not possible to verify or deny that Lawrence had been physically abusive to Fanny from any other known source or letter. The other correspondence from this time is missing. Was it burned? It is unfortunate that we don't have Fanny's letters from this period to hear her side of the story.

THIS IS ALSO a moment when observations from Rev. Adams would be illuminating. But from September 12, 1868, until January 3, 1869, he did not write in his diary—a very unusual absence for a man who wrote almost daily in his diary.

The marriage of Lawrence and Fanny functioned within the power dynamics of nineteenth-century marriages, where the husband was the head of the family. When it came to what was often called "marital cruelty," legislatures and courts were advancing slowly and often leniently to deal with the often unreported problem.[45]

After sending this letter, when Lawrence returned to Brunswick, it seems that he and Fanny lived separately for some time. But again we wish we knew more.

.   .   .

EVEN AS HIS marriage to Fanny struggled, Chamberlain spent time with his children. In February 1869, when Chamberlain journeyed to Philadelphia to speak at the Academy of Music, he took twelve-year-old Daisy with him. Becoming a young lady, she now asked to be called Grace. The love and appreciation Grace and her father shared was blossoming into a special lifelong relationship. Writing home to "Darling Bill," her younger brother, Grace regaled him with the scene of their father speaking in Philadelphia. "The snowy cap of the Sacred Mountain still looms above all. Father perfect in every way." Describing the speech and its reception: "Good voice—and the same presence. Our path is strewn with Generals and Admirals and old friends galore."[46]

Lawrence added a postscript to her letter. "The academy of music was packed to its utmost . . . I got on pretty well." Yet, amid the elation, he admitted, "I am tired and my head swimming," surely from the aggravation of his invisible wounds, which caused him physical and emotional distress.[47]

ON HIS RETURN to Maine, the pain from his wounds prompted him to visit physician J. W. Toward in Augusta. The physician wrote a report that offered a full description of Chamberlain's condition: "Bladder very painful & irritable—whole of lower part of abdomen tender & sensitive— Large urinal fistula at base of penis in front of scrotum, which is exceedingly troublesome—suffers constant pain in both hips from wound." The physician added a final estimation: "I think his general health much affected from his wounds, especially the first named & that it will materially abridge his life."[48] "Abridge" meant the physician believed Chamberlain's life would surely be diminished and shortened.

As THE 1869 Maine Republican convention approached, Chamberlain reiterated that he would serve only three terms; he would not run again. Only two of the previous thirty-one governors had served more than three terms. But with no good alternative candidates emerging, party leaders persuaded Chamberlain to break with the unofficial three-term rule and his own instinct, and run for a fourth term.

He was nominated in Bangor in June. The Republican convention hailed him as "one of our most eminent citizens, distinguished for his scholarship, his patriotism, and his undying military record."[49]

This time the opposition came not just from the Democrats, who nominated Franklin Smith, but from temperance advocates who nominated N. G. Hichborn as a third-party candidate. In the general election in September, Chamberlain received 54,314 votes, Smith 39,033, and Hichborn 4,736.[50]

BELIEVING THIS WOULD be his final term, in January 1870, in his fourth inaugural address, he used the issue of temperance to lay out his understanding of law and liberty, whose relationship he had sought to address fifteen years earlier in the speech at the Bowdoin commencement that won him his teaching position. Now, as governor, he stated, "Any law which proposes to abridge personal rights should be ventured upon with the utmost caution and administered with the utmost charity."[51]

If Chamberlain wanted to express his political ethic, the *Bangor Whig and Courier* did not think Chamberlain spoke with tact. No fervent supporter of prohibition, it nevertheless did not want to debase the idealism of the temperance reformers, nor did it think that local law enforcement in small towns was up to the task of enforcing the Maine liquor laws. The *Whig* wrote that the governor's "ideas of enforcing temperance are of questionable wisdom or expediency, scarcely worthy an able public officer."[52] The *Portland Transcript* went further, writing that in Chamberlain's desire to defend himself from the charge that he was an opponent of temperance, the governor took on "a censorious tone towards those citizens who saw fit to support a temperance candidate."[53] This would not be the last time tact became an obstacle to Chamberlain's idealism.

. . .

As CHAMBERLAIN BEGAN his final term, many wondered if he would seek another political office. With the 1869 death of Senator Fessenden, speculation arose that the governor might appoint a temporary placeholder and then run for the Senate himself in 1870. But those who speculated did not know Chamberlain. Ambitious, yes, but self-serving, no. He appointed former governor Lott Morrill to fill out Fessenden's term.[54]

IN THE SUMMER of 1870, Chamberlain joined Americans in following the war in Europe between the Second French Empire and the North German Federation, led by the Kingdom of Prussia. Restless about what he might do next, Chamberlain wrote a letter to William, the King of Prussia, the day after the war broke out, offering his service to the Prussian army. At almost forty-two, he stated his qualifications: "His last two promotions were made on the field of battle under circumstances which warrant him in referring to them as testimony of his capacity." Chamberlain's Maine constituents would have been shocked to read, "The office he now holds as Governor of the State of Maine he proposes to resign in case your Majesty shall be pleased to accept his service."[55]

After four years of being in the limelight as governor of Maine, Chamberlain's greater pleasure with his career in the Union army surfaced once more in a most unusual way. But Chamberlain was not the only former soldier looking to return to the battlefield. General Philip Sheridan became an advisor to the Prussian army in 1870.

No response to his letter has been found. Chamberlain had found his greatest purpose and meaning in the Civil War and the letter to the King of Prussia seems to be his effort to relocate that meaning.

THAT SAME SUMMER, an important link in Chamberlain's family circle was broken. In August, Rev. Adams said goodbye to First Parish after more than forty years of ministry in Brunswick. It had to be an agonizing decision, with much protestation from his parishioners. He accepted a call to the new Trinity Congregational Church in

East Orange, New Jersey. There would be no more Thanksgiving and Christmas family gatherings at the home Fanny grew up in.[56]

Perhaps Rev. Adams's departure at age sixty-eight made Chamberlain reckon with his own parents' ages. With his father and mother now seventy and sixty-seven, Chamberlain contracted with a portrait artist to paint them in their family home in Brewer.[57]

AT THE END of four terms and four years in Augusta, Chamberlain felt both fulfilled and frustrated as governor. He consistently led with principle—sometimes stubbornly so. He had managed to fulfill, or at least place on firm footing, some of the goals announced in his first inaugural address in January 1867. He worked hard to bolster new industries by offering public assistance. In his four years as governor, he extended railroads across Maine, even into hitherto uninhabited northern areas in order to promote settlement.

His encouragement of emigration from Sweden to Maine had borne fruit. In the spring of 1870, William W. Thomas, who previously had served as American consul in Sweden, and now appointed Maine's first commissioner of immigration, sailed on the steamship *City of Brooklyn* for Gothenburg. From there he traveled throughout Sweden recruiting "worthy" immigrants. Each applicant brought recommending "credentials" from their pastor.[58]

After only forty days in Sweden, Thomas returned with fifty-one Swedes aboard the steamship *Orlando*, landing in Halifax, Nova Scotia, before traveling south to Maine. On July 23, the immigrants reached their new home, which they called New Sweden, in northern Maine. One hundred acres were assigned to each family. A Maine historian, writing four years later in 1875, observed, "Gov. Chamberlain had taken a deep interest in this enterprise." Furthermore, the governor "had fostered it with truly parental care."[59]

THROUGHOUT HIS FOUR terms, public education had been central to Chamberlain's administration. We can see a through line from his youthful teaching at the Milford and Wiscasset common schools to his experience as a professor at Bowdoin to his efforts as governor.

In 1867 he stated the problem: "There is much to be done before our schools can be regarded as best subserving their ends." Sitting in the governor's chair changed his perspective: "We must begin at the bottom and build up rather than begin at the top and build down. Institutions of learning of high grade doubtless have an important influence in the community, but the hundreds of modest little schools in many nook and corner of the State are the real foundations of knowledge and power."[60] He strengthened the common schools of the state by insisting on standards for teachers and encouraging more thoughtful methods of learning.

As governor he had to learn to deal with financial constraints, but argued, "Improvements in the course and methods of instruction should not be regarded as impossible." Focusing on the quality of teachers, he wrote, "The idea is somewhat new that teachers of common schools require especially instruction and training for their profession."[61]

In his fourth inaugural in January 1870, Chamberlain took a victory lap on education: "There is probably no branch of our public interests where such improvement has been made as in that our common schools." The former teacher stated, "The spirit of our institutions, the demands of our times have necessitated aims, objects, and methods which render education altogether a different business from what it was a generation ago." What did he mean? "It no longer seeks to cram the mind with strange forms and aggravated facts, without harmony, relation, life of permanence; it now teaches the mind from the very start to observe, compare, analyze, assimilate—to master and make it its own."[62] These words sounded like the Bowdoin professor speaking.

As FOR HIS frustrations, in his four terms Chamberlain learned that politics could be a harsh endeavor. Civility too often gave way to criticism. Government was slow-moving to solve problems, especially in the face of opposition. His idealism was tempered quickly by forces he had not fully understood as a candidate. As governor, he did not always have as much power to lead as he originally thought he would.

. . .

AT THE END of 1870, at age fifty-two, Chamberlain had served an almost unprecedented four terms as governor. Each year he had won reelection to successive terms decisively. At the beginning of 1871, still restless, wanting to repair and renew his marriage to Fanny, what new vocation could offer him purpose and meaning?

SIXTEEN

President of Bowdoin College

The college still seemed to have need of something—not quite well defined—some hold on the public confidence, some share in the living sympathies through which alone a college can find its life and work.
—JOSHUA LAWRENCE CHAMBERLAIN, INAUGURAL ADDRESS, JULY 1872

Joshua L Chamberlain

WHEN CHAMBERLAIN STEPPED DOWN AS GOVERNOR OF Maine after four terms, he did not have to wait long before another entity sought his leadership. Those who pursued him in 1871 felt no need to do any due diligence.

In spring 1871, Bowdoin College president Samuel Harris, weary from the duties of his office, especially the raising of money, resigned after only four years. The Bowdoin trustees and overseers knew immediately who they wanted to be their next president: they elected Chamberlain unanimously. The position would begin with the new school year. They offered him a salary of $2,600 ($63,510 today).[1]

In Chamberlain's four years as governor, he had maintained close connections with the college. In 1867, he had been elected a trustee. In 1869, Bowdoin awarded him an honorary doctor of laws degree. Starting in 1870, he chaired the alumni committee.

Chamberlain had experienced Bowdoin as student, professor, and trustee, and briefly as acting president. He had experienced mixed feelings about his seven years as a professor, but especially enjoyed the challenge of encouraging young men to think for themselves. Yet from the vantage point of his three adventure-filled years as a soldier, the academic life seemed confined and tame.

But by 1871 it had been nine years since he taught there, and

FACING PAGE: *Chamberlain as Bowdoin College president in 1875*

nineteen years since he graduated as a student. Most of the faculty Chamberlain had known were either retired or dead. Thomas Upham, a spiritual heart of the college, retired in 1867 and moved to New York. William "Chalkboard" Smyth, the college's antislavery advocate, died in 1868.

Tired of politics, Chamberlain accepted the invitation to embark on a fourth career.

Leaving Augusta, Chamberlain began living again full-time with Fanny and his children in Brunswick. Before assuming his new duties, in May 1871 he realized a long-held dream by purchasing a twenty-six-foot, six-ton sloop named *Wildflower*. He sailed it on Casco Bay, sometimes all the way to Portland.

CHAMBERLAIN BECAME PRESIDENT at a moment when winds of change were blowing swiftly through America's colleges. The historical narrative about higher education in the nineteenth century has often focused on changes initiated at Harvard and Yale, the nation's two oldest colleges, but that is a limited picture. There were two-hundred-odd American colleges in existence after the Civil War, the majority established by Protestant denominations.[2]

Colleges large and small wondered what their institutions would look like in a rapidly changing postwar America. In an increasingly competitive market, many struggled to be financially viable, some not surviving to the end of the century. At the same time, some alumni resisted change. They wanted their colleges to remain as they sentimentalized their memories of their college years.

But for many, the system wasn't working. Limited by the small number of faculty, students were taught by the same teachers again and again. As for the range of subjects, students were still subjected to a curriculum with few choices, as in Chamberlain's student days.

Harvard president Charles William Eliot expressed disappointment that even after substantial revisions of curriculums, "the great majority of American colleges . . . make no requirement in history for admission, and have no teacher of history whatever."[3] Tedious recitations remained the basic method of instruction—something Chamberlain sought to change when a professor. He joined progressive educators who believed these recitations turned competent faculty into drillmasters, and deadened student interest in what should be thought-provoking subjects.[4]

As Chamberlain began his new duties, he wrote his mother, as he did each year on his birthday, September 8: "I have been full of business all day & it is almost twelve at night." He thanked her for "the right care & training which have given me a strong constitution and cheerful mind." As for his new responsibilities as president, he hoped to open "a larger field for the college to work in," which he would soon elaborate upon.[5]

He began his presidency with numerous obstacles facing the college.

He would need to deal with the differing constituencies and mindsets of two governing boards. A bicameral system of governance, trustees and overseers, was part of the 1794 articles of incorporation. By the time of Chamberlain's presidency, only Harvard, Brown, and Bates retained the bicameral governance system. (Bowdoin would not do away with the dual system until 1996.)

The body of trustees, smaller in number, more prestigious, and more liberal, was more apt to be made up of lawyers, judges, legislators, and businessmen, in addition to clergy. In its religious orientation, in addition to Congregationalists, it included Methodists and Unitarians. The overseers, larger in number, more conservative in orientation, would include a larger representation of Congregational ministers.[6]

In a paradox of Chamberlain's presidency, even though as a Congregational layman he shared the traditional Christian beliefs of many of the overseers, as president of Bowdoin, and an educator, he found himself often in line with the attitudes of the trustees. He appreciated that they would be more open to the innovations he planned to propose. Yet to advance his educational goals would require him to be cognizant of the different sensibilities of the two boards.

IN HIS FIRST fall as president of Bowdoin, Chamberlain was pleased to welcome Grant back to Maine. President Grant came for the dedication of the European and North American Railway, which was to take place in Bangor. The idea of the E&NA as a single system connecting the United States and Canada's Maritime Provinces was conceived at an 1850 railway conference in Portland. Two decades later, Mainers were excited that the train would link Portland— the eastern terminus of the U.S. rail network—with an ice-free Atlantic port in Nova Scotia. From there, goods could be shipped on fast transatlantic ships going to and from Europe.[7]

Grant's special train stopped in Brunswick, where the president was welcomed by Chamberlain. Grant invited his former comrade in arms to join him as the train continued north to Bangor. The entire Bowdoin student body gave the two presidents a rousing send-off.[8]

The city of eighteen thousand, just across the Penobscot River from Chamberlain's birthplace of Brewer, outdid itself in its welcome. The *Bangor Daily Whig and Courier* devoted many columns to the occasion. "Dense crowds of people occupied every available inch of space in the streets through which the procession passed." Troops marched, bands played, and firemen held aloft two hundred torches. It was a great honor for Bangor to welcome the president of the United States, but on this fall day citizens were also excited to greet Maine war hero Chamberlain. For a boy who long ago climbed the masts of boats anchored at the Bangor waterfront, he now stood proudly beside the president.[9]

CHAMBERLAIN, IN HIS inaugural address as president, which he titled "The New Education," tipped his hat to the values of "Old Bowdoin," while enthusiastically pointing to his hopes for a new Bowdoin. Using a military metaphor, he declared he had been given a "commission." However, in accepting the commission it was evident that something was wrong. He believed "the times had shot past the college. Left out of the current of living sympathies . . . she stood still, while the world at full flood and flushed with new life swept on." Telling his audience "The college had touched bottom," he asked two questions: "How to rise again? And how to begin?"[10] The easier path would have been to affirm the old Bowdoin, of which he was a beneficiary, but he came into the presidential office believing the college was at a critical juncture in a rapidly changing culture.

He answered with two options. The first: "We might confine our efforts chiefly to holding our own, 'strengthening the things that remain,' and feel our way by cautious and imperceptible degrees." The second: "We might accept at once the challenge of our times, advance boldly to the key point of the position, and begin in right earnest to entrench, before we had force enough to hold it at all hazards." He put the question in bold language: "Should the college conquer, or should it die?"[11] In exploring these two options, the master rhetorician, suddenly thrust into the presidency, hoped to bring along his multiple constituencies to join him in creating a Bowdoin in conversation with the ideas of post–Civil War America.

Near the end of his address, he surprised his audience when he declared, "Woman too should have part in this high calling. Because in this sphere of things her 'rights,' her capacities, her offices, her destiny, are equal to those of man."[12] But he did not elaborate on how he envisioned women becoming part of the college. In these years the desire of women for higher education was typically met by the creation of female schools, often called female seminaries or institutes.

Chamberlain concluded his address by calling for a "new Elizabethan age," by which he meant "dazzling discoveries, broadening science, swift-following invention, arts multiplying, civilization advancing, new fields of thought and labor, new prizes of courage." One can imagine Chamberlain's voice rising when he declared, "This is my hope and ideal for the college. I fear not the age."[13]

Chamberlain presented a vibrant vision for what he hoped would be the modern Bowdoin. Many alumni and supporters of the college would admit that the college must adjust to changing times, but how much change would they ultimately support?

BEFORE TRYING TO create change, the new president would need to raise money to support the changes he envisioned. The State of Maine had not contributed financially to the college since 1831. In order to raise new funds, Chamberlain believed it necessary to reach out more broadly than previous Bowdoin presidents had done.

In doing so, he was fully aware of the presence of rival colleges

in New England, especially in Maine. As governor, he had backed
the establishment of the state agricultural college at Orono. Maine
was also home to two colleges with Baptist origins: Colby College in
Waterville and Bates College in Lewiston. While both colleges were
more geographically distant than Bowdoin from Portland, and what
one Colby alumnus called "the city's well-heeled Congregationalists,"[14] Chamberlain took both colleges seriously as competitors.

The Congregationalists of Maine continued to think of Bowdoin
as "their" college. Their church members had been key financial
contributors over the decades. However, Woods, Bowdoin's previous president, had not wanted the college to be viewed as narrowly
sectarian, and angered Congregationalist ministers by absenting
himself from their meetings.[15]

In Chamberlain, the college elected its first president who was
not a Congregational minister. Yet in the eyes of the Bowdoin overseers and trustees, Chamberlain's seminary degree and his ability to
articulate the Christian faith persuasively did not make him different from his predecessors. As the new president he believed his
challenge was to maintain the college's Christian identity, but at the
same time to broaden its appeal to prospective students and donors.

IN RESPONSE TO these challenges, Chamberlain sought to enlarge
the curriculum, a move he thought could help raise money, attract
students, and enlarge the college's influence. He understood that
in the broader American culture scientific developments were challenging old ideas and offering new ways of thinking. There had
been science courses at Bowdoin before, but Chamberlain wanted
to set up an entire science department. He believed expanded offerings would help attract new students. Some alumni, however,
viewed science with alarm as a threat to their religious faith.

The *Bowdoin Orient,* the Bowdoin student newspaper, begun in
1871, agreed with Chamberlain. In September 1872, the biweekly
welcomed the new offerings in science even as it criticized some
in the college for "refusing to believe that times had changed."
The paper described those who objected to the teaching of science: "like Canute upon the seashore, Bowdoin really imagined

she could turn back the irresistible tide of progress beating against her walls."[16]

The president also wanted to enlarge the college's offerings in modern languages. He was convinced that French and German were the primary languages an educated person needed to know in the modern world. He encouraged the continued reading of ancient Greek and Latin texts but in modern translations.[17]

He also wanted to establish Bowdoin's first graduate program and degree. A master of arts would be offered for a two-year course in science, philosophy, and letters. In offering the MA degree, Bowdoin became one of the earliest American colleges to do so.

Enlarging the curriculum meant increasing the faculty. In his first three years as president, Chamberlain expanded the faculty from sixteen to twenty-six.[18] Of course, enlarging the faculty meant increasing the budget, but Chamberlain, ever optimistic, believed he could increase the student body enough to pay for the new faculty.

CHAMBERLAIN ALSO MADE extensive changes in the daily life of the college.

He altered the format for class rankings. Until 1871, a student's class ranking was based on both scholarship and behavior.[19] He decided to divide the two, so that in the future, a prank—like his caper as a sophomore—could not damage a senior's academic standing.

Listening to student feedback, he changed elements of Bowdoin's daily schedule. Morning prayers were transferred from before to after breakfast. Henceforth no recitations would be held before morning chapel. He did away with evening prayers, except on Sundays. Library hours for students were increased. He moved the long vacation from winter to summer. Commencement would now be held in June instead of August. Finally, Chamberlain instituted a Thursday evening reception where he and Fanny welcomed students into their home.[20]

In Chamberlain's first report to the two boards, he revealed some of his philosophy behind these changes, speaking at length about his relationship with the students. He wanted to change the hostile dynamic that often existed between high-spirited students

and faculty acting to police the campus: "In establishing my relations with the students, I made them see and understand that I
should deal with them as gentlemen, and that I should hold a man's
word of honor as better than foreign testimony, that I should allow
neither spy nor suspicion to hold any place between me and them,
and that I should not abandon my confidence in them until they
were false to themselves." Chamberlain knew that some on the
boards and some of the faculty were dubious of his approach. He
reassured them: "But where a man dealt untruthfully, I regarded
him as rotten at heart and good for nothing."[21]

The new president intended to treat students as young men
rather than boys, but these young men needed to live up to the
trust he put in them. He concluded, "I have found little less than
the most perfect frankness and honor among these young men
throughout the year."[22]

It would be informative to learn how the faculty responded to
their new president's first initiatives. Regrettably, the faculty minutes only sparingly captured these conversations. They usually recorded only official actions taken by the faculty.

The *Bowdoin Orient* provided more substantive commentary. It
admired the value the new president placed on the "thinking and
the formation of independent judgment" of the students. It appreciated his emphasis on the "larger and needed infusion of the
living and available truths to the present age." The student newspaper declared "that the college courses in the past have been
shaped too much in the interests of a particular class, the education of clergymen, and on their account the classical element has
largely predominated." Finally, with great praise, "He proposes to
root out the erroneous idea that a student is not to be considered
a companion of professors until he can affix an A.B. to his name."[23]
The student newspaper understood that the new president was
willing to challenge the hierarchical structure long in place at
Bowdoin.

NOW LIVING IN Brunswick again, Chamberlain turned his attention to enhancing his family's living situation. He chose not to move
into the president's house at 85 Federal Street, but instead he and

Fanny embarked on an immense project. They would raise their cape house by constructing a new first story. The term "cape," describing a single- or two-story frame house with a moderately pitched gabled roof, was first used in the early nineteenth century by Yale president Timothy Dwight, after seeing such homes on a visit to Massachusetts's Cape Cod.

Chamberlain painted the frame house a stylish stone beige trimmed in dark red. He painted red Maltese crosses, the symbol of the Fifth Corps, on the chimneys. The original colors of the 1871 house were established by the analysis of modern restoration experts. An iron fence bordered the front lawn. In the back was a barn for Charlemagne and a garden. In what he called his "greenhouse," probably a glassed-in porch located on the south side of the house, the man with the green thumb would end up growing approximately fifty kinds of flowers.[24]

Lawrence and Fanny raised their home on Maine Street, across the street from the Bowdoin campus, to make it a two-story house.

Chamberlain wanted the new first floor to be more expansive than the original first floor, so that it could function as a commodious space to entertain students, professors, and guests. He designed a splendid grand hall entrance with a Gothic arch of dark oak wood. He installed a hanging brass lamp. A spiral staircase wound up to the second floor. At the front of the staircase, he placed a portrait of his mother, dressed in the black dress decorated with Spanish lace that she wore at his inauguration as governor.

He took great care in planning a large library and a smaller adjoining study where he would do the writing of his lectures for the college and beyond. He would ultimately collect two thousand books that ranged across his multiple interests of history, politics, literature, poetry. For countless Bowdoin students, a high moment in their college years was the day President Chamberlain invited them to meet with him in his library or study.

The library, filled with Civil War memorabilia, became a special place for Chamberlain to work, and where he enjoyed meeting guests and students.

Conscious of the history of the house, Chamberlain preserved the rooms on the second floor where, as a young professor, Longfellow brought his bride. The whole architectural project brought the size of the renewed home to twenty rooms, a large house for that time.[25]

Fanny utilized her artistic abilities to furnish and decorate the home. She began by installing colonial furniture that had been passed down from her family. She then purchased antiques and other items, like elaborate oriental rugs, from her shopping trips to Boston, New York, and some of Maine's small towns.

She was especially proud of the blue-and-white drawing room. She designed the crystal candelabra that hung near the fireplace

herself. With music still central in the lives of both Fanny and Lawrence, her magnificent piano dominated the gaze of the visitor. She
placed her husband's bass viol against it. Nearby sat a lute that had
long been in her family. The emphasis on music was not simply
nostalgia for the beginnings of their courtship; she and Lawrence
continued to play music and attend musical concerts at the college
and the church.

Fanny also selected the many paintings that decorated the walls
of every room. She especially treasured the portrait of her maternal
grandmother painted by artist John Trumbull. Called "the Painter
of the Revolution," Trumbull was well-known for his paintings of
that earlier American war.

For Lawrence, the act of transforming his home into a place of
warm hospitality was a work of devotion. For Fanny, who had honed
her artistic crafts as a young woman in Portland's "painting rooms,"
the act of decorating the house became a vessel for her years of
aesthetic education.

The many decisions involved in this huge project seemed to be
an elixir for their marriage.

AT THE BEGINNING of Chamberlain's presidency, his and Fanny's
children were becoming high-spirited teenagers. In 1872, Grace,
now fifteen, was shy with people she did not know but an affectionate tease with her father, addressing him as "darling boy." That summer, she spent less time than usual sailing with her father, wanting
instead to be with her friends. In July she wrote him playfully, "How
do you do, and what kind of voyage did you have? It was ugly in me
not to go with my good Boy, but leave him to go back without any
girl!" After an outing in Portland, she told her father that the
mother of one of her friends "does not wonder I am such a *splendid
girl* having such a father & mother!" She assured her father, "So you
see I am behaving well."[26]

Wyllys, thirteen, interested in science, spent his summers enlarging his private zoo. The proud owner of a rat and four mice, he
hunted all around Brunswick for deserted bird nests and eggs.[27]

Although his professional and familial lives seemed to be thriv-
ing, Chamberlain privately struggled daily with the effects of his

wounds. By day, he often worked reclining on the sofa in his office to alleviate the pain in his hips and groin. At night, his suffering made it difficult to sleep.

THE NEW PRESIDENT had an opportunity to put his ideas about the equality of women expressed in his inaugural address to the test in 1872. "Half a dozen young women, graduates of Brunswick High School, have applied for admission to a select course of study [at Bowdoin] and their request will no doubt be granted," reported the *Portland Transcript* on October 7.[28]

Their applications were accepted, but evidently they were never officially enrolled. The young women probably ended up auditing a few courses.

The ante was upped later that fall when another young woman, C. F. Low, applied for admission to the dean of Bowdoin's medical school. She stated her "wish to graduate on equal terms with my brother students."[29]

Her request for admission was passed up to the president. Chamberlain replied to Low, "I perceive the reasonableness of your proposition, and regret that not having contemplated such applications we cannot make such arrangements as would be fit & proper." To soften his response, he told her, "I am sure that with the high character & earnest purpose you evince, women will soon find those equal terms which they so justly desire."[30] Having spoken words about the equality of women in his inaugural address, his real-time answer: no.

Chamberlain did not say more about the reasons behind his response. Was he reacting to pressure from the faculty? From the two boards? It is unknown what happened to C. F. Low after she was denied admission, but as for "soon," it would not be until ninety-nine years later, in 1970, that Bowdoin would welcome women into its student body.

IN THE 1870s, the national government, concerned about entering a future war with an untrained military, as it did in 1861, pushed for the establishment of military units at the nation's colleges. In his second year as president, General Chamberlain, the title by which everyone called him (common for many retired officers), recommended that mandatory military drill be instituted at Bowdoin. He believed its benefits went beyond teaching technical skills to developing character. He worried about the "softness" of young men growing up postwar in a more comfortable middle-class life. Willing to stand behind his beliefs, Chamberlain accepted the position of major general to lead the Maine state militia, in actuality a mostly honorary position in a barely functioning organization. At Bowdoin he made gymnastic physical activity a required part of the curriculum. In the nineteenth century, the term "gymnastics" was an all-inclusive name for physical exercise and training. It could encompass dumbbells, calisthenics, running, various games, and sometimes military drill.[31] The president's move was greeted with enthusiasm by the students.

In January 1872, selecting from a list supplied by the War Department, Chamberlain invited Major Joseph P. Sanger to lead the new military drill. Sanger, who began his service in the Civil War in the First Michigan Volunteer Infantry, came to Bowdoin with a splendid military record.

A member of the class of 1875 would write of Sanger, "He was a diminutive man physically, but mentally he was clear and strong and a finely equipped officer. The boys all liked him, and he displayed great tact and kindness in his treatment of them."[32]

Sanger organized the students into four companies. The state of Maine lent the college four twelve-pound Napoleon cannons to train with. A local tailor made uniforms similar to ones worn at West Point.

Gen. Joseph P. Sanger, hired by Pres. Chamberlain, led Bowdoin's military drill.

Students took to the military drill with enthusiasm. This same student remembered the enjoyment of "marching around in military maneuvers and handling the gun in manual of arms." He believed it "splendid exercise for the body."[33] The students joked with one another about pointing the cannon at the partially completed Memorial Hall.

Pleased with student responses, Chamberlain invoked a classic hero in writing to the two boards that the drill was "the kind of exercise particularly recommended by Plato."[34]

Bowdoin students in their military uniforms

But enthusiasm in 1872 turned to complaints in 1873. Students worried that Bowdoin was being turned into a military school. They grumbled that the drill was taking up too much time in their schedules. Graffiti criticizing the drill began appearing on the walls of the chapel.[35]

At this time Chamberlain's initiative to establish military drill was supported by a committee made up of members of the trustees and overseers. They concluded the military drill was a positive addition to the curriculum. It fitted the student "for active contact with the world and for performing efficiently his part in it."[36]

. . .

AT THIS SAME time, Chamberlain was stepping up his efforts to raise money for Bowdoin. In January, he appealed to influential and wealthy Mainers in a flurry of letters, insisting in one letter that Bowdoin "cannot keep up" with "the powerful influence of Colleges outside the State, which surpass us only in pecuniary means, unless the strong men of Maine come to her support."[37]

He invited Governor Abner Coburn to give his name and money for a Coburn School of Science and Art.[38] In his fundraising letter to former Democratic U.S. senator James W. Bradbury, an 1825 Bowdoin graduate, Chamberlain was forthcoming about the uphill battle he felt he was facing: "Nothing but a sense of duty & good faith towards the friends who have placed me here, makes me willing to work in a cause which looks likely to fail in the end, for want of a suitable endowment."[39]

Bradbury ended up making a pledge of two thousand dollars, but not payable until 1875. Chamberlain's initial fundraising efforts were so far bearing little fruit.

IN THE SUMMER of 1873 Chamberlain suddenly announced he was no longer willing to work for a faltering cause. He decided to resign as president. His decision, after only two years as president, seemed out of character for the man who loved the college that had educated him.

Still, on July 8, the day before commencement, he offered the trustees and overseers his resignation.

> When I assumed the duties to which you honored me on your election, I was aware that they involved difficulties and trials from which older and abler men than I had [retired] in despair. I have exerted myself beyond any previous experience to be equal to this place and meet your wishes. I hoped to succeed, but I have not met my own expectation. A spirit seems to possess the College with which I cannot harmonize, and under which I cannot advantageously work. I owe the world some better service, and it is my duty to seek it.[40]

Chamberlain packed a lot into these five sentences. He reminded the two boards that his predecessor, Harris, had resigned
"in despair" after only four years. He stated that he had "exerted"
himself beyond any previous vocations, by which he meant teaching, the Civil War, and as governor. The most intriguing allusion in
his letter was to a "spirit" that possessed the college. He was not
specific about the definition of that "spirit."

The trustees and overseers may have wondered what he meant
when he told them he had not measured up to his own expectations. But to know Chamberlain is not to be surprised. This is the
attitude with which he enlisted in the Union army. It was his high
expectation of himself when he agreed to enter the world of politics knowing he was starting a steep learning curve.

The trustees and overseers did not accept his resignation. How
we wish we could eavesdrop on their conversations when they came
to this decision.

As CLASSES RESUMED in the fall of 1873, student complaints grew
over military drill. The overseers and trustees called a special joint
meeting to discuss the controversy. One week before they met, each
member of the two boards received a letter from the students:

Bowdoin College, Nov. 12, 1873

Dear Sir:

At the approaching meeting of the Boards of Trustees and
Overseers, students of Bowdoin ask leave to present the following petition.

We, the undersigned, Students of Bowdoin College will ask
leave to present the following petition that the Military Department in this institution be abolished for the following reasons: First. Injury to the institution from loss of students.
Second. Abundant facilities for more popular and profitable
exercise. Third. Expense incurred in purchasing otherwise
useless equipment. Fourth. Its intense and growing unpopu-
larity and other subordinate reasons.

One hundred twenty-six students signed the letter. Only seven students did not.[41]

A committee of the two boards met with a student committee. No action was taken. The two boards met again in January 1874, but again took no action. This lack of response by the boards angered the students.

Chamberlain's name has always been associated as the main actor in what came to be called the Drill Rebellion, but an understanding of the governance of the college at that time would have placed the faculty and the two boards as actors also. For many faculty, the issue was not primarily about military drill—they knew that at least twenty other colleges had instituted similar military programs—the issue became the rebellious attitude of the students.

BY NOW THE story of the Drill Rebellion was being discussed not only by newspapers across Maine, but as far away as Boston and New York.

Letters to the Maine newspapers generally condemned the students. One writer rejected the student argument that drill was too taxing: "These picked youth, the flower of the State . . . are misled and have put themselves in a false position, untrue to their manhood."[42] To members of the generation that remembered their sons patriotically and obediently marching off to war, the notion of "rebellion" was particularly odious.

The Portland *Argus,* a Democratic newspaper, editorialized, "The revolt of all three classes . . . shows that something is radically wrong and needs to be reformed."[43] Chamberlain was not the focus of either of the newspaper articles.

A writer calling herself "Granny" urged a unique compromise. Half of the rebellious students "should be expelled and the other half pardoned." She went on to argue that both military drill and gymnastic activities should be abolished, and Bowdoin should become coeducational.[44]

Bowdoin College historian Charles C. Calhoun believes different notions of "manliness" were key to understanding the dispute. Chamberlain understood manliness to mean "military prowess and a willingness to make sacrifices in the name of duty." For many students, manliness "meant independence and forthright expression of one's point of view."[45] The distinction reflected a generational difference in play by the middle of the 1870s.

In the midst of the controversy a rumor started that Dartmouth College was ready to accept the Bowdoin strikers. Chamberlain, wishing to stifle this rumor, wrote Dartmouth president Asa Dodge Smith. President Smith, a preacher for 29 years at the 14th Street Presbyterian Church in New York, was elected Dartmouth's seventh president in 1866. Destined to preside over tremendous growth at Dartmouth, he replied immediately that the rumor was false, and that he agreed with the stance of his fellow New England president.[46] Smith's letter to Chamberlain was made public.

IN SPRING 1874, the rebellion escalated. On May 19, faculty records reported "there was much shouting and profanity on dispersing from the Artillery Drill, on the part of the Junior class." Within days the junior class voted not to participate in the drill again. The sophomore class soon followed suit. As did the freshmen.[47]

It was the faculty's turn to act. They summoned all of the students, one by one, and asked them if they intended to abide by the college rules. Upon their refusal, they sent each student home.

On May 28, Chamberlain, with the authorization of the faculty, sent a letter to the parents of each student who had refused to drill, giving their sons ten days to return to Bowdoin and pledge to adhere to all college rules and take part in the drill or be permanently expelled.[48]

Ultimately, all but three students returned within the prescribed time limit. The upheaval ended. Christopher Wells, class of 1875, would write later, "Of course we were wrong, and we all went back and submitted to the rules of the college, but the backbone of the drill was broken, and it died a speedy and unregretted death as a Bowdoin institution."[49]

At this point a joint committee of the two boards issued a new report. This time they stated the drill should become voluntary. They offered evaluations of all the stakeholders: "Attention should be paid to the feelings, even the prejudices of the students, and of their parents and friends, until further knowledge of the question permitted a decided opinion." They backed up Chamberlain. "The President of a college must deal both with Faculty and Students face to face with unswerving directness of statement, and in a manner of one doing the duties of his station, because they are duties and not because his station is superior." As for the faculty, they "must avoid cabals, refrain from depreciating one another, either carelessly or maliciously . . . and guard most carefully against sowing among the undergraduates the sense of distrust or want of confidence in the President of the college." As for the boards, they "also have duties, among which are to remember that variety of opinions temperately expressed is a good and not an evil." Yet, "in the stress of weather the good seaman sticks to his ship."[50]

CHAMBERLAIN DID NOT agree with the judgment of the faculty and boards to end the required military drill, but was ready to accept the decision.

He may not have been prepared for the headwinds he encountered as president of Bowdoin. After the weak leadership of President Harris, when Chamberlain was hired, members of the boards and the faculty probably told him that they wanted strong leadership. But once he began exercising that kind of leadership, he began receiving pushback. This was seen in the drill debacle, but also in his curriculum initiatives.

THAT SUMMER HE unburdened himself in a letter to his mother. "More thanks than I can speak for the kind words. It seems as if I have not heard anything like them for a long time." He told her, "Have had to work 14 hours a day for three weeks. I am not very easily cast down & don't mean to be now." And yet: "I am going to carry this point for I can do good. Am in the right place for now."[51]

The year 1875 brought criticism, celebration, and sadness.

Critics of Chamberlain charged the college should not have expanded its offerings in science until the program was undergirded financially. He was coming to realize that expanding donations to the college was a gradual process built on developing relationships

Henry Wadsworth Longfellow, Bowdoin class of 1825, returned for his fiftieth reunion in 1875, and accepted Chamberlain's offer to stay in the house where he once had rooms.

with potential donors, and responded tartly it was "a slow way and some of us into our graves before any land of promise was reached."[52]

On a celebratory note, Chamberlain presided over the 1875 commencement, in which William Wadsworth Longfellow came back to Bowdoin with his 1825 class for the fiftieth anniversary of their graduation. Chamberlain wrote to Longfellow inviting him to make "my house your 'base of operations' while at Bowdoin."[53]

Longfellow offered his poem "Morituri Salutamus"—"We Who Are About to Die Salute You." Written for the occasion, he told the young graduates,

> *And ye who fill the places we once filled,*
> *And follow in the furrows that we tilled,*
> *Young men, whose generous hearts are beating high,*
> *We who are old, and are about to die,*
> *Salute you; hail you; take your hands in ours,*
> *And crown you with our welcome as with flowers!*[54]

The poem conveyed Longfellow's belief that while the inevitable march of time cannot be stopped, learning while traveling through life can assuage its effects. If in the poem he argued that maturity brings understandings not possible in youth, at sixty-eight he also voiced his conviction that there is a great deal remaining to achieve in old age.

SADNESS CAME THAT same summer when word arrived that Rev. Adams, five years into his ministry at the Congregational church in Orange, New Jersey, had fallen gravely ill. He died on Christmas

Day. His funeral service was held in black-draped First Parish in Brunswick, where he'd ministered to both town and college for forty years.[55]

Rev. Adams had not immediately taken to young Lawrence when he courted Fanny, but in the years that followed, he became one of Chamberlain's greatest admirers. The feeling was mutual. Seven years after Adams's death, Chamberlain gave to First Parish its largest stained-glass window in memory of his father-in-law. He asked it to be placed right behind the pulpit.[56]

CHAMBERLAIN, WHO HAD always appreciated Rev. Adams's preaching, and had enjoyed his preaching classes at Bangor Theological Seminary, took ownership of the baccalaureate sermons delivered each year in commencement week. He did not hand off this assignment to anyone else.

Taken together, his baccalaureate sermons reveal his attempts to translate his Christian faith to what he believed were the challenges facing the graduating students, the college, and American society. In each address, he began with a contemporary problem or issue and then brought his considerable learning to bear on it.

Speaking at 4 P.M. on Sunday, July 5, 1874, in the sanctuary of the First Parish Church, he spoke to the contemporary debate about the relationship of science and religion. Referring to the philosophers Kant, Hegel, and Fichte, he declared, "It is sometimes said to be the duty of the scholar to resist the tendency of the times." Chamberlain declared this was not quite correct. He believed what was needed at this moment was "to keep things in wholesome balance." He encouraged the graduating seniors "to balance and harmonize the thought of the age," but to "keep up the spiritual side of the question."[57]

In his 1877 baccalaureate sermon Chamberlain spoke about the modern tension of the relationship of the individual to society. After beginning with a survey of this tension in ancient Greek and Roman civilizations, he invoked John Stuart Mill, the most influential English-language philosopher of the nineteenth century, who had died just four years earlier. Chamberlain said Mill argued that "society is advancing at the expense of the power of the individual."[58]

He followed with one of his favorite rhetorical devices: presenting a position he wished to counter. In this baccalaureate sermon it was Herbert Spencer, the English philosopher, who argued that because the state was "infringing" on the "liberties of the individual," man "has a right to ignore the State." Chamberlain, who regularly taught a class on government, declared that Spencer's argument was "based on a wrong conception of government."[59]

In his conclusion, with the controversy of the Hayes-Tilden presidential election still raw, Chamberlain, a Republican and former governor, lifted up a positive view of government. He wished "to enforce the high view of the part" the graduates "were to take as citizens." Always intent on translating Christian faith into public service, he told the graduates that as individuals, "Whatever their calling in life, they were enjoined to be true ministers of Christ" in society.[60]

MATTERS OF FAITH became a conversation within the Chamberlain family once again. Chamberlain had long ago made peace with the fact that Fanny did not share his commitment to traditional Christian faith when she told her adoptive father that she could not join Brunswick's First Parish. A quarter century later, Chamberlain found himself in a difficult conversation about religious beliefs with another family member.

It began in 1876 when Grace was attending the Gannett Institute in Boston. When her school refused her request to attend the South Congregational Church, led by Edward Everett Hale, renowned Boston Unitarian minister, she became angry. Starting in the 1830s, nearly all of Boston's Congregational Churches had become Unitarian. Little Daisy, now nineteen, valued her ability to make her own decisions.[61]

At this same time, Grace visited with the family of Stephen Allen, Fanny's old friend, who lived in Boston. There she met Stephen and Ann Maria's son, Horace, who was in his final year at Harvard Law School. The two soon became romantically involved.

The incident over the church not only caused a row at her school but also upset her father. He found it difficult to reconcile himself to her differing religious beliefs. He may have worried that Horace was affecting Grace's religious attitudes. He decided to come to Boston. Grace warned Horace, "We *shall* have a tear if he comes!"[62]

In a letter to his daughter, it is apparent that they quarreled when he came in April. At the end of May, with the hindsight of distance and time, the father recognized, "You do not tell me everything. You have good reasons." His long letter began with affirmation and affection: "I don't love you too much because you are my daughter—this is a mere physical law of time & earth—a mechanical management. I love you because you are a splendid soul & belong to eternity."[63]

He knew his views were not her views. His conclusion revealed his inner turmoil. "If you don't like this burn it up & me too." He told her, "I wrote a long letter & burned it! It did me just as much good and you no hurt."

Chamberlain concluded his letter to Grace: "Written in 10 minutes after—3 days of small hell-torment." To what is he referring? The pain of his wounds? The difficulties within the college?[64]

Unfortunately, we don't have records of Fanny's reaction to this turmoil with Grace and her changing religious beliefs. It may well have prompted memories of difficult conversations she herself had as a young woman with her adoptive father.

In the end, Chamberlain's love for his daughter far overcame his concerns about her religious beliefs.

ONE MONTH LATER, on June 26, 1876, Chamberlain wrote another letter of resignation to the Bowdoin trustees and overseers: "All that has actually been accomplished during the last five years does not yet fully appear, and some labor has perhaps been wasted. But I am happy to leave the College in so good condition, as will be apparent if anyone is disposed to consider it." Unlike his first letter of resignation, this time he enumerated what he believed to be his accomplishments: "Our funds are nearly doubled; our Buildings greatly improved; our means of instruction and the number of students largely increased; and we have every prospect of an unusually large entering class, and of continued additions to our funds."[65]

Chamberlain had given five years to the leadership of the college, one year more than he served as governor. Yet he does not really say why he made the decision to resign.

ONCE AGAIN, THE trustees and overseers refused to accept his resignation. Once again, we do not know why.

It is too simple to say that General Chamberlain was used to giving orders and the college—faculty, students, the two boards—unlike the military, was not used to receiving orders. His predecessor, Samuel Harris, had found the task of fundraising not to his liking. Did this assignment, not with great results, also become a burden for Chamberlain?

As WITH HIS reasons for resigning, he did not tell us why he decided to soldier on—but he did. Perhaps, upon reflection, he believed there was still more he could accomplish as president.

SEVENTEEN

Twelve Days in 1880

I cannot bear to think of our fair and orderly state plunged into
the horror of a civil war.

—JOSHUA LAWRENCE CHAMBERLAIN TO JAMES G. BLAINE,
DECEMBER 29, 1879

Joshua L Chamberlain

CHAMBERLAIN, HAVING MADE THE DECISION TO CONTINUE AS
president, now exerted greater effort at raising money to boost
Bowdoin's underwhelming endowment.

This challenging venture continued to be met by headwinds
caused by the Panic of 1873, whose impact would last until the end
of the decade. After eight years of post–Civil War business boom,
warnings of financial instability went unheeded. What Mark Twain
dubbed the Gilded Age spawned a speculative spirit. A surge in railroad construction became the primary edge of this enthusiasm.
Growing industries in oil, iron, and steel bolstered this expansion.
Extravagance ran rampant. The nation had not experienced a serious financial depression since 1837, and couldn't imagine one now.

Everything collapsed in September 1873. Banks, caught up in
the speculation, had lent money with insufficient collateral. Modern economists and politicians use less emotional words—
"recession" and "depression"; in the 1870s, "panic" was the word
that captured the frenzied feeling across the nation.[1] "A financial
thunderbolt," shouted the *New-York Tribune*.

IN THIS COMPLICATED economic environment, Chamberlain believed he needed to reach beyond alumni to achieve his fundraising
goals. In January 1875, he wrote Adelbert Ames, now governor of

Mississippi, inviting him to make a gift to Bowdoin.[2] Old military friendship notwithstanding, no gift ever came.

When Chamberlain approached William Drew Washburn, class of 1854, whose brother, Israel, when governor of Maine, appointed Chamberlain lieutenant colonel of the Twentieth Maine in 1862, he discovered that responses often depended upon the donors' understanding of the school's religious identity.

W. D. Washburn's enterprises in lumber and flour milling made him a wealthy man in Minnesota. After planning to give Bowdoin a large gift, he wrote Chamberlain telling him why he changed his mind: "Bowdoin is too sectarian, that she is not yet out of the hands of *Old Foggies,* and that you, Sir, are too strong a sectarian to manage its concerns." He told the president, "What canvassing I have done convinces me that some radical changes yet remain before Bowdoin can command the monies of all persons."[3]

If Chamberlain had done his due diligence, he would have learned the Minnesota businessman was a founder of the First Universalist Church of Minneapolis, the religious tradition at odds with traditional Congregational churches that were the main supporters of Bowdoin.

The president next courted Henry Winkley, a wealthy Philadelphia businessman who made his money importing Chinese crockery. He secured from Winkley a gift of $10,000 in 1878, and an additional sum of $30,000 in 1880 ($30,000 in 1880 is worth $875,000 today). In his letter, the philanthropist attached a condition to his gift: that Bowdoin "adhere to the Theological teachings of the Orthodox Congregational or Presbyterian Church."[4]

Chamberlain procured a fifty-thousand-dollar gift from Mrs. Valeria Stone of Malden, Massachusetts. Widow of Daniel P. Stone, a Bostonian who built a two-million-dollar dry goods business, she endowed the Stone Professorship of Mental and Moral Philosophy. Mrs. Stone attached a similar condition: that the professor occupying the chair be "in doctrinal and religious sympathy with the orthodox Congregational Churches in New England."[5]

Attaching conditions like this to gifts was not unusual at the time. In a changing educational and religious landscape, with the fear of Unitarianism in the air, these two philanthropists wanted their money to support what they called "orthodox" Christian institutions. Each gave smaller gifts to Bangor Theological Seminary and Andover Theological Seminary.

After initial discouragement in fundraising, Chamberlain was finally beginning to see some results.

FOR THE PEOPLE of Maine, Chamberlain continued to be the leading person in the state. Thus it was no surprise when Governor Selden Connor invited Chamberlain to speak at the 1876 American Centennial Exposition in Philadelphia on "Maine Day." Having built a national reputation with his speeches about the Civil War over the past decade, he set aside many hours to prepare his address.

The exposition, timed to celebrate the one hundredth anniversary of the signing of the Declaration of Independence, was held between May 10 and November 10 and focused on the growth of American industry. President Grant intended for the exposition to symbolize national healing after the Civil War. Ultimately, it would draw 8,804,631 visitors. In a nation of forty million, even factoring in repeat visitors, that meant approximately one in fifteen Americans paid the fifty cents to enter.[6]

The 1876 Centennial Exposition in Philadelphia celebrated the 100th anniversary of the signing of the Declaration of Independence.

Chamberlain spoke in the last week of the exposition, on November 4, 1876. He titled his address "Maine, Her Place in History."

Conscious that neighboring Massachusetts had claimed pride of place in the historical memory of colonial New England, in reminding his audience of the feats of Maine's pioneers, Chamberlain declared there had been "no bard to sing their story."[7] He became that bard, singing the story in multiple keys. His presentation was not the panegyric that characterized other state speeches—he offered both praise and critique of his native state.

In a first key he stated that "history traces the acts of men rather than the fate of lands." He put forth a thesis that "the land has much to do with man. It remains a moral as well as a physical relation to him."[8] He wove his knowledge of the distinctive geographical features of Maine—"this shoreland . . . so battered and frayed by sea and storm"—with stories of the "adventurous spirits . . . drawn to these waters and shores."[9]

In a second key, sensitive to the ambiguities of historical memory, he believed both "unjust blame and unjust praise have been lavished on the Puritans." The Bangor Theological Seminary graduate demonstrated his knowledge of religious history by deftly discussing the differences between the community-minded Puritans and the individualistic and separatist Pilgrims.[10] Chamberlain affirmed that nineteenth-century Congregationalists, heirs to the seventeenth-century Puritans, continued to emphasize community.

Turning to the present, the former governor did not hide his concern about the "slackening" of the state's population that began in the 1860s. After gold was discovered in California, he worried that for the easternmost state in the Union, "Everything is west of her; drawing her like a magnet."[11]

Chamberlain did not allow the lure of the West to become an excuse. "The fact of the matter is, that in our way of doing business Maine has become an old and exhausted state." He offered a stark critique. "The nation that relies solely on the sale of her raw products will find that when they are gone, she is gone."[12]

Toward the end of his address Chamberlain circled back to the centrality of the land. "It is right no doubt to avail ourselves of the gratuities of nature. But you may be blind and brutish about it." To the Pine Tree State, known for its splendid forests, he offered an environmental warning. "Always you must consider the extent of her stores and her powers of recuperation. Otherwise, you will sap her life, and leave her and yourself at the end wretched companions in poverty."[13]

"I pass over the story of the war."[14] If Chamberlain's speech is remarkable for what it contains, it is notable for what is absent. He resisted the opportunity to regale his audience on his favorite subject, the Civil War, and his role in it. He decided that at the 1876 Exposition, the story of Maine would be his single focus.

The address received high praise. In response, Governor Connor invited him to deliver it to the Maine state legislature on February 6, 1877.

ALTHOUGH CHAMBERLAIN WAS seeing some positive results in fundraising, he still faced significant obstacles in his efforts to revitalize the college's curriculum. The two boards removed his right to use newly acquired funds for the expansion of science offerings; they believed the study of science would undercut the college's reputation for offering students a classical curriculum.[15]

Still determined to encourage offerings in science, in the summer of 1877 Chamberlain found the funds to initiate a six-week summer school of science, offering courses in chemistry, zoology, and mineralogy. He wanted to attract a new audience of college graduates and teachers. The summer courses were open to female students. Of the twenty-seven students, eleven were women.[16] Chamberlain hoped that positive results of the summer school might change the minds of the doubters and critics in both the faculty and the boards.

The college provided similar summer courses in 1878, but then dropped the program. The official explanation was that the summer program was meant to be an "experiment."[17]

By the end of 1878, Chamberlain accepted the fact that Bowdoin's emphasis on science could no longer be sustained. He did not like to give up on ideas he advanced. He tried to put a good face on what he believed to be a shortsighted decision by the boards: "We may console ourselves with having made an earnest effort to meet what was a demand of the times, with having done good work and earned a good fame."[18] Although the science department lasted not quite a decade, in those years 25 percent of Bowdoin graduates would earn a bachelor of science degree.[19] Yet, at the same time, as word of this action trickled down to students, some transferred to colleges where they could be confident science rested on steadier ground.

A WELCOME RESPITE from the burdens of the Bowdoin presidency came in February 1878, when President Hayes appointed Chamberlain to serve as the U.S. commissioner for education at the 1878 Exposition Universelle in Paris. The exposition was meant to celebrate France's recovery after the 1870–71 Franco-Prussian War.

Chamberlain was appointed U.S. commissioner for education for the 1878 Paris Exposition Universelle.

Since a student at Bowdoin, Chamberlain had looked beyond Maine to Europe. He had engaged English and European history, literature, and culture in the classes he taught. He had looked forward to the two-year sabbatical in Europe the college offered him in 1862, but instead volunteered for the Civil War. Finally, he could travel there for five months to engage these diverse cultures in person.

Chamberlain almost declined, worried about the expense of the trip. But in March he wrote Fanny, "I may go to Paris after all." It would probably cost three thousand dollars "for all of us." As Fanny was away shopping in New York, he teased her, "You shall go, if you will be good! & I want Grace to go. Wyllys can't."[20]

But in June the entire Chamberlain family, including Wyllys, who was a freshman at Bowdoin, boarded the five-thousand-ton steamer *England*. Once aboard, Chamberlain wrote his mother and father that he intended to spend three weeks in London, then on to Paris where they would "*keep house* with a French housekeeper. We can learn how they do it."[21]

Once in Paris, Chamberlain was eager to learn about the philosophies and patterns of education in all countries represented at the exposition. His assignment was to write a report on education based on his observations in France, and later travel to Germany, Switzerland, and Italy.

He observed Europeans making education "obligatory, gratuitous, and neutral in religion." By comparison, some states in the United States lagged in making education required. He appreciated that France "sees that popular education is fundamental to the strength of the modern state." He noted primary education in Europe continued to be taught by men, whereas women had become the main teachers in America. The United States was ahead of Europe in the education of girls. But he found his nation "far behind" in the study of political and social science. He appreciated that European countries emphasized continuing education for adults beyond formal education: "The college should not only be a place where a student can get an education; it should be a light set on a hill, to shine into the dark places below it."[22]

Chamberlain's 165-page report showed that his five months abroad was not a boondoggle, but an opportunity to enhance his knowledge of varied ways to improve education. The French government appreciated the report and awarded him a medal for it.[23]

In the family's travel after the close of the exposition, with Chamberlain's knowledge of French, German, and Italian, they were far more able than typical Americans to appreciate the cultures of these nations. The best commentary on the Chamberlain family's time in Europe came from daughter Grace, who wrote to her boyfriend, Horace Allen, "Many fun things happen in this family, I assure you."[24]

Upon their return in December 1878, the Chamberlains were met at the Brunswick train station by Bowdoin students, including a band. The students accompanied the family to their home, where Chamberlain offered a short speech of thanks. The student newspaper, the *Bowdoin Orient,* reported, "The air was rent with cheers for President Chamberlain and B-o-w-d-o-i-n." A few days later, at the chapel, the president was welcomed home on behalf of the faculty by their most senior member, Chamberlain's former professor Alpheus Spring Packard.[25] Despite his two efforts to resign, and differences of opinion over the priority of science in the school's curriculum, the enthusiastic welcome home spoke to the appreciation by students and faculty of their president.

THE EUROPEAN TRIP was the lead-in to a special year in Chamberlain's personal life in 1879. He bought a ten-ton, two-masted schooner he named *Pinafore,* taking the name from Gilbert and Sullivan's hugely popular operetta, *H.M.S. Pinafore,* which opened in London on May 25, 1878.[26]

That same summer, he purchased a five-acre projection of land at Simpson's Point that jutted into Middle Bay. It was located four miles from his Brunswick home. Once the location of a shipbuilding yard, with the advent of the railroad, the land was abandoned, along with nearly all shipbuilding in Maine. Chamberlain restored the large house and rebuilt the wharf to make it a summer home for his family. He named it Domhegan in honor of the Native American chief who once lived on the land. Wishing to enjoy more leisure time going forward, he decided to resign his position as major general in the state militia, but Governor Connor, a fellow Civil War hero, persuaded him to continue in this peacetime service to the state.[27]

In subsequent summers, Chamberlain would enjoy the house and property. He harnessed Charlemagne to a light plow to map

In 1879 Chamberlain purchased a ten-ton, two-masted schooner he named Pinafore, *choosing the name from his appreciation for Gilbert and Sullivan's operetta* H.M.S. Pinafore.

out a path next to the bank above Morningside Cove. With his green thumb, he planted flowers in the late spring in order to enjoy varied colors throughout the summer.[28]

WHILE CHAMBERLAIN WAS in Europe, Maine politics heated up. Republicans had controlled Maine since the party began in the 1850s. The party held the governorship since 1856, including Chamberlain's four terms. But in the late 1870s, Maine politics were about to become more competitive.

A national third party, the Greenbacks, which supported soft money as opposed to gold and silver, came late to Maine. In 1862, the federal government had issued paper money to help fund the war effort. After the war, it determined to redeem the "greenbacks" with hard currency. Farmers and other hard-pressed debtors resisted the move. With the founding of a national Greenback Party in 1874, those experiencing debt agitated for issuing more greenbacks. In the midst of the economic downturn of the Panic of 1873, the party believed the issuing of greenback paper money to be the best way to restore economic prosperity.

.   .   .

IN 1878, THE question of greenbacks became central in the Maine campaign for governor. The September election did not yield a clear winner. Incumbent governor Connor received the highest number of votes, a plurality but not a majority; second was Greenback candidate, Joseph L. Smith, a rich lumberman, criticized by Republicans for his reputation for money manipulation. Placing

third was Democrat Alonzo Garcelon, whose service as Maine's surgeon general in the Civil War won him a large following of veterans.[29]

The Maine constitution stipulated that in the election for governor, if none of the candidates received a majority, the House of Representatives would choose two among the candidates, and the Senate would then elect one of the two.[30]

In the House, Greenbackers and Democrats combined their votes as a "Fusion" party to eliminate Connor. Though a distant third in the popular vote, Garcelon was ultimately

Maine governor Alonzo Garcelon, a Democrat, and Maine's surgeon general in the Civil War

elected, becoming the first Democratic governor in more than two decades.[31]

MAINE'S CONTENTIOUS 1878 election set the stage for an even more tumultuous election in 1879. As Chamberlain sat in his president's office in Brunswick, nearly a decade removed from his four terms as governor, he could not imagine that he was about to be pulled into a political civil war in Augusta.

The 1879 Maine state election was being scrutinized nationally as a possible preview of the 1880 national elections. Could Democrats once more break through solidly Republican New England? Blaine, while not on the ballot, was being rumored as a Republican presidential candidate in 1880. The performance of Republicans in Maine could help or hurt his national reputation.

At their convention in Bangor on June 2, the Republicans nominated young Daniel F. Davis. Only thirty-five years old, a relatively new state legislator from Corinth, Davis had one unassailable credential: he was a veteran of "the war."[32]

The Democrats renominated Governor Garcelon, as did the Greenbacks with Smith.

Republicans nominated Daniel F. Davis in the 1879 election for governor.

DURING THE SUMMER, the Republicans brought out their big guns. Maine senator Blaine and Congressman William P. Frye, as well as two future presidents, Ohio congressman James A. Garfield and William McKinley, spoke on behalf of Davis.[33]

September 8, 1879, the date of Chamberlain's fifty-first birthday, also happened to be the day of the election. Rainy skies across Maine did not discourage a large voter turnout.

Republicans cheered the election results. They increased their vote total by twelve thousand, while Democrats saw their vote shrink by seven thousand.

Nominee	Daniel F. Davis	Joseph L. Smith	Alonzo Garcelon
Party	Republican	Greenback	Democrat
Popular Vote	68,967	47,643	21,851

But even though Davis easily won the plurality, he'd missed winning the 50 percent majority by 840 votes. Following the Maine constitution, the election would go to the House.[34]

The Republicans were optimistic. They'd won majorities in both the Maine House and Senate. Even if Democrats and Greenbacks decided once more to combine their votes as Fusionists, Republicans were confident the results would be in their favor:

	Senate	House
Republicans	19	90
Fusionists	12	61

But now began what would be called the Great Count-Out. On October 28, as towns and county districts sent in their popular vote totals to the Maine secretary of state, Governor Garcelon and his seven-man Fusionist executive counsel immediately intervened and began to disqualify ballots on various technicalities.

In one town, five representatives and one senator lost their seats because the results were not signed in an open town meeting. In another, five representatives were eliminated because candidates' names were listed with initials, not their full names. Votes in strongly Republican Skowhegan were disqualified because the ballot was printed in two columns rather than one. In another town two representatives were counted out because of a misspelling of their names. In Portland, a problem with 143 votes meant all the votes were thrown out. In Lewiston, Saco, Bath, and Rockland, all the votes were dismissed because three aldermen instead of four signed the returns.[35]

Republican anger spread across Maine. On November 17, the *Bangor Whig and Courier* headline blared:

THE CONSPIRACY
REVOLUTION ACTUALLY AFOOT!
ONLY AWAITING THE FINAL ACT!
WILL THEY DARE COMMIT THE MONSTROUS CRIME?[36]

On December 16, C. A. Boutelle, the *Whig and Courier* editor, a right-hand man to Blaine, announced the count-out as overseen by Garcelon's cronies had reversed the results:

	House	Senate
Fusionists	78	20
Republicans	58	11

A few Fusionist returns were shrewdly counted out, but not so many as to alter the overall large Fusionist majority.[37] Republican Davis had lost.

Blaine, realizing that the political turmoil in Maine could damage his presidential ambitions, hurried home from Washington. He urged holding "indignation meetings" across the state to protest that Republicans were being denied their voting rights. He asked Chamberlain to "get up an indignation meeting in Brunswick."[38]

But the Bowdoin president, worried about what was emerging from the indignation meetings, refused. After learning that armed men were heading toward Augusta, he told Blaine, "What we need to do is not to add to the popular excitement, which is likely to lead to disorder and violence, but to aid in keeping the peace by inducing our friends to speak and act as sober and law-abiding citizens." From his war experiences, Chamberlain knew how a few hot tempers could trigger mass violence—and casualties. He recognized Blaine's role as chairman of the state Republican Party, but cautioned, "I hope you will do all you can to stop the incendiary talk which proposes violent measures." He admonished the erstwhile 1880 presidential candidate: "I cannot believe you sympathize with this."[39]

Chamberlain wrote Garcelon, who he barely knew, encouraging him to submit the controversy to the state supreme court for adjudication.

Governor Garcelon, worried by reports of anger growing across the state, ordered 120 rifles and 20,000 rounds of ammunition moved from the state arsenal in Bangor to Augusta. He assembled a paramilitary force to defend the state house, which the *Portland Daily Press* called "Fort Garcelon." This force was described popularly as "state police," but actually none of the men were regular army or police. By the end of December, more men and arms began arriving in Augusta in support of one side or the other, reporting either to Blaine's home or to the Fusion headquarters at a local hotel.[40]

In the midst of all this turmoil, Chamberlain expressed his strong displeasure to Blaine, the powerful leader of the Republican Party in Maine. Well acquainted with bloodshed on the battlefields of the Civil War, he was horrified to imagine that violence might take place in the capital of his native state.

As 1880 dawned, with a new governor slated to be sworn in on January 7, Garcelon, a Democrat, wrote to the one man in the state,

314 LEADER, 1866 TO 1883

a Republican, whom he believed could calm this dangerous situation and restore order. The governor issued a special order: "Major-General Joshua L. Chamberlain is authorized and directed to protect the public property and institutions of the State until my successor is duly qualified."[41]

Duty called once more.

CHAMBERLAIN ARRIVED IN Augusta on January 5. He found the state house barricaded with heavy wood planks. He entered and established himself in a small office. In his first orders, he dismissed the governor's paramilitary force and replaced them with Augusta mayor Charles Nash's official police force, who were lightly armed. He sent the rifles and ammunition back to the Bangor armory.

He described this period in Augusta as a "three-cornered fight." Republicans congregated at Blaine's house; Fusionists gathered at a downtown hotel; Chamberlain, joined by Nash, in his fourth year as the mayor of Augusta, made their headquarters inside the capitol.[42]

Chamberlain now became, in effect, the military governor of the state. In his wholly unanticipated position, the former Civil War general locked up the governor's and the legislature's rooms and placed important papers in vaults. He decided to keep clear of all civilian political decisions. He also determined not to call up any militia unless the deteriorating situation called for it. Chamberlain's hesitancy to employ the militia was undoubtedly due to his assessment of the readiness of Maine's citizen-soldiers. He had spent seven years leading the state's ramshackle militia and had grown discouraged when the state refused to pay members when they took time away from their jobs to train. The state even declined to appropriate money for uniforms. The twenty-eight militias, scattered across the state, drilled infrequently.[43]

He did not have the authority to determine which of the counted-out or counted-in lawmakers made up the legal governing legislature of the state. But in these first days of January, that didn't stop both sides from ratcheting up the pressure on him to recognize their side. In what he saw as his only option, Chamberlain urged both Republicans and Fusionists to present their case as to who was the rightfully elected governor to the state supreme court.

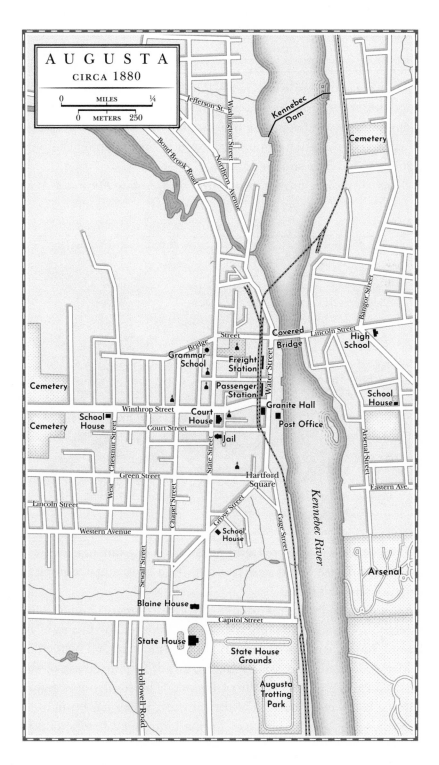

AUGUSTA
CIRCA 1880

0   MILES   ¼

0   METERS   250

Jefferson St.

Washington Street

Bond Brook Road

Northern Avenue

Kennebec Dam

Cemetery

Bangor Street

Bridge   Street   Covered   Lincoln Street   High
                                Bridge   School

Grammar   Freight   Water Street
School   Station

Cemetery

Passenger   School
Station   House

Granite Hall

Winthrop Street   Court   Post Office
School   House
House

Cemetery   Court Street

Chestnut Street   State Street   Jail

Green Street   Hartford   Eastern Ave.
                                          Square

West

Lincoln Street   Chapel Street   Arsenal Street

Western Avenue   Grove Street   School   Kennebec River
                                              House

Sewall Street   Gage Street

Arsenal

Blaine House

Capitol Street

Hollowell Road   State House

State House
Grounds

Augusta
Trotting
Park

. . .

"Everything is confusion here," Lawrence wrote to Fanny on January 7. He tried to assure her—"Although I succeeded yesterday in getting a good many awkward things straightened out." At the same time, he was beginning to recognize what he was up against: "What vexed me is that some of our own people (Republicans) do not like to have me straighten things."[44]

This confusion was captured by *Frank Leslie's Illustrated Newspaper.*

"Confusion in State House" was captured in this illustration in Frank Leslie's Illustrated Newspaper *in January 1880.*

Two days later he wrote Fanny again. "I do not dare to leave here a moment. There would most assuredly be a coup d'état, ending in violence and bloodshed."[45]

A January 10 letter by Portland U.S. congressman Thomas Reed offered a portrait of Chamberlain in the midst of the turmoil: "At last, we have peace broad, white winged beneficent and headed by a Major General." He told George Gifford, former editor of the *Portland Press,* and a close ally of Blaine, "The resplendent figure shining like one of the sons of the morning which has brought us this tranquil joy is the figure of Joshua Lawrence Chamberlain to whom Lee surrendered." He described Chamberlain as one who "walks the State House stairs master of the situation."[46]

Although Chamberlain understood his role to be that of a nonpartisan mediator, he was assailed from all sides—by Democrats, Fusionists, and Republicans. With rumors afloat of plans of discontent on all sides to overpower the police and kidnap him, Chamberlain began sleeping in different offices each night.

On the morning of January 12, one week after Chamberlain had assumed command, Fusionists and their candidate for governor, Greenbacker Joseph L. Smith, barged into the state house. Republicans sent Thomas Hyde, president of the Bath Iron Works, to inform Chamberlain that the Republicans were prepared to meet the Fusionists with force. When Hyde told Chamberlain the Republicans intended to "pitch the Fusionists out the window," Chamberlain was reported to have responded, "Tom, you are as dear to me as my own son. But I will permit you to do nothing of the kind. I am here to preserve the peace. There will be no fighting."[47]

It seems that Chamberlain's strong words stopped the Republicans in the moment, but it also raised their antagonism against him. Resentment toward Chamberlain was high from the Fusionists as well. When he refused to recognize Smith as governor, Smith tried to arrest Chamberlain for treason. The attempt proved unsuccessful.[48]

In the afternoon, Republicans began entering the state house in groups of twos and threes. It was not long before they had a large body gathered in Representative Hall. In the end, cooler heads prevailed. The Republican senators wrote up a list of questions to be presented to the supreme court and voted to adjourn until January 17.[49]

In the midst of ongoing confusion, Blaine sent a confidential message to Chamberlain telling him that if he could make it possible for the Republicans to "recognize the Republican organization of the two Houses," Blaine would see that the general could "go to the Senate"—specifically offering to back his election to the U.S. Senate.[50]

Once again, Blaine, ever the ambitious politician, did not judge Chamberlain correctly. The Bowdoin College president and leader of the state militia did not come to Augusta to trade for some future political office.

Adjournment did not end the wrangling and bitterness. In a January 15 letter to Fanny, Lawrence confided to her of a "bitter attack" on him in the Republican *Bangor Commercial* calling him a "traitor" to the Republican cause.[51] He had even heard of threats to her. "If you are afraid," he told her to contact Thomas Eaton, a local police officer, "to have the police keep an eye to you & the house."[52]

Chamberlain did receive support from veterans, especially from those who had served with him. Frank Ward wrote, "At a very short notice we can raise a Company here for you (mostly Veterans) that can be relied upon & would stand by you as we of the old 20th did at Round Top." Ward told his former commander, "I lost a leg in that Charge & if you require it am ready & willing to risk the other either in *your defense* or that of our rights."[53]

On a particularly frantic day, a member of Mayor Nash's staff rushed into Chamberlain's office to tell him a crowd of angry men was gathering, threatening to kill him. Chamberlain buttoned his coat and walked to the rotunda of the capitol, near where Maine's Civil War battle flags were displayed. He ascended two steps, and almost like a scene out of a Western movie, declared:

> Men, you wish to kill me, I hear. Killing is no new thing to me. I have offered myself to be killed many times, when I no more deserved it than I do now. Some of you, I think, have been with me in those days. You understand what you want, do you? I am here to preserve the peace and honor of this State, until the right government is seated—whichever it may be, it is not for me to say. But it is for me to see that the laws of this State are put into effect, without fraud, without force, but with calm thought and sincere purpose. I am here for that, and I shall do it. If anybody wants to kill me for it, here I am. Let him kill![54]

With those stunning words, in a dramatic gesture, Chamberlain opened his coat and challenged his threateners.

Witnessing the event, Nelson Dingley, Jr., who had served as Maine's thirty-fourth governor, recalled, "There was a breathless silence for a moment."[55]

Then a veteran in the crowd thundered, "By God, old General, the first man that dares lay a hand on you, "I'll kill him on the spot."[56]

The crowd drifted away.

BY 1880 CHAMBERLAIN had given hundreds of speeches across Maine and throughout the nation. But he had never given a speech like this one. As military governor, he made it clear-cut that he was not present to choose sides. But he also made it very clear that the mob would have to kill him if they intended to get their way by force. If all his previous addresses had been met with thunderous applause, this one-of-a-kind speech was met with stunned silence.

For Chamberlain, it was a near reprisal of that dramatic moment at Little Round Top seventeen years earlier. Indeed, he wrote Fanny, "Yesterday was another Round Top."[57]

ON JANUARY 16, the supreme court, replying to the questions sent to it by the Republicans, offered its ruling. The court declared the actions of Governor Garcelon and his council to count out or decertify votes unconstitutional. The court validated, unanimously, the election of a Republican governor and legislature.[58]

The next day, the legislature elected Davis governor of Maine. The new governor thanked Chamberlain personally: "In common with all the citizens of this State, I have watched with great anxiety the events of the past few days, and rejoice with them in the good results of the wise and efficient measures adopted by you for the preservation of the peace and protection of the property and institutions of the State."[59]

The "Twelve Days" in January were over.

"SUCH REJOICING WAS never before witnessed at the Capitol," Augusta's *Kennebec Journal* reported about the January 17 celebration. "What mighty manifestations of joy!"[60]

Further afield, in Philadelphia, *The Times*, a newspaper founded in 1875 to oppose machine politics and corruption, opined, "Chamberlain of Maine is a 'bigger man than Blaine,' and that it will be a glad day for the State when she turns from the Blaines and the Hamlins to a 'scholar and statesman like Chamberlain.' "[61]

During and after these tumultuous twelve days a cascade of letters from individuals arrived for Chamberlain.

Samuel Harris, Chamberlain's predecessor as president of Bowdoin, now professor of systematic theology at Yale, wrote that he had been "amused" a year earlier when he read that his successor had taken command of the ragtag Maine militia. "But to some men small positions are great opportunities, and so it seems in your case."[62]

Lewis Pierce, a Bowdoin classmate who went on to graduate from Harvard Law School, wrote with appreciation, "Looking at it from this distance it seems to us that no other man could have prevented bloodshed."[63]

L. T. Carleton, a lawyer in Winthrop, Maine, penned, "You have too long hidden yourself away from public gaze—let me assure you that the old-time enthusiasm for you has not abated in the least."[64]

Chamberlain had to be gratified to receive many letters from Civil War veterans. Ellis Spear, now U.S. commissioner of patents, wrote from Washington, "I must write you to add my word of congratulation, and my testimony as it what all good men here are saying." He told Chamberlain, "I laughed when I saw and heard the threats against you. The men who made them did not see you in the hell-fire of Petersburg."[65]

Dennis M. Shapleigh, remembering his participation in the surrender at Appomattox, wrote, "Gen. Chamberlain we were never so proud of you as now—not even when you stood upon the boundary lines and received the surrender of our vanquished brave foe."[66]

People were talking about Chamberlain even beyond Maine. John W. Chadwick wrote from Boston, "At this time of severe trial, perhaps it may afford some satisfaction to know how you are regarded in Boston."[67] Veteran Alfred L. Pearson wrote from Pittsburgh, "The people of this end of Pennsylvania are high in their praise."[68] On January 17, J. Warren Brown, mining executive in Maine, in business in Washington, commended Chamberlain, "The events of this day in Maine must ever be memorable in its history."[69]

Horace Allen, now Grace's fiancé, inquired whether she had seen what people in Massachusetts were saying about her father.

"What the press says of your father, all decent people in Massachusetts, irrespective of party, *think* of him." He went on: "Well you may be proud of your father, to whom the whole militia in Maine sent word, 'We take orders, from you alone.' "[70]

The twelve days in Augusta may have been Chamberlain's finest hour—even greater than Little Round Top. At Gettysburg, he acted spontaneously with courage in a battle that took minutes. At Augusta, he acted with deliberate calculation and courage in a battle that lasted twelve days.

WHEN CHAMBERLAIN RETURNED, exhausted, to Bowdoin, the student newspaper offered up praise of their president: "The whole strain of government came upon him at a time when the strain was the greatest." *The Orient* commended, "It is a high compliment to his integrity, and a certain proof of their confidence in him, that both sides felt the State was safe in his hands, and submitted willingly to his authority."[71] If Chamberlain had not always been honored in his own college, these students, too young to hear of his feat at Little Round Top in 1863, now praised him in 1880.

But Chamberlain also returned restless. He was beginning to think of life beyond Bowdoin once more. He was newly open to business ventures that had begun to approach him. But he would be slow to make any vocational changes.

That same year, on August 10, 1880, his father died in Brewer at the age of seventy-nine. Lawrence credited the senior Chamberlain, a taciturn man of unending Christian faith, as a huge influence in the formation of his values, teaching him from an early age to encounter difficulties directly and bravely. Two years before his father's death, he had written his mother, "My respect and affection for you & father increase the longer I live, & the more I know."[72]

In the spring of 1881, Grace married Horace Allen. Chamberlain's children had grown into adults during his college presidency. The wedding took place in First Parish, the church where her parents had been married twenty-six years earlier. Grace and Horace made their home in Boston, where Fanny was a frequent visitor. The always busy Chamberlain was a less frequent but no less welcome guest.[73]

Wyllys graduated from Bowdoin in 1881. Although not the student his father was, father and son marched proudly in the same commencement.

On March 12, 1883, the secretary of the faculty wrote a terse sentence in the faculty minutes: "The President announced that the condition of his health made it imperative for him to be absent for the remainder of the term."[74]

Wyllys Chamberlain graduated from Bowdoin in 1881.

In early 1883, feeling especially fatigued, Chamberlain contacted Boston surgeon Joseph H. Warren, a graduate of Bowdoin's medical school.

On March 2, Warren responded emphatically: "You must absolutely stop your work, for a time at least; You must have surgical treatment for your wounds. Both these things should have been done before. The condition is now critical." He concluded, "I shall not be responsible unless you obey these orders." The doctor suggested Chamberlain consider a shift of climate, proposing Florida.[75]

Chamberlain complied with Warren's urgency. The surgery was performed in Boston on April 19, 1883.

Chamberlain may have hoped the extent of his wounds would remain private, but the *Portland Transcript* reported on the surgery. "Portions of living flesh were taken in minute subdivisions from places where the opening could be spared." Furthermore, the flesh was "delicately applied to the reconstruction of the natural canal which had been taken away." After nineteen years his invisible wounds became visible. This painful, intimate revelation allowed people to see a much-admired man in a new light.

Even all these years after the end of the Civil War, the public remained captivated by the wounds of Union veterans. They were reminders of the terrible cost of the war. These wounds were both individual and communal. Chamberlain's wounds, individual and invisible up till this point, now entered the communal consciousness.[76]

Reading of the surgery, John Bigelow, former captain of the Ninth Massachusetts Battery, wrote to Chamberlain of his surprise that the general's wound was still so disruptive. "From time to time when I have had the pleasure of meeting you, you have spoken so lightly about your Petersburg wound, that I was led to believe it was not causing you trouble."[77]

Fanny did not accompany her husband to Boston, perhaps because of her own health issues; her lifelong problem with her eyes was becoming more acute. Two days after the surgery she wrote him, "I'm afraid [I've had] ignorance of your illness for a long time."[78] Even knowing that Chamberlain was a man who tried to hide his pain, her words are startling, perhaps offering insight into the distance that had sprung up between them over the years.

CHAMBERLAIN OFFERED HIS resignation as president for a final time, just prior to the 1883 commencement. This time the trustees and overseers accepted it, while asking him to continue as a lecturer in political science and public law.[79]

With his resignation, though still feeling the effect of his wounds, Chamberlain felt open to new challenges. Rumors circulated that several colleges approached him about their presidencies. But he was not interested in remaining in the academic world.

In early 1884, he wrote to twenty-seven-year-old Henry Johnson, an 1874 Bowdoin graduate just then completing a PhD in Germany: "I want to caution against your young ambition, that however pleasant and useful the life of a College Professor may be, that of a president, in I may say any of our best New England colleges even, is about the most thankless wearing wasteful life that can be undertaken. . . . no more of that sort of thing for me if I can help it."[80]

An exhausted man wrote these words. In time, he and others would offer a far more favorable narrative of his twelve years as president of Bowdoin and what he had accomplished, against difficult odds and opposition, but for now he was ready to move on.

Chamberlain was open to a new and very different chapter in his life. He was eager to pursue opportunities in business. And to do so beyond the boundaries of Maine.

EIGHTEEN

Second Civil War

The People made their recollections fit in with their sufferings.
—THUCYDIDES, *History of the Peloponnesian War*

I n 1883, THE YEAR CHAMBERLAIN STEPPED DOWN AS PRESIDENT of Bowdoin, if someone had asked him about his most gratifying experiences in the eighteen years since the Civil War, he might not mention his time as college president, or serving as governor. Rather, he might talk about the rewarding experiences of offering various lectures about the Civil War and the challenges facing his state and nation in a rapidly changing post–Civil War culture, something he did regularly. In speaking in towns across Maine, at various veterans' reunions, and in Boston, New York, and Philadelphia, his eloquent speeches brought audiences to their feet. This long parallel vocation in his life deserves more attention, analysis, and appreciation.

IN THE YEARS following the Civil War, countless soldiers spoke and wrote about those life-changing years. Initially, returning soldiers described the war as a crusade, with themselves as saviors in a magnificent campaign to preserve the Union.

Yet these memories quickly transitioned into a "second civil war." This war would be fought not with guns but words, as these veterans argued over facts and facets of the battles of Antietam, Shiloh, Gettysburg, and Vicksburg. In the ensuing years, this second war would be fought on many fronts: public speeches, newspapers, magazines, and reminiscences, as well as military courts of inquiry. Publishers quickly discovered a Northern public eager for stories about these

OVERLEAF: *Chamberlain returned to Gettysburg in 1888 to participate in the twenty-fifth reunion of the 1863 battle.*

heroes. But almost as quickly, veterans who felt slighted or maligned in these accounts responded with criticisms and rebuttals, offering their versions of a battle, or support or critique of a specific military leader.

WHEN CHAMBERLAIN CAME home in 1865, he quickly became one of the most sought-after public speakers about the Civil War. The professor of oratory devoted countless hours to developing a repertoire of speeches. He offered some of his speeches again and again. But he did not simply repeat them. He edited and revised them based on new information and his evolving insights. Audiences quickly discovered that Chamberlain brought to his speeches an ability unmatched by any other Union hero.

Audiences accustomed to speeches that basically were chronological accounts of different battles heard something quite distinct from Chamberlain. The soldier-professor drew examples from Greece, Rome, England, France, Germany, Switzerland, and Italy. He quoted frequently from the Bible. For military examples, he invoked not simply Grant, but also Lord Wellington and the Duke of Marlborough of England and Prince Eugene Francis of Savoy-Carignano of the Holy Roman Empire. He likened battle tactics to chess: "In the great game we are playing we could not afford to 'exchange queens.'"[1] He quoted from Dante, John Milton, Lord Byron, and Abraham Lincoln. The master of nine languages, he regularly used Latin words and French and Italian idioms and recited German poetry. He was a maestro of grammatical elements. He regularly enriched his speeches with alliteration, anaphora, simile, and assonance. To be sure, his audiences did not know these terms, but he used them seamlessly to enliven their listening experience.

IN ONE OF Chamberlain's first speeches, "The Battle of Gettysburg," which he gave for the first time in 1865 for the Bangor Freedman's Aid Society, he contended that the accomplishments of the Twentieth Maine at Gettysburg were still not fully understood and appreciated. During his description of the back-and-forth of the epic battle, he employed one of his favorite literary devices, a simile: the comparison of one thing with another. Thus, "Bullets hissed like spray. The lines were like resurgent seas."[2]

In his conclusion, he declared, "In the hour of battle they knew the meaning of '*Dirigo*' on your state escutcheon, and their record is as unsullied as your fame; may their memory be as green as your Pines!"[3] If at the outset he had lightly chided his audience for not fully appreciating the accomplishments of the Twentieth Maine, in his conclusion, using the Latin word *dirigo*—to lead—he skillfully connected his Bangor audience to the legendary Twentieth Maine regiment.

Three years later, in 1868, Chamberlain offered another version of "The Battle of Gettysburg" in Boston. Early on, as he described the Union and Confederate forces clashing at Little Round Top, he offered another simile: "The two hostile columns met . . . like two vast serpents in the desert."[4] He also employed metaphor, a figure of speech in which a word or phrase is applied to an object or action to which it is not literally applicable. Thus, he compared "the furious onset of the rebel army to the surging tide of the ocean that crept around and swept down the weak obstacles, only to be shivered in the last spray and recoil upon itself as it swept against invincible barriers of rock."[5]

As HIS SPEECHES took flight into history one of his favorite rhetorical strategies was to ask questions at the outset of his various speeches. In his 1866 address in Philadelphia to the Military Order of the Loyal Legion of the United States (MOLLUS), after focusing on the central word in his host's name, he asked a cascade of questions about its meaning. "Loyal whom? To the flag? To the people? To the Union?" He answered by employing examples of loyalty from England, the Netherlands, and Spain, invoking Greek history, and referencing Latin phrases: "The nation must make her heart ready to receive her lessons . . . she must cherish reverence, honor, truth, and brotherly love." In repetition—anaphora—he declared, "Loyalty to great memories; loyal to our new-plighted faith; loyal to the greater hope that this world's advancing edge shall touch the better one."[6]

Chamberlain wanted his audiences to experience events in what he called "present moments." Thus, he would begin in the past tense, then in the climax of a battle switch to the present tense, thus increasing the narrative tempo.

Chamberlain, concerned about the possibilities and problems of reconciliation between North and South in the immediate post-war years, wanted his audiences to leave feeling empathy rather than resentment toward the Confederate soldiers. Toward the conclusion of an 1866 speech, when commenting on the surrender at Appomattox: "They move along our front, face inward towards our lines . . . and then reluctantly, painfully, furl their flag, and lay them down, some kneeling and kissing them with tears in their eyes."[7]

A DECISIVE MOMENT in Chamberlain's budding parallel career as a public speaker occurred in 1869 when the Society of the Army of the Potomac invited him to be the keynote speaker for their founding meeting in New York. The invitation came not because of his military rank in the Civil War but because of his growing postwar reputation as a public speaker.

His first words: "Comrades: You bid me speak for you." Then, turning his invitation back on itself: "Rather you speak to me; you, who return my greeting, and you, unseen and silent to mortal sense, comrades in soul tonight! And drown my faltering words in your vast accord."[8]

After beginning with praise of the Army of the Potomac, he switched the tone of his address. "It is charged upon us that our campaigns were feeble, our battles indecisive, and even our victories barren." In the following minutes he described the obstacles facing the army, foremost, "The enemy were in their own country."[9] Chamberlain understood his audience and knew his remarks would resonate with them.

Pivoting again, he praised the commanders of the Army of the Potomac: "McClellan, the magic name, Burnside, the magnanimous, Hooker, the chivalrous, Meade, the victorious."[10] The hero of Little Round Top was always fulsome in his praise of others.

In this address Chamberlain had an important decision to make. General Sheridan, the newly elected president of the society, was present. It had long lingered in Chamberlain's mind that Sheridan had relieved General Warren of command of the Fifth Corps in the midst of the Battle of Five Forks. He had long thought "Little Phil's" decision impulsive and unfair.

Now, Chamberlain plunged ahead: "Pardon me, comrades, if I venture here to express the hope, knowing all the pains and penalties of so doing, that tardy justice (if that can be called justice which is tardy) may be done to officers whose character and service on behalf of the republic, deserving something better than its hasty and lasting rebuke."[11]

"Pardon me." Chamberlain well understood he was breaking protocol for such a celebratory evening, but he decided to do so.

BY 1878, AFTER thirteen years of speeches, one senses Chamberlain began to weary from telling the same stories. At the Music Hall in Boston, he began a speech, "The Old Flag: What Was Surrendered? What Was Won?" by saying to his audience, "You have often honored me by listening to stories of the war. Now that you asked me here again, I could easily relate more of them—too many—but what would be the use?" He went on: "To stir up unavailing sorrows. God pity our helplessness! To rouse up bitter hates. God forbid!" He then made his transition. "So, pardon me if I bring you nothing exciting or sensational tonight, but ask you rather to walk with me an hour in mind."[12]

He had a knack for sensing the mood of his audiences. He respected their intellect. "It will not be wasting your time to listen, because if you do not agree with me, you will know the reason why you do not, and that will be, perhaps, quite as well."[13]

That evening, instead of retracing the stories of familiar battles, Chamberlain brought contemporary politics into his speech. He understood that emotions were still smarting a year after the contentious 1877 election, in which Rutherford B. Hayes won a disputed victory over Samuel Tilden, in part because the Republican victor promised to pull federal troops from the South, in effect ending Reconstruction. Aware of the criticisms of Hayes's policy in New England, Chamberlain stated that he recognized the freed slaves were "abused," but "so are the Chinese in California, so are 40,000 poor girls in London, and so are the Indians. We must do the best we can for the negroes."[14]

There is a notable absence in Chamberlain's speeches. He almost never spoke about the outrages formerly enslaved African Americans faced in the South. As the situation for African Americans deteriorated, and the Ku Klux Klan swept forward in its reign of terror, Chamberlain remained optimistic about the ability of leaders of the South to deal fairly with the freed African Americans, despite evidence to the contrary.

Even considering that Chamberlain was geographically distant from Reconstruction's debates and actions, his silence is striking. In his speeches, it was one thing to commend the courage of Confederate soldiers in the Civil War; it was something else to trust the attitudes and actions of some of these same soldiers as they became leaders during Reconstruction.

OCCASIONALLY ONE OF his speeches sparked controversy. In Lewiston on Memorial Day 1879, in "The Heroes of the War," Chamberlain told the story of a Virginia father with two sons. First printed in *Harper's Weekly*, the tale was picked up and used by a number of speakers. According to the story, one son fought for the Union, the other for the Confederacy. Chamberlain asked, "Which of the boys was right?" then answered, "God indeed knows, and he alone. Into men's motives, which constitute one essential element in the character of actions, men cannot see. Both were right, perhaps neither, perhaps one." He went on to cite Jesus's Sermon on the Mount as the capstone of his story: "With what judgment ye judge ye shall be judged." He concluded by stating only God knows motives: "But God will be the final judge, and inevitably will weigh the differences between 'the just cause and the unjust.' "[15]

If the audience applauded Chamberlain's speech, two quite different Maine newspapers did not. *The Oxford Democrat* in Paris, an organ of the state Democratic Party, perhaps wishing to tamp down talk of the Republican Chamberlain becoming a future candidate for the U.S. Senate, thundered, "Does not God always fight for the right, and make it triumphant."[16] The newspaper charged that Chamberlain was questioning the Union cause.

SECOND CIVIL WAR 333

The *Bangor Whig and Courier,* a Republican newspaper that had always previously given Chamberlain favorable press, on this occasion wrote his speech "was shameful to the living and insulting to the dead."[17]

The next day the *Whig and Courier* published a response from Chamberlain, who wanted to set the record straight: "No one who heard me . . . could fail to see that the reverse of what is charged was the exact point of the passage referred to."[18]

THE MOST ENDURING controversy surrounding Chamberlain's speaking and writing concerns the surrender at Appomattox. He first spoke of it in one of his most popular speeches, "The Surrender of General Lee's Army," delivered on January 3, 1868, at the City Hall in Portland and a month later at the Norumbega Hall in Bangor.

Early in the speech Chamberlain stated that one of his purposes was to "relate many things which did not fall under the observation of the reporters."[19] He meant that at the time of the April 12, 1865, surrender, many newspaper reporters had left Appomattox, and thus did not report on the actual surrender ceremony. Chamberlain believed this left what happened that day open to conflicting accounts.

The surrender at Appomattox has become the subject of recent criticisms of Chamberlain. Historian William Marvel contends, "Chamberlain was the only original source of the claim he commanded the surrender ceremony; he offered no witnesses or documentation, and none has been found." Marvel alleges that, in Chamberlain's "apocryphal account," he invented the story of his magnanimous "shoulder arms" salute to Gordon's demoralized Confederates. Furthermore, he argues that Chamberlain waited for all the other participants to pass away, and then "exaggerated his role" at the surrender at Appomattox in the final speeches and writings of his life.[20]

From a different vantage point, English professor Stephen Cushman has offered a detailed literary analysis of the six of Chamberlain's speeches and writings over the years in which he talked of the surrender. Cushman tracks the changes in emphasis and wording in each speech. He notes that "Chamberlain's spellbinding descriptions combine the interest of romance and the value of history," which are the kinds of writings that Marvel "would censure."[21]

Cushman is critical of some of Marvel's conclusions. "For Marvel the fact that Chamberlain revised and improved his subsequent narratives of the salute is the end of the story," whereas "these later revisions and improvements" are part of the story of a master orator reflecting over the meaning of these battles in both a historical and literary way over many years. In the end, Cushman offers a measured assessment of Chamberlain's role and accounts of the surrender and concludes: "The simple truth is we just do not know for sure what happened."[22]

Patrick Schroeder, historian at the Appomattox Court House National Historical Park in Virginia, has studied many aspects of the surrender for years. In visiting Appomattox, I found his extensive research enormously helpful in determining the truth of the surrender. In contrast to the claims of Marvel and Cushman, Schroeder discovered that contemporary newspapers did report on Chamberlain leading the surrender. On June 5, 1865, the *Boston Evening Transcript* wrote, "Gen. Chamberlain, (formerly a Professor of Bowdoin College, Maine), a man of eminent attainments and valor, was designated by Gen. Grant to receive the surrender of the Generals of Lee's army at Appomattox Court House."[23] A month later, *The New York Times* wrote, "General Chamberlain was selected, it will be remembered, as the officer to receive the actual surrender."[24] In July 1865, the Washington *Evening Star* also wrote of Chamberlain's lead role at Appomattox.[25]

Thus, after sifting the evidence, Chamberlain's core story, first shared with his sister, narrated in one of his earliest speeches, remains trustworthy.

IT IS TRUE that Chamberlain made changes to his speeches. As with many Civil War veterans, he remembered more details. He made changes whenever new information merited correcting earlier versions. As he visited battlefields, as he corresponded with former soldiers, as he read memoirs and regimental histories, he collected new details that he would incorporate into future versions of his speeches.

Sometimes, Chamberlain's memory was confirmed. Theodore Gerrish, a member of Company F at Little Round Top, who after the war became a Protestant minister, wrote about the surrender at Appomattox in his 1882 *Army Life: A Private's Reminiscences of the Civil War:* "Our commander, with the true courtesy of a chivalrous spirit, gave the command Shoulder arms, and thus we saluted our fallen enemies. They returned the salute."[26]

On other occasions, his memory was corrected. Chamberlain remembered that Andrew Tozier, the Twentieth Maine's color-bearer, had courageously stood at the center of the regiment at a critical moment at Little Round Top. In May 1899, William Livermore wrote Chamberlain to tell him that both he and Elisha Coan were also guarding the colors. Livermore did not write to criticize Chamberlain, but to point out that the "smoke" might have hindered everyone's vision at that chaotic moment.[27] At the next opportunity to write about Little Round Top, Chamberlain incorporated Livermore's information in his story "Through Blood and Fire at Gettysburg" for *Hearst's Magazine.*[28]

It is fascinating to compare two speeches on the surrender at Appomattox given fourteen years apart—in 1868 and 1882. To do so is to see a man who was changed by time and age.

In 1868, Chamberlain depicts a bitter Confederate General Wise, who, at the surrender at Appomattox spit at Chamberlain, whereas in 1882 he omits Wise's "We hate you, sir," and instead describes an air of reconciliation: "There was something like a half-fraternal feeling towards these men." By the 1880s, reconciliation with former Confederate soldiers had become a main theme of almost all his speeches. Make no mistake: Chamberlain never soft-pedaled his opposition to the cause for which the Confederates fought, but he commended their courage.

Fourteen years later, Chamberlain was more aware that with the end of the war something had been lost: "When we took up our weary march homeward, it was dull to plod on without skirmishes ahead." And finally, "But though sometimes the heart will yearn for those stirring duties and those high companionships of the field."

He concludes with a vision of the martyred Lincoln keeping vigil over the nation, whispering through the night "All is well."[29]

ANOTHER OF CHAMBERLAIN'S battles in this second civil war did not take place on the lecture circuit but rather in a highly publicized military court of inquiry.

General Gouverneur Warren, stripped of his command of the Fifth Corps at the Battle of Five Forks on April 1, 1865, had long sought redress in a court of inquiry. But during the eight years of Grant's presidency, all his efforts were turned away. It may have been that President Grant believed he could not authorize such a court without offending his close friend Sheridan. When Hayes succeeded Grant as president in 1877, the new president did authorize a court of inquiry to look afresh at Warren's "conduct" at Five Forks.[30]

For Chamberlain, Warren's plight had long been personal. The former Bowdoin College professor admired the former West Point professor. He would never forget that July 1863 day when engineer Warren was the first to understand the danger to the Union army's tenuous hold of Little Round Top.

After speaking of Warren obliquely in his speech at the founding of the Society of the Army of the Potomac in 1869, eleven years later, Chamberlain traveled to Governors Island in New York Harbor in 1880 to be a witness at the court of inquiry.

He arrived with no illusions about Warren's prospects. As he wrote Fanny, "The traditions of the whole War Department were for sustaining military order." He believed, "We would not expect a Court to bring in a verdict of censure of General Sheridan or anything that would amount to that. Nor would it be easy to find officers who were willing to testify."[31] Chamberlain understood it was one thing to gossip or grouse privately about Sheridan's unfair treatment of Warren, quite something else to say so publicly in a court of inquiry. He expected he would undergo rigorous cross-examination, yet concluded, "We are bound to have the true history of this thing out now."[32]

After days of testimony by Sheridan and his side, Chamberlain took the stand on May 15. He was questioned by Warren's lawyer,

SECOND CIVIL WAR   337

Albert Stickney. A highly acclaimed lawyer, at age twenty-three he had persuaded one hundred young men at Harvard to form a company to serve in the Union army. On this day he questioned Chamberlain about Warren's deportment as the Fifth Corps assembled on the morning of April 1, 1865. Sheridan had testified that Warren was passive, even apathetic, but admitted under cross-examination that he did not know Warren and had never served with him before Five Forks. By contrast, Chamberlain testified, "General Warren's temperament is such that he, instead of showing excitement, generally shows an intense concentration in what I call important moments." He continued, "Those who do not know him . . . might take it as apathy when it is deep-concentrated thought and purpose." Finally, "I do not think he was apathetic that morning. He was energetic."[33]

As a witness Chamberlain offered powerful testimony about both Warren's character and his demeanor. He understood Warren's understated demeanor—deliberative but outwardly unemotional—because in some ways he shared the same traits.

The court of inquiry, with frequent interruptions, continued into the fall of 1880. In November, Chamberlain was called back to Governors Island. Stickney, recognizing the quality of both his presence and his testimony, called him as a major rebuttal witness. Questioned once more about Warren's demeanor, he answered that it was "peculiar to himself—a deeply earnest manner."[34] He understood that the gentle Warren was the antithesis of the explosive Sheridan. Warren and Stickney could not have asked for a more credible and persuasive witness.

As the court of inquiry dragged on, a Boston newspaper printed a story in December 1880 that claimed Grant and Sheridan were angry with Sherman, general of the army, for allowing the court to take place, arguing that the court put both of them on trial. Sherman was reported to have replied that he favored the court because "it would smooth over old difficulties and differences in the army."[35] Actually, the long proceedings of the court were dividing the Union triumvirate.

In July 1881, Stickney gave his final summation. Of the witnesses he had called, he chose to cite Chamberlain's testimony about Warren's demeanor as the most conclusive in his closing argument.[36]

The findings of the court were finally authorized to be published by President Chester Arthur in November 1882. They largely exonerated Warren.

It was too late for Warren. He had died three months earlier.[37]

The much-publicized Warren court of inquiry is a prime example of how the Civil War did not end in 1865. It also showcases the way in which Chamberlain was a central actor in one of the crucial battles of this second war.

THREE YEARS AFTER the verdict in the Warren court of inquiry Chamberlain's hero, Grant, died on July 23, 1885. *The New York Times* wrote, "The name of General Grant will be remembered by Americans as that of the savior of their country in a crisis more appalling than any it has passed through since the United States became a nation."[38] The *New-York Tribune* went further: "The foremost man of the nation has closed a career second to no other in the history of the republic."[39]

In the second civil war, everyone knew that the general, terminally ill with cancer, in his last battle had fought off death to complete his memoir, which would be published by Mark Twain.[40]

On August 8, one and a half million people congregated in New York for the funeral of the sixty-three-year-old Grant. Five hundred thousand came from outside the city by train and boat. Starting at city hall at 10 A.M., with the bells of old Trinity Church ringing, the nine-and-a-half-mile funeral procession snaked through the streets of the island city to finally arrive at Riverside Park, where a temporary tomb had been built.

Symbolizing Grant's commitment to restoring the Union, the four leading pallbearers included his two favorite Union generals, Sherman and Sheridan, who rode in a carriage with two leading surviving Confederate generals, Joe Johnston and Simon Bolivar Buckner. General Winfield Hancock, asked by President Grover Cleveland to be in charge of the procession, led a group of horsemen that included ex-Confederate Fitzhugh Lee, nephew of Robert E. Lee.[41]

Chamberlain traveled from Brunswick to be present for America's largest public gathering to date. He had long admired Grant

*One and a half million people congregated in New York for the August 8, 1886,
funeral of Ulysses S. Grant.*

and had welcomed him into his home in Brunswick in August 1865
when the general received an honorary doctorate from Bowdoin.
To his surprise, as he wrote Fanny, "By Genl Hancock's kind attention, I was treated with marked distinction—too much in fact. I had
a carriage directly in the group of Cabinet ministers & the most
distinguished men of the country." He also told her, "I would not
have chosen that position because it was too much. But Genl Hancock's staff officer did not seem to understand that I was only a
private citizen."[42]

Deeply emotional, Chamberlain went on and on to Fanny about
what he saw and experienced: "The great scene is over. Grant is laid
in his tomb. You may imagine—few others can—how strange that
seems to me. That emblem of strength & stubborn resolution yield-
ing to human weakness & passing helplessly away to dust." He believed "the pageant and the tribute of honor were grand—Worthy
of a nation." He had one regret. "I wish now very much that I had
brought Wyllys with me. This is the last of the great scenes."[43]

IN 1888, CHAMBERLAIN returned to Gettysburg for the twenty-fifth
reunion of the epic 1863 battle. Twenty-five thousand participants

attended the events. Invoking religious language, Chamberlain called them "pilgrims."

General Daniel Sickles had encouraged veterans of the Army of Northern Virginia to attend, so that once-clashing armies "might on that occasion record in friendship and fraternity the sentiments of good will, loyalty, and patriotism which now unite all in sincere devotion to the country." Only a few came, but these included General James Longstreet, who commanded Lee's First Corps, and General John Brown Gordon, who surrendered to Chamberlain at Appomattox.[44]

To his surprise, the Society of the Army of the Potomac elected Chamberlain their president, even though he had not been a candidate. He wrote his daughter Grace, "It was a remarkable honor, on such a field & such an occasion, for one who was only a colonel on that field."[45] The veterans present all knew of his heroism at Little Round Top, but he owed his election to his increasingly visible role in the past twenty-five years as a leading speaker about the meaning of the war.

CHAMBERLAIN RETURNED TO Gettysburg one year later on October 3, 1889, for an event much more personal. This time he came to

Returning in 1888, Chamberlain was pleased to see a new statue of Gen. Gouverneur Warren, field glasses in hand, looking up toward Little Round Top.

commemorate the battle of Little Round Top with the survivors of the Twentieth Maine.

Upon his arrival, he had to be pleased to see a bronze statue of General Gouverneur Warren. Veterans of the Fifth New York volunteer regiment had paid for its erection the previous August. The eight-foot-tall statue was mounted on a boulder with sword in one hand and binoculars in the other. This was the spot where Warren looked up and recognized that Little Round Top was unoccupied except for a small signal corps. Finding Vincent's and Weed's brigades, which included the Twentieth Maine, he redirected them in what became the battle to hold the Union army's left flank.[46]

In the afternoon, Chamberlain spoke briefly at the dedication of the monument, one of Maine granite, remembering the ground where the Twentieth Maine fought and prevailed at Little Round Top. Inscribed on the stone were the names of the young Maine volunteers who had given their lives so long ago.

In preparing his remarks, Chamberlain had become painfully aware of quarreling that signified that the second civil war had broken out, sadly, among the survivors of Little Round Top. As he arrived that day, and as he prepared his remarks, he knew that aspects of the Twentieth Maine's courageous stand had festered among those who were arriving for the reunion. Even the exact placement

In 1889 Chamberlain spoke at the Twentieth Maine reunion at Little Round Top.

The monument at Little Round Top was erected in 1889.

of the new monument provoked debate. He worried that acrimony among the veterans threatened to spoil the celebration.

One simmering argument concerned who, in the chaos of that July afternoon, deserved credit for first alerting Chamberlain of the enemy's movements. Seeking to quiet the controversy, on this October afternoon he answered deftly, "Now, as might will be believed of such gentlemen and soldiers, they are all right; no one of them is wrong." Ever the reconciler, he also wanted to set to rest the claim that some men did not charge with their fellow soldiers: "No man hesitated."[47]

In his evening address at the courthouse on the town square, he spoke directly against what he believed to be a falsehood: "There is a phrase abroad which obscures the legal and moral questions involved in this issue,—indeed which distorts and falsifies history: 'The War Between the States.' There are no states outside the Union. Resolving them out does not release them."[48] Once again, in 1889, Chamberlain sought to affirm the solidarity of the Union.

Yet, in a concession to the soldiers of the South, "No one of us would disregard the manly qualities and earnest motives among those who permitted themselves to strike at the life of the Union we held so vital and so dear." But Chamberlain responded, "Truly it has been said that the best of virtues may be enlisted in the worst of causes."

In his conclusion, Chamberlain put the meaning of the battle at Gettysburg in lyric language.

> In great deeds, something abides. On great fields something stays. Forms change and pass; bodies disappear, but spirits linger, to consecrate the ground for the vision-place of souls. And reverent men and women from afar, and generations that know us not and that we know not of, heart-drawn to see where and by whom great things were suffered and done for them, shall come to this deathless field, to ponder and dream.[49]

In this deeply emotional speech, spoken to comrades in arms but with the memory of those not present, Chamberlain offered words that, more than he knew, would echo across the years.

NINETEEN

The Entrepreneur

*I am still active and full of courage, & I cannot but believe some of the
things I have in hand will be brought to results before very long.*
—JOSHUA LAWRENCE CHAMBERLAIN, LETTER TO FANNY, 1891

Joshua L Chamberlain

WHEN CHAMBERLAIN STEPPED DOWN AS PRESIDENT OF BOW-
doin College in 1883, he was fifty-four years old. With only his
small military pension for income, he knew he needed a new avenue to make money for himself and Fanny. He dreamed of becoming successful in business.

While still president, in December 1881, he had sailed to Florida
at the invitation of the Florida West Coast Improvement Company
to explore an entrepreneurial opportunity. He traveled south with
enthusiasm, but with no business experience.

FLORIDA, UNDER SPANISH and British colonial rule from the sixteenth to the nineteenth centuries, became the twenty-seventh state
in 1845. Before the Civil War, Floridians lived primarily bunched
along the state's northern border. Its economy of cotton, farmed by
enslaved people, mirrored the economies of neighboring Georgia
and Alabama.[1]

At the end of Reconstruction, with a population of only 250,000,
Florida ranked as the least populated and most sparsely settled state
east of the Mississippi River. But in the 1870s, the *Florida New Yorker*
magazine began to promote the state to both investors and settlers,
and over the next four decades, the state would grow at a rate twice
as fast as the population of the United States.[2]

Chamberlain disembarked at Fernandina, a town on Florida's
east coast. He traveled by train to Ocala, a town founded in 1849.

GEORGIA

Okeefenokee
Swamp

St. Marys

Fernandina

Monticello   ·Clifton
·Madison   ·Jasper
Ocala R.

Live Oak
Welborn   ·   Lake City   Callahan

Baldwin   Jacksonville

Stark
St. Johns R.

Suwannee R.   Santa Fe R.

Picolata
Tocoi   St. Augustine

Waldo
Gainesville
Archer   Palatka   Matanzas Inlet

Deadmans
Bay   Clay
Landing·
Bronson·   Flemington   ·Welaka

Ocklawaha R.   L. George
Volusia   Halifax R.

Ocala
St. Johns R.   Port Orange
Smyrna

Wacasasse Bay   Withlacoochee R.

Homosassa·   Mosquito Lagoon
Enterprise

Springhill
Bayport·   ·Pierceville   L.
Apopka   Cape Canaveral
Spring Hall

Pittitochoscolee·
Indian River

Clear Water·   Tampa
Alafia   Cypress
Bartow   L. Kissimmee

Tampa Bay   Indian River
Inlet

Little Sarasota I.   Kissimmee R.

Sarasota R.   Peace Cr.   L. Istokpoga

Charlotte
Harbor   Lake
Okeechobee   L. Worth

Captiva I.   Caloosahachee R.
Sanibel I.   ·Punta Rassa

GULF

OF

MEXICO

ATLANTIC   OCEAN

Caximbas Bay
Gallivan's Bay   EVERGLADES

Thousand
Islands   Biscayne
Bay   Key
Biscayne
Bahia Ponce
de Leon   Capo's
Sound

Cape Sable   Barnes
Sound

Florida Bay

Dry Tortugas   Pine Islands

Key West   FLORIDA KEYS

FLORIDA
IN THE 1870s

Based on a map published
in 1870 by C. Drew

0   MILES   60

0   KILOMETERS 60

Rail service had reached Ocala in 1881.[3] "Never before in the history of Ocala was there as much building going on as now," boasted *The Ocala Banner*. Chamberlain traveled by horse and buggy forty-five miles to Homosassa. As a lover of nature, he found the undeveloped land's lush vegetation wonderful and entirely different from the forests and rocky fields of Maine. The north-central area of Florida grew sweet oranges, budded from sour orange stock imported many years earlier from Spain. Where the Homosassa River emptied into the Gulf of Mexico, he observed giant cypress trees ornamenting both banks of the river.[4]

Chamberlain learned the Florida West Coast Improvement Company aimed to build the Silver Springs, Ocala, and Gulf Railroad to extend rail service in Florida. The directors envisioned great opportunities in land speculation, with the company becoming one of the earliest leaders in Florida real estate. With the completion of the railroad, they were convinced prices would shoot up, but they understood they needed funding from northern investors to advance their plans. The directors also believed they needed a well-known northerner to be titular head of the company—a common practice at the time. Enter Chamberlain.[5]

His visit to Florida also brought Chamberlain into contact with men who had fought for the Confederacy, and who were now intent on building the economy of a postwar new South. He was especially impressed with John F. Dunn, who had fought in a Confederate Florida regiment. Dunn was the leading director of Ocala's first financial institution, the Bank of Ocala.[6]

"I MADE QUITE a visit to Florida," an enthusiastic Chamberlain wrote Sae on his trip home. "Saw much there to invite energetic & resolute young men," and "had many invitations to take positions of responsibility." He shared with her his motivations if he decided to accept any of the offers: "I always wanted to be at the head of some enterprise to transform the wilderness into a garden." But he saw an opportunity for something more. He could "be a missionary of civilization & Christianity at once." The person who went to seminary to consider becoming a missionary wrote, "Here is a chance to do it, & in my own country."[7] Chamberlain's sister, with great respect for her idealistic older brother, may have wondered about how he intended to combine business and Christianity.

On his way back north, Chamberlain stopped in Petersburg, his first visit since the battle in 1864. In the letter to his sister: "I visited the battlefields of Petersburg & spent 4 hours trying to identify the spot where I fell on the 18 of June [1864] in leading a charge upon the Rebel works."[8] Chamberlain wrote emotionally of "standing & musing there remembering how I thought of Mother in that calm ebbing away of life amidst the horrible carnage."[9]

He also stopped in Washington, where he experienced mixed sentiments. "Here is the little world around which the whole great country moves." Disappointed, "Self-seeking marks too many faces, & all the strife of peaceful times, less noble often than those of war—are seen here in their little play, or great one, as the case may be." If initially disheartened, he did encounter another side: "All is not evil here, however, I went to a church thronging with earnest people this morning, & heard words of deep impressiveness."[10] Disappointed by the actions of politicians, Chamberlain found encouragement in the people of faith.

AFTER HIS EXPLORATORY trip, Chamberlain decided to pursue business interests in Florida when he completed his presidency of Bowdoin. He became vice president of the Florida West Coast Improvement Company and president of the Homosassa Company, which became the engine for development in Citrus County in the 1880s.[11]

In the next years Chamberlain would spend most of his time not in Florida but working out of an office on Wall Street. He arrived in New York at a time of tremendous growth and development in the nation's largest city. The 1880s would see the completion of the Brooklyn and George Washington bridges and the dedication of the Statue of Liberty. It was the beginning of the skyscraper— a slang term borrowed from the highest mast or stack of a sailing ship. "Still higher" became the watchwords of the city's architects. Elevated trains cost five cents a ride. The first subway in New York would not open until 1904.[12]

In this Gilded Age New York, Chamberlain found himself in a

hub for speculation and the growth of commerce. Well-known American author James D. McCabe, in his 1882 book *New York by Sunlight and Gaslight,* described the "mad race for wealth" in the city.[13] For Chamberlain, a man who spent most of his life in Maine, living and working in fast-paced New York must have been a viscerally different experience from living in Brunswick.

From his New York office he became president of several other companies, including the Kinetic Power Company, which produced motors for streetcars, and the Mutual Town and Bond Company. Chamberlain was mostly a figurehead in these companies. He was fine with the understanding that he would not be in charge of day-to-day operations. The directors wanted his name at the head of the business.[14]

He tried to persuade Fanny to join him at his apartment at 101 West Seventy-fifth Street. Although in earlier years she enjoyed her visits to New York, she seldom came. No specific explanation is offered by her, but, struggling more with her eyes, it appears that she preferred to stay in their beautiful home in Brunswick.

IN SEPTEMBER 1885, Chamberlain made a trip to Florida. He traveled south because his plans to build a hotel in Homosassa had been frustrated by the difficulty of acquiring materials for such an isolated spot. In contrast with his typical optimism, he admitted to Fanny, "It is dull and lonely here." If he had been initially attracted to Florida's natural beauty, he now wrote that "though soft & sweet [it] lacks richness & body" and "fails to fill my spirit to perfect satisfaction." Most importantly, sounding like the romantic Chamberlain of old, "I should delight to have you here."[15]

He had also begun to realize another reality of doing business in faraway Florida: "The worst now is the great expenses that have been run up for the company in my absence."[16] It was clear that he could not simply be the titular head, but needed to be present to manage the affairs of his business investments. It also seemed clear that the earlier promise of money to be made in Florida was proving elusive.

He looked forward to Fanny coming to Florida in November. Ending on his usual positive note, he wrote her, "Our enterprises here are full of promise, & really are worthy of my best powers."[17]

If Chamberlain tried to put his best face on for Fanny, his sister did not buy it. In January 1886, Sae replied to a letter he'd written their mother: "[Your letter] conveys the impression that you are undergoing hardship and privation down there— To what end? simply of business enterprise?" She wrote bluntly, "If so, it seems to me you might do better with yourself." Sae was always the realist in the family.[18]

Fanny did come in November, anticipating the pleasures of a warm winter. Unfortunately, her first trip to Florida coincided with the Great Freeze of 1885–1886. With the unusual below-freezing temperatures, the state suffered a loss of one million dollars' worth of oranges.[19]

In the winter of 1886 Chamberlain bought the one-hundred-foot-long steamer *Mistletoe* in the hopes of improving reliable transportation along the Gulf Coast. The *Mistletoe* was much larger than the *Pinafore*, which he enjoyed sailing along the Maine coast. In Florida he relished being the boat's pilot, taking freight and passengers from Cedar Key to Homosassa.[20] Now more easily able to secure materials, he completed a scaled-back Homosassa Inn.

In March, Chamberlain became afflicted with malaria, a disease common in nineteenth-century Florida. But medical science was not yet aware that the painful illness was transmitted by anopheles mosquitoes.

The malaria hung on, so that he and Fanny were not able to start for Maine until July. The continuing effects of the disease forced them to stop for two weeks in Chattanooga, and again in New York. As Chamberlain headed north, his son Wyllys headed south to Ocala, intending to practice law and fill in during his father's absence.[21]

In February 1887, back in New York City without Fanny once more, father confided to daughter, "The Doctor of course thinks my trouble is simply '*malaria.*' I know it better. It is overwork." He told twenty-year-old Grace, in whom he now confided as he always did with Sae, "But I do miss 'Mamma' very much. New York without her is desolation."[22]

Undaunted, not willing to let his Civil War wounds, malaria, or loneliness slow him down, he returned to Florida in 1887 and again in 1888, still determined to make a go of his several business enterprises.

. . .

AT THE END of 1888, Chamberlain grieved the loss of his mother, who died on November 5 at age 85. He had written his mother every year on his September 8 birthday. Most of these letters have not survived, but one dating from 1887 spoke of her influence on him: "This is my birthday, and I must write you my letter, as I always do to bless and thank you for my life; for all your suffering for me & tender care, and faithful guidance & good instruction." He concluded, "Your prayers for me are always in my heart."[23]

Mother Chamberlain was buried in Brewer's Oak Hill Cemetery beside her husband and sons Horace and John.

As CHAMBERLAIN CONTINUED to keep up his busy pace, he knew Fanny questioned his expenditure of energy, his long trips to Florida in his painful physical condition, and what she suspected were negligible returns on his business ventures. When in New York, he confided to his daughter, Grace, "I have to be out every evening to keep myself in good relations with the *gentlemen* I am associated with." If at first Chamberlain found these contacts energizing, by 1889 one hears a very different tone. He admitted ruefully, "it is very hard for me to break out & give *one* lecture when my mind is so absorbed in other business."[24] The networking he felt compelled to do was far beyond anything he had previously experienced in Maine. One also hears his unhappiness that he is not able to deliver the lectures that had for so long brought him such pleasure and respect.

In an emotional letter to Fanny, written while suffering yet another infection from his wounds, he sought to explain his efforts by telling her that all his endeavors were "to secure the command of the things necessary for this freedom." At sixty-two, with no retirement benefits from his service as Maine governor and Bowdoin president and only a minuscule army pension, he perceived business as the best route to a secure retirement for himself and Fanny. He acknowledged, "I have been delayed & baffled as to some of these plans. But I am still active and full of courage, & I cannot but believe some of the things I have in hand will be brought to results before very long."[25] Even when facing huge obstacles, Chamberlain could be, as ever, optimistic.

Yet the economic results of Chamberlain's entrepreneurial activities in Florida were not good. In March 1890, the directors were forced to sell the Homosassa Company to pay off its debts. Both the promise of business and a pleasurable life in Florida did not turn out as Chamberlain had hoped. He never acknowledged how much money he may have lost in his Florida investments. In the long run he faced a double dilemma: he did not have the skill set for this new venture in business, but also many of these speculative ventures seemed doomed to fail with or without his participation.

Wyllys, struggling with illness and financial troubles, made the decision to leave Florida in 1891.

In December 1892, Chamberlain endured yet another painful infection from his Petersburg wounds. He traveled to New York to receive care from urologist Dr. Robert Holmes Green. Still bedridden in early 1893, both he and his physician wrote to the Bureau of Pensions about his condition.[26]

If Chamberlain felt too weak to deliver lectures, he could still write. Interested as ever in participating in the debate about this or that battle in the Civil War, he wrote an essay about the battle at White Oak Road, especially the controversy surrounding Sheridan and Warren. Always open to feedback, especially correction, he sent his essay to Alexander Webb, who had been General Meade's last chief of staff, and now served as the second president of the City College of New York.

Webb replied, "It is a powerful little book and it is so full of repressed contempt for the mean plotting and sacrificing of men for a single purpose. I saw it all & Meade felt it night & day." He told Chamberlain, "It is all coming back to me—I can sit by the campfire & see & feel & hear it all over again."[27] Webb's appreciative response typified the effect Chamberlain's writing had on his readers. The professor of oratory had the ability to place people in the midst of the action.

· · ·

IN 1893, DURING this difficult period, Congress awarded Chamberlain the Medal of Honor. Aware of what Abraham Lincoln called

"the silent artillery of time," referring to the death of veterans of the American Revolutionary War, friends were making efforts to step forward with nominations while heroes of the Civil War were still alive.[28]

Several veterans nominated Chamberlain. Thomas H. Hubbard, Bowdoin class of 1857, wrote, "In Maine we have always thought General Chamberlain's military service deserved any reward the Government could bestow."[29] Close friend Webb, who received his Medal of Honor in 1891, believed Chamberlain should receive this recognition also. When Chamberlain was asked to supply witnesses, he named Ellis Spear and Joseph F. Land, both members of the Twentieth Maine.[30] Fitz-John Porter, grateful for Chamberlain's support in his court of inquiry, believed Chamberlain was one of the most deserving

Chamberlain received the Congressional Medal of Honor in 1893 for his "daring heroism and great tenacity."

members of the Fifth Corps. In his letter to Secretary of War Daniel S. Lamont, Porter, knowing of the severity of Chamberlain's wounds, stressed that he might not have long to live.[31]

His nation honored him with the Medal of Honor for "daring heroism and great tenacity in holding his position on Little Round Top against repeated assaults, and carrying the advance position on Great Round Top."[32]

AS CHAMBERLAIN SPENT the early months of 1893 recuperating, it became a rare opportunity to slow down and take a moment for introspection. He had been pursuing his business interests for a full decade, with little economic gain to show for his efforts.

In this same year the Panic of 1893 presented yet another road-block. The depression that followed led to a run on banks. Unemployment rates skyrocketed to 20 to 25 percent in some parts of the United States. The panic put a temporary crimp in Florida's development.

His health somewhat recovered, and through the urging of Webb, Chamberlain agreed to become president of the Institute for Artists-Artisans in New York.

On April 23, Chamberlain wrote a revealing letter to "Dearest friend—of friends"—probably Webb.

> Your kind and strengthening letter came this happy 'Lord's Day'—& gave me heart comfort & courage. I have 'burned my ships behind me' in turning away the offers elsewhere, of late, and clinging to New York & the sense of duty here—with it comes a sort of reaction from the strain. I feel very weak now, & in the hands of God. I have to be brought to this with patient trust & faith—It has always been my pride to be active, & trust too much (I fear) to my human strength.[33]

Approaching his sixty-fifth birthday, looking forward to working once more with young people, as he had done for so many years at

Chamberlain's summer home, Domhegan, which he named for an Indian chief who once lived on this land

Bowdoin, he concluded, "It is their Cause, Country, Civilization, City, their Young, their Commerce—"[34]

As a young man, Chamberlain had felt insecure around Fanny's artistic friends. Now he had the opportunity to lead an institution that provided courses by artists in architecture, illustration, painting, and sculpture. He was especially pleased to introduce an eight-week summer course at Domhegan. He savored being around artists and their students at his seaside home.

AT THE BEGINNING of 1894, Chamberlain struggled with another debilitating infection. He tried to hide his pain from Fanny, who was managing her own pain. But he broke this rule in a January letter: "You have not, I hope, been allowed to know how very hard a time I have had with sufferings and disabilities since Christmas." He confessed, "I have told Wyllys to write you such particulars as he thought proper, and he has no doubt, and rightly, softened the story down so as not to distress you."[35]

IN THE LAST decade of the century, Fanny's world had contracted as her lifelong struggle with her eyes worsened. Her deteriorating eyesight deprived her of the pleasure of reading, which she very much liked to do. Her husband tried to cheer her up: "I shall bring some good books to read to you," he wrote toward the end of 1894.[36]

Despite medical interventions, by her seventieth birthday in 1895, Fanny was blind in one eye. By the beginning of the new century, Fanny would be blind in both eyes.

Once a source of strength to her family, she gradually became an object of their concern and care. The way her husband and children thought of her is reflected by the way they referred to her: "little Ma" or "little one."[37]

Still, she continued to attend First Parish regularly. At the end of the morning service, friends would linger to speak with her. She would always turn to the direction of their voices to join the conversation.[38]

In 1896, the Chamberlain family diminished further when Lawrence's younger brother Tom died. Tom, although also a decorated veteran of the Civil War, had never quite found his footing in civilian life after the war. If always encouraged by Lawrence, one wonders if, in the dynamics of family systems, Tom might have found it difficult to be the younger brother of such a famous sibling. Tom died at age fifty-five of tuberculosis.

In 1897, Chamberlain was honored to receive an invitation from President William McKinley to attend the dedication of Grant's Tomb in New York to be held on August 27, the seventy-fifth anniversary of the general's birth. It would be attended by one million people, including President McKinley and Julia Grant. Twelve years earlier, Chamberlain had participated in Grant's funeral procession, but in 1897, exhausted by periodic infections from his wounds, he was forced to decline the invitation.[39]

DESPITE HIS INJURIES and business failures, Chamberlain was still eager to embrace new causes. An opportunity came unexpectedly in 1898 with the outbreak of the Spanish-American War. At 9:40 P.M. on February 15, 1898, the battleship *Maine* exploded in Havana harbor, killing 268 sailors and igniting the fury of the American public. The United States officially entered war with Spain two months later on April 21, 1898.[40]

Chamberlain volunteered the next day. At sixty-nine, he wrote to an old foe, William P. Frye, now senator of Maine, seeking a command: "I cannot but think that my day is not yet over for the service of my country."[41] Former Union friend Ames, age sixty-two, and former Confederate foe Oates, also sixty-two, received commissions, as did many Union and Confederate veterans. Chamberlain received a polite no from Secretary of War Russell A. Alger.[42]

A friend and admirer, George O. Cutler, eager to find an appropriate role for the Civil War hero, wrote to the Navy Department, urging that Chamberlain be appointed governor of the Philippines.[43] Of interest: William Howard Taft became governor of the Philippines in 1901.

IN THE MIDST of this disappointment, Chamberlain was surprised by a letter he received in the spring of 1899. Francis Fessenden had discovered a letter addressed to his father, Senator William Pitt Fessenden, who had died thirty years earlier. The letter, written on September 8, 1863, was from General James Rice and recommended Chamberlain for promotion. The younger Fessenden forwarded the letter to Chamberlain, writing, "The enclosed letter from Genl. Rice pays such a handsome tribute to your bravery and skill, that I think you ought to have it."[44]

Rice's recommendation declared, "My personal knowledge of this gallant officer's skill and bravery on the battlefield, his ability in drill and discipline, and his fidelity to duty in camp, added to a just admiration for his scholarship, and respect for his Christian character." Rice then spoke of Chamberlain's leadership of the Twentieth Maine: "The conduct of this Regiment at the Battle of Gettysburg has rendered, for all time, the prowess of the arms of your State, the imperishable conduct which, as an eye-witness, I do not hesitate, has its inspiration and great success from the moral power and personal heroism of Col. Chamberlain."[45]

Rice's words echoed from the distant past; he was mortally wounded at Spotsylvania Courthouse, Virginia, in May 1864. Chamberlain replied to Fessenden, "I thank you for the kind letter enclosing that of Genl Rice, as brave and true a man as ever went 'booted & spurred' from the field to report to the God of battles." Chamberlain concluded, "His letter does me more good now than it did then."[46]

BY THE END of the decade, Chamberlain cut off his last connections with business in both Florida and New York. The entrepreneurial spirit which launched him into a completely different chapter in his life in the early 1880s had come to an end without the results for which he had hoped.

The best appraisal of this adventure and these years came in a letter from Wyllys to his mother. "I am coming to realize better than ever what you have seen so long; that our man can't be best at *everything;* and Father cannot ever be relied to look out for himself, but always for the other fellow."[47] Wyllys deftly juxtaposed two realities from these years. He recognized his father's shortcomings as a businessman, but his final appraisal expressed his admiration for a father who was always concerned about the welfare of others.

RETURNING TO MAINE, Chamberlain determined to look out for himself.

On Thanksgiving Day, November 23, 1899, the Chamberlain family gathered at their home on Maine Street across from Bowdoin College. Lawrence and Fanny were there. Grace and Horace, with their three children, came up from Boston. Wyllys was also present. The next day, Chamberlain wrote to Sae sharing his happiness that "the circle, long broken," was finally together.[48]

TWENTY

"Remember and Go Forward"

In every great crisis his idealism not only held him true;
but became a contagious inspiration.

—DR. WILLIAM DEWITT HYDE, PRESIDENT, BOWDOIN COLLEGE

[signature: Wm D Hyde]

I T WAS 1900. PERHAPS TO HIS SURPRISE, AND CERTAINLY TO THE
surprise of his doctors and some of his family and friends, Chamberlain was still alive at age seventy-one after all he had suffered in the thirty-six years since doctors told him he would die from his "mortal" wounding at Petersburg.

Now Chamberlain hungered for new employment in the new century. He had been unsuccessful at business. The army didn't want him back. So he decided to lobby for the position of collector of the Port of Portland, which was the second-leading New England port, after Boston. Since colonial times, the person appointed to be the executive overseeing the many activities of the Custom House was traditionally a leading community figure or otherwise well-connected in political patronage.

Chamberlain received endorsements from many old friends. Petitions were initiated in Portland and Brunswick, one signed by 390 citizens. Ellis Spear offered an effusive recommendation to Amos Allen, 1860 Bowdoin graduate and Maine member of the U.S. House of Representatives: "His is the most conspicuous and singular case in the State of distinguished service in the war." His Twentieth Maine colleague added, "Chamberlain is also 'solid' with the old soldiers, in Maine and elsewhere, and they would feel gratified if he were favored."[1]

Chamberlain did not receive the position. Instead, President

FACING PAGE: *Chamberlain riding in parade in Portland in early twentieth century*

William McKinley offered him a lesser post: surveyor of the Port of Portland. Chamberlain was disappointed, but Dr. Abner Shaw, the Twentieth Maine physician who saved his life at Petersburg, encouraged Chamberlain to accept it: "Your best friends advise this."[2]

He did. After the highs and more frequent lows of his multiple business engagements, Chamberlain needed the $4,500 annual income ($160,000 today).

He accepted the post and began working at the Portland Custom House, where he helped record and facilitate the movement of goods in and out of the busy port.

He quickly discovered that the work was not all-consuming. The position allowed him to commute regularly to Brunswick on weekends, and left time for a few speaking engagements, writing projects, and hours spent sailing *Pinafore* on the Maine coast. Sardonically, he commented to a friend that the position had "no responsibilities, no duties, no power, no prominence . . . and requiring no ability."[3] If his lament spoke to the fact that the

position did not provide him the meaning he was seeking, he would soon discover that it allowed him the time he never had in his years in business to restart his writing project about the Union armies in the final months of the Civil War.

Chamberlain as surveyor of the Port of Portland in 1905

As HE SETTLED into his new position, a letter arrived from old friend Sarah Sampson, the Maine "angel of mercy" who nursed him at the Annapolis hospital in 1863 after his near-mortal wounding at Petersburg. After the death of her husband in 1881, she had gotten a job at the Pension Bureau in Washington through the recommendation of General Howard. Believing she and Chamberlain might both be nearing the end of their lives, she wanted him to know, "Since I first knew you, you have given me more encouragement and assistance in my life work than any other person living. . . . I appreciate all your kindnesses to me in so many ways—ways that you have forgotten but I never shall."[4]

In the fall of 1900, having negotiated a two-month leave of absence before accepting his position with the port, Chamberlain prepared to embark on a long-desired trip to Italy and Egypt. Before sailing from New York, he wrote Fanny, "You remember we are 'engaged' again." We cannot know exactly what his amorous words referred to, but he may have been trying to assuage her hurt feelings over the fact that he was choosing to be separated from her once more. He urged her "not to sink down under any evils in our absence, but to keep whole and well for other days to come." Quoting one of his favorite poets, Dante, he added, " 'And other songs in other keys, God willing.' "[5]

With government credentials from Secretary of State John Milton Hay (who long ago had been one of President Abraham Lincoln's secretaries) in hand that would provide introduction to local leaders,[6] Chamberlain visited Genoa, Pisa, and Florence. He became ill in Rome and, seeking a warmer winter climate, sailed from Naples to Egypt, lodging in Cairo.

In Cairo he began reading the Koran, desiring to better understand the Muslim religion. He read it in its original language, classical Arabic, which he had studied while a student at Bangor Theological Seminary when he considered becoming a missionary. As he told a friend in a letter published in the *Portland Press* and *Brunswick Telegraph*, each evening he read from both the Bible and the Koran.[7]

His readings only made him want to learn more. The British proconsul, Lord Cromer, opened doors for him in Egypt. He made the acquaintance of Muslim leader Fordure, a lineal descendant of the Prophet Muḥammad, and Syrian lawyer Nicholas Nimr. His health recovered, he visited the ruins of Heliopolis, one of the major cities of ancient Egypt. This lengthy visit to Italy and Egypt reconnected Chamberlain with his lifelong interest in the history, architecture, art, painting, and literature of classical culture.

Because of his convalescence, the trip lasted longer than expected, so he did not arrive home until March 1901. He returned with scarabs—Egyptian amulets—as well as impression seals and statues of Cupid and Hermes, all of which would enjoy places of honor in the library of his Brunswick home.[8]

ALONGSIDE HIS CUSHY job at the port, Chamberlain stepped up his civic engagement. He agreed to serve as a senior vice president of the American Bible Society. A daily reading of the Bible was central to his life, and he appreciated that during the Civil War the American Bible Society kept its printing presses running twenty-four hours a day, and distributed nearly one million Bibles or portions of Bibles, such as the Gospel of John, to Union troops.[9]

He became a life member of the American Board of Commissioners for Foreign Missions, an organization dear to the heart of his father-in-law, Rev. George Adams. Sensitive to Fanny's condition, he became a director of the Maine Institute for the Blind. With his abiding interest in history, he became a member of the American Historical Association, the Maine Historical Society, the Colonial Society of Massachusetts, and the Military Historical Society of Massachusetts.[10]

AFTER DECADES OF involvement with Union veterans, the turn of the century found Chamberlain discussing and debating the Civil War with former Confederate foes.

These connections began in 1896 when Chamberlain was invited to participate in a commission researching and writing a new book, *Maine at Gettysburg*. He was asked to edit the chapter on the Twentieth Maine at Little Round Top written by Howard Prince, the Twentieth Maine's historian.

He was immediately concerned that Prince, who was not present at Little Round Top, had not contacted Chamberlain to inquire about the voluminous research he had collected over the years. The bulk of Prince's material came from a trip he made to Gettysburg with Spear in 1882, part of a group of soldiers from both sides. Oates, leader of the Fifteenth Alabama in 1863, had planned to be present but at the last moment was not able to come. Instead, Spear and Prince went to Washington to consult with Oates, now an Alabama congressman. They were received graciously by their former foe.[11]

When Chamberlain read the chapter, he believed that Prince and Spear had been overly influenced by Oates. Corresponding with Spear, Chamberlain voiced his concerns: "Quite a number of things have been put in distorted perspective lately. The influence of Col. Oates's statements has extended to color the accounts of the whole engagement." He was especially concerned with a central narrative of Oates's account: "to reduce our whole fight to an encounter with his regiment is to falsify history." He reminded Spear that the Eighty-third Pennsylvania participated in the fight, and that Confederate prisoners also included men from the Fourth Alabama and the Fourth and Fifth Texas regiments.[12]

Chamberlain did significant work reconciling the various accounts, and believed it one of his most difficult literary tasks. He also footnoted the chapter twice with "Statement of Colonel Oates."[13]

Chamberlain's edits, including his footnotes, were accepted. *Maine at Gettysburg* was published in 1898 to a readership still very interested in the memory of the Civil War.

As THE LINES between friend and foe continued to blur, Chamberlain was invited to be present when General John Brown Gordon, who had surrendered Robert E. Lee's troops to Chamberlain at Appomattox, lectured in New York in November 1893. Like Chamberlain, Gordon was elected to political office in the years after the war. He won a seat in the U.S. Senate as a Democrat from Georgia in 1873. In 1886, he was elected governor of Georgia, and in 1891 was elected again to the Senate. When the United Confederate Veterans, a patriotic veteran organization, the equivalent of the Union Grand Army of the Republic, was founded in 1889 as a merger of a number of local and state Confederate organizations, they selected Gordon as their first commander in chief.[14]

In New York, when Gordon stepped to the stage to deliver his signature lecture, "Last Days of the Confederacy," *The New York Times* reported that he invited a group of well-known Union military veterans, including Chamberlain, to sit on the stage.[15]

In his lecture Gordon defended the virtues of the Southern people with a call for a new spirit of reconciliation and nationalism.[16]

For two and a half hours, interrupted frequently by applause, he captivated the five thousand in attendance at the Tabernacle in Brooklyn.

At the conclusion of the lecture, as he told the story of the surrender at Appomattox, he spoke of the "Union officer" who led the

When John Brown Gordon lectured in New York in 1893, he invited Chamberlain to be present onstage.

surrender without giving his name. Then, Gordon turned to the military veterans sitting behind him and in a dramatic gesture said, "And now I take a sincere pleasure in shaking the hand of that man, who was afterward Governor of the State of Maine—Gen. Chamberlain."[17]

In this long second civil war this had to be one of the most emotional moments for Chamberlain. In his lectures across the North, he had long talked about reconciliation with Southern soldiers. Now, the Confederate general who had surrendered his troops to Chamberlain at Appomattox had returned his spirit of reconciliation.

During the next years Gordon would deliver this lecture in hundreds of venues on extensive speaking trips. He invited Chamberlain to join him for a joint speaking tour, but because of his declining health, Chamberlain did not accept the offer.

TEN YEARS LATER, in 1903, Gordon published *Reminiscences of the Civil War*. Of that long-ago day at Appomattox, he wrote, "One of the knightliest soldiers of the Federal army, General Joshua L. Chamberlain of Maine, who afterward served with distinction as governor of his State, called his troops into line, and as my men marched in front of them, the veterans in blue gave a soldierly salute to those vanquished heroes—a token of respect from Americans to Americans, a final and fitting tribute from Northern to Southern chivalry."[18]

Both Chamberlain and Gordon described the story of the surrender with similar detail. A recent critic has argued, "Gordon made no mention of it until he saw Chamberlain's published account, nearly four decades later."[19] But Gordon confirmed Chamberlain's account ten years earlier in his lecture in New York. And as for Chamberlain, in a letter to Bangor businessman Frank A. Guernsey in 1899, he confirmed, "Neither of us knew of the other's writing on the subject." He then went on to write, "I presume it is as true of his as of mine, that nothing is changed from the original account. No new light was needed by either of us. We spoke from knowledge."[20]

In the summer of 1903, Gordon, although in poor health, traveled all the way from Atlanta to Brunswick to call upon his onetime foe and now friend.[21]

Less than one year later, at the age of seventy-one, Gordon died. An estimated seventy-five thousand people came to pay their final respects at Central Presbyterian Church in Atlanta. Upon hearing the news, it was reported that at the Portland Custom House, Chamberlain "wept bitterly."[22]

A SECOND ENCOUNTER with a former Confederate foe began in August 1903 when Chamberlain received an unexpected letter from John Page Nicholson, chairman of the commission in charge of the new national battlefield park at Gettysburg. Nicholson, a Civil War veteran who served in the Twenty-eighth Pennsylvania, had received a request from Oates that a memorial stone be placed at the farthest point of the Fifteenth Alabama advance on July 2, 1863.[23]

The Gettysburg National Military Park was established in 1895. In that same year, parks were established at Chickamauga and Chattanooga, Shiloh, and Vicksburg. All were under the authority of the War Department. Before he left Congress in 1894, Oates enthusiastically supported the legislation. But right away commissions at each park were faced with a thorny question: who and what deserved to be memorialized?

Three years later, while serving in the Spanish-American War, Oates was stationed at Fort Meade near Harrisburg, Pennsylvania. That fall, he traveled forty miles to the new military park at Gettysburg. He saw there the two monuments to the Twentieth Maine.

Wanting to memorialize his own brave men, especially his younger brother John, who died in the battle for Little Round Top, he determined to erect a monument to the Fifteenth Alabama. He believed he had an ally in William Robbins, a veteran of the Fourth Alabama,

one of three persons on the Gettysburg commission.[24]

Throughout 1903 and 1904, Oates wrote the commission continuously, asking about the status of his application. Robbins expressed concern that Oates's application implied that other regiments, including his own Fourth Alabama, were not also meritorious of commendation. Nicholson worried about the accuracy of the Oates account detailed in his submission.[25]

William C. Oates, stationed in Pennsylvania while serving in the Spanish-American War, visited Gettysburg in his campaign to establish a monument honoring the Fifteenth Alabama Regiment.

Nicholson came up with a strategy to get the commission and the War Department out of the dilemma they found themselves in with Oates: they would invite an outside expert to comment on Oates's application. Who better than Chamberlain?

The Gettysburg commissioner did not know Chamberlain personally, but understood his reputation as a highly respected post–Civil War figure, prominent in the Society of the Army of the Potomac, the Grand Army of the Republic, and Military Order of the Loyal Legion of the United States. In his letter to Chamberlain, he wrote of Oates's application, "Some of the statements are so much at variance with the records we thought we would ask your opinion on the subject."[26]

Chamberlain, unlike Spear and Prince, had never met Oates. He had corresponded with him in 1897 when editing Prince's chapter for *Maine at Gettysburg,* asking him a question about "our respective movements" on July 2. At that time, he told Oates he was "much gratified to find so close an agreement between our impressions and recollections as to our contest there."[27] But in 1903 Chamberlain was troubled by Oates's recollections as expressed in his application.

He replied to Nicholson immediately: "I should feel no objection to the erection of a monument to the honor of a regiment that had pushed its way so far around the flank of the Union line and made so gallant an attack." Yet that is not what Chamberlain believed was reflected by reality: "I should expect it to be placed on ground where it actually stood at some time during the battle,—at the extreme point of its advance, if desired—so that it might not only represent the valor of the regiment but the truth of history."[28] Chamberlain, in his typical posture of reconciliation, was quite willing, even eager, to commend the courage of the Confederate soldiers, but as a soldier and historian, he wanted the story of Little Round Top to be accurate for all those who would come to visit the sacred place in future years.

Oates visited Gettysburg in July 1904 to press his case in person, but was once more rebuffed.

In the winter of 1905, after twenty years of research, Oates published *The War between the Union and the Confederacy and Its Lost Opportunities, with a History of the 15th Alabama.* The eight-hundred-page volume attempted to rally its audience around the legitimacy of secession, the righteousness of slavery, and the justification for the Confederacy.[29]

The book received quite different reviews in the North and the South. The Memphis *Commercial Appeal* praised Oates's argument that the "Confederacy should have succeeded." By contrast, New York's *Literary Digest* deemed it "a human document testifying to the provincials' capacity to hug closely the corpse of an issue long since dead."[30]

Despite the controversy his book produced, Oates continued to press his case for a memorial at Gettysburg. To that end, he initiated correspondence with Chamberlain. In Chamberlain's reply, it was clear that he and Oates differed on how far the Fifteenth Alabama had driven back the left and right wings of the Twentieth Maine. Oates offered to meet Chamberlain at Gettysburg; surely they could agree if they looked together at their former battleground.[31]

On May 18, 1905, Chamberlain wrote Oates he would be willing to meet him "again" at Little Round Top: "It is really my desire to have your monument set up, only let us make sure of our ground for the sake of historical fact."[32]

Chamberlain mailed a copy of his letter to Nicholson. The Gettysburg commissioner replied, "I wish to congratulate you upon the dignified, manly, soldierly and gentlemanly way in which you replied to him."[33]

But in the end, Chamberlain and Oates never met at Gettysburg. William Howard Taft, now secretary of war under President Theodore Roosevelt, never made a ruling. Despite Oates's endless efforts, a monument to the Fifteenth Alabama was never erected.

IN THAT SAME year, three days before her eightieth birthday, on August 4, 1905, Fanny fell and broke her hip. In a letter, Lawrence wrote her, "although your condition is far from being what I could wish . . . Your husband & children 'rise up & call you blessed'—as the old scriptures represent the crowning grace of a good woman."[34]

Fanny died on October 18, 1905, just six weeks shy of Lawrence and Fanny's fiftieth wedding anniversary. Her funeral service took place at First Parish, the church where she first met Lawrence, and where the young couple was married. She was buried at Pine Grove Cemetery on the Old Bath Road.

The marriage of Fanny and Lawrence was at times difficult but enduring. She brought to it her quest to find her true self in the midst of frequent depression and lifelong problems with her eyes. As a young woman she admired Lawrence's remarkable abilities, but as the years passed found herself too much alone as his various vocations took him to Augusta, New York, and Florida. Over time passion transitioned into companionship. Both their children loved their mother and admired her resilience in the face of what finally became total blindness. If she never officially joined First Parish, she was admired by many friends in the congregation where she and Lawrence met and were married.

CHAMBERLAIN'S LIFE SHIFTED after the death of Fanny. He bought a two-story white house at 211 Ocean Avenue in Portland (the house still stands and is numbered 499 today). From it, he had a wonderful view of Back Cove, an estuary basin on the north side of the city, and beyond it to the ocean.

He became a well-known person in Portland. By his own admission, he had lost one and a half inches of height in his older age, but he remained trim. He dressed formally but smartly: a black suit, a white shirt with a starched collar, a black tie, and on Portland's many cold days, a black overcoat. Always convivial, he greeted everyone he encountered on the trolley he took to work at the Custom House or when walking throughout the city. His frequent canine companions with their distinctive historical names, Tiberias Caesar and Henry of Navarre, only added to his pleasure in these walks.[35]

Chamberlain with another of his classical-named pets, his dog Tiberias Caesar, in Portland

He traveled often to spend time with Grace and Horace and his three granddaughters, Eleanor, Beatrice, and Rosamond, in Boston. "Gennie's coming, Gennie's coming," the little girls would shout. Everyone addressed Chamberlain as "General," but in his granddaughters' pronunciation, it became "Gennie."

In the summers, he would open his home in Brunswick and invite the girls to visit him there. Just as he used to write to Grace or "Daisy" when she was young, now he wrote to the youngest granddaughter, brown-eyed eleven-year-old Rosamond: "You must come to me in the summer, with the birds and flowers, when all the brown-eyed things are building nests. We will build one too!"[36]

IN 1909, THE nation looked forward to celebrating the centennial of the birth of Abraham Lincoln. Chamberlain, despite frequent illnesses that kept him from doing much speaking anymore, looked forward to participating.

The year-long events began with prayers in churches on Sunday, February 7. In the following days, and especially on February 12, Lincoln's birthday, events were held in many cities. In Chicago, the president of Princeton University, Woodrow Wilson, was one of many speakers. In Springfield, William Jennings Bryan, "the Great Commoner" and three-time Democratic presidential candidate, spoke. Retiring president Theodore Roosevelt spoke at Lincoln's birthplace in Kentucky. Julia Ward Howe, author of *The Battle Hymn of the Republic,* read a poem in Boston. Parades, concerts, school programs, and plentiful oratory continued throughout the year.[37]

Chamberlain was invited to speak in Philadelphia on February 12. He traveled there with his daughter, Grace. Forty-three years earlier, he had traveled to Philadelphia to speak for MOLLUS, then a brand-new organization, on February 22, George Washington's birthday.

Now, speaking at the Academy of Music, he gave an address titled "Abraham Lincoln: Seen from the Field in the War for the Union." He focused not on Lincoln's achievements, but rather on how Lincoln embodied what was central to Chamberlain's understanding of all great leaders. "The heroes of history are not self-seekers; they are saviors. They give their strength to the weak, the wronged, the imperiled. Suffering and sacrificice that take on themselves." As to Lincoln's character: "Courtly manners and culture of the schools he did not bring. But moulded and seasoned strength, calm courage, robust sense, he brought; and a heart to humanize it all." He went on: "His inherent and potential greatness was the power of his reason and sense of right, and a magnanimity which regarded the large and long interests of man more than the near and small of self."[38] Chamberlain had long been impressed with Lincoln's "magnanimity" toward the South, a model for his similar attitude.

Now in his early eighties, Chamberlain no longer accepted many invitations to speak. But in 1910, he agreed to appear at the YMCA in Brunswick. So many students showed up at the event that it had to be switched to the larger Bowdoin chapel. Chamberlain wrote Sae, "The entire assembly rose at my entrance & remained standing until I was seated, & the greeting was repeated with emphasis at the Conclusion of my address."[39] Even in his old age, Chamberlain never lost his love for the young men of the college.

THAT YEAR, WYLLYS moved to Portland to be with his father in the white house on Ocean Avenue. His father also invited Lillian Edmunds, a distant relative who had served as Chamberlain's secretary

and later Fanny's caretaker, and who had most recently been looking after the home in Brunswick, to come to Portland. She came
initially to serve as housekeeper, but as Chamberlain's illnesses became more frequent, she doubled as a nurse.

During the Christmas season in 1910, Chamberlain sent greet-
ings to old friends, including Spear. His comrade in the Twentieth
Maine responded, "Your dear Christmas greeting helps, and gives
me an impulse upward." Spear invited Chamberlain to come to
Washington for a visit and concluded his letter, "Many years &
peaceful to you— You have seen enough of War."[40]

THE YEAR 1911 brought both pain and pleasure to Chamberlain.
January found Chamberlain confined to his house and bed due to
poor health.

But his spirits rose in April with the beginning of the fiftieth
commemoration of the Civil War. The anniversary brought numerous invitations for Chamberlain to write about the Civil War in national magazines. In his old age, Chamberlain found meaning in
his memories of the war.

In December, he enjoyed visits to "Gennie" from Eleanor and
Beatrice, two of his three granddaughters. Although he found "each
lovely in her way and words," in a letter to their mother, he focused
on Eleanor, the eldest at eighteen. He deemed her "a distinct and
decided personality," language closely resembling the way he described Grace when she was of similar age. He encouraged Grace to
let Eleanor go to college, still unusual for girls at this time, and a
possibility he had not sanctioned at Bowdoin decades earlier.[41]

At Christmas, Chamberlain offered advice to his new young secretary, Catherine Zell. Chamberlain was a perfectionist at a time when
spelling remained uneven for most people. He gave his secretary a
dictionary in which he inscribed "Remember and Go Forward." If his
inscription was particular to her, he may have been giving advice to
himself at the end of 1911. For Chamberlain, both in his speaking and
writing, always sought to combine a balance between the lessons of
the past with an imperative to go forward with boldness.

On the next to the last day of the year, ex-governor Selden Connor, keenly aware of Chamberlain's frequent health issues, wrote to

advise his eighty-two-year-old friend to slow down and curb his busy schedule.[42]

BUT CHAMBERLAIN WAS never one to fully slow down. At age eighty-three, he could still write. In 1912, the editor of *Cosmopolitan* magazine approached Chamberlain about writing an article. The magazine, founded in 1886, began life as a family magazine aimed at women. In 1905, it was purchased by businessman and newspaper publisher William Randolph Hearst, who pushed the magazine to find new audiences. Aware of the diminishing number of Civil War veterans, and believing their reminiscences appealing to a wider audience, the magazine asked Chamberlain to write "My Story of Fredericksburg" on the fiftieth anniversary of the epic battle.

The old soldier could still summon prose that put the reader in the midst of the hellish retreat in the eastern theater of the Civil War.

> We had to pick our way over a field strewn with incongruous ruin; men torn and broken and cut to pieces in every inde-scribable way, cannon dismounted, gun-carriages smashed or overturned, ammunition chests flung wildly about, horses dead and half-dead still held in harness, accouterments of every sort smashed as by whirlwinds.[43]

The enthusiastic response to his article elicited a subsequent re-quest for an essay on Gettysburg for *Hearst's Magazine,* a newly ac-quired title in the growing Hearst publishing empire.

Given his health issues, Chamberlain was not certain he could contribute. He was now afflicted with neuritis, a painful inflamma-tion of the nerves that led him to complain to one correspondent: "The pain was excruciating, and the disability attendant complete. I could do nothing but *scream.*" In the same letter, Chamberlain re-ferred, with a morbid sense of humor, to "my practical extinction in February."[44] Dr. Shaw now looked in on him almost every day.

Despite his physical limitations, Chamberlain summoned his strength and submitted a short essay on Gettysburg, a much-abridged version of what he had originally envisioned.

The magazine accepted the piece, though the editors changed quite a bit of Chamberlain's language, adhering to Hearst's mandate to use plenty of the florid writing that he believed readers loved. The final dramatic title was "Through Blood and Fire at Gettysburg." The essay was published in June 1913, one month in advance of the fiftieth anniversary of the battle at Gettysburg.[45]

Chamberlain was not happy with the final version; he believed the editors "mutilated and 'corrected' my 'Gettysburg.'" Disappointed, he did not order any copies of the essay to give to friends.[46]

Even if Chamberlain's original wording was sometimes changed by editors, his emotional fingerprints are present, and several points in his account are worth noting.

Some have charged that Chamberlain, in his various recountings of the story of Little Round Top, did not give sufficient credit to brigade commander Strong Vincent.[47] Yet in "Through Blood and Fire at Gettysburg," he wrote of Vincent, "He rushed in among the broken companies in desperate effort to rally them, man by man. By sheer force of his superb personality, he restored a portion of his line, and was urging up the rest."[48]

Although the editors requested that he write his essay in the first person, he gives credit to others in a summary sentence: "How men held on, each one knows—not I."[49]

As for the crucial moment, which he knew had been long debated, Chamberlain narrated, "One word was enough,—BAYONET!" He quickly added, "It was vain to order 'Forward.' No mortal could have heard it."[50]

CHAMBERLAIN'S TWO ESSAYS triggered an unanticipated response. Longtime friend and fellow veteran Spear, a mere three years after his warm invitation for Chamberlain to visit him in Washington, turned on him.

In March 1913, Spear criticized Chamberlain in a very long letter in *The National Tribune,* the newspaper of the Grand Army of the Republic, commenting on Chamberlain's account of Fredericksburg almost sentence by sentence. At the outset, he commended the article as "written in his charming style," but went on to cast Chamberlain's descriptions as "pure imagination," "gross exaggeration," and "nothing of the kind happened to us there." He faulted Chamberlain for not making Ames and other members of the Twentieth Maine "more prominent in this 'Story.'" Spear concluded, "if it is intended and offered for history, it is misleading and unjust," then adds a final jab: "It may be a 'literary way' of writing history."[51]

WHAT TO MAKE of Spear's lengthy response? Is it the reaction of an embittered old man? Did Spear feel that in "My Story," others, including himself, were not getting credit for their roles at Fredericksburg and Gettysburg?

Tom Desjardin, historian of the Twentieth Maine, offers the most helpful explanation of Spear's response. He believes Chamberlain saw his participation in the Civil War as a mark of honor and heroism, whereas for Spear the war was and remained a terrible reality that left so many of his friends and their families dead and injured. Over the time of this long second civil war, Spear had come to believe the "vain glorying" of many veterans, including Chamberlain, exasperating and wrong.[52]

There is no record that Chamberlain ever replied to Spear's critique.

DESPITE CHAMBERLAIN'S DISSATISFACTION with the final version of his Gettysburg piece, two publishers were impressed and approached him with propositions. Houghton Mifflin of Boston and G. P. Putnam's Sons of New York expressed interest in any book he would write about the Civil War. In fact, as he cut down on public speaking, and despite his frequent illnesses, Chamberlain had been working for some time on the book that he had preliminarily titled *The Last Campaign of the Armies*. He ultimately accepted the offer from G. P. Putnam's Sons.[53]

IN MAY OF 1913, Chamberlain traveled to Gettysburg for a final time. He had been invited to be one of fourteen members of the committee planning a fiftieth reunion of the Battle of Gettysburg in July. Dr. Shaw accompanied him on this strenuous trip.

But in July, with great sadness, he was not able to join the more than fifty-four thousand Union and Confederate veterans, plus family members, journalists, and visitors, who came from all over the nation for the reunion. Respecting Dr. Shaw's counsel, Chamberlain agreed to avoid what promised to be intense summer heat in southern Pennsylvania (it would be 102 degrees on July 2).[54] He did see the Maine group off at Portland's Union train station.

Days later, Chamberlain learned of the magnificent fireworks display that took place above Little Round Top on the night of July 3. The presentation included a 200-foot-wide, 120-foot-tall American flag released from a balloon that floated over the veterans. Balloon figures of a Union and Confederate soldier also shook hands with each other high in the sky.[55]

Despite his absence, the official report, the *Fiftieth Anniversary of the Battle of Gettysburg*, included a photograph of Chamberlain. It captured his still-commanding presence. At the age of eighty-four, his name and the story of his achievement at Little Round Top continued to have great significance in the historical memory of the Civil War.[56]

THE BEGINNING OF 1914 found Chamberlain bedridden and in decline. He had long refused opiates to alleviate his frequent pain and continued to do so. In a dictated letter to Sae on January 20, he described the "unspeakable agony," but reassured her, "if the dear Lord has appointed me to live a little longer, I am resolved it shall be of good to me and others. I am trying to get a little closer to God and to know him better."[57]

ON FEBRUARY 24, 1914, succumbing at last to infections of his old war wounds and to pneumonia, eighty-five-year-old Chamberlain died at his home in Portland, a full half century from when a minie ball ripped through his body at Petersburg. Grace was at her father's side at the moment of his death; Wyllys arrived several hours later from Boston.

In Brunswick, the news spread across the Bowdoin campus and in the stores and offices on Maine Street. "Grand Old Hero Is Dead" headlined Portland's *Daily Eastern Argus*.[58] By order of Governor William T. Haines, all American flags flew at half-staff across Maine.

Chamberlain, a man who did not like ostentation, had requested a simple funeral. Grace and Wyllys, however, acquiesced to appeals from their father's friends to hold a large but modest public service under the auspices of MOLLUS and the GAR.

On the morning of February 27, a funeral cortege consisting of a horse-drawn hearse, accompanying carriages, four companies of Maine militia, and Portland's famous Chandler's Band departed from Chamberlain's Ocean Avenue home. Despite the bitterly cold temperatures, multitudes of people with heads bared in respect, lined the snowy route to Portland's city hall.[59]

Two thousand five hundred people filled every seat in the city hall, the largest building in Maine at the time, while hundreds more stood outside. Chamberlain's sword lay atop the old soldier's casket. Ever a lover of music, he had asked to have Ludwig van Beethoven's "Funeral March on the Death of a Hero" and "The Death of Åse" from Norwegian composer Edvard Grieg's *Peer Gynt* suite played at his funeral; they were performed on the auditorium's large organ. Chamberlain's friend, the Rev. Jesse M. Hill, pastor of Portland's Williston Church, offered the funeral sermon. He told the assemblage, "There was a texture to his mind, a color to his soul, a certain quality to his personality that would have made him conspicuous and lovable without the titles and robes of the earth."[60]

At the conclusion of the service, the funeral procession moved to the Union train station to the notes of Chopin's "Funeral March," as more Portland citizens lined the streets to pay their respects.

There, Chamberlain's body was placed upon a special train, which carried it to Brunswick, where all the town's businesses had closed and classes at Bowdoin College canceled. More than a thousand town residents, plus the entire Bowdoin student body, formed a walkway as the casket was carried from the train station to the sanctuary at First Parish.

So much of Chamberlain's life took place within the sanctuary of the old church, with its beautiful oak arches. He both attended and led worship services across the years. He participated in Bowdoin commencements as student, professor, president, and trustee. It was where he met and married Frances Caroline Adams.

Here too, he had chosen the hymns in advance: "Abide with Me" and "Nearer My God to Thee," both nineteenth-century hymns evoking personal faith in life and in death, to be sung by a soloist. A musician also played Chamberlain's favorite instrument, the cello, in a rendition of Handel's solemn "Largo."

Dr. William DeWitt Hyde, who had succeeded Chamberlain as president of Bowdoin College, offered a eulogy to his predecessor as student, professor, soldier, governor, president, and memoirist. He particularly emphasized Chamberlain's role as educator: "He advocated the very reforms, using often the very phrases, which are now the commonplaces of progressive educational discussion. Modern languages, science, classics in translation, political and social sciences, research, individual instruction." Yet, knowing of Chamberlain's disappointment when these reforms were not accepted during his tenure, he declared Chamberlain never "hauled down his flag to the low level of what he or any man could easily do or habitually be."[61]

At the conclusion of the service, a procession formed and started east on the Old Bath Road, the same road the nineteen-year-old Lawrence had traveled from the opposite direction to enroll at Bowdoin College sixty-six years earlier. The procession stopped at the Pine Grove Cemetery, where Joshua Lawrence Chamberlain was buried beside Fanny.

The simple red granite gravestone designed by Chamberlain at the Pine Grove Cemetery

He had designed the three-foot gravestone himself.
The epitaph might easily have included such appellations as

HERO OF LITTLE ROUND TOP
CONGRESSIONAL MEDAL OF HONOR RECIPIENT
GOVERNOR OF MAINE
PRESIDENT OF BOWDOIN COLLEGE

But instead, in death, this simple gravestone bespoke a man comfortable in life and trusting in eternal life.

Epilogue

In every great crisis his idealism not only held him true;
but became a contagious inspiration.

—DR. WILLIAM DEWITT HYDE, PRESIDENT, BOWDOIN COLLEGE, 1914

AFTER CHAMBERLAIN'S DEATH IN 1914, HIS VOICE DID NOT GO silent. He left behind an almost completed manuscript about the final campaigns of the Army of the Potomac in the spring of 1865, already under contract with G. P. Putnam's Sons of New York. Grace and Wyllys finalized the book for publication, and it was released in April 1915. *The Passing of the Armies: An Account of the Final Campaign of the Army of the Potomac, Based upon Personal Reminiscences of the Fifth Army Corps* was the culmination of the writing project Chamberlain had first envisioned when he returned to Brunswick after the Civil War in August 1865.

Chamberlain's last literary hurrah can be appreciated on many levels. He offers riveting historical accounts of the battles in the final days of Grant's overland campaign. It is an opportunity to experience Chamberlain's elegant writing, brimming with classical and biblical allusions and quotations. Although some twenty-first century readers may initially find his writing overly flowery, Chamberlain describes wanting "the literal, the legal, the moral, the figurative, the poetic, the florid, the transcendental" to emerge in his account.[1] Perhaps of greatest interest to contemporary readers, he sets forth a riveting set of final judgments on various Civil War generals. Sheridan: "dark and tense." Warren: "like a caged eagle." Griffin, promoted to lead the Fifth Corps after Warren was summarily dismissed: "alert and independent."[2] Elaborating on Griffin, Chamberlain captures what he perhaps admired most in military leadership: Griffin "took it all modestly; like a soldier and man he was, thinking more of duty and service than of self."[3] Indeed, Chamberlain could have been writing of himself.

In the book's conclusion, Chamberlain quotes the order of June 28, 1865, which declared that the Army of the Potomac "ceases to exist." At this point we can almost hear the old general shout in defiance: "Ceases to exist! Are you sure of that!" He then declares, "This army will live, and live on, so long as soul shall answer soul, so long as that flag watches with its stars over fields of mighty memory, so long as its red lines a regenerated people read the charter of its birthright, and in the field of white God's covenant with man."[4] In this final encomium, at the beginning of the twentieth century, Chamberlain offers his salute to the great generation that fought and won the Civil War.

YET IT WOULD not be long after *The Passing of the Armies* that the memory of Chamberlain was passed by. In 1932, William C. Storrick, superintendent of the guides at Gettysburg, writing in *Gettysburg: The Place, The Battles, The Outcome of Little Round Top*, gave center stage to Gouverneur Warren and Strong Vincent, making no reference to Chamberlain. And in 1954, Frederick Tilberg's *Gettysburg National Military Park, Pennsylvania,* the National Park Service handbook did not mention Chamberlain once in the section titled *Warren Saves Little Round Top.*[5] Outside of Maine, Chamberlain was largely forgotten until his tale reemerged more than a half century later, through the influence of Shaara's novel, Burns's documentary, and Maxwell's movie. In that way, the story of our unlikely hero, Joshua Lawrence Chamberlain, is also a story of America's ever-shifting memory.

Today, Chamberlain's influence can be felt around the country, from Maine to Gettysburg.

At his death, Chamberlain left his house in Brunswick to his daughter Grace. Residing in Boston, she put the house up for rent. With her death in 1937, her daughter, Rosamund Allen, inherited the house. In 1939, she sold it to Emery Booker, a local businessman. He divided the home into seven apartments, which he rented to Bowdoin married students. In 1983, after Booker's death, the Pejepscot Historical Society purchased the home for $75,000. In succeeding years, the house was deconstructed and renovated with the aim of returning it to the way it looked when Joshua, Fanny, and their children lived there and entertained students and guests over the years.[6] Chamberlain would be pleased that today his old house welcomes visitors once more.

In 2003, a bronze statue of Chamberlain was dedicated in Brunswick. (An interesting side fact: Chamberlain is now the leading subject of the major Civil War artists, depicted more frequently than Grant, Sherman, Sheridan, McClellan, and Meade.[7]) Created by Maine sculptor Joseph Query and standing eight feet tall, the statue portrays Chamberlain as a brevet major general in military dress. The statue was funded by a commission of private citizens and donated to the town of Brunswick. The accompanying plaza has an installation focusing on Chamberlain's roles as scholar and statesman. The statue is situated directly across the street from the Chamberlain home, in front of Bowdoin College, and facing the First Congregational Church of which Chamberlain was a devoted member.

At Gettysburg, Chamberlain's legacy is felt today in several ways.

Chamberlain's leadership at Little Round Top has so inspired West Point instructors that they now bring cadets each year on what they call military staff rides—three-day exercises where cadets are asked to play Chamberlain, Vincent, Oates, and other leaders—to learn the lessons of military direction.

The ongoing interest in Chamberlain has continued to make Little Round Top the most visited place at Gettysburg. Starting in 2022, Little Round Top is undergoing the latest and largest of several recent rehabilitations. The goals of the project are to reestablish, preserve, and protect the features that make up the Little Round Top landscape. The project will also improve interpretive signage, and create new accessible trail alignments and gathering areas. These initiatives will allow visitors to better understand Chamberlain and the pivotal one-and-a-half-hour battle at Little Round Top.[8] This is particularly remarkable considering the omission of Chamberlain's heroic actions from William C. Storrick and Frederick Tilberg's Gettysburg guidebooks.

I AM GRATEFUL for the restoration of Chamberlain's story to our collective body of wisdom. A man of unswerving religious and moral conviction, Chamberlain was not a spotless hero. He could be head-strong and susceptible to grand schemes in his tenure as governor and college president. As a risk-taker, he sometimes put himself and the men he commanded in danger. In adhering to a strict code of duty for himself, he sometimes failed to understand the points of view of others who differed from him in their understanding of what duty demanded.

But for me, Chamberlain remains a hero nonetheless, a leader committed to magnanimity in the divided nation of his time. As bitterness rose in the years following the Civil War, Chamberlain worked to foster reconciliation between North and South. Again and again, he stated that he did not support the cause but admired the courage of the Confederate soldiers. Empathy became his lodestone, the prism through which he tried to put himself in the shoes of the defeated Confederate soldiers.

In the great "count out crisis" of 1880, Helen E. Kilham, a leader of the woman's club movement in Massachusetts, characterized Chamberlain's leadership from a broader perspective: "We see it possible for a man to be at once a statesman, a soldier, a scholar, a gentleman and a Christian."[9]

In his old age, Chamberlain recalled the heading frequently printed upon his copy books: "Be virtuous and you will be happy." In his long and varied life, he had come to see that it is no simple task to embrace virtue. In fact, in his memoirs, he lingered on this thought, rewriting the mandate to read, "Be virtuous and you will pass through pain, and suffer evil, but at the end of the grievous passage, you will find the good."[10] Chamberlain self-consciously and deliberately cultivated virtue, in the steadfast belief that he could build a bridge between the American society as it was and America as it could be.

I've come away from Chamberlain's compelling and complex life story believing it to be much more than a nineteenth-century or Civil War tale—at its heart, it poses a question with many possible answers: What makes a hero—what background, what behavior, what beliefs, what circumstances, what records, what outcomes? At the end of this book, I turn that question over to you.

ACKNOWLEDGMENTS

THE IDEA FOR A BIOGRAPHY OF JOSHUA LAWRENCE CHAMBER-
lain began when I was speaking at a "Meet the Author" evening
at the Jonathan Club in downtown Los Angeles in March 2017. During the Q and A portion of the event, a man in the back left corner
of the audience called out: "What is your next biography?"

"I don't know," I replied. "Do you have a suggestion?"

Mark Lipis shouted, "Joshua Lawrence Chamberlain!" Thank
you, Mark.

Every biography is a journey into partially unknown territory.
Joshua Lawrence Chamberlain has been lionized by legions of Civil
War folk in recent decades, but he has also experienced pushback
from some who argue that his recently revived reputation masks
some endemic flaws. I learned quickly that these schools of thought
were also alive in Chamberlain's lifetime. But that only encouraged
me to take a closer look at this courageous, complex, and at times
contradictory American leader.

In July 2017, I began that closer look by traveling 3,097 miles
from Pasadena, California, to Brunswick, Maine, the start of a six-
year journey of discovery.

Bowdoin College president Clayton Rose invited me to breakfast
on my first day in Brunswick. Before the morning was out, he had
written to various members of the college community requesting
that they help me in my endeavors.

Many Bowdoin people did so over the next six years, and I especially wish to thank John Cross, secretary of development and college relations. John, Bowdoin class of 1976, is a remarkable man I
now call my friend. He offered his enormous understanding of
Bowdoin and Chamberlain in countless telephone calls, emails,
and in-person conversations during Brunswick summers.

My research took me to numerous libraries and historical cen-
ters. At Bowdoin College, I spent many hours doing research in the
George J. Mitchell Special Collections and Archives of the

Hawthorne-Longfellow Library. I thank Roberta Swartz and Caroline Mosely for their guidance and assistance.

Another Brunswick jewel is the Pejepscot History Center.

I thank Larissa Vigue Picard, executive director, for graciously providing an accommodating place to do research, offering her counsel, and, when I was back in California, promptly answering all my queries. In July 2021, Larissa sponsored and hosted my first presentation on JLC: "Joshua Lawrence Chamberlain: Pieces of the Puzzle." The PHC also owns the Joshua L. Chamberlain Home and Museum. John Murchie guided in my initial tour of the Chamberlain house.

In attempting to trace Chamberlain's faith journey, I turned early on to his involvement in First Parish Church in Brunswick. I thank Liz Newman, the congregation's historian, and archivist, who opened the Rev. George Adams's diaries for me.

Librarians and archivists at other Maine libraries and historical societies became important persons in my pursuit of Chamberlain.

That initial summer, my first stop beyond Brunswick was Brewer, Maine, where Chamberlain was born and grew up. I am grateful to the late David Hanna, director of the Brewer Historical Society, for orienting me to the role of the Chamberlain family in that community. I also thank Katie Conner, director of the Brewer Public Library, for allowing me to see the Chamberlain family Bible.

Brittany Goetting, then a PhD student at the University of Maine, offered to assist me. She had organized the papers of Brewer's First Congregational Church and later would succeed David Hanna as director of the Brewer Historical Society. She and I also explored the Chamberlain collections at the Raymond H. Fogler Library at the University of Maine in Orono.

It is always a priority for me to search for stories that may have been left out of previous biographies and histories. Chamberlain's three years as a student at Bangor Theological Seminary after graduating from Bowdoin is an important but overlooked story. After one hundred years, the seminary closed its doors in 2013, but fortunately its papers have been preserved at the Brown Research Library of the Maine Historical Society in Portland. Jamie Rice and Tiffany Link aided me in accessing the massive seminary collection.

While on the trail of the seminary, I appreciated telephone calls with the Rev. Bill Imes, who served as president of Bangor Theological Seminary from 2001 to 2008.

At the Maine State Archives in Augusta, I was grateful to archivist Heather Moran.

Beyond Maine, a central place in the contested Chamberlain story proved to be the Appomattox Court House National Historical Park in Virginia. Patrick A. Schroeder, park historian, generously offered his research and insights into the April 1865 surrender at Appomattox.

To understand Chamberlain at Petersburg, historians Jonathan White and Timothy Orr proved to be extremely knowledgeable tour guides on a bright fall day. Thank you, Jon and Tim.

At Gettysburg, military historian Carol Reardon guided me across the battlefield in May 2019 and shared her knowledge of what took place at Little Round Top. John Heiser, National Park Service historian at Gettysburg, offered his counsel as I consulted the extensive Gettysburg records about both the Twentieth Maine and the Fifteenth Alabama, as well as Oates's attempt in the early twentieth century to establish a monument to his Alabama regiment.

In Harrisburg, the National Civil War Museum is a treasure for the Civil War enthusiast. I thank Wayne Motts, president, and Brett Kelley, curator of collections, for their assistance during my visit. I also thank Rich Baker at the U.S. Army Heritage and Education Center at Carlisle, Pennsylvania.

At the Library of Congress, Michelle Krowl, Civil War and reconstruction specialist, once again offered her assistance. I also thank Jeff Flannery, head of the Reference and Readers Services Section in the Manuscript Division.

At the National Archives, Trevor K. Plante, chief of Reference Services, assisted me in working in Chamberlain's army retirement records.

The Schlesinger Library, Radcliffe College, Harvard University, is an important repository of the correspondence between Joshua and Fanny. I thank Diana Carey, research librarian, for her assistance.

Andrea R. Cuccaro at the Citrus County Historical Society in Inverness, Florida, provided information about Chamberlain's Florida adventures in business.

At West Point, Peter Madsen described the staff rides he led at Gettysburg, in which he took battalion officers to walk the battlefield. Each officer was responsible for knowing and playing out what their assigned officer did during the battle at Little Round Top. He wanted his cadets and officers to learn lessons on leadership, decision-making, logistics, intelligence, use of terrain, weapons technology, information flow, courage—and more.

The Chamberlain biography was fortunate to have a cadre of advance readers: Jim McPherson, my Princeton teacher; Gary Gallagher, Civil War historian extraordinaire; the aforementioned John Cross of Bowdoin; Appomattox Court House historian Patrick Schroeder, and Ernesto Cortez, co-president of the Industrial Areas Foundation, who has offered his astute comments on every version of the manuscript. Of course, I assume responsibility for the biography.

In Maine, Bill Quigley and Leslie Cargill offered their friendship and hospitality.

Over these six years I have received encouragement, counsel, and many kindnesses from Richard Wightman Fox, General David Petraeus, Diana Nixon, Nat Read, Madelon Maupin, and Jeff Paule.

Once more I have been privileged to have David Lindroth execute the maps for a biography. Conversations with him always result in maps with just the right detail to enhance the narrative.

Karen Needles, director of the Lincoln Archives Digital Project, has once again proved a talented colleague. She is remarkable in both suggesting and finding photographs, artwork, and cartoons to include alongside my text.

I thank Jon Meacham for recommending Victoria Hinshaw, who joined the Chamberlain project midstream, and provided valuable research assistance.

I am especially indebted to Nancy Macky. A dear friend, she has been a conversation partner once more. She brought an English professor's pen to the content and style of the manuscript. She provided invaluable insight as we sought to understand Fanny by careful reading of her letters.

Mary Evans, my literary agent for more than two decades, is a treasured colleague. I have benefitted from her knowledge of the world of publishing. Her editing eye has been a resource to me now for six books.

I am privileged to serve as Scholar in Residence at the San Marino Community Church. I thank Senior Minister Jessica Vaughn Lower for her invitation to serve this thoughtful, vibrant congregation. At SMCC I am grateful for the support of Rev. Erik Wiebe, Bong Bringas, Skip Ober Miller, and many others.

This is my fifth book with Random House, and I am more impressed than ever with the talented people who work the magic of their publishing process. I wish to particularly thank Andy Ward, Tom Perry, Carlos Beltran, Elizabeth Rendfleisch, Rachel Parker, Greg Kubie, Stasia Whalen, Erica Gonzalez, Windy Dorresteyn, and Michael Hoak. Sheryl Rapée-Adams put the biography through a thorough copyedit. Noa Shapiro has adroitly managed the many stages of Chamberlain.

My profound thanks to my editor at Random House, the remarkable Caitlin McKenna. She inspires me with her abilities and her care for Chamberlain and me. I laughed when Caitlin told me that on a recent vacation, she regaled her friends with Chamberlain stories. In this, our third book together, I instinctively trust her sense of narrative, balance, and tempo.

Finally, my wife, Cynthia, has long learned to live with my living in the nineteenth century. Her love and support, and critical reading, makes what I do meaningful and joyful.

Ron White
Pasadena, California

NOTES

ABBREVIATIONS EMPLOYED IN THE NOTES

AL Abraham Lincoln

BC George J. Mitchell Department of Special Collections and Archives, Hawthorne-Longfellow Library, Bowdoin College, Brunswick, ME

CW Collected Works of Abraham Lincoln

FCA Francis Caroline Adams Chamberlain

FPC First Parish Church, Brunswick, ME

GDC Grace Dupee Chamberlain

GEA Rev. George E. Adams

GNMPL Gettysburg National Military Park Library

JLC Joshua Lawrence Chamberlain

LOC Library of Congress, Gettysburg, PA

MHS Maine Historical Society, Portland, ME

MSA Maine State Archives, Augusta, ME

NA National Archives

OR *War of the Rebellion: A Compilation of the Official Records of the Union and Confederate Armies*

PHC Pejepscot History Center, Brunswick, ME

RC Chamberlain-Adams Collection, Arthur & Elizabeth Schlesinger Library, Radcliffe College, Harvard University, Cambridge, MA

SBC Sarah Brastow Chamberlain [Sae]

SDB Sarah Dupee Brastow Chamberlain

UMO Raymond H. Fogler Library, University of Maine, Orono, ME

USG Ulysses S. Grant

YU Yale University, Manuscripts and Archives Library, New Haven, CT

PROLOGUE: A COURAGEOUS AND CONTROVERSIAL LEADER

1. Michael Shaara, *The Killer Angels* (New York: David McKay Co., 1974); *The Civil War,* the 1990 Ken Burns television documentary miniseries, was broadcast on PBS on five consecutive evenings in September 1990; the 1993 movie *Gettysburg,* about the Battle of Gettysburg, was written and directed by Ronald F. Maxwell. The film was adapted from the historical novel *The Killer Angels*; in 1996, Shaara's son, Jeff, published *Gods and Generals,* the story of events leading up to Gettysburg, in which Chamberlain is again a central character.

ONE: "DO IT! THAT'S HOW!"

1. *"Blessed Boyhood!": The 'Early Memoir' of Joshua Lawrence Chamberlain,* with annotations by Thomas A. Desjardin and David K. Thompson (Brunswick, ME: Bowdoin College,

2011), 42–43. The original typescript of the *Early Memoir* is in the Joshua Lawrence Chamberlain Collection, George J. Mitchell Department of Special Collections & Archives, Bowdoin College Library. The page numbers of the original and the printed versions differ. The page numbers of the printed versions will be used because it can be accessed by readers. Chamberlain wrote his memoir in the early years of the twentieth century. It is undated. He wrote in the third person, a custom used by some writers, including Abraham Lincoln, in his time. For a discussion of possible dating and various publications, see JLC, *Early Memoir*, vi–vii.

2. JLC, *Early Memoir*, 43.

3. I am grateful to the late David Hanna, President of the Brewer Historical Society, who explained these early one-hundred-acre farms and their relation to the river and the town. He also took me to see the Chamberlain home in June 2018; JLC, *Early Memoir*, 7; Richard R. Shaw, *Images of America: Brewer* (Charleston, SC: Arcadia Publishing, 2000), 61; homes in Maine were not numbered until after the Civil War.

4. Chamberlain Family Bible, Brewer Public Library, Brewer, Maine.

5. Andrew Lambert, *The Challenge: Britain Against America in the Naval War of 1812* (London: Faber and Faber, 2012), 168–85; C. S. Forester, *The Naval War of 1812* (London: Michael Joseph, 1957), 141–45; Theodore Roosevelt, *The Naval War of 1812* (New York: G. P. Putnam's Sons, 1901), 182–94. See also Albert Gleaves, *James Lawrence, Captain, United States Navy, Commander of the "Chesapeake"* (New York: G. P. Putnam's Sons, 1904), 177–95.

6. JLC, *Early Memoir*, 5.

7. Willard M. Wallace, *Soul of the Lion: A Biography of General Joshua L. Chamberlain* (New York: T. Nelson, 1960), 17; Michael Golay, *To Gettysburg and Beyond: The Parallel Lives of Joshua Lawrence Chamberlain and Edward Porter Alexander* (Rockville Center, NY: Sarpedon publishers, 1994), 3–4.

8. Alice Rains Trulock, *In the Hands of Providence: Joshua L. Chamberlain & the American Civil War* (Chapel Hill: University of North Carolina Press, 1992), 25.

9. Ronald C. White, *A. Lincoln: A Biography* (New York: Random House, 2009), 8–9.

10. Chamberlain Association of America, *Joshua Lawrence Chamberlain: A Sketch.* N.P. (1906) (reprint, compiled by Brian L. Higgins, Bangor, ME: Bangor Letter Shop, 1995), 1; hereafter, *"JLC: A Sketch."*

11. Wallace, *Soul of the Lion*, 18; for the Huguenots, see Geoffrey Treasure, *The Huguenots* (New Haven, CT: Yale University Press, 2013); Samuel Smiles, *The Huguenots in France after the Revocation of the Edict of Nantes* (New York: Harper & Bros., 1874), especially 94–95, 224–35.

12. Diane Monroe Smith, *Fanny & Joshua: The Enigmatic Lives of Frances Caroline Adams and Joshua Lawrence Chamberlain.* Gettysburg, PA: Thomas Publications, 1999. Smylie, James H., *A Brief History of the Presbyterians* (Louisville, KY: Geneva Press, 1996), 13.

13. JLC, *Early Memoir*, 6.

14. Diana Halderman Loski, in *The Chamberlains of Brewer* (Gettysburg, PA: Thomas Publications, 1998), 1–2.

15. Shaw, *Images of America*, 60.

16. For the story of Bangor, see Trudy Irene Scee, *City on the Penobscot: A Comprehensive History of Bangor, Maine* (Charleston, SC: History Press, 2010).

17. Golay, *To Gettysburg and Beyond*, 7.

18. "Then and Now: The Penobscot River," *Bangor Daily News,* June 27, 2017.

19. The vote was 17,091 to 7,132; the best study of Maine's efforts to become a state is Ronald F. Banks, *Maine Becomes a State: The Movement to Separate Maine from Massachu-*

setts, 1785–1820 (Middletown, CT: Published for the Maine Historical Society by Wesleyan University Press, 1970). See also Charles E. Clark, *Maine: A Bicentennial History* (Nashville, TN: American Association for State and Local History, 1977), 74–78; Louis Clinton Hatch, editor, *Maine: A History* (New York: American Historical Society, 1919), vol. I, 107–43; Robert E. Hall, "Maine's Admission to the Union," *Sprague's Journal of Maine History*, vol. VIII, June 1920, no. 1, 8–14.

20. For the struggle in Congress, see Banks, *Maine Becomes a State*, Chapter 18, "The Missouri Compromise: 'The Mother Has Twins,'" 184–204; Clark, *Maine: A Bicentennial History*, 79–80; for an excellent summary of this debate, see Daniel Walker Howe, *What Hath God Wrought: The Transformation of America, 1815–1848* (New York: Oxford University Press, 2007), 147–63.

21. Banks, *Maine Becomes a State*, 202; Clark, *Maine: A Bicentennial History*, 81; Howe, *What Hath God Wrought*, 150–54.

22. *JLC: A Sketch*, 2.

23. Ibid., 26. See also Calvin Montague Clark, *History of the Congregational Churches in Maine*, vol. 2 (Portland, ME: The Congregational Christian Conference of Maine, 1935), 302–03.

24. *Historical Sketch, First Congregational Church* (Brewer, ME: First Congregational Church, 1928), 10.

25. JLC, *Early Memoir*, 7–8. The Beatitudes, often called the Sermon on the Mount, constituted Jesus's ethical teaching in Matthew 5–7.

26. For the Westminster Assembly, see Robert Letham, *The Westminster Assembly: Reading Its Theology in Historical Context* (Phillipsburg, NJ: P&R Publishing, 2009); John H. Leith, *Assembly at Westminster: Reformed Theology in the Making* (Atlanta, GA: John Knox Press, 1973); Robert S. Paul, *The Assembly of the Lord: Politics and Religion in the Westminster Assembly and the 'Grand Debate'* (Edinburgh, Scotland: T&T Clark, 1985).

27. Westminster Shorter Catechism, *Book of Confessions*, Study Edition, Revised (Louisville, KY: Westminster John Knox Press, 2017), 175.

28. JLC, *Early Memoir*, 8. For an excellent essay on the value of memorization, see Brad Leithauser, "Why We Should Memorize," *The New Yorker*, January 25, 2013.

29. JLC, *Early Memoir*, 8.

30. *Historical Sketch*, 16.

31. JLC, *Early Memoir*, 47; *JLC: A Sketch*, 3.

32. Isaac Watts (1674–1748), recognized as the "father of English hymnody," is credited as the hymn writer of some 750 hymns. Chamberlain calls the edition of hymns he sang as a youth "Watts and Select," which refers to *Hymns and Spiritual Songs*, first published in London in 1707. Samuel Worcester (1770–1821), a Massachusetts Congregational minister, published *Watts's Entire and Select Hymns* in 1818, in which he added hymns composed by others. JLC, *Early Memoir*, 8.

33. *JLC: A Sketch*, 3.

34. JLC, *Early Memoir*, 27.

35. George Hood, *A History of Music in New England, and Biographical Sketches of Reformers and Biographical Sketches of Reformers and Psalmists* (Boston: Wilkins, Carter & Co., 1846), 140–41; Irving Sablosky, *American Music* (Chicago: University of Chicago Press, 1969), 12, 67.

36. JLC, *Early Memoir*, 16.

37. Ibid., 16–17.

38. Ibid., 7, 18–19.

39. Ibid., 7, 21–22.

40. *JLC: A Sketch*, 4.

41. JLC, *Early Memoir*, 30; Trulock, *In the Hands of Providence*, 32.

42. JLC, *Early Memoir*, 23–24.

43. See William E. Campbell, *The Aroostook War of 1839* (Fredericton, New Brunswick: Goose Lane Editions and the New Brunswick Military Heritage Project, 2013), 11; Mark Perry, *Conceived in Liberty: Joshua Chamberlain, William Oates, and the American Civil War* (New York: Viking, 1997), 40.

44. *JLC: A Sketch*, 3–4; John Alfred Coulter II, *Cadets on Campus: History of Military Schools of the United States* (College Station, TX: Texas A & M University Press, 2017), 84.

45. JLC, *Early Memoir*, 26–27.

46. Edward G. Longacre, *Joshua Chamberlain: The Soldier and the Man* (Conshohocken, PA: Combined Publishing, 1999), 18–19.

47. *Historical Sketch*, 12–20.

48. Walter L. Cook, *Bangor Theological Seminary: A Sesquicentennial History* (Orono, ME: University of Maine Press, 1971), 26–27; Calvin Montague Clark, *History of Bangor Theological Seminary* (Boston: Pilgrim Press, 1916), 54–63.

49. Clark, *History of the Congregational Churches in Maine*, vol. 2, 303.

50. JLC, *Early Memoir*, 36.

51. Ibid., 36–37.

52. Ibid., 36–38.

53. Ibid., 39.

54. See Charles C. Calhoun, *A Small College in Maine: Two Hundred Years of Bowdoin* (Brunswick, ME: Bowdoin College, 1993). For older studies, see Nehemiah Cleaveland, edited and completed by Alpheus Spring Packard, *History of Bowdoin College: With Biographical Sketches of Its Graduates, from 1806 to 1879* (Boston: J. R. Osgood & Co., 1882); Louis C. Hatch, *The History of Bowdoin College* (Portland, ME: Lording, Short & Harmon, 1927).

55. *Catalogue of Officers and Students of Bowdoin College, and the Medical School of Maine* (Brunswick, ME: Press of Joseph Griffin, 1847), xix.

56. JLC, *Early Memoir*, 46; Longacre, *Joshua Chamberlain*, 20–21.

57. JLC, *Early Memoir*, 46.

58. Cleaveland, *History of Bowdoin College*, 570.

59. Raphael Kühner, *Grammar of the Greek Language*, translated from the German by B. B. Edwards and S. H. Taylor (Andover, MA: Allen, Morrill and Wardwell, 1844).

60. JLC, *Early Memoir*, 46; Perry, *Conceived in Liberty*, 47.

61. JLC to Sara Shepard, February 8, 1847, UMO.

62. JLC, *Early Memoir*, 47–48; White, *A. Lincoln*, 115–16.

63. JLC, *Early Memoir*, 47.

64. Ibid., 47–48.

TWO: A BOWDOIN MAN

1. Holmes quotation cited in Caroline Winterer, *The Culture of Classicism: Ancient Greece and Rome in American Intellectual Life, 1780–1910* (Baltimore, MD: The Johns Hopkins University Press, 2002), 78.

2. JLC, *Early Memoir*, 49.

3. Ibid.

4. Patricia McGraw Anderson, *The Architecture of Bowdoin College* (Brunswick, ME: Bowdoin College Museum of Art, 1988), 1; Cleaveland, *History of Bowdoin College,* 4–5; Hatch, *The History of Bowdoin College,* 1–5.

5. A brief history of the founding is on the Bowdoin College website, bowdoin.edu under "About: 1794 to the Present." The succeeding James Bowdoins did not use roman numerals after their names; to keep the generations straight, the successive Bowdoins received numerals by historians and by the college. See https://www.bowdoin.edu /about/history-traditions/historical-sketch.html.

6. George Augustus Wheeler and Henry Warren Wheeler, *History of Brunswick, Topsham, and Harpswell, Maine, Including the Ancient Territory Known as Pejepscot* (Boston: Alfred Mudge & Son, 1878), 104–07.

7. *General Catalogue of Bowdoin College and the Medical School of Maine, 1794–1894* (Brunswick, ME: Bowdoin College, 1894), 59–61.

8. Calhoun, *A Small College in Maine,* 113–17. The medical school closed its doors in 1921.

9. JLC, *Early Memoir,* 52.

10. Anderson, *The Architecture of Bowdoin College,* 17–18.

11. *Catalogue of Bowdoin College and the Medical School of Maine,* Spring Term, 1849 (Brunswick, ME: Press of Joseph Griffin, 1849), ix–xx.

12. Carl J. Richard, *The Founders and the Classics: Greece, Rome, and the American Enlightenment* (Cambridge, MA: Harvard University Press, 1994); for the study of the importance of classicism in American colleges, see Caroline Winterer, *The Culture of Classicism: Ancient Greece and Rome in American Intellectual Life, 1780–1910* (Baltimore: Johns Hopkins University Press, 2002).

13. Winterer, *The Culture of Classicism,* 78–79.

14. Ibid., 69, 81. Felton served as both professor and president at Harvard.

15. Calhoun, *A Small College in Maine,* 101–05.

16. Hatch, *The History of Bowdoin College,* 53–57.

17. Thompson Eldridge Ashby, *A History of the First Parish Church in Brunswick, Maine,* edited by Louise R. Helmreich (Brunswick, ME: J. H. French and Son, 1969), 303–05.

18. Ibid., 302–03.

19. Newman Smyth, *Recollections and Reflections* (New York: Charles Scribner's Sons, 1926), 43. For the attempt in 1835 to remove Smyth as a professor at Bowdoin because of his radicalism on the slavery question, see James Plaisted Webber, "An Inquisition of 1835," in *Tales of Bowdoin* (Augusta, ME: Press of Kennebec Journal, 1901), 275–78.

20. Golay, *To Gettysburg and Beyond,* 34. William Smyth's son, Newman, recalled that his father and Upham thought "that so great a wrong as slavery could not be settled without the shedding of blood." Smyth, *Recollections and Reflections,* 10.

21. Thomas Cogswell Upham, *Principles of the Interior or Hidden Life* (Boston: D. S. King, 1843).

22. Ibid., 117, 224, 332.

23. JLC, *Early Memoir,* 57.

24. Ibid., 57–58.

25. *Laws of Bowdoin College* (Brunswick, ME: Press of Joseph Griffin, 1844), 18.

26. Ernst Christian Helmreich, *Religion at Bowdoin College: A History* (Brunswick, ME: Bowdoin College, 1981), 39.

27. Visiting Committee, 1845–1850, Report of 1847, 20, cited by Helmreich, *Religion at Bowdoin College,* 37, 174, footnote 11.

28. Calhoun, *A Small College in Maine,* 124–25.

29. Ibid., 125.

30. JLC, *Early Memoir,* 51.

31. Ibid., 51–52.

32. Oliver O. Howard, who entered Bowdoin two years before Chamberlain, describes the religious life at the college in great detail. O. O. Howard, *Autobiography of Oliver Otis Howard, Major-General, United States Army* (New York: Baker & Taylor, 1907), vol. 1, 31.

33. Ashby, *A History of the First Parish Church,* 93–94.

34. Ibid., 203–207. Professor William Smyth chaired the building committee that supervised the construction.

35. Ibid., 184–87.

36. Ibid., 156–57.

37. Wheeler and Wheeler, *History of Brunswick, Topsham, and Harpswell, Maine,* 711–12.

38. Ashby, *A History of the First Parish Church,* 271.

39. JLC, *Early Memoir,* 61.

40. Cyrus Hamlin, *My Life and Times* (Boston: Congregational Sunday School and Publishing Society, 1893), 97.

41. Helmreich, *Religion at Bowdoin College,* 51–54. The society did not elect its president, but rather awarded the position to the student with the highest academic record.

42. Ibid., 54.

43. JLC to "My Dear Pastor" (Rev. Stephen Thurston), May 5, 1848, Bowdoin College.

44. Upham, *Principles of the Interior or Hidden Life,* 14.

45. Ibid., 15, 18.

46. JLC, *Early Memoir,* 55.

47. JLC to "My Dear Pastor," May 5, 1848, BC.

48. Trulock, *In the Hands of Providence,* 39.

49. JLC, *Early Memoir,* 52.

50. *Catalogue of Bowdoin College and the Medical School of Maine,* 1849, xx.

51. Calhoun, *A Small College in Maine.*

52. Cleaveland, *History of Bowdoin College,* 431. Later, Goodwin would also study for the Episcopal ministry.

53. JLC, *Early Memoir,* 59.

54. Ibid., 60.

55. Ibid.

56. For a discussion of the origin and growth of the Peucinian Society, see Hatch, *The History of Bowdoin College,* 304–11.

57. Calhoun, *A Small College in Maine,* 105–06.

58. George Thomas Little, "Historical Sketch," *General Catalogue of Bowdoin College, 1794–1894,* lxxxviii.

59. JLC, *Early Memoir,* 59; Golay, *To Gettysburg and Beyond,* 32.

60. Golay, *To Gettysburg and Beyond,* 28; Trulock, *In the Hands of Providence,* 39.

61. JLC, *Early Memoir,* 55.

62. Ibid., 55–56.

63. A popular eighteenth and nineteenth century word, "scruple" has fallen out of popular use. Congregational and Presbyterian ministers employed it as a verb. They would "scruple" certain portions of the Westminster Confession of Faith about which they had questions or problems.

64. JLC, *Early Memoir,* 56–57.

65. Ibid., 52.

THREE: "BE VIRTUOUS"

1. JLC, *Early Memoir,* 61–62.

2. Golay, *To Gettysburg and Beyond,* 54–55.

3. JLC, *Early Memoir,* 62.

4. For Clay, see Robert V. Remini, *Henry Clay: Statesman for the Union* (New York: W. W. Norton and Company, 1991), 730–33; For a description of the debate, see Fergus M. Bordewich, *America's Great Debate: Henry C. Clay, Stephen A. Douglas, and the Compromise That Preserved the Union* (New York: Simon & Schuster, 2013).

5. Remini, *Henry Clay,* 737; Bordewich, *America's Great Debate,* 141–42, 225–26, 257, 286.

6. Bordewich, *America's Great Debate,* 320, 323.

7. *The Liberator* 1 (January 1, 1831); Daniel Walker Howe, *What Hath God Wrought: The Transformation of America, 1815–1848* (New York: Oxford University Press, 2007), 425.

8. Edward O. Schriver, *Go Free: The Antislavery Impulse in Maine, 1833–1855* (Orono, ME: University of Maine Press, 1970), 4–5.

9. The presidential election results in Maine:
       1832: Andrew Jackson (Democrat) 54.7%; Henry Clay (National Republican) 44.0%
       1836: Martin Van Buren (Democrat) 58.9%; William Henry Harrison (Whig) 38.2%
       The lone exception, barely, was 1840: William Henry Harrison (Whig) 50.23%; Martin Van Buren (Democrat) 49.8%
       1844: James K. Polk (Democrat) 53.8%; Henry Clay (Whig) 40.5%; James Gillespie Birney (Liberty) 5.7%
       1848: Lewis Cass (Democrat) 45.9%; Zachary Taylor (Whig) 40.3%; John P. Hale (Free Soil) 9.8%. By contrast, the results in Massachusetts in 1848: Lewis Cass (Democrat) 26.2%; Zachary Taylor (Whig) 45.3%
       The American Presidency Project at presidency.ucsb.edu.

10. Golay, *To Gettysburg and Beyond,* 39.

11. The Minutes of the General Conference of Maine, 1850, Appendix (Portland, ME: William H. Cushing, 1850). The smaller number of Methodists in Maine also struggled to act, again over fear of alienating their Southern members. The Methodists split over the issue in 1844, with the Methodist Episcopal Church, South, organized in 1845. Maine Baptists, with a little more enthusiasm, organized the Maine Baptist Antislavery Convention in 1840. By 1845 the Baptists also split, with Southerners organizing the Southern Baptist Convention. Schriver, *Go Free,* 80–86.

12. Oliver O. Howard to his mother, November 19, 1851, quoted in William S. McFeely, *Yankee Stepfather: General O. O. Howard and the Freedmen* (New Haven, CT: Yale University Press, 1968), 29.

13. Joan D. Hedrick, *Harriet Beecher Stowe: A Life* (New York: Oxford University Press, 1994), 194. At that time the street was called Back Street.

14. Harriet Beecher Stowe, *The May Flower, and Miscellaneous Writings* (Boston: Phillips, Sampson, 1843).

15. Stowe, "Frankness," *The May Flower,* 122; Hedrick, *Harriet Beecher Stowe,* 141–42, is insightful in analyzing Stowe's writings.

16. Bordewich, *America's Great Debate,* 361–67.

17. Hedrick, *Harriet Beecher Stowe,* 205–06.

18. Ibid., 206.

19. Nancy Koester reminds us that during her lifetime Stowe offered different versions of when she began writing *Uncle Tom's Cabin.* See Koester, *Harriet Beecher Stowe: A Spiritual Life* (Grand Rapids, MI: William B. Eerdmans Publishing Company, 2014), 113–14.

20. Koester, *Harriet Beecher Stowe,* 108–109. Harriet first met Bailey in Cincinnati during the volatile Lane Seminary debates over slavery when Stowe's father, Lyman, was president of the seminary.

21. Harriet Beecher Stowe to Gamaliel Bailey, March 9, 1851, cited in Hedrick, *Harriet Beecher Stowe,* 208.

22. JLC, *Early Memoir,* 65.

23. Hedrick, *Harriet Beecher Stowe,* 208, 223.

24. JLC, *Early Memoir,* 63. The story of Jacob marrying Leah and Rachel is in Genesis 29.

25. *Catalogue of Bowdoin College and the Medical School of Maine,* Spring Term, 1849 (Brunswick, ME: Press of Joseph Griffin, 1849), xxi.

26. JLC, *Early Memoir,* 63.

27. Ibid.

28. Ibid., 67.

29. Ibid., 59.

30. Wallace, *Soul of the Lion,* 22.

31. JLC, *Early Memoir,* 63.

32. Ibid., 67.

33. Trulock, *In the Hands of Providence,* 46.

34. Nathaniel Hawthorne, *The House of the Seven Gables: A Romance* (Boston: Ticknor, Reed, and Fields, 1851). Chamberlain, in his *Early Memoir,* remembered that he read Hawthorne's novel at the end of his sophomore year, but since it was not published until 1851, he would have read it during his junior year.

35. George Gordon Byron, "The Prisoner of Chillon," stanza 10, Perry, *Conceived in Liberty,* 45, 355.

36. JLC essay, "The Monomaniac," September 11, 1849, in *Joshua L. Chamberlain: A Life in Letters,* edited by Thomas Desjardin (Oxford, U.K.: Osprey Publishing, 2012), 11–12.

37. "Easter Morning," n.d., in Desjardin, *Joshua L. Chamberlain: A Life in Letters,* 16.

38. *Catalogue of Bowdoin College and the Medical School of Maine,* Spring Term, 1849, xxi.

39. JLC, *Early Memoir,* 54. JLC, copybook, BC.

40. George M. Marsden, *Jonathan Edwards: A Life* (New Haven, CT: Yale University Press, 2003), 78.

41. Ibid., 464–71; Edwards died in 1758. *The Nature of True Virtue* was published in 1765.

42. JLC, *Early Memoir,* 58.

43. Of the contemporary witnesses to Chamberlain's speech, Rev. Adams confided to his

diary, "Chamberlain did well, but his memory failed at the end." GEA, diary, September 1, 1852.

44. JLC, *Early Memoir,* 67–68; Golay, *To Gettysburg and Beyond,* 37; Trulock, *In the Hands of Providence,* 47.

FOUR: FANNY

1. D. M. Smith, *Fanny & Joshua,* 2–4; Jennifer Lund Smith, "The Reconstruction of 'Home': The Civil War and the Marriage of Lawrence and Fannie Chamberlain," *Intimate Strategies of the Civil War: Military Commanders and Their Wives,* edited by Carol K. Bleser and Lesley J. Gordon (New York: Oxford University Press, 2001), observes, "Fannie grew up in a gray area between two families, not feeling clearly a part of either," 57.

2. D. M. Smith, *Fanny & Joshua,* 3.

3. J. L. Smith, "The Reconstruction of 'Home,'" 159; Trulock, *In the Hands of Providence,* 50.

4. FCA to {Mr. Pike}, June 8, 1843, RC; D. M. Smith, *Fanny & Joshua,* 6.

5. Wallace, *Soul of the Lion,* 26; Trulock, *In the Hands of Providence,* 44; Longacre, *Joshua Chamberlain,* 28; Perry, *Conceived in Liberty,* 70–71.

6. Deborah Folsom to FCA, February 17, 1853, MHS.

7. Annette Blaugrund, "The Evolution of American Artists' Studios, 1740–1860," *The Magazine Antiques* (January 1992): 214–25, describes the transmission and development of painting rooms from England to America. D. M. Smith, *Fanny & Joshua,* 2. The Kennebec and Portland Railroad completed its line from Brunswick to Portland in 1847.

8. George Thornton Edwards, *Music and Musicians of Maine* (Portland, ME: The Southworth Press, 1928), 82–86.

9. Richard A. Easterlin, George Alter, and Gretchen A. Condran, "Farms and Farm Families in Old and New Areas: The Northern States in 1860," in *Family and Population in Nineteenth-Century America,* edited by Tamara K. Hareven and Maris A. Vinovskis (Princeton, NJ: Princeton University Press, 1978), 40. This study focused on farm families.

10. D. M. Smith, in *Fanny & Joshua,* is insightful in exploring the early romance of Lawrence and Fanny. See 20–25.

11. JLC to FCA, n.d. (early 1851), RC.

12. D. M. Smith, *Fanny & Joshua,* 25–26.

13. Peter Tufts Richardson, *Universalists and Unitarians of Maine: A Comprehensive History* (Rockland, ME: Red Barn Publishing, 2017), 97–100, 577.

14. FCA to JLC, June 14, 1851, RC.

15. Ibid.

16. FCA to JLC, n.d. (Summer 1851), RC.

17. Upon his return from Chicago, Adams wrote, "Returned from Chicago. Absent 9 weeks this Morning. My longest absence since I kept house." GEA, diary, August 12, 1851, FPC.

18. D. M. Smith, *Fanny & Joshua,* 22–23; J. L. Smith, "The Reconstruction of 'Home,'" 160–61.

19. Trulock, *In the Hands of Providence,* 45; D. M. Smith, *Fanny & Joshua,* 23.

20. JLC to FCA, December 30, 1851, RC.

21. Ibid.

22. FCA to JLC, January 1, 1852, RC.

23. Ibid.

24. Stephen Allen to FCA, January 8, 1852, RC. Allen attended Harvard Law School, receiving an LLB in 1846. *The New England Historical and Genealogical Register* (Boston: New England Historic Genealogical Society, 1894 XLVIII), 472–73.

25. JLC to FCA, May 21, 1852, RC; D. M. Smith, *Fanny & Joshua,* 24–25.

26. GEA, diary, March 29, 1852, FPC.

27. D. M. Smith, *Fanny & Joshua,* 24–25, 29.

28. JLC to FCA, June 7, 1852, MHS; Trulock, *In the Hands of Providence,* 54.

29. Rev. Adams, diary, March 13, 1852, FPC.

30. See George F. Root, *The Story of a Musical Life: An Autobiography* (Cincinnati: The John Church Co., 1891).

31. JLC to FCA, May 16, 1852, RC.

32. JLC to FCA, May 17, 1852, RC.

FIVE: BANGOR THEOLOGICAL SEMINARY

1. Walter L. Cook, *Bangor Theological Seminary: A Sesquicentennial History* (Orono, ME: University of Maine Press, 1971), 3, 9, 11–13; Clark, *History of Bangor Theological Seminary,* 9–13, 21; Scee, *City on the Penobscot: A Comprehensive History of Bangor, Maine,* 43, 170. The land was donated by Isaac Davenport.

2. The first professional school of medicine was established in 1765 by the College of Philadelphia; the first professional study of law was established at William and Mary College in 1779; for the establishment of theological seminaries, see Lefferts A. Loetscher's chapter "Ministers as Professionals," 139–49, in *Facing the Enlightenment and Pietism: Archibald Alexander and the Founding of Princeton Theological Seminary* (Westport, CT: Greenwood Press, 1983).

3. William Warren Sweet, "The Rise of Theological Schools in America," *Church History,* 6, no. 3 (September 1937): 261; Williston Walker, *A History of the Congregational Churches in the United States* (New York: Christian Literature Company, 1894), 299–300.

4. Daniel Walker Howe, *The Unitarian Conscience: Harvard Moral Philosophy, 1895–1861* (Cambridge, MA: Harvard University Press, 1970), 4–5.

5. Leonard Woods, *History of the Andover Theological Seminary* (Boston: James R. Osgood and Co., 1885), 485–86.

6. Ibid., 27; James W. Fraser, *Schooling the Preachers: The Development of Protestant Theological Education in the United States, 1740–1875* (Lanham, MD: University Press of America, 1988), 31.

7. Sweet, "The Rise of Theological Schools in America," 266. See also Henry K. Rowe, *History of Andover Theological Seminary* (Boston: Thomas Todd Company, 1933), 1–22, and John H. Giltner, "The Fragmentation of New England Congregationalism and the Founding of Andover Seminary," *Journal of Religious Thought* 20, no. 1 (2008): 27–42.

8. Rowe, *History of Andover Theological Seminary,* 12, 20.

9. *Catalogue of the Theological Seminary* (Bangor, ME: Samuel S. Smith, 1853), 9.

10. Ibid., 7.

11. Trulock, *In the Hands of Providence,* 51.

12. Charlotte Amelia Adams to FCA, September 10, 1852, RC.

13. D. M. Smith, *Fanny & Joshua*, 33.

14. FCA to JLC, October 10, 1852, Desjardin, *Joshua L. Chamberlain: A Life in Letters*, 57–58.

15. FCA to JLC, October 24, 1852, *Joshua L. Chamberlain: A Life in Letters*, 60.

16. James C. Bonner, *Milledgeville: Georgia's Antebellum Capital* (Athens, GA: University of Georgia Press, 1978), 17–21.

17. D. M. Smith, *Fanny & Joshua*, 33.

18. GEA, diary, December 22, 1852, FPC.

19. FCA to Charlotte Adams, January 10, 1853, MSH; J. L. Smith, "The Reconstruction of 'Home,'" 162; James C. Bonner, *Milledgeville*, 41.

20. Trulock, *In the Hands of Providence*, 48.

21. When the cornerstone for a new church building was laid in 1904 the name of the church was changed to the First Presbyterian Church of Milledgeville.

22. *Catalogue of the Theological Seminary*, Bangor, 1854, 4, Bangor Theological Collection, MHS.

23. Enoch Pond, *The Autobiography of the Rev. Enoch Pond* (Boston: Congregational Sunday-School and Publishing Society, 1883), 71–72.

24. JLC, *Early Memoir*, 69.

25. Enoch Pond, *The Mather Family* (Boston: Massachusetts Sabbath Society, 1844), v.

26. JLC, class notes from Professor Enoch Pond's Bangor Seminary Theology class, UMO.

27. Clark, *History of Bangor Theological Seminary: 1816–1916*, 141, 155–56, 164–65.

28. Ibid., 156.

29. JLC to FCA, no date (probably autumn 1852), MHS.

30. JLC to FCA (January 1853), RC.

31. Ibid.

32. JLC, *Early Memoir*, 68–69.

33. Ibid., 69; *JLC: A Sketch*, 10.

34. *JLC: A Sketch*, 8.

35. Cook, *Bangor Theological Seminary*, 26–27; D. M. Smith, *Fanny & Joshua*, 14, 16, 17.

36. For contrasting views of the evangelical voluntary societies, published in the same year, see Charles I. Foster, *An Errand of Mercy: The Evangelical United Front, 1790–1837* (Chapel Hill: University of North Carolina Press, 1960), and Clifford S. Griffin, *Their Brothers' Keepers: Moral Stewardship in the United States, 1800–1865* (New Brunswick, NJ: Rutgers University Press, 1960).

37. GEA, diary, September 24, 1848, FPC. There are regular comments about the various voluntary societies in the Adams diaries.

38. Ibid., September 12, 1848.

39. Minutes, Records of Society of Missionary Inquiry, June 27, 1853, Bangor Theological Seminary Collection, MHS.

40. General Correspondence, Society of Missionary Inquiry, Bangor Theological Seminary Collection, MHS.

41. Rhetorical Society, Order of Exercises, August 29, 1853, Bangor Theological Seminary Collection, MHS.

42. GEA, diary, February 21, 1853, FPC.

43. Ibid., February 22, 1853.

44. JLC to FCA, June 3, 1853, RC.

45. FCAto JLC, June 23, 1853, RC.

46. JLC to FCA fragment, undated (June, 1853), RC.

47. JLC to FCA, August 19, 1853, Desjardin, *Joshua L. Chamberlain: A Life in Letters*, 86–87.

48. FCA to JLC, June 23, 1853, RC.

49. JLC to FCA, March 14, 1854, RC.

50. Ibid.

51. JLC, *Early Memoir*, 69.

52. Historical Catalogue Inquiry Form, Bangor Theological Seminary Collection, MHS.

53. JLC, *Early Memoir*, 69–70.

54. On August 11, Fanny's adoptive father wrote, "Called on Fanny." GEA, diary, August 11, 1855, FPC.

55. JLC, *Early Memoir*, 70.

56. Ibid.

57. Ibid.

58. Joseph P. Thompson was also well known as the minister of the Broadway Tabenacle in New York.

SIX: " 'GETTING AT' THE STUDENT'S MIND (& HEART)"

1. JLC, *Early Memoir*, 70; JLC, *A Sketch*, 11; Trulock, *In the Hands of Providence*, 52.

2. GEA to JLC, n.d. (late summer), BC.

3. D. M. Smith, *Fanny & Joshua*, 44, 69, 73; Trulock, *In the Hands of Providence*, 44.

4. SDC to JLC, October 8, 1855, RC.

5. For the large place of Sunday schools in the nineteenth century, see Anne M. Boylan, *Sunday School: The Formation of an American Institution, 1790–1880* (New Haven, CT: Yale University Press, 1988).

6. Sabbath students to JLC, November 19, 1855, BC.

7. JLC, *Early Memoir*, 70–71; Trulock, *In the Hands of Providence*, 53–54; D. M. Smith, *Fanny & Joshua*, 78.

8. GEA diary, November 29–December 7, FPC.

9. D. M. Smith, *Fanny & Joshua*, 80.

10. SDB, October 8, 1855, RC.

11. Golay, *To Gettysburg and Beyond*, 53.

12. Charles Chesley to JLC, March 27, 1856, Desjardin, *Joshua L. Chamberlain: A Life in Letters*, 135–36.

13. Edwin Beamon to JLC, May 13, 1856, *Joshua L. Chamberlain: A Life in Letters*, 137–38.

14. Edward Cutter to JLC, February 18, 1856, RC.

15. Aristotle's *Treatise on Rhetoric*, translated by Theodore Buckley (London, 1857), Chapter II, 11. See also Charles Sears Baldwin, *Ancient Rhetoric and Poetic* (New York, 1924), 6–36.

16. For a summary of books on rhetoric used at this time, see Albert R. Kitzhaber, *Rhetoric in American Colleges, 1850–1900* (Dallas, TX: Southern Methodist University Press, 1990), 49–73.

17. James A. Berlin, *Writing Instruction in Nineteenth-Century American Colleges* (Carbondale: Southern Illinois University Press, 1984), 7–9.

18. Kitzhaber, *Rhetoric in American Colleges*, 55.

19. Ibid., 9. Campbell, a Scottish Calvinist, minister of the Church of Scotland, a product of the eighteenth-century Scottish Enlightenment, was a professor of divinity at Marischal College in Aberdeen. Blair was a minister of the Church of Scotland (Presbyterian) and occupied the chair of rhetoric at the University of Edinburgh. Whately, an English theologian, taught rhetoric at Trinity College, Oxford.

20. JLC, *Memoirs*, 74; Hatch, *The History of Bowdoin College*, 106–07.

21. JLC, *Early Memoir*, 64.

22. JLC to Nehemiah Cleaveland, October 14, 1859, BC.

23. Ibid.

24. Ibid.

25. GEA, diary, October 17, 1856, FPC.

26. GEA to JLC, October 21, 1856, Desjardin, *Joshua L. Chamberlain: A Life in Letters*, 140.

27. JLC, *Early Memoir*, 72; Trulock, *In the Hands of Providence*, 54; D. M. Smith, *Fanny & Joshua*, 81–82.

28. D. M. Smith, *Fanny & Joshua*, 86.

29. JLC to FCA, January 26, 1857, RC.

30. JLC to FCA, May 27, 1857, MHS.

31. JLC, *Early Memoir*, 72, Trulock, *In the Hands of Providence*, 20, 54; D. M. Smith, *Fanny & Joshua*, 81–82.

32. JLC to FCA, May 20, 1857, MHS.

33. D. M. Smith, *Fanny & Joshua*, 91.

34. On transcendentalism and religion, see Philip F. Gura, *American Transcendentalism: A History* (New York: Hill and Wang, 2007).

35. Smyth, *Recollections and Reflections*, 74.

36. D. M. Smith, *Fanny & Joshua*, 85; Golay, *To Gettysburg and Beyond*, 55.

37. Hatch, *The History of Bowdoin College*, 107.

38. JLC, *Early Memoir*, 73; Golay, *To Gettysburg and Beyond*, 53.

39. *Portland Transcript*, August 14, 1858.

40. Calhoun, *A Small College in Maine*, 166; Perry, *Conceived in Liberty*, 87–88; Golay, *To Gettysburg and Beyond*, 57; Trulock, *In the Hands of Providence*, 4, 400, note 14.

41. For the views of Southern contemporaries, see James M. McPherson, *Embattled Rebel: Jefferson Davis as Commander in Chief* (New York: The Penguin Press, 2014), 5–7.

42. Jefferson Davis, "Speech at the Portland Serenade," *Speeches of the Hon. Jefferson Davis, of Mississippi, Delivered During the Summer of 1858* (Baltimore: n.p., 1859), 12, 16.

43. Perry, *Conceived in Liberty*, 88; Golay, *To Gettysburg and Beyond*, 57.

44. William C. Davis, *Jefferson Davis: The Man and His Hour* (New York: HarperCollins, 1991), 263.

45. William J. Cooper, Jr., *Jefferson Davis, American* (New York: Alfred A. Knopf, 1991), 291–92.

46. *Portland Advertiser*, August 5, 1858; Caroline E. Vose, "When Bowdoin College Conferred the LL.D. Degree on Jefferson Davis" (originally published in *Lewiston Journal Illustrated Magazine*, April 18, 1925), *A Distant War Comes Home: Maine in the Civil War Era*, edited by Donald W. Beattie, Rodney M. Cole, Charles G. Waugh (Camden, ME: Down East Books, 1991), 33.

47. Vose, "When Bowdoin College Conferred the LL.D. Degree on Jefferson Davis," 34.

48. Ibid.

49. *Charleston Mercury,* July 30, 1858; *New Orleans Daily Delta,* July 31, 1858, cited in Davis, *Jefferson Davis: The Man and His Hour,* 266.

50. *New Orleans Daily Delta,* July 31, 1858. For more on Southern newspaper responses, see also Cooper, *Jefferson Davis, American,* 293.

51. D. M. Smith, *Fanny & Joshua,* 96.

52. Horace Chamberlain to JLC, July 7, 1858, RC.

53. Horace Chamberlain to JLC, May 9, July 7, August 1858, RC; Trulock, *In the Hands of Providence,* 56.

54. D. M. Smith, *Fanny & Joshua,* 91–92.

55. Graph of child mortality rate (under five years old) in the United States, from 1800 to 2020, statista.com/statistics/1041693/united-states-all-time-child-mortality-rate/.

56. Trulock, *In the Hands of Providence,* 20.

57. Allan M. Levinsky, *At Home with the General: A Visit to the Joshua L. Chamberlain Museum* (Gettysburg, PA: Thomas Publications, 2001), 5, 12; Golay, *To Gettysburg and Beyond,* 54–55.

58. JLC, *Personal Memoir,* 73–74; Wheeler and Wheeler, *History of Brunswick, Topsham, and Harpswell, Maine,* 715–16.

59. D. M. Smith, *Fanny & Joshua,* 83.

60. Perry, *Conceived in Liberty,* 100.

61. Golay, *To Gettysburg and Beyond,* 56.

62. Perry, *Conceived in Liberty,* 100.

63. FCA to JLC, January 1859, RC; JLC, *Memoir,* 74.

64. JLC to FCA, n.d. (late January), RC.

65. JLC to FCA, February 2, 1859, RC.

66. en.wikipedia.org/wiki/1860_United_States_presidential_election_in_Maine.

67. GEA, diary, November 6 and 7, 1860, FPC.

68. Ibid., December 11, 1860.

SEVEN: "DUTY CALLED ME"

1. JLC to Fanny, April 22, 1861, RC.

2. John Furbish, *"Darkness Is Over Our Land . . .": Civil War Perspectives from the Journals of John Furbish,* edited by Judith Kenoyer Stoy (Brunswick, ME: Pejepscot Historical Society, 2018), April 13, 17. There are no page numbers in his journal.

3. Ibid., April 26, 1861.

4. Calhoun, *A Small College in Maine,* 171.

5. Charles A. Curtis, "Bowdoin Under Fire," in *Tales of Bowdoin,* edited by John Clair Minot and Donald Francis Snow (Augusta, ME: Press of Kennebec Journal, 1901), 262. For more on Curtis, see *Obituary Record of the Graduates of Bowdoin College and the Medical School of Maine for the Decade Ending 1 June 1909* (Brunswick, ME: Bowdoin College Library, 1911), 399–400.

6. Curtis, "Bowdoin Under Fire," 268.

7. Ibid., 266.

8. Ibid., 266–68.

9. Ibid., 269.

10. John A. Carpenter, *Sword and Olive Branch: Oliver Otis Howard* (New York: Fordham University Press, 1999), 18; William S. McFeeley, *Yankee Stepfather: General O. O. Howard and the Freedmen* (New Haven, CT: Yale University Press, 1968), 33.

11. Oliver Otis Howard, *Autobiography of Oliver Otis Howard*, vol. 1 (New York: Baker & Taylor, 1907), 123–24.

12. My thanks to John Cross of Bowdoin College for supplying records of all the Bowdoin students who served in the Civil War.

13. Bowdoin *Bugle*, July 1861. The *Bugle* began in 1858.

14. JLC to Nehemiah Cleaveland, October 14, 1859, RC.

15. Walter S. Poor to JLC, October 13, 1861, LOC.

16. Golay, *To Gettysburg and Beyond*, 60.

17. Ibid., 61.

18. JLC to SBC, February 4, 1861, BC.

19. JLC, "Notes of my little speeches & doings which led to my going into the army in the war 1862," BC.

20. For the Peninsula Campaign, see Stephen W. Sears, *To the Gates of Richmond: The Peninsula Campaign* (New York: Ticknor and Fields, 1992); Gary W. Gallagher, editor, *The Richmond Campaign of 1862: The Peninsula and the Seven Days* (Chapel Hill: University of North Carolina Press, 2008).

21. Allen C. Guelzo, *Robert E. Lee: A Life* (New York: Knopf, 2021), 229–36; James M. McPherson, *Battle Cry of Freedom: The Civil War Era* (New York: Oxford University Press, 1988), 461–71.

22. JLC to Governor Israel Washburn, Jr., July 4, 1862, MSA; Trulock, *In the Hands of Providence*, 7.

23. James M. McPherson, *For Cause and Comrades: Why Men Fought in the Civil War* (New York: Oxford University Press, 1997), viii.

24. JLC to Governor Israel Washburn, July 14, 1862, MSA.

25. For descriptions of Washburn's physical appearance and personality, see Howard, *Autobiography of Oliver Otis Howard*, 114, 117; Hatch, *Maine*, 425ff.

26. *JLC: A Sketch*, 12.

27. "War Meeting at Brunswick," *Portland Daily Advertiser*, July 19, 1862.

28. Ibid.

29. Ibid.

30. Catherine T. Smith interview, "Brunswick's 'Soldier Statesman,'" *Brunswick Times Record*, September 7, 1976; Trulock, *In the Hands of Providence*, 8–9. For more on Catherine Zell Smith, see D. M. Smith, *Fanny & Joshua*, 364–65, note 17.

31. *Bangor Daily Whig and Courier*, July 22 and 23, 1862.

32. *Portland Daily Press*, July 21, 1862.

33. JLC to Governor Israel Washburn, July 22, 1861, MSA.

34. *Portland Daily Press*, July 21, 22, 1862.

35. Records of the Executive Government, Bowdoin College, 1862, BC; JLC, *Early Memoir*, 76–77.

36. Attorney General Josiah Drummond to Governor Israel Washburn, July 22, 1862, MSA.

37. Ibid.

38. John D. Lincoln to Governor Israel Washburn, July 17, 1862, MSA.

39. Governor Israel Washburn to JLC, August 8, 1862, LOC; JLC to Governor Israel Washburn, August 8, 1862, MSA.

40. Furbish, *"Darkness Is Over Our Land . . ."* August 14, 1862.

EIGHT: THE TWENTIETH MAINE

1. Harriet Beecher Stowe to Georgiana May (1833), *Life and Letters of Harriet Beecher Stowe,* edited by Annie Fields (Boston: Houghton, Mifflin, and Co., 1898), 72–73.

2. Walter Holden, William E. Ross, Elizabeth Slomba, *Stand Firm and Fire Low: The Civil War Writings of Colonel Edward E. Cross* (Hanover, NH: University Press of New England, 2002), 1–4.

3. Ibid.

4. Ibid., 51; Allen C. Guelzo, *Gettysburg: The Last Invasion* (New York: Alfred A. Knopf, 2013), 38.

5. Thomas A. Desjardin, *Stand Firm Ye Boys from Maine: The 20th Maine and the Gettysburg Campaign* (New York: Oxford University Press, 1995), 169–180, provides a "Roster of 20th Maine Soldiers at Gettysburg" that lists both the "Residence" and the "Occupation" of the five hundred members at the time of Gettysburg. Desjardin indicates that he has assembled his information from several sources, but chiefly from the *Annual Reports of the Adjutant General of Maine, 1861–1865, Maine at Gettysburg,* and from the correspondence and papers of the veterans.

6. Carol Reardon and Tom Vossler, *A Field Guide to Gettysburg: Experiencing the Battlefield Through Its History, Places, and People* (Chapel Hill: University of North Carolina Press, 2013), 11–12; William H. Powell, *The Fifth Army Corps (Army of the Potomac): A Record of Operations During the Civil War in the United States of America, 1861–1865* (New York: G. P. Putnam's Sons, 1896), 261; Francis Augustín O'Reilly, *The Fredericksburg Campaign: Winter War on the Rappahannock* (Baton Rouge: Louisiana State University Press, 2003), 6; John J. Pullen, *The Twentieth Maine* (Philadelphia: Lippincott, 1957), 19.

7. Perry, *Conceived in Liberty,* 142–43; Trulock, *In the Hands of Providence,* 13.

8. *The Civil War Recollections of General Ellis Spear,* co-edited by Abbott Spear, Andrea C. Hawkes, Marie H. McCosh, Craig L. Symonds, and Michael H. Albert (Orono: University of Maine Press, 1997), 7.

9. "Presentation to Brunswick Officer," *Portland Advertiser,* September 1, 1862; GEA, diary, September 1, 1862, FPC. A member of the regiment, William Livermore, would report later that the splendid horse cost nine hundred dollars. William Livermore diary, October 5, 1863, UMO.

10. "Presentation to Brunswick Officer," *Portland Advertiser,* September 1, 1862.

11. Blanche Ames, *Adelbert Ames: 1835–1933, General, Senator, Governor, the Story of His Life and Times and His Integrity as a Soldier and Statesman in the Service of the United States Throughout the Civil War and in Mississippi in the Years of Reconstruction* (New York: Argosy-Antiquarian, 1964), 98; Pullen, *The Twentieth Maine,* 36.

12. Joshua Chamberlain, Jr., to JLC, n.d. (fall 1862), RC.

13. GEA, diary, September 1, 1862, FPC.

14. For insights on the two wars, battlefield and home front, see Gerald F. Linderman, *Embattled Courage: The Experience of Combat in the American Civil War* (New York: The Free Press, 1987).

15. Theodore Gerrish, *Army Life: A Private's Reminiscences of the Civil War* (Portland, ME: Hoyt, Fogg & Donham, 1882), 6.

16. Ibid., 9–10.

17. Ibid., 18–19.

18. O'Reilly, *The Fredericksburg Campaign*, 7.

19. Gerrish, *Army Life*, 24–25.

20. For the description and analysis of the Battle of Antietam, see James M. McPherson, *Crossroads of Freedom: Antietam* (New York: Oxford University Press, 2002), 116–18; Powell, *The Fifth Army Corps*, 274–76; Guelzo, *Robert E. Lee: A Life*, 255–56.

21. Powell, *The Fifth Army Corps*, 279–80; McPherson, *Crossroads of Freedom*, 124–29.

22. McPherson, *Crossroads of Freedom*, 118–19; Powell, *The Fifth Army Corps*, 276–77; Guelzo, *Robert E. Lee: A Life*, 257–59.

23. George B. McClellan to Henry W. Halleck, September 17, 1862, George B. McClellan, *The Civil War Papers of George B. McClellan: Selected Correspondence 1860–1865*, edited by Stephen W. Sears (New York: Ticknor & Fields, 1989), 464. McClellan and other commanding generals wrote to Lincoln through Halleck, who at the time was general-in-chief.

24. McPherson, *Crossroads of Freedom*, 124–29; Powell, *The Fifth Army Corps*, 282–83; Guelzo, *Robert E. Lee: A Life*, 257.

25. Gerrish, *Army Life*, 33.

26. JLC to FCA, September 17, 1862, in private collection, cited by D. M. Smith, *Fanny & Joshua*, 125.

27. McPherson, *Crossroads of Freedom*, 129.

28. The quotation from the letter of the Pennsylvania soldier is from Stephen W. Sears, *Landscape Turned Red: The Battle of Antietam* (New Haven, CT: Yale University Press, 1983), 315.

29. McPherson, *Crossroads of Freedom*, 1.

30. Powell, *The Fifth Army Corps*, 301; Theodore Gerrish commented that Chamberlain "sat coolly upon his horse." Gerrish, *Army Life*, 27.

31. JLC to FCA, September 21, 1862, the Pearce Civil War Documents Collection, Navarro College, Corsicana, Texas.

32. White, *A. Lincoln*, 518–19.

33. JLC to FCA, November 22, 1862, LOC; JLC to FCA, October 26, 1862, LOC.

34. Thomas D. Chamberlain to Sarah Chamberlain, October 14, 1862, BC; Pullen, *The Twentieth Maine*, 37.

35. JLC to FCA, November 3, 1862, LOC.

36. JLC to FCA, November 4, 1862, LOC.

37. Ibid.

38. Ibid.

39. FCA to JLC, November 27, 1862, RC. For the separation by war of Lawrence and Fanny, see J. L. Smith, "The Reconstruction of 'Home,'" 157.

40. For the Battle of Fredericksburg, see O'Reilly, *The Fredericksburg Campaign: Winter War; The Fredericksburg Campaign: Decision on the Rappahannock,* edited by Gary W. Gallagher (Chapel Hill: University of North Carolina Press, 1995); James K. Bryant II, *The Battle of Fredericksburg: We Cannot Escape History* (Charleston, SC: The History Press, 2010).

41. McPherson, *Battle Cry of Freedom*, 571–74.

42. Bryant, *The Battle of Fredericksburg*, 77–79.

43. Guelzo, *Robert E. Lee: A Life*, 270–77; O'Reilly, *The Fredericksburg Campaign: Winter War*, 104–06; Bryant, *The Battle of Fredericksburg*, 153.

44. Luther C. Furst, diary, Harrisburg Civil War Roundtable Collection, U.S. Army Heritage and Education Center.

45. Fowler, letter, December 20, 1862, New London Historical Society, cited in O'Reilly, *The Fredericksburg Campaign: Winter War*, 125.

46. JLC, "My Story of Fredericksburg," *Cosmopolitan* magazine 54 (December 1912): 148–59. Also, "The Last Night at Fredericksburg," in *Camp-fire Sketches and Battlefield Echoes of 61–65*, compiled by W. C. King and W. P. Derby (Springfield, MA: King, Richardson, 1888), 131–35.

47. JLC to FCA, December 17, 1862, Desjardin, *Joshua L. Chamberlain: A Life in Letters*, 179; Pullen, *The Twentieth Maine*, 52–53.

48. Robert Goldthwaite Carter, *Four Brothers in Blue: Or Sunshine and Shadows of the War of the Rebellion: A Story of the Great Civil War from Bull Run to Appomattox*, foreword by Frank Vandiver, introduction by John M. Carroll (Austin: University of Texas Press, 1978), 196. This volume is based on letters and diaries by the author and his three brothers. The first part of this work was first published serially in the Maine *Bugle* from July 1896 to October 1898, at which point the *Bugle* suspended publication.

49. JLC to FCA, December 17, 1862, Desjardin, *Joshua L. Chamberlain: A Life in Letters*, 179.

50. Ibid.

51. George C. Rable, "It Is Well That War Is So Terrible: The Carnage at Fredericksburg," 55–56, in *The Fredericksburg Campaign: Decision on the Rappahannock*.

52. Chamberlain was not happy with the editing of his article "My Story at Fredericksburg" by editors at *Cosmopolitan* magazine. The author's proof version contained the conversation with Hooker, but it was omitted in the published edition. See JLC, author's proof, UMO. Trulock, *In the Hands of Providence*, 428, footnote 42.

53. Ambrose Burnside to President Abraham Lincoln, January 1, 1863, *The Collected Works of Abraham Lincoln*, edited by Roy P. Basler (New Brunswick, N.J.: Rutgers University Press, 1953–55) 6:32; William G. Marvel, *Burnside* (Chapel Hill: University of North Carolina Press, 1991), 209–11.

54. Marvel, *Burnside*, 211–14.

55. President Abraham Lincoln, "Emancipation Proclamation," January 1, 1863, *Collected Works of Abraham Lincoln*, 6:28–31.

56. Marvel, *Burnside*, 211–14.

57. O'Reilly, *The Fredericksburg Campaign: Winter War*, 476–77; Trulock, *In the Hands of Providence*, 106; Golay, *To Gettysburg and Beyond*, 126–27.

58. O'Reilly, *The Fredericksburg Campaign: Winter War*, 478.

59. Ibid., 478–82; Pullen, *The Twentieth Maine*, 68–69.

60. O'Reilly, *The Fredericksburg Campaign: Winter War*, 488–89.

61. Trulock, *In the Hands of Providence*, 107; Golay, *To Gettysburg and Beyond*, 126–27.

62. Walter H. Hebert, *Fighting Joe Hooker* (Indianapolis, IN: Bobbs-Merrill, 1944), 65, 91, 153–61.

63. Ibid., 178–80; Pullen, *The Twentieth Maine*, 66, 71.

NINE: "AS GOOD A COL AS IN THE ARMY OF THE POTOMAC"

1. GEA, diary, February 10, 12, 13, 17, 1863, FPC.

2. Pullen, *The Twentieth Maine*, 19.

3. GEA, diary, February 10, 17, FPC; JLC to Governor Abner Coburn, February 26, 1863, MSA; *Official Records of the Union and Confederate Armies* (Washington, D.C.: Government Printing Office, 1880–1901), hereafter *OR*, vol. 25, part 2, 262, 269; Trulock, *In the Hands of Providence*, 199.

4. Golay, *To Gettysburg and Beyond*, 129.

5. Hebert, *Fighting Joe Hooker*, 178–80; Pullen, *The Twentieth Maine*, 72.

6. GEA, diary, February 22, 1863, FPC; D. M. Smith, *Fanny & Joshua*, 135. For life in wartime Washington, see Noah Brooks, *Washington, D.C., in Lincoln's Time* (New York: The Century Company, 1895), 15–16.

7. D. M. Smith, *Fanny & Joshua*, 135. For life in a Union camp, see T. J. Stiles, *Custer's Trials: A Life on the Frontier of a New America* (New York: Alfred A. Knopf, 2015), 127.

8. Pullen, *The Twentieth Maine*, 72.

9. Carole Emberton, "The Minister of Death," *The New York Times*, August 17, 2012.

10. See Terry Reimer, "Smallpox and Vaccination in the Civil War," National Museum of Civil War Medicine, November 9, 2004, civilwarmed.org/surgeons-call/small_pox/. From May 1861 to June 1866, 12,236 cases of smallpox were reported among white troops in the Union Army, and 6,716 cases among U.S. African American troops. The death rate among white troops was approximately 23 percent, for African American troops, 35 percent.

11. Pullen, *The Twentieth Maine*, 74–75.

12. JLC to FCA, April 24, 1863, LOC.

13. Desjardin, *Stand Firm Ye Boys from Maine*, 7–8.

14. Trulock, *In the Hands of Providence*, 110–11.

15. Powell, *The Fifth Army Corps*, 534; Trulock, *In the Hands of Providence*, 110–11.

16. JLC to Governor Abner Coburn, May 25, 1863, MSA.

17. "Horse[s] shot under me," a list of horses in JLC's hand, JLC letter book, PHC. The fate of Prince is not clear. One month after Chancellorsville, John Chamberlain came to visit his brother, writing in his diary that he looked forward to riding "a gray horse." Later, after Gettysburg, he wrote of taking his brother's "valuable horse" to be shod at Frederick, Maryland. He does not name Prince, but his reference to Lawrence's "valuable horse" certainly points to Prince. John Chamberlain's diary remained unknown until it was found in 1986 in the summer cottage of JLC's granddaughter, Rosamond Allen, when she closed the cottage. Trulock, *In the Hands of Providence*, 111, 431, footnote 66.

18. William Swinton, *Campaigns of the Army of the Potomac* (New York: C. B. Richardson, 1866), 280.

19. Brooks, *Washington, D.C., in Lincoln's Time*, 57–58.

20. JLC to Daisy Chamberlain, May 1863, BC; Trulock, *In the Hands of Providence*, 112–13.

21. Ellis Spear, diary, May 24, 1863, *The Civil War Recollections of General Ellis Spear*, 210.

22. Meade quotation, Trulock, *In The Hands of Providence*, 115.

23. Tom Huntington, *Maine Roads to Gettysburg* (Guilford, CT: Stackpole Books, 2018), 193.

24. JLC, "Through Blood and Fire at Gettysburg," in *Bayonet! Forward: My Civil War Remembrances* (Gettysburg, PA: Stan Clark Military Books, 1994), 23–24.

25. JLC to Governor Abner Coburn, May 25, 1863, MSA.

26. D. M. Smith, *Fanny & Joshua*, 137; Trulock, *In the Hands of Providence*, 121–22.

27. D. M. Smith, *Fanny & Joshua*, 137.

28. SBC to Tom Chamberlain, May 26, 1863, RC.

29. Deborah Folsom to FCA, June 3, RC.

30. Trulock, *In the Hands of Providence*, 118.

31. Stephen W. Sears, *Gettysburg* (Boston: Houghton Mifflin, 2003), 58.

32. Emory M. Thomas, *Robert E. Lee: A Biography* (New York: W. W. Norton, 1995), 279; Sears, *Gettysburg*, 12–14.

33. James H. Nevins and William B. Styple, *What Death More Glorious: A Biography of General Strong Vincent* (Kearny, NJ: Belle Grove Publishing, 1997), 61.

34. Powell, *The Fifth Army Corps*, 497; Pullen, *The Twentieth Maine*, 84.

TEN: LITTLE ROUND TOP

1. Richard M. Lee, *Mr. Lincoln's City: An Illustrated Guide to the Civil War Sites of Washington* (McClean, Virginia: EPM Publications, 1981), 114–15.

2. AL to Joseph Hooker, June 16, 1863, *Collected Works of Abraham Lincoln*, 6:281; Mark, 12:38–44; Luke: 20:45–47, 21:1–4.

3. Glenn W. LaFantasie, *Gettysburg Requiem: The Life and Lost Causes of Confederate Colonel William C. Oates* (New York: Oxford University Press, 2006). See also, Philip Thomas Tucker, *Storming Little Round Top: The 15th Alabama and Their Fight for Higher Ground* (Boston: De Capo Press, 2002), and Perry, *Conceived in Liberty*. These "cotton state" soldiers came from seven counties in the Chattahoochee River Valley of Alabama.

4. Tucker, *Storming Little Round Top*, 49.

5. Ibid., 16–19.

6. In *Gettysburg Requiem*, LaFantasie offers a splendid character study of the Alabama colonel.

7. Tucker, *Storming Little Round Top*, 53–57; Perry, *Conceived in Liberty*, 79–83.

8. Pullen, *The Twentieth Maine*, 84.

9. Spear, diary, June 18, 1863, *The Civil War Recollections of General Ellis Spear*, 213.

10. Ibid., 214.

11. Pullen, *The Twentieth Maine*, 87.

12. William Livermore diary, June 1863, UMO.

13. Tom Huntington, *Searching for George Gordon Meade: The Forgotten Victor of Gettysburg* (Mechanicsburg, PA: Stackpole Books, 2013), 147–49; Cleaves, *Meade of Gettysburg*, 122–25; Sears, *Gettysburg*, 121–22; Guelzo, *Gettysburg: The Last Invasion*, 88–90.

14. Freeman Cleaves, *Meade of Gettysburg* (Norman: University of Oklahoma Press, 1960), 103–15, 123–24.

15. Sears, *Gettysburg*, 125–29.

16. For the Confederates in and around Chambersburg, see Edward L. Ayers, *In the Presence of Mine Enemies: Civil War in the Heart of America, 1859–1864* (New York: W. W. Norton, 2004), 10, 395–407; Sears, *Gettysburg*, 112; and Tucker, *Storming Little Round Top*, 76–78; Perry, *Conceived in Liberty*, 2–4.

17. John Chamberlain diary, n.d. [June 29], PHC.

18. Wallace, *Soul of the Lion*, 76.

19. Desjardin, *Stand Firm Ye Boys from Maine,* 25.

20. McPherson, *Battle Cry of Freedom,* 653; Sears, *Gettysburg,* 142–44, 162–63; John Buford to Alfred Pleasanton, June 30, 1863, *OR,* 27, pt. 1, 923; James M. McPherson, *Hallowed Ground: A Walk at Gettysburg* (New York: Crown Publishers, 2003), 18–21.

21. Guelzo, *Gettysburg: The Last Invasion,* 129–35; McPherson, *Battle Cry of Freedom,* 653–54.

22. McPherson, *Hallowed Ground,* 26.

23. Oliver W. Norton, *The Attack and Defense of Little Round Top, Gettysburg, July 2, 1863* (New York: Neal Publishing Co., 1913), 285; Gerrish, *Army Life,* 65; Nevins and Styple, *What Death More Glorious,* 67.

24. Gerrish, *Army Life,* 65.

25. John Chamberlain, diary, 48–49, PHC.

26. *Maine at Gettysburg: Report of Maine Commissioners* (Portland, Maine: Lakeside Press, 1898), 252.

27. Gerrish, *Army Life,* 66.

28. John Chamberlain, diary, n.d. [June 29], PHC.

29. JLC, "Through Blood and Fire at Gettysburg," *Hearst's Magazine,* 23 (June 1913): 896; *Maine at Gettysburg,* 253. Trulock, *In the Hands of Providence,* 124.

30. McPherson, *Hallowed Ground,* 50.

31. Pullen, *The Twentieth Maine,* 97.

32. Tucker, *Storming Little Round Top,* 72–78; Gary J. Laine and Morris M. Penny, *Law's Alabama Brigade in the War Between the Union and the Confederacy* (Shippensburg, PA: White Mane Publishing, 1996), 76–77.

33. LaFantasie, *Gettysburg Requiem,* 82–85.

34. James Longstreet, *From Manassas to Appomattox: Memoirs of the Civil War in America* (Philadelphia: J. B. Lippincott, 1896), 365.

35. Livermore, diary, July 2, 1863, UMO; Desjardin, *Stand Firm Ye Boys from Maine,* 31.

36. David M. Jordan, *"Happiness Is Not My Companion": The Life of General G. K. Warren* (Bloomington: Indiana University Press, 2001), 4–6, 80.

37. Jordan, *"Happiness Is Not My Companion": The Life of General G. K. Warren,* 90–92; McPherson, *Battle Cry of Freedom,* 657–59.

38. Jordan, *"Happiness Is Not My Companion": The Life of General G. K. Warren,* 92; Powell, *The Fifth Army Corps,* 521.

39. Guelzo, *Gettysburg: The Last Invasion,* 254–56, 262–64.

40. James A. Hessler, *Sickles at Gettysburg: The Controversial Civil War General Who Committed Murder, Abandoned Little Round Top, and Declared Himself the Hero of Gettysburg* (El Dorado Hills, CA: Savas Beatie, 2009), 1–20.

41. Jordan, *"Happiness Is Not My Companion": The Life of General G. K. Warren,* 92; Powell, *The Fifth Army Corps,* 522.

42. Harry W. Pfanz, *Gettysburg: The Second Day* (Chapel Hill: University of North Carolina Press, 1987), 208; Desjardin, *Stand Firm Ye Boys from Maine,* 36–37; Guelzo, *Gettysburg: The Last Invasion,* 257–58.

43. Jordan, *"Happiness Is Not My Companion": The Life of General G. K. Warren,* 92–93; Norton, *The Attack and Defense of Little Round Top,* 263–64, 285; William Swinton, war correspondent for *The New York Times,* known for his aggressive reporting, wrote, "General Warren assumed the responsibility of detaching from the force the brigade of Vincent and this he hurried up to hold the position." Swinton, *Campaigns of the Army of the Potomac,* 346–48.

44. JLC, "Through Blood and Fire at Gettysburg," *Hearst's Magazine,* 898–99.

45. Ibid., 899; Norton, *The Attack and Defense of Little Round Top,* 264–66; Desjardin, *Stand Firm Ye Boys from Maine,* 37.

46. JLC, "Through Blood and Fire at Gettysburg," *Hearst's Magazine,* 899; Gerrish, *Army Life in Chamberlain's 20th Maine,* 70–71.

47. Pullen, *The Twentieth Maine,* 110–12; Desjardin, *Stand Firm Ye Boys from Maine,* 42–44; Golay, *To Gettysburg and Beyond,* 157–58; Guelzo, *Gettysburg: The Last Invasion,* 270–71.

48. Tucker, *Storming Little Round Top,* 96–97; Laine and Penny, *Law's Alabama Brigade,* 79. The men filled the canteens from a well at Anew Curran's home on Emmitsburg Road.

49. LaFantasie, *Gettysburg Requiem,* 87; William C. Oates, *The War Between the Union and the Confederacy* (New York: The Neale Publishing Co., 1905), 210–11; Tucker, *Storming Little Round Top,* 137–48; Laine and Penny, *Law's Alabama Brigade,* 99–100.

50. LaFantasie, *Gettysburg Requiem,* 89-93; Oates, *The War Between the Union and the Confederacy,* 210–11; Tucker, *Storming Little Round Top,* 169–72.

51. LaFantasie, *Gettysburg Requiem,* 93-94; Oates, *The War Between the Union and the Confederacy,* 212; Tucker, *Storming Little Round Top,* 172–73.

52. LaFantasie, *Gettysburg Requiem,* 94; Oates, *The War Between the Union and the Confederacy,* 212–13; Tucker, *Storming Little Round Top,* 180–83; Laine and Penny, *Law's Alabama Brigade in the War Between the Union and the Confederacy,* 100–01.

53. JLC, "Through Blood and Fire at Gettysburg," *Hearst's Magazine,* 900.

54. Howard L. Prince address, *Dedication of the Twentieth Maine Monuments, Oct 3, 1889* (Waldoboro, ME: News Stream Job Print, 1891).

55. Desjardin, *Stand Firm Ye Boys from Maine,* 51.

56. JLC, "Through Blood and Fire at Gettysburg," *Hearst's Magazine,* 900.

57. *The Civil War Recollections of General Ellis Spear,* 34; Pfanz, *Gettysburg: The Second Day,* 232.

58. JLC, "Through Blood and Fire at Gettysburg," *Hearst's Magazine,* 901–02; JLC, report, July 6, 1863, *OR,* vol. 27, part 1, 623; Pullen, *The Twentieth Maine,* 116–18.

59. *The Civil War Recollections of General Ellis Spear,* 33.

60. JLC, "Through Blood and Fire at Gettysburg," *Hearst's Magazine,* 902; Wallace, *Soul of the Lion,* 94–95.

61. Oates, *The War Between the Union and the Confederacy,* 218.

62. Nevins and Styple, *What Death More Glorious,* 77–78.

63. JLC, "The Maine 20th at Gettysburg," *The Maine Farmer,* December 28, 1865; JLC, "Through Blood and Fire at Gettysburg," *Hearst's Magazine,* 904; Pullen, *The Twentieth Maine,* 120; Desjardin, *Stand Firm Ye Boys from Maine,* 63.

64. Holman S. Melcher, *With a Flash of His Sword: The Writings of Major Holman S. Melcher 20th Maine Infantry,* edited by William B. Styple (Kearny, NJ: Belle Grove Publishing, 1994), vii–xii.

65. *The Civil War Recollections of General Ellis Spear,* 317; Desjardin, *Stand Firm Ye Boys from Maine,* 55.

66. JLC, "Through Blood and Fire at Gettysburg," *Hearst's Magazine,* 903.

67. Ibid., 907; Pullen, *The Twentieth Maine,* 122.

68. Herbert Heath to JLC, February 7, 1903, MHS; Pullen, *The Twentieth Maine,* 125.

69. John Chamberlain to Charles Desmond, July 11, 1863, BC.

70. William C. Oates, "Gettysburg: The Battle on the Right," *Southern Historical Society Papers,* 6 (1878).

ELEVEN: PETERSBURG

1. Adelbert Ames to JLC, July 3, 18673, LOC.

2. JLC to FCA, July 4, 1863, LOC.

3. D. M. Smith, *Fanny & Joshua,* 137–40.

4. JLC, July 6, OR, XXVII, Pt. 1, 622–26. See also William Edward S. Whitman and Charles Henry True, *Maine in the War for the Union* (Lewiston, ME: Dingley Publishers, 1865).

5. James C. Rice, July 31, *OR*, XXVII, Pt. 1, 616–20.

6. JLC to FCA, July 17, 1863, LOC.

7. Elizabeth R. Varon, *Armies of Deliverance: A New History of the Civil War* (New York: Oxford University Press, 2019), 171–75; McPherson, *Battle Cry of Freedom,* 609–11.

8. JLC to FCA, July 17, 1863, LOC.

9. Ibid.

10. Ibid.

11. Spear, diary, July 25, 1863, Civil War Diaries, 1863–1865, *The Civil War Recollections of General Ellis Spear,* 220.

12. JLC to Lt. John. M. Clark, July 30, 1863, National Archives; JLC, Military Service Records, National Archives.

13. D. M. Smith, *Fanny & Joshua,* 145–46.

14. Robert F. Lord, *Downeast Depots: Maine Railroad Stations in the Steam Era* (Hartford, CT: W. E. Andrews, 1986), 93.

15. GEA, diary, August 6, 1863, FPC.

16. Ibid.

17. John D. Lincoln, MD, Affidavit, August 17, 1863, PHC; JLC order book, 39, PHC.

18. Trulock, *In the Hands of Providence,* 163.

19. For Rice, see Ezra J. Warner, *Generals in Blue: Lives of the Union Commanders* (Baton Rouge: Louisiana State University Press, 1964), 400–01.

20. Eugene Arus Nash, *A History of the Forty-fourth Regiment, New York Volunteer Infantry, in the Civil War, 1861–1865* (Chicago: R. R. Donnelley & Sons, 1911), 226.

21. JLC to Governor Abner Coburn, August 25, 1863, MSA.

22. JLC to FCA, September 12, 1863, LOC.

23. R. G. Carter, September 3, 1863, *Four Brothers in Blue,* 348–49; Trulock, *In the Hands of Providence,* 166.

24. JLC to FCA, August 31, 1863, LOC.

25. James Clay Rice to William Pitt Fessenden, September 8, 1863, NA; also, Chamberlain Papers, LOC.

26. General Charles Griffin to General Seth Williams, October 7, 1863, MSA. The original recommendation, with an endorsement on the back, is at the National Archives. Trulock, *In the Hands of Providence,* 167, 450–51, note 29.

27. Golay, *To Gettysburg and Beyond,* 200.

28. Trulock, *In the Hands of Providence,* 170.

29. Bierle, Sarah Kay, "The Generals' Horses," January 13, 2017, gazette665.com/2017/01/13/chamberlains-charlemagne/.

30. Civil War and Reconstruction Era Court Martial Records, Paperless Archives.com—BACM Research.

31. Oliver W. Norton, *Army Letters, 1861–1865* (Chicago: O. L. Deming, 1903), 293; Nash, *A History of the Forty-fourth Regiment*, 172; Trulock, *In the Hands of Providence*, 173.

32. JLC to Lt. Col. Locke, surgeon's certificate, November 15 and 16, 1863, NA; JLC medical records, NA, JLC order book, 39, PHC.

33. Malaria and Wars and Victims, malariasite.com/wars-victims/#:~:text=During%20the%20American%20civil%20war,black%20soldiers%20got%20malaria%20annually. Our understanding of a great deal about the Union army's medical history owes to the publication of the six volumes of *The Medical and Surgical History of the War of the Rebellion, 1861–65*, between 1870 and 1888.

34. Lt. William E. Donnell to FCA, November 16, 1863, LOC.

35. Trulock, *In the Hands of Providence*, 173–74; D. M. Smith, *Fanny & Joshua*, 149; Perry, *Conceived in Liberty*, 155.

36. "Malaria," Center for Disease Control and Prevention, cdc.gov.

37. *Scientific American*, July 20, 1861.

38. Malaria and Wars and Victims, malariasite.com/wars-victims/#:~:text=During%20the%20American%20civil%20war,black%20soldiers%20got%20malaria%20annually. Our understanding of a great deal about the Union army's medical history owes to the publication of the six volumes of *The Medical and Surgical History of the War of the Rebellion, 1861–65* between 1870 and 1888.

39. Medical Certificate, November 28, 1863, JFC Medical Records, NA; GEA, diary, November 24, 28, 1863, FPC; Jack D. Welsh, *Medical Histories of Union Generals* (Kent, OH: Kent State University Press, 1996), 63.

40. See Libby MacCaskill, *Ladies on the Field: Two Civil War Nurses from Maine on the Battlefields of Virginia* (Livermore, ME: Signal Tree Publications. 1996), 51–80.

41. D. M. Smith, *Fanny & Joshua*, 149.

42. Ibid.

43. GEA, diary, December 19, 1863, FPC.

44. Ibid., diary, January 14, 1864, FPC.

45. biggestuscities.com.

46. Margaret Leech, *Reveille in Washington: 1860–1865* (New York: Harper, 1941), 350–51.

47. Brooks, *Washington, D.C., in Lincoln's Time*, 14, 16.

48. Leech, *Reveille in Washington: 1860–1865*, 341.

49. Ibid., 340–44; lincolnconspirators.com/2014/01/19/grovers-theatre-and-the-lincoln-assassination/.

50. Ibid., 34–44; Brian Anderson, *Images of America: Ford's Theatre* (Charleston, SC: Arcadia Publishing, 2014), 7, 21.

51. D. M. Smith, *Fanny & Joshua*, 150.

52. Gary Wills, *Lincoln at Gettysburg: The Words That Remade America* (New York: Simon & Schuster, 1992), 21–22.

53. FCA to Deborah Folsom, April 14, 1864, MSA.

54. White, *American Ulysses*, xxi–xxiii.

55. Charles Francis Adams, Jr., to Charles Francis Adams, Sr., May 1, 1864, in Worthing-

ton Chauncey Ford, editor, *A Cycle of Adams Letters, 1861–1865* (Boston: Houghton Mifflin, 1920), 2:128.

56. JLC to Deborah Folsom, April 14, 1864, MSA.

57. George Gordon Meade to Margaret Meade, March 14, 1864, in *The Life and Letters of General George Gordon Meade,* vol. 2 (New York: Charles Scribner's Sons, 1913), 178.

58. Ulysses S. Grant to George Gordon Meade, April 9, 1864, *The Papers of Ulysses S. Grant,* edited by John Y. Simon and John F. Marszalek (Carbondale: Southern Illinois University Press, 1967–2017), 10:274.

59. White, *American Ulysses,* 328.

60. Sylvanus Cadwallader, *Three Years With Grant,* edited by Benjamin P. Thomas (New York: Alfred A. Knopf, 1955), 174–75.

61. White, *American Ulysses,* 336–37.

62. JLC to Col. E. D. Townsend, May 9, 1863, JLC Military Personnel file, NA.

63. Trulock, *In the Hands of Providence,* 177.

64. Years later, asked to write the introduction to *A History of the Forty-Fourth Regiment,* Chamberlain remembered that as he rode to the top of Little Round Top with Rice on July 2, 1863, the indomitable Rice exclaimed, "Colonel, we are making world-history today." JLC, introduction, Nash, *A History of the Forty-fourth Regiment,* ix.

65. Gerrish, *Army Life,* 113.

66. Trulock, *In the Hands of Providence,* 188; Golay, *To Gettysburg and Beyond,* 226–27; Whitman and True, *Maine in the War for the Union,* 499.

67. McPherson, *Battle Cry of Freedom,* 733; casualty statistics are estimates.

68. For the battle at Cold Harbor, see Gordon C. Rhea, *Cold Harbor: Grant and Lee, May 26–June 3, 1864* (Baton Rouge: Louisiana State University Press, 2002), and *Cold Harbor to the Crater: The End of the Overland Campaign,* edited by Gary W. Gallagher and Caroline E. Janney (Chapel Hill: University of North Carolina Press, 2015), especially the introduction, ix–xvii.

69. Horace Porter, *Campaigning with Grant.* Introduction by Brooks D. Simpson (Lincoln: University of Nebraska Press, 2000 [Originally published New York: Century Co., 1897]), 179. Years later, in his *Personal Memoirs,* Grant wrote, "I have always regretted that the last assault at Cold Harbor was ever made . . . At Cold Harbor no advantage whatever was gained to compensate for the heavy loss sustained." Ulysses S. Grant, *The Personal Memoirs of U. S. Grant,* 2 vols. (New York: Charles L. Webster & Co., 1885), 2:276.

70. Rhea, *Cold Harbor: Grant and Lee, May 26–June 3, 1864 (Baton Rouge Lousiana State University Press, 2002),* 41; White, *American Ulysses,* 364–66.

71. A. Wilson Greene, *A Campaign of Giants: The Battle for Petersburg, Volume One: From the Crossing of the James to the Crater* (Chapel Hill: University of North Carolina Press, 2018), 135–36; Dennis A. Rasbach, *Joshua Lawrence Chamberlain and the Petersburg Campaign* (El Dorado Hills, CA: Savas Beatie, 2016), 24–27; Diane Monroe Smith, *Chamberlain at Petersburg: The Charge at Fort Hell June 18, 1864* (Gettysburg, PA: Thomas Publications, 2004), 38–41.

72. McPherson, *Battle Cry of Freedom,* 740–41.

73. White, *American Ulysses,* 366–69.

74. R. G. Carter, *Four Brothers in Blue,* 438.

75. Greene, *A Campaign of Giants,* vol. 1, 194.

76. Ibid., 182–83; Powell, *The Fifth Army Corps,* 700–01. For a contemporary account of the Petersburg campaign, see *New York Times* war correspondent Swinton, *Campaigns of the Army of the Potomac,* 497–511.

77. Pullen, *The Twentieth Maine*, 203.

78. Charlemagne was badly wounded in the hindquarters, but he would recover. Bierle, "The Generals' Horses," January 13, 2017, gazette665.com/2017/01/13/chamberlains-charlemagne.

79. Pullen, *The Twentieth Maine*, 210; Greene, *A Campaign of Giants*, vol. 1, 194.

80. Greene, *A Campaign of Giants*, vol. 1, 195.

81. Chamberlain recounted this incident years later in "The Charge at Fort Hell," 1899, William Henry Noble Papers, Special Collections, Library, Duke University, Durham, North Carolina. D. M. Smith, recovering this manuscript, made it the basis of her *Joshua Lawrence Chamberlain at Petersburg*, 56.

82. Chamberlain would write of this incident four times in future years: "The Charge at Fort Hell" in 1899; "The Hero of Gettysburg," *Lewiston Evening Journal* (Maine), September 1, 1900; *Brunswick Record*, February 5, 1904; and "Reminiscences of Petersburg and Appomattox: October, 1903," *War Papers* (Portland, ME: Lefavor-Tower, 1908 [Reprinted Wilmington, NC: Broadfoot Publishing, 1992, v. III, 161–82]). He had made a copy of the letter, or a paraphrase of the letter, which he retained.

83. JLC, "The Charge at Fort Hell," in D. M. Smith, *Chamberlain At Petersburg*, 56–57. It is not clear whether Meade received Chamberlain's reply. The fact that his response did not make it into the *War of the Rebellion: Official Records of the Civil War* was not unusual—many short field notes and responses did not.

84. Greene, in *A Campaign of Giants*, vol. 1, 194, argues that "the notion that Meade would send direct orders to a lowly brigade commander bypassing both Warren and Griffin in the process is illogical." See also Rasbach, *Joshua Lawrence Chamberlain and the Petersburg Campaign*, 4, footnote 5. I thank historian Jim McPherson for helping me think through this question. What Meade did at Petersburg—asking for reports from his commanders—was consistent with his command practice. Although Greene argues "No evidence exists of any order," it is well known that not all orders made it years later into the official *War of the Rebellion: Official Records of the Civil War*.

85. Patrick DeLacy, Manuscript, n.d., LOC. DeLacy wrote that he corresponded with M. L. Blair, also of the 143rd Pennsylvania, who had written down Chamberlain's speech, and then reviewed DeLacy's manuscript to verify its accuracy. See also DeLacy to JLC, January 15, 1904, LOC; Trulock, *In the Hands of Providence*, 462, footnote 46.

86. JLC, "The Charge at Fort Hell," in D. M. Smith, *Chamberlain at Petersburg*, 60.

87. Rasbach, *Joshua Lawrence Chamberlain and the Petersburg Campaign*.

88. JLC, "The Charge at Fort Hell," D. M. Smith, *Chamberlain at Petersburg*, 62–65; Trulock, *In the Hands of Providence*, 209.

89. JLC, "The Charge at Fort Hell," D. M. Smith, *Chamberlain at Petersburg*, 65–66.

90. Rasbach, *Joshua Lawrence Chamberlain and the Petersburg Campaign*, 60.

91. JLC, "The Charge at Fort Hell," D. M. Smith, *Chamberlain at Petersburg*, 67.

92. Trulock, *In the Hands of Providence*, 214; D. M. Smith, *Fanny & Joshua*, 152–53.

93. Nash, *A History of the Forty-Fourth Regiment*, 112.

94. Wallace, *Soul of the Lion*, 134.

95. Robert F. Reilly, MD, "Medical and Surgical Care During the American Civil War, 1861–1865," *Baylor University Medical Center Proceedings*, 29, no. 2, 138.

96. JLC, "The Charge at Fort Hell," in D. M. Smith, *Chamberlain at Petersburg*, 71.

97. JLC to FCA, June 19, 1864, BC. This letter is on display outside the George J. Mitchell Department of Special Collections & Archives in the Hawthorne-Longfellow Library at BC.

98. *JLC: A Sketch,* 16; JLC Pension Record, NA; H. C. Henries, chaplain, to *Bangor Whig and Courier,* June 28, 1864, newspaper clipping; JLC letter book, PHC.

99. *OR,* 40, pt. 2, 2, 216–17.

100. Ibid., 40 (2); 216–17, 236. Grant forwarded his order to Secretary of War Edwin Stanton.

101. Ulysses S. Grant, *The Personal Memoirs of U. S. Grant,* 2:381–82.

TWELVE: APPOMATTOX

1. Melcher's letter was undated. Herman Melcher (to Chamberlain family), n.d. 1864, RC.

2. SBC to JLC, June 23, 1864, RC.

3. For an excellent summary of the wounds Chamberlain incurred in the Civil War, see Jack D. Welsh, *Medical Histories of Union Generals* (Kent, OH: Kent State University Press, 1996), 63–65.

4. Mary Clark to JLC, July 11, 1865, RC.

5. Lt. Col. Charles D. Gilmore to General John L. Hodsdon, Maine adjutant general, July 5, 1864, MSA.

6. JLC to Governor Samuel Cony, August 31, 1864, MSA.

7. GEA to JLC, September 6, 1864, RC.

8. Ibid.

9. *Bangor Daily Whig and Courier,* October 18, 1864.

10. Adelbert Ames to JLC, October 18, 1864, LOC.

11. JLC to SDC, October 26, 1864, RC; Trulock, *In the Hands of Providence,* 219; D. M. Smith, *Fanny & Joshua,* 155–56.

12. en.wikipedia.org/wiki/1864_United_States_presidential_election_in_Maine; White, *A. Lincoln,* 644–45.

13. *OR,* 42 (3): 633 records Chamberlain's arrival.

14. Thomas Chamberlin, *History of the One Hundred Fiftieth Regiment, Pennsylvania Volunteers* (Philadelphia: Lippincott, 1895), 278–79.

15. Pullen, *The Twentieth Maine,* 232–34.

16. JLC to SBC, December 14, 1864, BC.

17. Francis B. Jones to JLC, January 15, 1865, RC.

18. JLC order book, 41, PHC. Chamberlain provides no first name for Dr. Pancoast, so there is no way of knowing whether it was Dr. Joseph Pancoast or his son, Dr. William Henry Pancoast. For the Pancoasts, see Howard A. Kelly, *Dictionary of American Medical Biography* (New York: D. Appleton, 1928), 934–37.

19. Trulock, *In the Hands of Providence,* 224.

20. JLC to Joshua Chamberlain, Jr., February 12, 1865, BC.

21. Ibid.

22. Ibid.

23. JLC to SBC, March 9, 1865, BC.

24. Ibid.

25. Ronald C. White, *Lincoln's Greatest Speech: The Second Inaugural* (New York: Simon & Schuster, 2002).

26. Chris M. Calkins, *The Appomattox Campaign, March 29–April 9, 1865* (Lynchburg, VA: Schroeder Publications, 2018), 11; Powell, *The Fifth Army Corps,* 776.

27. William Tecumseh Sherman, *Memoirs of General William T. Sherman, by Himself* (New York: D. Appleton, 1875), vol. 2, 326.

28. Calkins, *The Appomattox Campaign,* 14.

29. Michael J. McCarthy, *Confederate Waterloo: The Battle of Five Forks, April 1, 1865, and the Controversy that Brought Down a General* (El Dorado Hills, CA: Savas Beatie, 2017), 24; A. Wilson Greene, *The Final Battles of the Petersburg Campaign: Breaking the Backbone of the Rebellion* (Knoxville: University of Tennessee Press, 2008), 158.

30. *JLC: A Sketch,* 16–17; E. M. Woodward, *History of the One Hundred and Ninety-Eighth Pennsylvania Volunteers* (Trenton, NJ: MacCrellish & Quigley, 1884), 36–37; Powell, *The Fifth Army Corps,* 776; Calkins, *The Appomattox Campaign,* 20; McCarthy, *Confederate Waterloo,* 24.

31. Calkins, *The Appomattox Campaign,* 20; McCarthy, *Confederate Waterloo,* 24–25.

32. JLC, *The Passing of the Armies,* 45–46; Wallace, *Soul of the Lion,* 144; Trulock, *In the Hands of Providence,* 235.

33. JLC, *The Passing of the Armies,* 46; *JLC: A Sketch,* 17.

34. JLC, *The Passing of the Armies,* 45–48.

35. *A Diary of Battle: The Personal Journals of Colonel Charles S. Wainwright, 1861–1865,* edited by Allan Nevins, new foreword by Stephen W. Sears (Boston: Da Capo Press, 1998 [Original publication: New York: Harcourt, Brace, & World, 1862]), 507–08.

36. Ibid., 508.

37. JLC, *The Passing of the Armies,* 48–49.

38. *OR* 46 (1) 845.

39. JLC, *The Passing of the Armies,* 56.

40. *OR* 46 (1) 800.

41. *JLC: A Sketch,* 17; JLC, *The Passing of the Armies,* 56.

42. Ibid., 57.

43. Woodward, *History of the One Hundred and Ninety-Eighth Pennsylvania Volunteers,* 38.

44. Sherman, *Personal Memoirs,* 2:143–45; Joseph Wheelan, *Terrible Swift Sword: The Life of Philip H. Sheridan* (Cambridge, MA: Da Capo Press, 2012), 174–75; White, *American Ulysses,* 402.

45. Greene, *The Final Battles of the Petersburg Campaign,* 182–84; Calkins, *The Appomattox Campaign,* 27–28.

46. McCarthy, *Confederate Waterloo,* 92; Golay, *To Gettysburg and Beyond,* 258.

47. Greene, *The Final Battles of the Petersburg Campaign,* 184–86; McCarthy, *Confederate Waterloo,* 74–76.

48. JLC remembers this dialogue years later in *The Passing of the Armies,* 104.

49. There are many accounts of Sheridan's displeasure with Warren. For the story from Warren's point of view, see Jordan, *"Happiness Is Not My Companion": The Life of General G. K. Warren.*

50. McCarthy, *Confederate Waterloo,* 91; Golay, *To Gettysburg and Beyond,* 257.

51. McCarthy, *Confederate Waterloo,* 76–78, 87–102.

52. Ibid., 102.

53. *New York World,* April 4, 1865; JLC letter book, PHC. Gravelly Run was the name then used for the March 31 battle of White Oak Road.

54. Davis, *Jefferson Davis*, 603.

55. Pullen, *The Twentieth Maine*, 258–59; Trulock, *In the Hands of Providence*, 285–85.

56. McPherson, *Battle Cry of Freedom*, 847–48.

57. JLC, *The Passing of the Armies*, 223–24.

58. USG to Robert E. Lee, April 7, 1865, *Grant Papers*, 14:361.

59. Ibid., April 8, 1865, 367; Robert E. Lee to USG, April 8, 1865, Note. White, *American Ulysses*, 404–05.

60. JLC, *The Passing of the Armies*, 246.

61. For Appomattox, see Elizabeth R. Varon, *Appomattox: Victory, Defeat and Freedom at the End of the Civil War* (New York: Oxford University Press, 2017); White, *American Ulysses*, 405–06.

62. White, *American Ulysses*, 406.

63. Douglas Southall Freeman, *R. E. Lee: A Biography* (New York: Charles Scribner's Sons, 1934–35), 4:138; Varon, *Appomattox*, 77–78.

64. Horace Porter, *Campaigning with Grant* (Lincoln: University of Nebraska Press, 2000). Originally published New York: Century Co., 1984, 486.

65. Newspaper headlines, without attribution to specific newspapers, in Ruel H. Stanley and George O. Hall, *Eastern Maine and the Rebellion* (Bangor, ME: R. H. Stanley, 1887), 190.

66. GEA, diary, April 10, 1865, FPC.

67. Furbish, *"Darkness Is Over Our Land . . . ,"* Furbish did not continue his journal after 1862. Starting in 1863 he wrote "Facts About Brunswick," often apparently writing his facts at the end of 1863, 1864, and 1865.

68. GEA, diary, April 10, 1865, FPC.

69. Furbish, *"Darkness Is Over Our Land . . . ,"* 1865.

70. Stanley and Hall, *Eastern Maine and the Rebellion*, 199.

71. Varon, *Appomattox*, 77.

72. Patrick A. Schroeder, *More Myths About Lee's Surrender* (Lynchburg, VA: Schroeder Publications, 1998), 22–23; Wallace, *Soul of the Lion*, 186; Trulock, *In the Hands of Providence*, 302.

73. For Gordon, see Ralph Lowell Eckert, *John Brown Gordon: Soldier, Southerner, American* (Baton Rouge: Louisiana State University Press, 1989); John W. Primomo, *The Appomattox Generals: The Parallel Lives of Joshua L. Chamberlain and John B. Gordon* (Jefferson, NC: McFarland. 2013).

74. Eckert, *John Brown Gordon*, 121–22.

75. JLC, *The Passing of the Armies*, 260.

76. Eckert, *John Brown Gordon*, 122.

77. Pullen, *The Twentieth Maine*, 274; Trulock, *In the Hands of Providence*, 309.

78. JLC, *The Passing of the Armies*, 266–67.

79. JLC to SBC, April 13, 1865, BC.

80. JLC to FCA, April 19, 1865, PHC.

THIRTEEN: THE GRAND REVIEW

1. JLC to FCA, April 19, 1865, PHC.

2. JLC, *The Passing of the Armies*, 289; Golay, *To Gettysburg and Beyond*, 278–79.

3. JLC, *The Passing of the Armies*, 318.

4. GEA, diary, May 18, 1865, FPC.

5. Ibid., May 20, 1865.

6. Ibid., May 21, 1865.

7. Ibid., May 22, 1865.

8. Ibid.

9. JLC, *The Passing of the Armies*, 322–24.

10. GEA, diary, May 22, 1865, FPC; JLC, *The Passing of the Armies*, 324; Trulock, *In the Hands of Providence*, 320.

11. GEA, diary, May 22, 1865, FPC.

12. Taps was composed by General Daniel Butterfield in 1862 to replace the usual firing of three rifle volleys at the end of burials during battle.

13. *The Grand Review: The Civil War Continues to Shape America* (York, PA: Bold Print, 2000), 42. Chapters on day one and day two of the Grand Review by George R. Sheets.

14. Leech, *Reveille in Washington*, 511; Charles Royster, *The Destructive War* (New York: Knopf, 1991), 406.

15. Royster, *The Destructive War*, 407; Porter, *Campaigning with Grant*, 505–06.

16. *The Grand Review*, 42.

17. Porter, *Campaigning with Grant*, 506.

18. *The Grand Review*, 43.

19. Ibid., 49.

20. T. J. Stiles, *Custer's Trials: A Life on the Frontier of a New America* (New York: Alfred A. Knopf, 2015), 214.

21. JLC, *The Passing of the Armies*, 339–40.

22. *The Grand Review*, 52; Leech, *Reveille in Washington*, 510; Trulock, *In the Hands of Providence*, 325–26.

23. GEA, diary, May 23, 1865, FPC.

24. Gary W. Gallagher, in *The Union War* (Cambridge, MA: Harvard University Press, 2011), recovers the meaning of the Union for the Civil War generation, even as it has disappeared from popular understanding and recent scholarship in favor of choosing to depict the Civil War as a war to end slavery. *Harper's Weekly,* June 10, 1865, 353, 356–58, 364–65; *New York Herald,* May 24, 1865, in J. Cutler Andrews, *The North Reports the Civil War* (Pittsburgh, PA: University of Pittsburgh Press, 1955), 12–13.

25. JLC to SBC, June 6, 1865, BC.

26. Ibid.

FOURTEEN: DECISIONS

1. Howard has been the subject of two quite different biographies. Carpenter, *Sword and Olive Branch: Oliver Otis Howard*, 82, praises Howard's efforts, whereas McFeely, *Yankee Stepfather: General O. O. Howard and the Freedmen*, portrays the "ambiguous role played by Howard," 57, 328.

2. Stephen Budiansky, *The Bloody Shirt: Terror After the Civil War* (New York: Viking, 2007), 66.

3. Amers, *Adelbert Ames*, 267.

4. Budiansky, *The Bloody Shirt*, 72–73; Ames, *Adelbert Ames, 267*.

5. Theda Skocpol, *Protecting Soldiers and Mothers: The Political Origins of Social Policy in the United States* (Cambridge: Harvard University Press, 1992), 104.

6. Sarah Handley-Cousins illuminates what she calls Chamberlain's "nonvisible disability." See her " 'Wrestling at the Gates of Death': Joshua Lawrence Chamberlain and Nonvisible Disability in the Post–Civil War North," *Journal of the Civil War Era*, 6, no. 2 (January 2016): 220–42.

7. "Commencement at Bowdoin," a clipping of a newspaper article in the JLC order book without the name of the newspaper, PHC.

8. A clipping from another newspaper, JLC order book, PHC.

9. JLC to USG, July 31, 1865, JLC order book, PHC.

10. *The New York Times* reported on Grant's movements on August 1 and 2. See the extensive note in *The Papers of Ulysses S. Grant*, vol. 15, 271.

11. *The New York Times*, August 9, 1865; Hatch, *The History of Bowdoin College*, 121–22.

12. Furbish, *"Darkness Is Over Our Land . . .,"* 1865.

13. Hatch, *The History of Bowdoin College*, 116–17.

14. Michael Haines, "Fertility and Mortality in the United States," Table 1, eh.net /encyclopedia/fertility-and-mortality-in-the-united-states/.

15. Levinsky, *At Home with the General: A Visit to the Joshua L. Chamberlain Museum*, 19–20.

16. JLC, "Address of Joshua Lawrence Chamberlain," August 1865, MHS.

17. Wallace, *Soul of the Lion*, 203.

18. D. M. Smith, *Fanny & Joshua*, 172. Griffin would serve briefly in Maine before being deployed to Galveston, Texas.

19. Receipt from Tiffany jewelers, December 5, 1865, BC.

20. Governor Samuel Cony to Senator Lott Morrill, September 5, 1865, JLC Military Personnel File, NA; application of Maine delegation to President Andrew Johnson, December 20, 1865, endorsed by General U. S. Grant and Secretary of War Edwin Stanton, January 16, 186, LOC.

21. For Blaine, see Neil Rolde. *Continental Liar from the State of Maine: James G. Blaine* (Gardiner, ME: Tilbury House, 2006).

22. For a list of the governors of Maine, see en.wikipedia.org. Beginning in 1880, Governors would serve two-year terms; finally in 1962, they would serve four-year terms.

23. Richard White, *The Republic for Which It Stands: The United States During Reconstruction and the Gilded Age, 1865–1896* (New York: Oxford University Press, 2017), 63.

24. Stiles, *Custer's Trials*, 213–15.

25. SBC to JLC, "First Day 66," RC.

26. JLC to FCA, March 20, 1866, RC.

27. The *Portland Press* is quoted in Hatch, *Maine*, vol. 2, 533.

28. Hamlin was a central figure in Maine politics for decades. See Harry Draper Hunt, *Hannibal Hamlin of Maine: Lincoln's First Vice-President* (Syracuse, NY: Syracuse University Press, 1969); Michael Kovacevich, *Hannibal Hamlin: The Story of the Anti-Slavery and Civil War Vice President Who Might Have Changed History* (Denver, CO, 2010).

29. *Bangor Whig*, April 22, 1866; White, *The Republic for Which It Stands*, 68–69.

30. JLC to FCA, April 7, 1866, RC.

31. FCA to JLC, April 15, 1866, RC.

32. Hatch, *Maine*, vol. 2, 533.

33. *Eben F. Pillsbury's Record! As Written with His Own Pen* (Augusta, ME: 1866), 1; "Maine," *The American Cyclopedia and Register of Important Events of the Year 1866* (New York: D. Appleton and Company, 1873), 467–68.

34. Ibid.

35. Trulock, *In the Hands of Providence,* 335.

36. G. K. Warren to JLC, August 28, 1866, LOC; Taylor, *Gouverneur Kemble Warren,* 237–39.

37. *Journal of the House of Representatives,* Maine, forty-sixth legislature (Augusta, ME: Owen & Nash, 1867), 13.

38. GEA, diary, September 11, 1866, FPC.

39. Alfred C. Godfrey to JLC, November 20, 1866, MHS.

FIFTEEN: GOVERNOR OF MAINE

1. GEA, diary, January 3, 1867, FPC.

2. Hatch, *Maine,* vol. 2, 533.

3. JLC, *Address of Governor Chamberlain to the Legislature of Maine,* January 1867 (Augusta, ME: Stevens and Sayward, 1867); *Portland Daily Press,* January 4, 1867.

4. Ibid.

5. White, *The Republic for Which It Stands,* 82–83; White, *American Ulysses,* 438–39.

6. For the Fourteenth Amendment, see Garrett Epps, *Democracy Reborn: The Fourteenth Amendment and the Fight for Equal Rights in Post–Civil War America* (New York: Henry Holt, 2006).

7. Bill Kenny, *A History of Maine Railroads* (Charleston, SC: The History Press, 2020), 9.

8. JLC, *Address of Governor Chamberlain to the Legislature of Maine, Portland Daily Press,* January 4, 1867.

9. Ibid.

10. Ibid.

11. JLC, *Address of Governor Chamberlain to the Legislature of Maine, Lewiston Evening Journal,* January 3, 1867.

12. *Portland Transcript,* January 12, 1867.

13. James G. Blaine to JLC, January 15, 1867, Chamberlain Papers, LOC.

14. Trulock, *In the Hands of Providence,* 339–40.

15. D. M. Smith, *Fanny & Joshua,* 185.

16. Hatch, *Maine,* vol. 2, 534.

17. Ian R. Tyrell, *Sobering Up: From Temperance to Prohibition in Antebellum America, 1800–1860* (Westport, CT: Greenwood Press, 1979), 4.

18. Liz Greene, "A Brief History of Women and Alcohol," lipmag.com/featured/a-brief-history-of-women-and-alcohol/.

19. Tyrell, *Sobering Up: From Temperance to Prohibition in Antebellum America, 1800–1860,* 252–54; Richard S. Westcott and Edward O. Schriver, "Reform Movements & Party Reformation, 1820–1861," in *Maine: The Pine Tree State From Prehistory to the Present,* edited by Richard W. Judd, Edwin A. Churchill, and Joel W. Eastman (Orono, ME: University of Maine Press, 1995), 201–03.

20. Hatch, *Maine,* 535.

21. Perry, *Conceived in Liberty,* 336.

22. *Bangor Whig and Courier,* January 17, 1868.

23. JLC, *Address of Governor Chamberlain to the Legislature of Maine, Bangor Whig and Courier,* January 3, 1868.

24. Ibid., 35; Michael Bailey, "Republican Ascendancy: The Gubernatorial Career of Joshua Lawrence Chamberlain, 1866–1881," *Maine History* 50, no.1 (2016): 47.

25. Brenda Wineapple, *The Impeachers: The Trial of Andrew Johnson and the Dream of a Just Nation* (New York: Random House, 2020), 260–66.

26. *Bangor Whig and Courier,* May 16, 1868.

27. Desmond, Jr., Eastman, Howe, Judd, and Schriver, "Defending Maine and the Nation," *Maine: The Pine Tree State From Prehistory to the Present,* 357–58.

28. Wineapple, *The Impeachers,* 297–99, 321–22, 363–66.

29. Desmond et al., "Defending Maine and the Nation," 358.

30. JLC, *A Sketch,* 18; Hatch, *The History of Bowdoin College,* 536–38; Wallace, *Soul of the Lion,* 215–16.

31. Hatch, *Maine,* vol. 2, 540.

32. Jason Finkelstein, "The Governor's Gallows: Joshua Lawrence Chamberlain and the Clifton Harris Case," *Maine History,* vol. 45, 2 (2010), 169–70.

33. Stuart Banner, *The Death Penalty: An American History* (Cambridge, MA: Harvard University Press, 2002), 5, 23.

34. Ibid., 88–111.

35. Ibid., 134. Edward Schriver, "Reluctant Hangman: The State of Maine and Capital Punishment, 1820–1887," *The New England Quarterly,* 63, no. 2 (June 1990): 276–78. Francis Couillard Spencer murdered the warden, Richard Tinker. Prisoner Spencer was the first person hanged at the state prison since it opened in 1824.

36. *Maine Farmer* (Augusta), February 6, 1869; Schriver, "Reluctant Hangman," 280.

37. Portland *Daily Eastern Argus,* January 8, 1869.

38. *Report of the Attorney General of the State of Maine, 1868,* Public Documents of Maine, 1868–69 (Augusta, ME: Sprague, Owen & Nash, 1869), 7; *Bangor Whig and Courier,* January 9, 1869.

39. JLC, *Address of Governor Chamberlain to the Legislature of the State of Maine,* January 1869 (Augusta, ME: Steves and Sayward, 1869).

40. JLC to SDB, January 27, 1869, BC.

41. Joshua Chamberlain, Jr., to JLC, January 30, 1869, BC.

42. JLC to FCA, November 20, 1868, YU.

43. Ibid.

44. Ibid.

45. Nicholas L. Syrett, "Responding to Domestic Violence in the Nineteenth-Century United States," *Journal of Women's History,* 33, no. 1 (Spring 2021): 158–62.

46. GDC to Harold Wyllys Chamberlain, February 15, 1869, BC.

47. Ibid.

48. "Application for Invalid Army Pension," December 26, 1868, and J. W. Toward, MD, Examining Surgeon's Certificate, February, 1869, JLC medical file, NA.

49. Wallace, *Soul of the Lion,* 219.

50. Trulock, *In the Hands of Providence,* 513, footnote 22.

51. JLC, Fourth Inaugural Address, Hatch, *Maine,* vol. 2, 563; Trulock, *In the Hands of Providence,* 513, footnote 22.

52. JLC, Fourth Inaugural Address, *Bangor Whig and Courier;* Hatch, *Maine,* vol. 2, 563.

53. Portland *Transcript,* January 15, 1870.

54. Trulock, *In The Hands of Providence,* 341.

55. JLC to William, King of Prussia, July 20, 1870. The letter is in Alice Rains Trulock papers, PHCepscot Historical Society. No response to the letter has been found.

56. Trulock, *In the Hands of Providence,* 350.

57. D. M. Smith, *Fanny & Joshua,* 212.

58. John C. Abbott, *The History of Maine* (Boston: Rand, Avery, and Co., 1875), 436–38.

59. Ibid., 444.

60. JLC, *Address of Governor Chamberlain to the Legislature of Maine,* January 1867 (Augusta, ME: Stevens and Sayward, 1867), 26.

61. Ibid., 5–6.

62. JLC, *Address of Governor Chamberlain to the Legislature of Maine,* January 1870 (Augusta, ME: Stevens and Sayward, 1870), 6.

SIXTEEN: PRESIDENT OF BOWDOIN COLLEGE

1. Hatch, *The History of Bowdoin College,* 129–30. Harris became professor of systematic theology at Yale.

2. John R. Thelin, *A History of American Higher Education* (Boston: Houghton Mifflin, 2004), 60–63. Before the early nineteenth century, Congregationalists, Presbyterians, and Anglicans (it became the Episcopal Church in 1789) founded American colleges. Starting in the 1820s, Methodists and Baptists began establishing colleges.

3. Charles William Eliot, *Educational Reform* (New York: Century Company, 1898), 105.

4. Richard Hofstadter, "The Revolution in Higher Education," in *Paths of American Thought,* edited by Arthur Schlesinger, Jr., and Morton White (Boston: Houghton Mifflin, 1963), 269–73.

5. JLC to SDB, September 8, 1871, BC.

6. I am grateful to John Cross, alumni secretary of Bowdoin College, for his knowledge of the makeup of the two boards in the nineteenth century.

7. Trudy Irene Scee, *City on the Penobscot: A Comprehensive History of Bangor, Maine* (Charleston, SC: The History Press, 2010), 132–33.

8. Fannie Harlow Robinson, *D.A.R., 1850–1930* (privately printed, 1968), 37.

9. Ibid., 37–38.

10. JLC, Bowdoin College Presidential Inaugural Address, "The New Education," September, 1871, 1–2, BC.

11. Ibid., 3.

12. Ibid., 7–8.

13. Ibid., 33.

14. Earl H. Smith, *Mayflower Hill: A History of Colby College* (Hanover, NH: University Press of New England, 2006), 5.

15. Hatch, *The History of Bowdoin College,* 90–91.

16. *Bowdoin Orient,* September 23, 1872; Hatch, *The History of Bowdoin College,* 157–58.

17. Calhoun, *A Small College in Maine,* 189.

18. George Thomas Little, *General Catalogue of Bowdoin College and the Medical School of Maine, 1794–1894,* xc, xci.

19. Ibid.

20. Trulock, *In the Hands of Providence*, 342–43.

21. Chamberlain's first annual report to the two boards; Hatch, *The History of Bowdoin College*, 131.

22. Ibid.

23. *Bowdoin Orient*, October 2, 1871.

24. Trulock, *In the Hands of Providence*, 348–49.

25. Ibid., D. M. Smith, *Fanny & Joshua*, 218–20.

26. G. D. Crace to JLC, July 24, 1872, August 8, 1872, RC.

27. D. M. Smith, *Fanny & Joshua*, 221.

28. *Portland Transcript*, October 7, 1872; Helmreich, *Religion at Bowdoin College*, 128.

29. C. F. Low to Cyrus F. Bracket, MD, September 30, 1872, RC.

30. JLC to C. F. Low, October 9, 1872, BC.

31. Lee Bjella, "Early Gymnastics in America," wanawgj.com/history/early-gymnastics-in-america/.

32. Christopher H. Wells, "Random Recollections of 1871–75," *Tales of Bowdoin: Told by Bowdoin Men*, 283.

33. Ibid.

34. Hatch, *The History of Bowdoin College*, 134.

35. Calhoun, *A Small College in Maine*, 191.

36. Hatch, *The History of Bowdoin College*, 135. Chamberlain sought to counter some of the criticisms by stating that the uniforms need be worn only during military drill.

37. JLC to Hon. L. K. Kersey, January 20, 1873, PHC; *The Grand Old Man of Maine: Selected Letters of Joshua Lawrence Chamberlain, 1865–1914*, edited by Jeremiah E. Goulka (Chapel Hill: University of North Carolina Press, 2014), 51.

38. JLC to Governor Abner Coburn, January 20, 1873, PHC; Goulka, *The Grand Old Man of Maine: Selected Letters of Joshua Lawrence Chamberlain, 1865–1914*, 55.

39. JLC to Hon. J. W. Bradbury, January 28, 1873, PHC; Goulka, *The Grand Old Man of Maine*, 52–53.

40. JLC to trustees and overseers, July 8, 1873, MHS; Goulka, *The Grand Old Man of Maine*, 59–60.

41. Student petition to abolish military drill, November 12, 1873, BC; Hatch, *The History of Bowdoin College*, 135–36.

42. Hatch, *The History of Bowdoin College*, 140–41.

43. Portland *Daily Eastern Argus*, May 25, 1874. President Chamberlain was not criticized in the article.

44. Calhoun, *A Small College in Maine*, 191–92.

45. Hatch, *The History of Bowdoin College*, 139–40.

46. Ibid.

47. Chamberlain sent a one-page letter to each parent on May 28, 1874, addressed "Dear Sir," with a space for the name of the son, BC.

48. Wells, "Random Recollections of 1871–1875," 286.

49. Hatch, *The History of Bowdoin College*, 143–44.

50. Philip S. Wilder, editor, *General Catalogue of Bowdoin College, 1794–1950* (Portland, ME: The Anthoensen Press, 1950), 99.

51. JLC to Sarah Dupee Brastow, July 4, 1874, BC.

52. Ibid.

53. JLC to Henry Wadsworth Longfellow, March 22, 1875, BC.

54. Henry Wadsworth Longfellow, "Morituri Salutamus"—"We Who Are About to Salute You."

55. Ashby, *A History of the First Parish Church,* 368.

56. Ibid., 367–68. Chamberlain took great care and spent considerable time designing the window. It was dedicated on December 17, 1882. Today it commands one's attention in entering the sanctuary.

57. JLC, Baccalaureate Address, *Bangor Whig and Courier,* July 7, 1874; *The New York Times,* July 12, 1874.

58. JLC, "Baccalaureate Address," *The New York Times,* July 9, 1877.

59. Ibid.

60. Ibid.

61. D. M. Smith, *Fanny & Joshua,* 231.

62. GDC to Horace Allen, April 5, 1876, BC.

63. JLC to GDC, May 29, 1876, MHS.

64. Ibid.

65. JLC, to trustees and overseers of Bowdoin College, June 26, 1876, MHS.

SEVENTEEN: TWELVE DAYS IN 1880

1. Charles W. Calhoun, *From Bloody Shirt to Full Dinner Pail* (New York: Hill and Wang, 2010), 34–36; Irwin Unger, *The Greenback Era: A Social and Political History of American Finance, 1865–1879* (Princeton, NJ: Princeton University Press, 1964), 213–33. The Panic of 1873 did not occur in the United States alone. From England to Germany to Russia, even to faraway South Africa and Australia, costly wars, overextended credit, and unwarranted construction of railroads, both preceded and accompanied the American homegrown economic turmoil.

2. JLC to Adelbert Ames, January 22, 1875, LOC.

3. William Drew "W.D." Washburn to JLC, June 29, 1874, MHS.

4. "Named Professorships at Bowdoin College," *Bowdoin College Bulletin,* no. 399 (December 1975): 25; *General Catalogue of Bowdoin College and the Medical School of Maine, 1794–1894,* xciv. The 1880 gift was to endow the Winkley Professorship of Latin Language and Literature.

5. Ibid., 22.

6. Dee Brown, *The Year of the Century: 1876* (New York: Charles Scribner's Sons, 1966), 112–13; Centennial Exposition of 1876: Pennsylvania Historical & Museum Commission, archive.org/details/CentennialExhibitionOf1876.

7. JLC, *Maine, Her Place in History* (Augusta, ME: Sprague, Owen & Nash, 1877), 13.

8. Ibid., 15.

9. Ibid., 4–5.

10. Ibid., 79.

11. Ibid., 96.

12. Ibid.

13. Ibid.

14. Ibid., 104.

15. General Catalogue of Bowdoin College and the Medical School of Maine 1794-1894, xci-xcii.

16. Hatch, *The History of Bowdoin College*, 156–58.

17. Ibid., 158–59.

18. Ibid., 160.

19. Wallace, *Soul of the Lion*, 231.

20. JLC to FCA, March 6, 1878, RC.

21. JLC to SDB and Joshua Chamberlain, Jr., June 14, 1878, BC.

22. Hon. Joshua L. Chamberlain, "Education as Represented at the Universal Exposition," in *Reports of the United States Commissioners to the Paris Universal Exposition, 1878* (Washington, D.C.: Government Printing Office, 1880), vol. II, 228, 342, 344, 347.

23. Chamberlain offered analysis of education in France, Belgium, the Netherlands, Norway, Sweden, Denmark, Finland, Russia, Greece, Switzerland, Algeria, Japan, Argentina, Uruguay, and Canada.

24. GDC to Horace Allen, September 28, 1878, BC.

25. *Bowdoin Orient*, December 18, 1878; Calhoun, *A Small College in Maine*, 193, 205, note 19.

26. D. M. Smith, *Fanny & Joshua*, 245–46.

27. Trulock, *In the Hands of Providence*, 347.

28. JLC, handwritten note on Domhegan, PHC.

29. Edward Schriver and Stanley Howe, "The Republican Ascendancy: Politics and Reform in Maine," in *Maine: The Pine Tree State from Prehistory to the Present* (Orono: University of Maine Press, 1995), 373–74.

30. Hatch, *Maine*, vol. 2, 593–95.

31. Ibid., 595.

32. Ibid., *Maine: A History*, 596–97; John J. Pullen, *Joshua Chamberlain: A Hero's Life & Legacy* (Mechanicsburg, PA: Stackpole Books, 1999), 78.

33. Rolde, *Continental Liar*, 201.

34. Hatch, *Maine*, 599.

35. Ibid., 602; Pullen, *Joshua Chamberlain*, 82–83; Tom Huntington, *Maine at 200: An Anecdotal History Celebrating Two Centuries of Statehood* (Camden, ME: Down East Books, 2020), 54–55.

36. *Bangor Whig and Courier*, November 17, 1879.

37. Pullen, *Joshua Chamberlain*, 81–82.

38. Rolde, *Continental Liar*, 202–03.

39. James G. Blaine to JLC, December 24 and 29, 1879; JLC to James G. Blaine, December 29, 1879, PHC; the Chamberlain quotes are also in *Twelve Days at Augusta, 1880* (Portland, ME: Smith and Dale, 1906). No author was listed, but the book was endorsed by Chamberlain.

40. *Portland Daily Press*, January 3, 1880; Pullen, *Joshua Chamberlain*, 87.

41. Alonzo Garcelon to JLC, January 1880, Desjardin, *Joshua L. Chamberlain: A Life in Letters*, 239.

42. Chamberlain provided no contemporary account of the crisis.

43. Wallace, *Soul of the Lion*, 260; Pullen, *Joshua Chamberlain*, 92–93.

44. JLC to FCA, January 7, 1880, Goulka, *The Grand Old Man of Maine*, 94.

45. JLC to FCA, January 9, 1880, Ibid., 94–95.

46. Thomas Reed to George Clifford, January 10, 1880, George Clifford Papers, Rubenstein Rare Book & Manuscript Library, Duke University; D. M. Smith, *Fanny & Joshua*, 246–47.

47. *Twelve Days in August*, 10.

48. Pullen, *Joshua Chamberlain*, 94.

49. Hatch, *Maine*, 612.

50. Rolde, *Continental Liar*, 207.

51. JLC to FCA, January 15, 1880, Goulka, *The Grand Old Man of Maine*, 96–97.

52. Ibid., 97.

53. F. B. Ward to JLC, January 15, 1880, LOC; Desjardin, *Stand Firm Ye Boys from Maine*, 93.

54. *Twelve Days in August*, 24–25.

55. Edward Nelson Dingley, *The Life and Times of Nelson Dingley, Jr.* (Kalamazoo, MI: Ihling Bros. & Everard, 1902), 171.

56. *Twelve Days in August*, 25.

57. JLC to FCA, January 15, 1880, Goulka, *The Grand Old Man of Maine*, 97.

58. Trulock, *In the Hands of Providence*, 359.

59. Daniel F. Davis to JLC, January 17, 1880, quoted in Wallace, *Soul of the Lion*, 266.

60. Augusta *Kennebec Journal*, January 21, 1880.

61. *The Times* (Philadelphia), n.d., JLC Scrapbook, UMO.

62. Samuel Harris to JLC, January 13, 1880, Desjardin, *Joshua L. Chamberlain: A Life in Letters*, 248–49.

63. Lewis Pierce to JLC, January 19, 1880, Ibid., 269.

64. L. T. Carleton to JLC, January 13, 1880, Ibid., 247.

65. Ellis Spear to JLC, January 17, 1880, Ibid.

66. D. M. Shapleigh to JLC, January 15, 1880, Ibid., 250.

67. J. W. Chadwick to JLC, January 15, 1880, Ibid., 251–52.

68. A. L. Pearson to JLC, January 16, 1880, Ibid., 253–54.

69. J. Warren Brown to JLC, January 17, 1880, Ibid., 259–60.

70. Horace Allen to GDC, January 18, 1880, BC.

71. *Bowdoin Orient* 9, no. 13 (February 4, 1880).

72. JLC to SDB, November 27, 1877, UMO.

73. D. M. Smith, *Fanny & Joshua*, 253.

74. Meeting of March 12, 1883, *Faculty Records, 1874–1886*, BC.

75. Joseph H. Warren to JLC, March 2, 1883, YU; Sarah Handley-Cousins, " 'Wrestling at the Gates of Death,' " *Journal of the Civil War Era*, vol. 6, no. 2 (June 2016): 228. Warren practiced medicine in Boston from 1856 to 1891.

76. Sarah Handley-Cousins writes of the communal nature of the Civil War wounds of veterans. See " 'Wrestling at the Gates of Death,' " 229–30.

77. John Bigelow to JLC, April 27, 1883, MHS.

78. FCA to JLC, April 21, 1883, copy in Alice Trulock Collection, PHC.

79. Wallace, *Soul of the Lion*, 270.

80. JLC to Henry Johnson, February 6, 1884, BC.

EIGHTEEN: SECOND CIVIL WAR

1. JLC, "The Army of the Potomac," July 4, 1869, reported in *Daily Eastern Argus,* July 9, 1869.

2. JLC, "The Battle of Gettysburg," *Bangor Whig and Courier,* December 20 and 22, 1865.

3. Ibid.

4. JLC, "The Battle of Gettysburg," *Boston Daily Journal,* November 13, 1868.

5. Ibid.

6. JLC, "Loyalty," February 22, 1866, 36, 38, 41–42, 54, BC.

7. "The Surrender of Gen. Lee," *Kennebec Journal* (Augusta), January 3, 1866.

8. JLC, Address at the First Reunion of the Army of the Potomac and the Organization of the Society of the Army of the Potomac, at New York, July 4, 1969, 1. Republished by request of members of the society.

9. Ibid., 2.

10. Ibid.

11. Ibid.

12. JLC, "The Old Flag: What Was Surrendered? What Was Won?" 1, *Boston Journal,* January 4, 1878.

13. Ibid., 2.

14. Ibid.

15. JLC, "The Heroes of the War," *Lewiston Evening Journal,* May 31, 1879. Ibid.

16. *Oxford Democrat* (Paris, Maine), June 10, 1879.

17. *Bangor Whig and Courier,* June 25, 1879.

18. Ibid., June 26, 1879.

19. JLC, "The Surrender of Gen. Lee," BC; *Kennebec Journal* (Augusta), January 3, 1868; *Bangor Daily Whig and Courier,* February 1, 17–18. Copies of both newspapers, BC.

20. William G. Marvel, "A Question of Rhetoric," *North & South,* vol. 2 (June 1999), 80–85; see also Marvel, *Lee's Last Retreat: The Flight to Appomattox* (Chapel Hill: University of North Carolina Press, 2002), 193-95; and Marvel, *A Place Called Appomattox* (Chapel Hill: University of North Carolina Press, 2000), 259-61; quote on page 358, footnote 38.

21. Stephen Cushman, *Belligerent Muse: Five Northern Writers and How They Shaped Our Understanding of the Civil War* (Chapel Hill: University of North Carolina Press, 2014), 151–52.

22. Ibid., 149. For Cushman's detailed response to Marvel, see 198–99, footnote 6.

23. *Boston Evening Transcript,* June 5, 1865.

24. *The New York Times,* July 22, 1865.

25. Washington *Evening Star,* July 25, 1865.

26. Gerrish, *Army Life,* 175.

27. William T. Livermore to JLC, May 22, 1899, MHS.

28. *Hearst's Magazine,* 23 (June 1913), 894–909; Coan had died in 1896.

29. Ibid., xxx.

30. Jordan, *"Happiness Is Not My Companion": The Life of General G. K. Warren,* 262.

31. JLC to Fanny, May 11, 1880, RC.

32. Ibid.

33. Jordan, *"Happiness Is Not My Companion": The Life of General G. K. Warren,* 272.

34. Ibid., 289.

35. *Boston Daily Advertiser,* December 22, 1880; Jordan, *"Happiness Is Not My Companion":* *The Life of General G. K. Warren,* 292.

36. Jordan, *"Happiness Is Not My Companion": The Life of General G. K. Warren,* 296.

37. Ibid., 308–10.

38. *The New York Times,* August 8, 1885.

39. The *New-York Tribune,* August 8, 1885.

40. White, *American Ulysses,* 635–49.

41. For the description and analysis of Grant's funeral procession, see Joan Waugh, "Pageantry of War: The Funeral of Ulysses S. Grant," in *Vale of Tears: New Essays on Religion and Reconstruction,* edited by Edward J. Blum and W. Scott Poole (Macon, GA: Mercer University Press, 2005), 212–34. For a contemporary account, see Benjamin Perley Poore and O. H. Tiffany, *Life of U. S. Grant* (Philadelphia: Hubbard Brothers, 1885), 549–71.

42. JLC to FCA, August 8, 1885, MSA.

43. Ibid.

44. The Blog of Gettysburg National Military Park, npsgnmp.wordpress.com/2015/10 /16/the-grand-reunion-of-1888/.

45. JLC to GDC, July 13, 1888, BC.

46. Jordan, *"Happiness Is Not My Companion": The Life of General G. K. Warren,* 313; Gettysburg.stonesentinels.com/monuments-to-individuals/Gouverneur-warren/.

47. JLC, *Address of Gen. Joshua L. Chamberlain at the Dedication of the Maine Monuments on the Battlefield of Gettysburg, October 3, 1889* (Augusta, ME: Maine Farmer's Almanac Press, 1895).

48. JLC, "Dedication of the Maine Monuments at Gettysburg, October 3, 1889," *Bayonet! Forward,* 192.

49. Ibid., 202.

NINETEEN: THE ENTREPENEUR

1. Thomas Graham, "The First Developers," *The History of Florida,* edited by Michael Gannon (Gainesville: University Press of Florida, 1996), 276.

2. Jerrell H. Shofner, "Reconstruction and Renewal, 1865–1877," *The History of Florida,* 268.

3. Eloise Robinson Ott and Louis Hickman Chazal, *Ocali Country, Kingdom of the Sun: A History of Marion County, Florida* (Ocala, FL: Greene's Printing, 1986), 115, 126–27.

4. W. Horace Carter, *Nature's Masterpiece at Homosassa* (Tabor City, NC: Atlantic Publishing, 1981), 5.

5. James Hoge, "The Silver Springs, Ocala, and Gulf: From Dream to Reality," Citrus County Historical Society, November–December, 1994, 5.

6. Ibid., 16. For more on Dunn, see Ott and Chazel, *Ocali Country,* 127.

7. JLC to SBC, January 29, 1882, UMO.

8. As noted earlier, Rasbach, in *Joshua Lawrence Chamberlain and the Petersburg Campaign,* determined a slightly different place where Chamberlain fought and was wounded.

9. JLC to SBC, January 29, 1882, UMO.

10. Ibid.

11. Hampton Dunn, *Back Home: A History of Citrus County, Florida* (Clearwater, FL: Artcraft Printing, n.d.), 100–01. This newly settled region officially became Citrus County in 1887.

12. Esther Crain, *The Gilded Age in New York, 1870–1910* (New York: Black Dog & Leventhal Publishers, 2016), 41–43.

13. James D. McCabe, *New York by Sunlight and Gaslight* (Philadelphia: Douglas Bros., 1882), 60.

14. Trulock, *In the Hands of Providence*, 366–67.

15. JLC to FCA, October 20, 1885, BC.

16. Ibid.

17. Ibid.

18. SBC to JLC, January 3, 1886, RC.

19. On the Great Freeze of 1885–86, see weather.gov/media/tbw/paig/PresAmFreeze1886.pdf.

20. Trulock, *In The Hands of Providence*, 367.

21. D. M. Smith, *Fanny & Joshua*, 266–67.

22. JLC to GDC, February 15, 1887.

23. JLC to SDB, September 8, 1887, LOC.

24. JLC to GDC, January 18, 1889, BC.

25. JLC to FCA, n. d. (1891), MSA.

26. JLC to Bureau of Pensions, February 6, 1893, NA; JLC Pension Record, NA; Robert Holmes Green, MD, to Bureau of Pensions, JLC Pension Record, NA.

27. Alexander Webb to JLC, April 4, 1893, LOC.

28. Lincoln used these words in his Young Men's Lyceum Speech of January 27, 1838, where he evoked the inheritance of the founders of the republic. Abraham Lincoln, "Address Before the Young Men's Lyceum of Springfield, Illinois, January 27, 1838," vol. 1:108; White, *A. Lincoln*, 87.

29. Thomas H. Hubbard to War Department, March 1, 1893, JLC Military Personnel File, NA.

30. JLC to Alexander Webb, May 18, 1893, Alexander Webb Collection, YU.

31. Fitz John Porter to Secretary of War Daniel S. Lamont, May 19, 1893, NA; affidavit of Fitz John Porter to Bureau of Pensions, NA.

32. Congressional Medal of Honor Society, cmohs.org/recipients.

33. JLC to unknown [probably Alexander Webb], April 23, 1893, MSA.

34. Ibid.

35. JLC to FCA, January 23, 1894, BC.

36. JFC to FCA, October 23, 1894, BC.

37. Trulock, *In the Hands of Providence*, 369–70.

38. Ibid., 371.

39. Wallace, *Soul of the Lion*, 288–89.

40. G.J.A. O'Toole, *The Spanish War: An American Epic 1898* (New York: W. W. Norton, 1986).

41. JLC to William P. Frye, April 22, 1898, JLC Military Personnel File, NA.

42. Secretary of War Russell A. Alger to JLC, April 30, 1898, JLC Military Personnel File, NA. The secretary of war wrote, "I have your patriotic letter of the 22nd instant offer-

ing your services in the impending war, which has been placed on file for consideration at the proper time should an opportunity occur making this possible."

43. George O. Cutler to the Navy Department, May 11, 1898, NA.

44. Francis Fessenden to JLC, March, 1899, LOC.

45. Ibid.

46. JLC to Francis Fessenden, March 9, 1899, LOC.

47. Wyllys to Fanny, n.d., probably early 1891, MSA.

48. JLC to SBC, December 24, 1899, LOC.

TWENTY: "REMEMBER AND GO FORWARD"

1. Ellis Spear to Hon. Amos Allen, House of Representatives, December 4, 1899, BC; Wallace, *Soul of the Lion*, 292.

2. Chief of the Division of Appointments, Treasury Department, to JLC, March 27, 1900, YU; A. O. Shaw to JLC, December 5, 1899, MHS.

3. JLC to John T. Richardson, December 26, 1899, MHS.

4. Sarah Sampson to JLC, November 2, 1900, MHS.

5. JLC to FCA, November 6, 1900.

6. JLC to Secretary of State John Milton Hay, October 25, 1900, YU; "Letter Received from Gen. Chamberlain Who Is in Egypt," newspaper clipping, PHC.

7. *Portland Press,* January 10, 1901; *Brunswick Telegraph,* January 12, 1901; Wallace, *Soul of the Lion*, 296–97.

8. L. C. Bateman, "At Home with Gen. Joshua Lawrence Chamberlain in Old Longfellow House, Brunswick," *Lewiston Journal Illustrated Magazine,* August 1907.

9. *JLC: A Sketch*, 34–35; for the story of the American Bible Society, see Paul C. Gutjahr, *An American Bible: A History of the Good Book in the United States, 1777–1880* (Stanford, CA: Stanford University Press, 1999).

10. *JLC: A Sketch*, 34–35.

11. D. M. Smith, *Fanny & Joshua*, 288–89.

12. JLC to Ellis Spear, November 27, 1896, BC.

13. *Maine at Gettysburg, Report of Maine Commissioners*, The Executive Committee (Portland, ME: Lakeside Press, 1898), 255, 257.

14. Eckert, *John Brown Gordon*, 324–26.

15. *The New York Times,* November 26, 1893; Cushman, *Belligerent Muse,* 159.

16. Eckert, *John Brown Gordon*, 315–17.

17. *The New York Times,* November 26, 1893.

18. John Brown Gordon, *Reminiscences of the Civil War* (New York: C. Scribner's Sons, 1903).

19. William G. Marvel is suspicious of Brown's account. Of the surrender, "each told it in flattering terms of the other." Marvel, *A Place Called Appomattox,* 261–62.

20. JLC to Frank A. Guernsey, January 18, 1899, Goulka, *The Grand Old Man of Maine,* 166–67.

21. Eckert, *John Brown Gordon*, 341–42; D. M. Smith, *Fanny & Joshua*, 316.

22. D. M. Smith, *Fanny & Joshua*, 316.

23. The story of Oates's initiative to place a memorial stone honoring the Fifteenth Alabama at Little Round Top is told in detail by LaFantasie, *Gettysburg Requiem,* 291. He

writes, "Beneath the surface of his excruciating fight to erect a monument on Little Round Top lay hidden the unreconstructed and unreconciled antagonisms of the war itself."

24. Ibid., 233.

25. Ibid., 263–64.

26. John P. Nicholson to JLC, August 6, 1903, GNMPL.

27. JLC to William C. Oates, February 27, 1897, BC.

28. JLC to John P. Nicholson, August 14, 1903, GNMPL.

29. Oates, *The War Between the Union and the Confederacy.*

30. *Memphis Commercial Appeal,* March 6, 1905; New York *Literary Digest,* April 8, 1905, cited in LaFantasie, *Gettysburg Requiem,* 295 and 363, footnote 21.

31. William C. Oates to JLC, April 14, 1905, GNMPL.

32. JLC to William C. Oates, May 18, 1905, GNMPL.

33. John P. Nicholson to JLC, May 22, 1905, GNMPL.

34. JLC to FCA, August 12, 1905, RC.

35. Trulock, *In the Hands of Providence,* 372.

36. JLC to Rosamond Allen, December 27, 1909, BC; Trulock, *In the Hands of Providence,* 372.

37. *Abraham Lincoln: The Tribute of a Century, 1809–1909,* edited by Nathan William MacChesney (Chicago: A. C. McClurg, 1910). Commemorative events were also held in Manchester, England; Berlin, Germany; Paris, France; and Rome, Italy.

38. JLC, "Abraham Lincoln: Seen from the Field in the War for the Union," (Commandery of the State of Pennsylvania, Military Order of the Loyal Legion of the United States, February 12, 1909); JLC, *Bayonet! Forward,* 244–46.

39. JLC to SBC, February 1910, UMO.

40. Ellis Spear to JLC, December 24, 1910, BC.

41. JLC to GDC, December 9, 1911, RC.

42. Selden Connor to JLC, December 30, 1911, MHS.

43. JLC, "My Story of Fredericksburg," *Cosmopolitan* 54 (December 1912): 56; *Bayonet! Forward,* 1–15.

44. JLC to Fanny Hardy Eckstrom, February 10 and March 2, 1913, UMO.

45. JLC, "Through Blood and Fire at Gettysburg," *Hearst's Magazine,* 894–909.

46. JLC to Fanny Hardy Eckstrom, August 28, 1913, UMO.

47. See H. G. Myers, *The Lion of Round Top: The Life and Military Service of Brigadier General Strong Vincent in the American Civil War* (Philadelphia: Casemate, 2022).

48. JLC, "Through Blood and Fire at Gettysburg," *Bayonet! Forward,* 27.

49. Ibid., 28.

50. Ibid., 33.

51. Spear's grandson, Abbott Spear (1907–1995), brought his grandfather's response to Chamberlain to contemporary readers by publishing " 'My Story of Fredericksburg' and Comments Thereon by One Who Was There," Abbott Spear and Ellis Spear, *The 20th Maine at Fredericksburg: The Conflicting Accounts of General Joshua L. Chamberlain and General Ellis Spear,* foreword by Tom Desjardin (Union, ME: Union Publishing Company, 1989), 45, 46, 49.

52. See Desjardin, foreword, Spear and Spear, *The 20th Maine at Fredericksburg,* 5–7.

53. Trulock, *In the Hands of Providence,* 374, 528, footnote 110.

54. James Rada, Jr., *No North, No South . . . : The Grand Reunion at the 50th Anniversary of the Battle of Gettysburg* (Gettysburg, PA: Legacy Publishing, 2013), 73.

55. Rada, *No North, No South*, 88–90.

56. *Fiftieth Anniversary of the Battle of Gettysburg: Report of the Pennsylvania Commission* (Harrisburg, PA: W. S. Ray, 1913), 6, 29. The committee meeting took place May 15–16, 1913.

57. JLC to SBC, January 20, 1914, UMO.

58. "Grand Old Hero Is Dead," Portland *Daily Eastern Argus*, February 25, 1914.

59. "Services City Hall Probable," *Portland Evening Express*, February 24, 1914; "Simple Services," Portland *Daily Eastern Argus*, February 26, 1914.

60. Portland *Daily Eastern Argus*, February 28, 1914.

61. *Lewiston Journal*, February 28, 1914; Hatch, *The History of Bowdoin College*, 131.

EPILOGUE

1. JLC, *The Passing of the Armies*, 146.

2. Ibid., 121, 381.

3. Ibid., 148.

4. Ibid., 391–92.

5. I am grateful to Civil War historian Gary Gallagher for informing me of these two books about Gettysburg. See Gary H. Gallagher, *The Enduring Civil War: Reflections on the Great American Crisis* (Baton Rouge: Louisiana State University Press, 2020), 21–22 and notes 246.

6. https://pejepscothistorical.org/chamberlain/historyhouse.

7. Gary W. Gallagher, *Causes Won, Lost, Forgotten: How Hollywood and Popular Art Shape What We Know About the Civil War* (Chapel Hill: University of North Carolina Press, 2008), 189–202.

8. I am grateful to Ben Hansford, senior director of philanthropy at The Gettysburg Foundation for information on the rehabilitation. See https://www.nps.gov/gett/learn/historyculture/little-round-top.htm.

9. Helen E. Kilham to JLC, January 18, 1880, Desjardin, *Joshua L. Chamberlain: A Life in Letters*, 265–66.

10. JLC, *Early Memoir*, 54.

SELECTED BIBLIOGRAPHY

MANUSCRIPT COLLECTIONS

Alabama Historical Society, Montgomery, AL
The Papers of Governor William C. Oates

Bowdoin College, Hawthorne-Longfellow Library, George J. Mitchell Special Collections & Archives, Brunswick, ME
Joshua Lawrence Chamberlain Collection

Brewer Historical Society, Brewer, ME
First Congregational Church, Brewer, ME, Papers

Duke University, Durham, NC, George Clifford Papers, Rubenstein Rare Book & Manuscript Library
Joshua Lawrence Chamberlain, "The Charge at Fort Hell," 1899, William Henry Noble
    Papers, Special Collections Library

First Parish Church, Brunswick, ME
George E. Adams Diaries

Gettysburg National Military Park Library, Gettysburg, PA
Gettysburg Battlefield Commission Map, Blueprint, 1893
William C. Oates Correspondence Scrapbook
Fifteenth Alabama Infantry Regiment File
Twentieth Maine Volunteer Infantry File
July 2: Little Round Top (Twentieth Maine Infantry vs. Fifteenth Alabama Infantry)
July 2: Little Round Top (Vincent & Weed vs. Law & Robertson) File
Ellis Spear, "Recollections" (typescript copy) Twentieth Maine Infantry Regiment File

The Huntington Library, San Marino, CA
John P. Nicholson Papers
Joshua Lawrence Chamberlain Papers

Library of Congress, Manuscripts Division, Washington, D.C.
Joshua Lawrence Chamberlain Papers
Twentieth Maine Muster Roll
Twentieth Maine Regimental Books

Maine Historical Society, Portland, ME
Bangor Theological Seminary Collection
Holman Melcher Papers

Holman Melcher Scrapbook
Joshua Lawrence Chamberlain Collection

Maine State Archives, Augusta, ME
Records of the Adjutant General of Maine
Civil War Correspondence, 1861–1866
Civil War Photographs
Gettysburg Reunion Records

National Archives, Washington, D.C.
Joshua Lawrence Chamberlain, Compiled Service Records

National Civil War Museum, Harrisburg, PA
Joshua Lawrence Chamberlain Collection

Pejepscot Historical Society, Brunswick, ME
Alice Trulock Collection
John Chamberlain Diary
Joshua Lawrence Chamberlain Files
Joshua L. Chamberlain Letter Book or Order Book
Photograph Collection

Radcliffe College, Schlesinger Library, Cambridge, MA
Chamberlain-Adams Family Correspondence

The Union League Club of Philadelphia
Military Order of the Loyal Legion of the United States, Philadelphia, PA, Papers

University of Maine, Raymond H. Fogler Library, Orono, ME
Chamberlain Family Papers
Joshua Chamberlain, Author's Proof, "My Story of Fredericksburg"
Joshua Chamberlain Scrapbook
William Livermore Diary

U.S. Army Heritage and Education Center, Carlisle, PA
Brake Collection (Joshua Lawrence Chamberlain Papers)
Harrisburg Civil War Roundtable Collection
Maine Twentieth Maine Infantry Regiment Papers

Yale University, Manuscripts and Archives Library
Frost Family Papers

BOOKS

A Diary of Battle: The Personal Journals of Colonel Charles S. Wainwright 1861–1865, edited by Allan Nevins, new foreword by Stephen W. Sears. Boston: Da Capo Press, 1998 (Original publication: New York: Harcourt, Brace, & World, 1862).

A Distant War Comes Home: Maine in the Civil War Era, edited by Donald W. Beattie, Rodney M. Cole, and Charles G. Waugh. Camden, ME: Down East Books, 1991.

Abbott, John C., *The History of Maine*. Boston: Rand, Avery, and Co., 1875.

Abraham Lincoln: The Tribute of a Century, 1809–1909, edited by Nathan William MacChesney. Chicago: A. C. McClurg, 1910.

Ames, Blanche, *Adelbert Ames: 1835–1933, General, Senator, Governor, the Story of His Life and Times and His Integrity as a Soldier and Statesman in the Service of the United States throughout the Civil War and in Mississippi in the Years of Reconstruction*. New York: Argosy-Antiquarian, 1964.

Anderson, Brian, *Images of America: Ford's Theatre*. Charleston, SC: Arcadia Publishing, 2014.

Anderson, Patricia McGraw, *The Architecture of Bowdoin College*. Brunswick, ME: Bowdoin College Museum of Art, 1988.

Annual Report of the Adjutant General, State of Maine, 1862. Augusta, ME: Stevens and Sayward, 1862.

Applebome, Peter, Georg R. Sheets, L. Douglas Wilder, and Charles Reagan Wilson, *The Grand Review: The Civil War Continues to Shape America*. York, PA: Bold Print, 2000.

Ashby, Thompson Eldridge, *A History of the First Parish Church in Brunswick, Maine*, edited by Louise R. Helmreich. Brunswick, ME: First Parish Church, 1969.

Ayers, Edward L., *In the Presence of Mine Enemies: Civil War in the Heart of America 1859–1864*. New York: W. W. Norton, 2004.

Banks, Ronald F., *Maine Becomes a State: The Movement to Separate Maine from Massachusetts, 1785–1820*. Middletown, CT: Published for the Maine Historical Society by Wesleyan University Press, 1970.

Battles and Leaders of the Civil War, 4 vols. New York: Century Company, 1887–1888.

Berlin, James A., *Writing Instruction in Nineteenth-Century American Colleges*. Carbondale: Southern Illinois University Press, 1984.

Bonner, James C., *Milledgeville: Georgia's Antebellum Capital*. Athens, GA. University of Georgia Press, 1978.

Book of Confessions, Study Edition, Revised. Louisville, KY: Westminster John Knox Press, 2017.

Boylan, Anne M., *Sunday School: The Formation of an American Institution, 1790–1880*. New Haven, CT: Yale University Press, 1988.

Brooks, Noah, *Washington, D.C., in Lincoln's Time: A Memoir of the Civil War Era by the Newspaperman Who Knew Lincoln Best*. New York: The Century Company, 1895.

Bryant, James K., II, *The Battle of Fredericksburg: We Cannot Escape History*. Charleston, SC: The History Press, 2010.

Calhoun, Charles C., *A Small College in Maine: Two Hundred Years of Bowdoin*. Brunswick, ME: Bowdoin College, 1993.

Calhoun, Charles W., *From Bloody Shirt to Full Dinner Pail: The Transformation of Politics and Governance in the Gilded Age*. New York: Hill and Wang, 2010.

Calkins, Chris M., *The Appomattox Campaign, March 29–April 9, 1865*. Lynchburg, VA: Schroeder Publications, 2008.

Campbell, William E., *The Aroostook War of 1839*. Fredericton, New Brunswick: Goose Lane Editions and the New Brunswick Military Heritage Project, 2013.

Carter, Robert Goldthwaite, *Four Brothers in Blue: Or Sunshine and Shadows of the War of the Rebellion: A Story of the Great Civil War from Bull Run to Appomattox*. Austin, University of Texas Press, 1978.

Carter, W. Horace, *Nature's Masterpiece at Homosassa: Where the Saltgrass Joins the Sawgrass*. Tabor City, NC: Atlantic Publishing Company, 1981.

Catalogue of Officers and Students of Bowdoin College and the Medical School of Maine. Brunswick, ME: Press of Joseph Griffin, 1847 and 1849.

Chamberlain Association of America, *Joshua Lawrence Chamberlain: A Sketch*. N.P. (1906) (Reprint, Compiled by Brian L. Higgins, Bangor, ME: Bangor Letter Shop, 1995).

Chamberlain, Joshua Lawrence, *Abraham Lincoln Seen from the Field in the War for the Union*. Philadelphia: Military order of the Loyal Legion of the United States, 1909.

_____, *Address of Gen. Joshua L. Chamberlain at the Dedication of the Maine Monuments Battlefield of Gettysburg, October 3, 1889*. Portland, ME: Lakeside Press, 1898. Augusta, ME: Farmers' Almanac Press, 1895.

_____, *Address of Governor Chamberlain to the Legislature of the State of Maine, January 1867*. Augusta, ME: Stevens and Sayward, 1867.

_____, *Address of Governor Chamberlain to the Legislature of the State of Maine, January 1868*. Augusta, ME: Stevens and Sayward, 1868.

_____, *Address of Governor Chamberlain to the Legislature of the State of Maine, January 1869*. Augusta, ME: Stevens and Sayward, 1869.

_____, *Address of Governor Chamberlain to the Legislature of the State of Maine, January 1870*. Augusta, ME: Stevens and Sayward, 1870.

_____, *"Blessed Boyhood!" The 'Early Memoir' of Joshua Lawrence Chamberlain*. With annotations by Thomas A. Desjardin and David K. Thomson. Brunswick, ME: Bowdoin College, 2013.

_____, *Five Forks: A Paper Read Before the Military Order of the Loyal Legion, Commandery of Maine, May 2, 1901*. Portland, ME: Lefavor-Tower Company, 1902.

_____, *Maine: Her Place in History*. Augusta, ME: Sprague, Owen & Nash, 1877.

_____, *The Passing of the Armies: An Account of the Final Campaign of the Army of the Potomac*. New York: G. P. Putnam's Sons, 1915.

Chamberlin, Thomas, *History of the One Hundred Fiftieth Regiment, Pennsylvania Volunteers*. Philadelphia: Lippincott, 1895.

Clark, Calvin Montague, *American Slavery and Maine Congregationalists: A Chapter in the History of the Development of Anti-Slavery Sentiment in the Protestant Churches of the North*. Bangor, ME: Calvin Montague Clark, 1940.

_____, *History of Bangor Theological Seminary*. Boston: Pilgrim Press, 1916.

_____, *History of the Congregational Churches in Maine*, vol. 2. Portland, ME: Southworth Press, 1935.

Clark, Charles, E., *Maine: A History*. New York: W. W. Norton, 1977.

Cleaveland, Nehemiah, edited and completed by Alpheus Spring Packard, *History of Bowdoin College: With Biographical Sketches of Its Graduates, from 1806 to 1879*. Boston: J. R. Osgood & Co., 1882.

Cleaves, Freeman, *Meade of Gettysburg*. Norman: University of Oklahoma Press, 1960.

Cold Harbor to the Crater: The End of the Overland Campaign, edited by Gary W. Gallagher and Caroline E. Janney. Chapel Hill: University of North Carolina Press, 2015.

Connor, Selden, Franklin M. Drew, and Abner O. Shaw, *In Memoriam: Companion Joshua Lawrence Chamberlain*. Portland, ME: Military Order of the Loyal Legion of the United States, 1914.

Cook, Walter L., *Bangor Theological Seminary: A Sesquicentennial History*. Orono: University of Maine Press, 1971.

Cooper, William J., Jr., *Jefferson Davis, American*. New York: A. A. Knopf, 2000.

Coulter, John Alfred, II, *Cadets on Campus: History of Military Schools of the United States*. College Station, TX: Texas A & M University Press, 2017.

Davis, Jefferson, *Speeches of the Hon. Jefferson Davis of Mississippi, Delivered During the Summer of 1858*. Baltimore: n.p., 1859.

Davis, William C., *Jefferson Davis: The Man and His Hour*. New York: HarperCollins, 1991.

Desjardin, Thomas A., *Stand Firm Ye Boys from Maine: The 20th Maine and the Gettysburg Campaign*. New York: Oxford University Press, 1995.

Desjardin, Thomas A., ed. *Joshua L. Chamberlain: A Life in Letters*. Oxford, U.K.: Osprey Publishing, 2012.

Dingley, Edward Nelson, *The Life and Times of Nelson Dingley, Jr.* Kalamazoo, MI: Ihling Bros. Everard, 1902.

Dorien, Gary, *The Making of American Liberal Theology: Imagining Progressive Religion, 1805–1900*. Louisville, KY: Westminster John Knox Press, 2001.

Dow, Neal, *The Reminiscences of Neal Dow*. Portland, ME: Evening Express Publishing Company, 1898.

Eben F. Pillsbury's Record! As Written with His Own Pen. Augusta, ME: n.p., 1866.

Eckert, Ralph Lowell, *John Brown Gordon: Soldier, Southerner, American*. Baton Rouge: Louisiana State University Press, 1989.

Edwards, George Thornton, *Music and Musicians of Maine*. Portland, ME: Southworth Press, 1928.

Edwards, Jonathan, *Two Dissertations, I. Concerning the End for Which God Created the World. II. The Nature of True Virtue*. Boston: S. Kneeland, 1765.

Epps, Garrett, *Democracy Reborn: The Fourteenth Amendment and the Fight for Equal Rights in Post–Civil War America*. New York: Henry Holt, 2006.

Fiftieth Anniversary of the Battle of Gettysburg: Report of the Pennsylvania Commission. Harrisburg, PA: W. S. Ray, 1913.

Foner, Eric, *Free Soil, Free Labor, Free Men: The Ideology of the Republican Party Before the Civil War*. New York: Oxford University Press, 1970.

————, *Reconstruction: America's Unfinished Revolution, 1863–1877*. New York: Harper & Row, 1988.

Foster, Charles I., *An Errand of Mercy: The Evangelical United Front, 1790–1837*. Chapel Hill: University of North Carolina Press, 1960.

Fraser, James W., *Schooling the Preachers: The Development of Protestant Theological Education in the United States, 1740–1875*. Lanham, MD: University Press of America, 1988.

Freeman, Douglas Southall, *R. E. Lee: A Biography*, 4 vols. New York: Charles Scribner's Sons, 1934–35.

Furbish, John, *"Darkness Is Over Our Land . . .": Civil War Perspectives from the Journals of John Furbish*, edited by Judith Kenoyer Stoy. Brunswick, ME: Pejepscot Historical Society, 2018.

Gallagher, Gary W., *Causes Won, Lost, and Forgotten: How Hollywood and Popular Art Shape What We Know About the Civil War*. Chapel Hill: University of North Carolina Press, 2013.

————, *The Enduring Civil War: Reflections on the Great American Crisis*. Baton Rouge: Louisiana State University Press, 2020.

————, *The Union War*. Cambridge, MA: Harvard University Press, 2011.

General Catalogue of Bowdoin College, 1794–1894. Brunswick, ME: Bowdoin College, 1894.

General Catalogue of Bowdoin College, 1794–1950, Philip S. Wilder, editor. Portland, ME: The Anthoensen Press, 1950.

Gerrish, Theodore, *Army Life: A Private's Reminiscences of the Civil War*. Portland, ME: Hoyt, Fogg & Donham, 1882.

Golay, Michael, *To Gettysburg and Beyond: The Parallel Lives of Joshua Lawrence Chamberlain and Edward Porter Alexander*. Rockville Center, NY: Sarpedon Publishers, 1994.

Gordon, John Brown, *Reminiscences of the Civil War*. New York: C. Scribner's Sons, 1903.

Grant, Ulysses S., *The Personal Memoirs of U. S. Grant*, 2 vols. New York: Charles L. Webster & Co., 1885.

Greene, A. Wilson, *A Campaign of Giants: The Battle for Petersburg*, vol. 1: *From the Crossing of the James to the Crater*. Chapel Hill: University of North Carolina Press, 2018.

_____, *The Final Battles of the Petersburg Campaign: Breaking the Backbone of the Rebellion*. Knoxville: University of Tennessee Press, 2008.

Griffin, Clifford S., *Their Brothers' Keepers: Moral Stewardship in the United States, 1800–1865*. New Brunswick, NJ: Rutgers University Press, 1960.

Guelzo, Allen C., *Gettysburg: The Last Invasion*. New York: Alfred A. Knopf, 2013.

_____, *Robert E. Lee: A Life*. New York: Alfred A. Knopf, 2021.

Gura, Philip F., *American Transcendentalism: A History*. New York: Hill and Wang, 2007.

Gutjahr, Paul C., *An American Bible: A History of the Good Book in the United States, 1777–1880*. Stanford, CA: Stanford University Press, 1999.

Halderman Loski, Diana, *The Chamberlains of Brewer*. Gettysburg, PA: Thomas Publications, 1998.

Hamlin, Cyrus, *My Life and Times*. Boston: Congregational and Sunday School Publishing Society, 1893.

Hatch, Louis C., *The History of Bowdoin College*. Portland, ME: Lording, Short & Harmon, 1927.

Hedrick, Joan D., *Harriet Beecher Stowe: A Life*. New York: Oxford University Press, 1994.

Helmreich, Ernst C., *Religion at Bowdoin College: A History*. Brunswick, ME: Bowdoin College, 1981.

Hessler, James A., *Sickles at Gettysburg: The Controversial Civil War General Who Committed Murder, Abandoned Little Round Top, and Declared Himself the Hero of Gettysburg*. El Dorado Hills, CA: Savas Beatie, 2009.

Hessler, James A. and Britt C. Isenberg, *Gettysburg's Peach Orchard: Longstreet, Sickles, and the Bloody Fight for the "Commanding Ground" Along the Emmitsburg Road*. El Dorado Hills, CA: Savas Beatie, 2019.

Historical Sketch, First Congregational Church. Brewer, ME: First Congregational Church, 1928.

Hood, George, *A History of Music in New England: With Biographical Sketches of Reformers and Psalmists*. Boston: Wilkins, Carter & Co., 1846.

Howard, Oliver Otis, *Autobiography of Oliver Otis Howard*, vol. 1. New York: Baker & Taylor, 1907.

Howe, Daniel Walker, *The Unitarian Conscience: Harvard Moral Philosophy, 1805–1861*. Cambridge, MA: Harvard University Press, 1970.

_____, *What Hath God Wrought: The Transformation of America, 1815–1848*. New York: Oxford University Press, 2007.

Hunt, Harry Draper, *Hannibal Hamlin of Maine: Lincoln's First Vice-President*. Syracuse, NY: Syracuse University Press, 1969.

Huntington, Tom, *Maine at 200: An Anecdotal History Celebrating Two Centuries of Statehood.* Camden, ME: Down East Books, 2020.

_____, *Maine Roads to Gettysburg: How Joshua Chamberlain, Oliver Howard, and 4,000 Men from the Pine Tree State Helped Win the Civil War's Bloodiest Battle.* Guilford, CT: Stackpole Books, 2018.

_____, *Searching for George Gordon Meade: The Forgotten Victor of Gettysburg.* Mechanicsburg, PA: Stackpole Books, 2013.

In Memoriam: Joshua Lawrence Chamberlain: Late Major-General U.S.V., Military Order of the Loyal Legion of the United States, Commandery of the State of Maine, circular no. 5, series of 1914, whole number, 328. Portland, ME: 1914.

James, Joseph B., *The Framing of the Fourteenth Amendment.* Urbana: University of Illinois Press, 1965.

Jermann, Donald R., *Fitz-John Porter, Scapegoat of Second Manassas: The Rise, Fall and Rise of the General Accused of Disobedience.* Jefferson, NC: McFarland & Company, 2008.

John, Arthur, *The Best Years of the Century.* Urbana: University of Illinois Press, 1981.

Jordan, David M., *"Happiness Is Not My Companion": The Life of General G. K. Warren.* Bloomington: Indiana University Press, 2001.

Joshua L. Chamberlain: A Life in Letters, edited by Thomas Desjardin. Oxford, U.K.: Osprey Publishing, 2012.

Joshua Lawrence Chamberlain: A Sketch. Place: Chamberlain Association of America, 1905.

Kelly, Howard A., *Dictionary of American Medical Biography.* New York: D. Appleton, 1928.

Kenny, Bill, *A History of Maine Railroads.* Charleston, SC: The History Press, 2020.

Kitzhaber, Albert R., *Rhetoric in American Colleges, 1850–1900.* Dallas, TX: Southern Methodist University Press, 1990.

Koester, Nancy, *Harriet Beecher Stowe: A Spiritual Life.* Grand Rapids, MI: William B. Eerdmans Publishing Company, 2014.

LaFantasie, Glenn W., *Gettysburg Requiem: The Life and Lost Causes of Confederate Colonel William C. Oates.* New York: Oxford University Press, 2005.

_____, *Twilight at Little Round Top: July 2, 1863—The Tide Turns at Gettysburg.* Hoboken, NJ: John Wiley & Sons, 2005.

Laine, J. Gary, and Morris M. Penny, *Law's Alabama Brigade in the War Between the Union and the Confederacy.* Shippensburg, PA: White Mane Publishing, 1996.

Laws of Bowdoin College. Brunswick, ME: Press of Joseph Griffin, 1844.

Lee, Richard M., *Mr. Lincoln's City: An Illustrated Guide to the Civil War Sites of Washington.* McClean, VA: EPM Publications, 1981.

Leech, Margaret, *Reveille in Washington: 1860–1865.* New York: Harper, 1941 (New York: New York Review of Books, 2011).

Leith, John H., *Assembly at Westminster: Reformed Theology in the Making.* Atlanta, GA: John Knox Press, 1973.

Letham, Robert, *The Westminster Assembly: Reading Its Theology in Historical Context.* Phillipsburg, NJ: P&R Publishing, 2009.

Levinsky, Allan M., *At Home with the General: A Visit to the Joshua L. Chamberlain Museum.* Gettysburg, PA: Thomas Publications, 2001.

Lewis, Lloyd, *Sherman: Fighting Prophet.* New York: Harcourt Brace, 1932.

Linderman, Gerald F., *Embattled Courage: The Experience of Combat in the American Civil War.* New York: The Free Press, 1987.

Longacre, Edward G., *Joshua Chamberlain: The Soldier and the Man*. Conshohocken, PA: Combined Publishing, 1999.

Longstreet, James, *From Manassas to Appomattox: Memoirs of the Civil War in America*. Philadelphia: J. B. Lippincott, 1896.

Loski, Diana Halderman, *The Chamberlains of Brewer*. Gettysburg, PA: Thomas Publications, 1998.

Lystra, Karen, *Searching the Heart: Women, Men, and Romantic Love in Nineteenth-Century America*. New York: Oxford University Press, 1989.

MacCaskill, Libby, *Ladies on the Field: Two Civil War Nurses from Maine on the Battlefields of Virginia*. Livermore, ME: Signal Tree Publications, 1996.

Maine: A History, edited by Louis Clinton Hatch. New York: The American Historical Society, 1919.

Maine at Gettysburg: Report of Maine Commissioners. Portland, ME: Lakeside Press, 1898.

Marszalek, John F., *Sherman: A Soldier's Passion for Order*. Carbondale: Southern Illinois University Press, 1993.

Marvel, William G., *A Place Called Appomattox: Community at the Crossroads of History*. Chapel Hill: University of North Carolina Press, 2000.

————, *Radical Sacrifice: The Rise and Ruin of Fitz John Porter*. Chapel Hill: University of North Carolina Press, 2021.

McCarthy, Michael J., *Confederate Waterloo: The Battle of Five Forks, April 1, 1865, and the Controversy That Brought Down a General*. El Dorado Hills, CA: Savas Beatie, 2017.

McConnell, Stuart, *Glorious Contentment: The Grand Army of the Republic, 1865–1900*. Chapel Hill: University of North Carolina Press, 1992.

McDonough, James Lee, *William Tecumseh Sherman: In the Service of My Country: A Life*. New York: W. W. Norton, 2016.

McFeely, William S., *Yankee Stepfather: General O. O. Howard and the Freedmen*. New Haven, CT: Yale University Press, 1968.

McPherson, James M., *Battle Cry of Freedom: The Civil War Era*. New York: Oxford University Press, 1988.

————, *Crossroads of Freedom: Antietam*. New York: Oxford University Press, 2002.

————, *Embattled Rebel: Jefferson Davis as Commander in Chief*. New York: The Penguin Press, 2014.

————, *For Cause and Comrades: Why Men Fought in the Civil War*. New York: Oxford University Press, 1997.

————, *Hallowed Ground: A Walk at Gettysburg*. New York: Crown Publishers, 2003.

Miller, Glenn T., *Piety and Intellect: The Aims and Purposes of Ante-Bellum Theological Education*. Atlanta, GA: Scholars Press, 1990.

Moorhead, James H., *Princeton Seminary in American Religion and Culture*. Grand Rapids, MI: William B. Eerdmans, 2012.

Munson, Gorham, *Penobscot: Down East Paradise*. Philadelphia: J. B. Lippincott, 1959.

Myers, H. G., *The Lion of Round Top: The Life and Military Service of Brigadier General Strong Vincent in the American Civil War*. Philadelphia: Casemate, 2022.

Nash, Eugene Arus, *A History of the Forty-fourth Regiment, New York Volunteer Infantry, in the Civil War, 1861–1865*. Chicago: R. R. Donnelley & Sons, 1911.

Nevins, James H., and William B. Styple, *What Death More Glorious: A Biography of General Strong Vincent*. Kearny, NJ: Belle Grove Publishing, 1997.

Norton, Oliver W., *Army Letters, 1861–1865*. Chicago: O. L. Deming, 1903.

_____, *The Attack and Defense of Little Round Top*. New York: Neale Publishing Co., 1913.

Oates, William C., *The War Between the Union and the Confederacy*. New York: The Neale Publishing Co., 1905.

Obituary Record of the Graduates of Bowdoin College and the Medical School of Maine for the Decade Ending 1 June 1909. Brunswick, ME: Bowdoin College Library, 1911.

O'Reilly, Francis Augustín, *The Fredericksburg Campaign: Winter War on the Rappahannock*. Baton Rouge: Louisiana State University Press, 2003.

Ott, Eloise Robinson, and Louis Hickman Chazal, *Ocali Country*. Ocala, FL: Greene's Printing, 1986.

Paul, Robert S., *The Assembly of the Lord: Politics and Religion in the Westminster Assembly and the 'Grand Debate.'* Edinburgh, Scotland: T&T Clark, 1985.

Perry, Mark, *Conceived in Liberty: Joshua Chamberlain, William Oates, and the American Civil War*. New York: Viking, 1997.

Petersburg to Appomattox: The End of the War in Virginia, edited by Caroline E. Janney. Chapel Hill: University of North Carolina Press, 2018.

Pfanz, Harry W., *Gettysburg: The Second Day*. Chapel Hill: University of North Carolina Press, 1987.

Pond, Enoch, *The Autobiography of the Rev. Enoch Pond*. Boston: Congregational Sunday School and Publishing Society, 1883.

_____, *The Lives of Increase Mather and Sir William Phipps*. Boston: Massachusetts Sabbath School Society, 1847.

_____, *The Mather Family*. Boston: Massachusetts Sabbath School Society, 1844.

Powell, William H., *The Fifth Army Corps (Army of the Potomac): A Record of Operations During the Civil War in the United States of America, 1861–1865*. New York: G. P. Putnam's Sons, 1896.

Primomo, John W., *The Appomattox Generals: The Parallel Lives of Joshua L. Chamberlain and John B. Gordon*. Jefferson, NC: McFarland, 2013.

Pullen, John J., *Joshua Chamberlain: A Hero's Life & Legacy*. Mechanicsburg, PA: Stackpole Books, 1999.

_____, *The Twentieth Maine*. Philadelphia: Lippincott, 1957.

Rable, George C., *God's Almost Chosen Peoples: A Religious History of the American Civil War*. Chapel Hill: University of North Carolina Press, 2010.

Rada, James, Jr., *No North, No South . . . : The Grand Reunion at the 50th Anniversary of the Battle of Gettysburg*. Gettysburg, PA: Legacy Publishing, 2013.

Remini, Robert V., *Henry Clay: Statesman for the Union*. New York: W. W. Norton and Company, 1991.

Rhea, Gordon C., *Cold Harbor: Grant and Lee, May 26–June 3, 1864*. Baton Rouge: Louisiana State University Press, 2002.

Richard, Carl J., *The Founders and the Classics: Greece, Rome, and the American Enlightenment*. Cambridge, MA: Harvard University Press, 1994.

Richardson, Peter Tufts, *Universalists and Unitarians of Maine: A Comprehensive History*. Rockland, ME: Red Barn Publishing, 2017.

Roberts, Kenneth, *Trending into Maine*. Boston: Little Brown and Company, 1938.

Robinson, David, *The Unitarians and the Universalists*. Westport, CT: Greenwood Press, 1985.

Robinson, Fannie Harlow, *D.A.R., 1850–1930. Daniel Arthur Robinson and Some of His Forefathers, Family and Friends Compiled by His Daughter*. Privately printed, 1968.

Rolde, Neil, *Continental Liar from the State of Maine: James G. Blaine.* Gardiner, ME: Tilbury House Publishers, 2007.

Rotundo, E. Anthony, *American Manhood: Transformations in Masculinity from the Revolution to the Modern Era.* New York: Basic Books, 1993.

Rowe, Henry K., *History of Andover Theological Seminary.* Boston: Thomas Todd Company, 1933.

Sablosky, Irving, *American Music.* Chicago: University of Chicago Press, 1969.

Scee, Trudy Irene, *City on the Penobscot: A Comprehensive History of Bangor, Maine.* Charleston, SC: History Press, 2010.

Schaff, Morris, *The Sunset of the Confederacy.* Lanham, MD: Cooper Square Press, 2002 (Originally published: Boston: J. W. Luce, 1912).

Schriver, Edward O., *Go Free: The Antislavery Impulse in Maine, 1833–1855.* Orono: University of Maine Press, 1970.

Schroeder, Patrick A., *More Myths About Lee's Surrender.* Lynchburg, VA: Schroeder Publications, 1995.

Scott, Winfield, *Infantry Tactics.* New York: Harper & Row, 1859.

Sears, Stephen W., *Gettysburg.* Boston: Houghton Mifflin, 2003.

_____, *Landscape Turned Red: The Battle of Antietam.* New Haven, CT: Yale University Press, 1983.

_____, *To the Gates of Richmond: The Peninsula Campaign.* New York: Ticknor and Fields, 1992.

Shaara, Michael, *The Killer Angels.* New York: David McKay Co., 1974.

Shaw, Richard R., *Images of America: Brewer.* Charleston, SC: Arcadia Publishing, 2000.

Smiles, Samuel, *The Huguenots in France After the Revocation of the Edict of Nantes.* New York: Harper & Bros., 1874.

Smith, Diane Monroe, *Chamberlain at Petersburg: The Charge at Fort Hell, June 18, 1864.* Gettysburg, PA: Thomas Publications, 2004.

_____, *Fanny & Joshua: The Enigmatic Lives of Frances Caroline Adams and Joshua Lawrence Chamberlain.* Gettysburg, PA: Thomas Publications, 1999.

Smylie, James H., *A Brief History of the Presbyterians.* Louisville, KY: Geneva Press, 1996.

Smyth, Newman, *Recollections and Reflections.* New York: Charles Scribner's Sons, 1926.

Spear, Abbott, and Ellis Spear, *The 20th Maine at Fredericksburg: The Conflicting Accounts of General Joshua L. Chamberlain and General Ellis Spear,* foreword by Tom Desjardin. Union, ME: Union Publishing Company, 1989.

Staley, Ruel H., and George O. Hall, *Eastern Maine and the Rebellion.* Bangor, ME: R. H. Stanley, 1887.

Stowe, Harriet Beecher, *The May Flower, and Miscellaneous Writings.* Boston: Phillips, Sampson, 1843.

_____, *Uncle Tom's Cabin; or, Life among the Lowly.* Boston: Phillips, Sampson, 1852.

Summers, Mark Wahlgren, *Rum, Romanism, and Rebellion: The Making of a President, 1884.* Chapel Hill: University of North Carolina Press, 2000.

Swinton, William, *Campaigns of the Army of the Potomac.* New York: C. B. Richardson, 1866.

Taylor, Emerson Gifford, *Gouverneur Kemble Warren: The Life and Letters of an American Soldier, 1830–1882.* Boston: Houghton Mifflin, 1932.

The American Presidency Project: presidency.ucsb.edu.

The Civil War Recollections of General Ellis Spear, co-edited by Andrea C. Hawkes, Marie H. McCosh, Craig L. Symonds, and Michael L. Alpert. Orono: University of Maine Press, 1997.

The Fredericksburg Campaign: Decision on the Rappahannock, edited by Gary W. Gallagher. Chapel Hill: University of North Carolina Press, 1995.

The Papers of Ulysses S. Grant, edited by John Y. Simon and John F. Marszalek. Carbondale: Southern Illinois University Press, 1967–2017.

The Story of a Musical Life: An Autobiography by Geo. F. Root. Cincinnati: The John Church Co., 1891.

Thelin, John R., *A History of American Higher Education.* Baltimore: Johns Hopkins University Press, 2004.

Thomas, Emory M., *Robert E. Lee: A Biography.* New York: W. W. Norton, 1995.

Through Blood & Fire: Selected Civil War Papers of Major General Joshua Chamberlain, edited by Mark Nesbitt. Mechanicsburg, PA: Stackpole Books, 1996.

Treasure, Geoffrey, *The Huguenots.* New Haven, CT: Yale University Press, 2013.

Trulock, Alice Rains, *In The Hands of Providence: Joshua L. Chamberlain & the American Civil War.* Chapel Hill: University of North Carolina Press, 1992.

Tucker, Philip Thomas, *Storming Little Round Top: The 15th Alabama and Their Fight for Higher Ground.* Boston: De Capo Press, 2002.

Twelve Days at Augusta, 1880. Portland, ME: Smith and Dale Printers, 1906.

Unger, Irwin, *The Greenback Era: A Social and Political History of American Finance, 1865–1879.* Princeton, NJ: Princeton University Press, 1964.

Upham, Thomas Cogswell, *Elements of Mental Philosophy: Embracing the Two Departments of the Intellect and the Sensibilities,* 2 vols. Portland, ME: William Hyde, 1837.

————, *Principles of the Interior or Hidden Life.* Boston: D. S. King, 1843.

Upton, Emory, *Tactics.* New York: D. Appleton, 1862.

Varon, Elizabeth R., *Appomattox: Victory, Defeat, and Freedom at the End of the Civil War.* New York: Oxford University Press, 2014.

————, *Armies of Deliverance: A New History of the Civil War.* New York: Oxford University Press, 2019.

Walker, Williston, *A History of the Congregational Churches in the United States.* New York: Christian Literature Company, 1894.

Wallace, Willard M., *Soul of the Lion: A Biography of General Joshua L. Chamberlain.* New York: T. Nelson, 1960.

Warner, Ezra J., *Generals in Blue: Lives of the Union Commanders.* Baton Rouge: Louisiana State University Press, 1964.

Welsh, Jack D., *Medical Histories of Union Generals.* Kent, OH: Kent State University Press, 1996.

Whately, Richard, *Elements of Rhetoric: Comprising an Analysis of the Laws of Moral Evidence and of Persuasion.* New York: Sheldon and Company, 1867.

Wheelan, Joseph, *Terrible Swift Sword: The Life of General Philip H. Sheridan.* Cambridge, MA: Da Capo Press, 2012.

Wheeler, George Augustus and Henry Warren Wheeler, *History of Brunswick, Topsham, and Harpswell, Maine.* Boston: Alfred Mudge & Son, Printers, 1878.

White, Richard, *The Republic for Which It Stands: The United States During Reconstruction and the Gilded Age, 1865–1896.* New York: Oxford University Press, 2017.

White, Ronald C., *A. Lincoln: A Biography.* New York: Random House, 2009.

————, *American Ulysses: A Life of Ulysses S. Grant.* New York: Random House, 2016.

————, *Lincoln's Greatest Speech: The Second Inaugural.* New York: Simon & Schuster, 2002.

Whitman, William Edward S., and Charles Henry True, *Maine in the War for the Union.* Lewiston, ME: Dingley Publishers, 1865.

Willey, Austin, *The History of the Antislavery Cause in State and Nation.* Portland, ME: Brown Thurston and Hoyt, Fogg & Donham, 1886.

Wineapple, Brenda, *The Impeachers: The Trial of Andrew Johnson and the Dream of a Just Nation.* New York: Random House, 2020.

Winterer, Caroline, *The Culture of Classicism: Ancient Greece and Rome in American Intellectual Life, 1780–1910.* Baltimore, MD: The Johns Hopkins University Press, 2002.

With a Flash of His Sword: The Writings of Major Holman S. Melcher 20th Maine Infantry, edited by William B. Styple. Kearny, New Jersey: Belle Grove Publishing, 1994.

Woods, Leonard, *History of the Andover Theological Seminary.* Boston: James R. Osgood and Co., 1885.

Woodward, E. M., *History of the One Hundred and Ninety-Eighth Pennsylvania Volunteers.* Trenton, NJ: MacCrellish & Quigley, 1884.

Wright, Conrad, *The Beginnings of Unitarianism in America.* Boston: Starr King Press, distributed by Beacon Press, 1955.

ARTICLES, CHAPTERS, ESSAYS, PAMPHLETS

Bailey, Michael, "Republican Ascendancy: The Gubernatorial Career of Joshua Lawrence Chamberlain and its Consequences, 1866–1881." *Maine History,* vol. 50, no. 1, 2016, 43–57.

Bierle, Sarah Kay, "The Generals' Horses," January 13, 2017. gazette665.com/2017/01/13/chamberlains-charlemagne/.

Bjella, Lee, "Early Gymnastics in America," wanawgj.com/history/early-gymnastics-in-america/.

Blaugrund, Annette, "The Evolution of American Artists' Studios, 1740–1860," *The Magazine Antiques,* January 1992, 214–25.

Carleton, Patrick W., *The Practice of Leadership: The Life and Times of Joshua L. Chamberlain,* 2001, 1–94, digitalscholarship.unlv.edu/sea_fac_articles/405.

Chamberlain, Joshua Lawrence, "Education at the Universal Exposition," in *Reports of the United States Commissioners to the Paris Universal Exposition, 1878,* Washington, D.C., Publisher, 1880, II, 181–347.

_____, "My Story of Fredericksburg," *Cosmopolitan* magazine, vol. 54, December 1912, 148–59.

_____, "The Last Night at Fredericksburg," in *Camp-fire Sketches and Battlefield Echoes of 61–65,* compiled by W. C. King and W. P. Derby. Springfield, MA: King, Richardson, 1888, 131–35.

_____, "Through Blood and Fire at Gettysburg," *Hearst's Magazine,* vol. 23, June 1913, 895–915 (Reprinted by Stan Clark Military Books, Gettysburg, 1994), 16–37.

Curtis, Charles A., "Bowdoin Under Fire," *Tales of Bowdoin,* edited by John Clair Minot and Donald Francis Snow. Augusta, ME: Press of Kennebec Journal, 1901, 261–72.

Dedication of the Twentieth Maine Monuments at Gettysburg, Oct. 3, 1889, Waldoboro, ME: News Stream Job Print, 1891.

Desjardin, Tom, "A Broken Bond? The Little Round Top Feud Between Joshua Chamberlain and Ellis Spear," July 2017. historynet.com/broken-bond.htm.

Desmond, Jerry R., Jr., Joel W. Eastman, Stanley R. Howe, Richard W. Judd, and Edward O. Schriver, "Defending Maine and the Nation," in *Maine: The Pine Tree State from Prehistory to the Present.* Orono: University of Maine Press, 1995, 342–69.

Easterlin, Richard A., George Alter, and Gretchen A. Condran, "Farms and Farm Families in Old and New Areas: The Northern States in 1860," in *Family and Population in Nineteenth-Century America,* edited by Tamara K. Hareven and Maris A. Vinovskis, Princeton, NJ: Princeton University Press, 1978, 22–73.

Finkelstein, Jason, "The Governor's Gallows: Joshua Lawrence Chamberlain and the Clifton Harris Case," *Maine History,* vol. 45, no. 2, 2010, 168–88.

Foley, Edward, "The Third Maine's Angel of Mercy: Sarah Smith Sampson," *Maine History,* vol. 36, no. 1, 1996, 38–53.

Gerrish, Theodore, "The Twentieth Maine at Gettysburg," *Portland Advertiser,* March 13, 1882.

Giltner, John H., "The Fragmentation of New England Congregationalism and the Founding of Andover Seminary," *Journal of Religious Thought,* vol. 20, no. 1, 2008, 27–42.

Greene, Liz, "A Brief History of Women and Alcohol," lipmag.com/featured/a-brief-history-of-women-and-alcohol/.

Hall, Robert E., "Maine's Admission to the Union," *Sprague's Journal of Maine History,* vol. VIII, no. 1, June 1920, 8–14.

Handley-Cousins, Sarah, " 'Wrestling at the Gates of Death': Joshua Lawrence Chamberlain and Nonvisible Disability in the Post–Civil War North," *Journal of the Civil War Era,* vol. 6, no. 2, January 2016, 220–42.

Harmon, William J., and Charles K. McAllister, "The Lion of the Union: The Pelvic Wound of Joshua Lawrence Chamberlain," *Journal of Urology,* 163, 2000, 713–16.

Hofstadter, Richard, "The Revolution in Higher Education," *Paths of American Thought,* edited by Arthur Schlesinger, Jr., and Morton White. Boston: Houghton Mifflin, 1963, 269–90.

LaFantasie, Glenn, "Gettysburg 1895–1995: The Shaping of an American Shrine: Memories of Little Round Top," npshistory.com/series/symposia/gettysburg_seminars/4/essay5.htm.

Leithauser, Brad, "Why We Should Memorize," *The New Yorker,* January 25, 2013.

"Malaria in Wars and Victims," malariasite.com/wars-victims/#:~:text=During%20the%20American%20civil%20war,black%20soldiers%20got%20malaria%20annually.

"Named Professorships at Bowdoin College," *Bowdoin College Bulletin,* December 1975, no. 399, 1–25.

Oates, William C., "Gettysburg: The Battle on the Right," Southern Historical Society Papers, vol. 6, 1878, 172–82.

Raymond, Harold B., "Joshua Chamberlain's Retirement Bill," *Colby Library Quarterly,* ser. 7, no. 8, December 1966, 342–54.

Reilly, Robert F., MD, "Medical and Surgical Care During the American Civil War, 1861–1865," *Baylor University Medical Center Proceedings,* vol. 29, no. 2, 138–42.

Reimer, Terry, "Smallpox and Vaccination in the Civil War," National Museum of Civil War Medicine, November 9, 2004, civilwarmed.org/surgeons-call/small_pox/.

Schriver, Edward, "Reluctant Hangman: The State of Maine and Capital Punishment, 1820–1887." *New England Quarterly,* vol. 63, no. 2, June 1990, 271–87.

Schriver, Edward, and Stanley Howe, "The Republican Ascendancy: Politics and Reform in Maine," in *Maine: The Pine Tree State from Prehistory to the Present.* Orono: University of Maine Press, 1995, 370–90.

Smith, Catherine T., "Brunswick's 'Soldier Statesman,' " Brunswick *Times Record,* September 7, 1976.

Smith, Jennifer Lund, "The Reconstruction of 'Home': The Civil War and the Marriage of Lawrence and Fannie Chamberlain," *Intimate Strategies of the Civil War: Military Command-*

ers and Their Wives, edited by Carol K. Bleser and Lesley J. Gordon. New York: Oxford University Press, 2001, 157–77.

Spear, Ellis, "The Left at Gettysburg," *National Tribune,* March 1913.

Sweet, William Warren, "The Rise of Theological Schools in America," *Church History,* vol. 6, no. 3, September 1937, 260–73.

Syrett, Nicholas L., "Responding to Domestic Violence in the Nineteenth-Century United States," *Journal of Women's History,* vol. 33, no. 1, Spring 2021, 158–62.

Vose, Caroline E., "When Bowdoin College Conferred the LL.D. Degree on Jefferson Davis," *Lewiston Journal Illustrated Magazine,* April 18, 1925.

Waugh, Joan, "Pageantry of War: The Funeral of Ulysses S. Grant," in *Vale of Tears: New Essays on Religion and Reconstruction,* edited by Edward J. Blum and W. Scott Poole. Macon, GA: Mercer University Press, 2005, 212–34.

Westcott, Richard S., and Edward O. Schriver, "Reform Movements & Party Reformation, 1820–1861," in *Maine: The Pine Tree State from Prehistory to the Present,* edited by Richard W. Judd, Edwin A. Churchill, and Joel W. Eastman. Orono: University of Maine Press, 1995, 193–216.

DISSERTATIONS AND PAPERS

Cross, Robert M., *Joshua Lawrence Chamberlain,* Bowdoin College, 1947.

Cuddy, John F., *Training Through Blood and Fire: The Leadership Development of Joshua Lawrence Chamberlain.* Master of Operational Arts and Sciences, Maxwell Air Force Base, Alabama, 2015.

NEWSPAPERS CONSULTED

Bangor Daily Commercial

Bangor Historical Magazine

Bangor Whig and Courier

Boston Daily News

Boston Herald

Boston Journal

Boston Post

Bowdoin Orient

Brunswick Record

Brunswick Telegraph

Brunswick *Times Record*

Colby Library Quarterly

Congregationalist and Boston Recorder

Cosmopolitan magazine

Daily Eastern Argus (Portland, Maine)

Hearst's Magazine

Kennebec Journal (Augusta, Maine)

Lewiston Journal

National Tribune (Washington, D.C.)

New York Herald

New-York Tribune

New York World

Oxford Democrat (Oxford, Maine)

Portland Daily Advertiser

Portland Daily Press

Portland Evening Express

Portland Sunday Telegram

Portland Transcript

Public Ledger (Philadelphia)

The New York Times

PHOTOGRAPHIC ARCHIVAL SOURCES

George J. Mitchell Department of Special Collections & Archives, Bowdoin College, Brunswick, ME

Library of Congress, Prints and Photographs Division, Washington, D.C.

Maine Historical Society, Portland, ME

Maine State Archives, Augusta, ME

Pejepscot History Center, Brunswick, ME

Raymond H. Fogler Library, University of Maine, Orono, ME

ILLUSTRATION LIST AND CREDITS

237   Reviewing Stand at the Grand Review, May 23–24, 1865. Library of Congress, Prints and Photographs Division.

238   Joshua Lawrence Chamberlain house, Brunswick, ME. Pejepscot History Center.

246   Joshua Lawrence Chamberlain Tiffany bracelet. George J. Mitchell Department of Special Collections & Archives, Bowdoin College.

248   James G. Blaine. Maine Historical Society.

249   President Andrew Johnson. Library of Congress, Prints and Photographs Division.

254   Maine State Capitol, Augusta, Maine. Maine State Archives.

255   Sarah Dupee Brastow Chamberlain. Pejepscot History Center.

259   Bernard Gillam temperance cartoon, 1882: *Between Two Evils*. Library of Congress, Prints and Photographs Division.

260   Portland mayor Neal Dow. Heritage Auction.

261   Governor Joshua Lawrence Chamberlain. George J. Mitchell Department of Special Collections & Archives, Bowdoin College.

263   Gallery at impeachment trial of Andrew Johnson, May 1868. Library of Congress, Prints and Photographs Division.

264   *"Dame Butler – Head boy!"* Boston Public Library, Boston, MA.

265   Clifton Harris. Maine State Archives.

266   Maine attorney General William P. Frye. Maine Historical Society.

276   Bowdoin president Joshua Lawrence Chamberlain. George J. Mitchell Department of Special Collections & Archives, Bowdoin College.

285   Joshua Lawrence Chamberlain house. Pejepscot History Center.

286   Joshua Lawrence Chamberlain house. Pejepscot History Center.

289   General Joseph P. Sanger. "In the Public Eye," *Munsey's Magazine,* November 30, 1899.

290   Bowdoin students in military uniforms. George J. Mitchell Department of Special Collections & Archives, Bowdoin College.

296   Henry Wadsworth Longfellow. Library of Congress, Prints and Photographs Division.

303   The Centennial Exposition of 1876 in Philadelphia. Library of Congress, Prints and Photographs Division.

306   Universelle Exposition of 1878. Library of Congress, Prints and Photographs Division.

309   The *Pinafore*. Pejepscot History Center.

308   Governor Alonzo Garcelon. Maine Historical Society.

311   Daniel F. Davis. Maine Historical Society.

316   "Confusion in State House." *Frank Leslie's Illustrated Newspaper,* January 1880.

322   Wyllys Chamberlain. George J. Mitchell Department of Special Collections & Archives, Bowdoin College.

324   Twenty-fifth reunion of the 1863 battle at Gettysburg. George J. Mitchell Department of Special Collections & Archives, Bowdoin College.

339   Funeral of Ulysses S. Grant in New York. Library of Congress, Prints and Photographs Division.

340   Statue of Gouverneur K. Warren dedicated at Gettysburg in 1888. Library of Congress, Prints and Photographs Division.

Grant's memoirs and, 338
Lee's surrender, conflicting accounts
and historical analysis, 333–34,
433n19
military court of inquiry on Warren's
conduct at Five Forks, 336–38
Oates's account of Little Round Top
and book on the Civil War, 362–63,
367
published accounts, 327–28, 332
quarreling among survivors, 341
Spears's criticism of Chamberlain and,
373–74, 434n51
war as a crusade, 327
Clark, John, 163
Clark, Mary, 206
Clay, Henry, 8, *42*, 42, 397n9
"American System," 257
Cleaveland, Parker, 26, *26*, 50
Cleveland, Grover, 338
Coan, Elisha, 335
Coburn, Abner, 144, *144*, 150, 291
Colby College, Waterville, Maine, 282
Cold Harbor, Battle of, 195, 415n69
College of New Jersey (later Princeton), 53
Compromise of 1850, 42–43, 47
Confederate Army, 110, 128, 156
casualties, 139, 195
Grant's magnanimous peace and, 223,
226
horses owned by their riders, 223
march to Gettysburg, 157
Petersburg and, 212
surrender at Appomattox, 222–27, *227*
unwillingness to surrender, 212
See also Army of Northern Virginia;
Fifteenth Alabama Regiment; *specific
battles*
Congregationalism, xviii, 9
abolitionism and, 44
antislavery wing of, 84
apprenticeships for ministers and,
67–68
Bangor Theological Seminary and, 74
Bowdoin College and, 23, 30, 97–98,
102, 104–5, 117, 282, 302–3
catechesis and, 10
Chamberlain joins the Brewer church,
10–11
founding of America's two earliest
colleges, 9
General Conference of Maine, 44
the "Great Revival" and, 9
missionary movement and, 15, 33,
69, 76

Puritanism and, 9, 30, 304
theological education and, 67–69
traditional teachings of, 60
values instilled by, 157–58
word "scruple" and, 38, 397n63
"Yankee singing schools," 11–12
See also Calvinism; *specific parish churches*
Connor, Selden, 303, 310, 371–72
Cony, Samuel, 206, 207, 247
Cooper, James Fenimore
The Deerslayer, 36–37
Cosmopolitan magazine, 372
"My Story of Fredericksburg"
(Chamberlain), 372
Crawford, Samuel W., 220
Cross, Edward E., 124
Crouch, Frederick N., 58–59, *59*
Culpeper, Virginia, 153, 192
Curtin, Andrew, 191
Curtis, Charles A., 109
Cushman, Stephen, 333–34
Custer, George, 235–36
horse, Don Juan, 236
Cutler, George O., 355

Daniels, Jeff, xvii
Dartmouth College, Hanover, New
Hampshire, 27, 73, 294
Davis, Anna, 57, 63, 70
Davis, Daniel F., 311, *311*, 312
Davis, Henry Winter, 263
Davis, Jefferson, 100, *100*
Bowdoin College awards honorary
degree, 99–101, 111, 244
evacuation of Richmond and, 221
Fessenden's shouting match with, 100
Portland, Maine, speech, 99, 100
service in the Pierce administration, 99
summer in New England, 99
Deerslayer, The (Cooper), 37
DeLacy, Patrick, 200, 416n85
Delamater, John, 57
Democratic Party
Civil War and, 106, 248
in Maine, 43–44, 106–7, 248, 252, 255,
310, 332, 311–14
Reconstruction measures opposed, 259
in the South, 158
Desjardin, Tom, 374
DeWitt, W. R., 232
Dictionary of Love, The (1858), 67
Dingley, Nelson, Jr., 318
Douglas, Stephen A., 42, 106
Dow, Neal, *260*, 260

Florida
  Chamberlain's interests in, 346, 347,
    348, 349, 356–57
  Chamberlain's visits to, 344, 346, 348–49
  Great Freeze of 1885–1886, 349
  history and economy, 344
  malaria and, 349
  map, 1870s, *345*
  Panic of 1893 and, 353
  population growth, 344
  railroads, 346
Florida West Coast Improvement
    Company, 344, 346
  Chamberlain as vice president, 347
Folsom, Deborah, 58, 61, 63, 70, 145, 152,
    182
Forbes, Edwin, etching of Little Round
    Top, *179*
Fort Donelson, Battle of, 112
Fort Stedman, Battle of, 212
Forty-fourth New York Regiment, 162, 172,
    175, 177, 202
Forty-seventh Alabama Regiment, *173*, 176,
    177–78
Fourth Alabama Regiment, 363, 366
Frank Leslie's Illustrated Newspaper
  "Confusion in State House," 316
Franklin, William, 136, 137
Frederick, Md., 162
Fredericksburg, Battle of, 123, 135–39,
    137, 157
  Burnside's flawed assault, 139
  Carter's description of the Twentieth
    Maine, 138, 408n48
  casualties, 138, 139
  Marye's Heights assault, 137–38
  Twentieth Maine Regiment and, 137–39,
    175, 180
  Union defeat at, 139
Fredericksburg, Virginia, 135
  Burnside's headquarters, 135
  looting by Union forces, 136–37
French, William H., 136
French and Indian War, 13
Frye, William P., *266*, 267, 268, 311, 355
Fugitive Slave Act of 1793, 42–43
  radicalizing New England moderates,
    45, 46
  Uncle Tom's Cabin and, 45–48, *47*
Funk, West, 201
Furbish, John, 108, 224, 244, 404n2, 419n67

G. P. Putnam's Sons, New York, 374, 379
Gallagher, Gary, 434n5

GAR (Grand Army of the Republic), 363,
    366, 376
  The National Tribune newspaper, 373
Garcelon, Alonzo, 310, *310*, 311, 312,
    313–14, 319
Garfield, James A., 311
Garrison, William Lloyd, *44*, 44
  The Liberator, 43
Gerrish, Theodore, 129, 131, 163, 194,
    407n30
  *Army Life: A Private's Reminiscences of the
    Civil War*, 335
Gettysburg (film), xvii, 380, 391n1
Gettysburg, Battle of, 156–80, 184
  Baltimore Pike, 166
  battle map: "Day 1, July 1, 1863," *165*
  battle map: "Opening Positions Day 2:
    July 2, 1863," *167*
  Berdan's Second U.S. Sharpshooters,
    174
  Big Round Top, 172, *172*, 174, 178
  Buford and Eighth Illinois Cavalry,
    162–63
  burial of the dead, 181, 191
  casualties, 164, 166
  cavalry battle by Jeb Stuart and Union
    horsemen, 164
  Cemetery Hill, 168
  Cemetery Ridge, 168, 169, 170
  Chamberlain and Twentieth Maine
    Regiment at, xvi, 164–80
  Chamberlain's cry of "Bayonet" and
    victory, xvi, 177, 373
  Chamberlain's speeches on, 245,
    328–29, 335, 342–43
  Chamberlain's written account, 335,
    373
  Confederate troops in, *165*, 166, *172*,
    172, *173*, 174, 175
  Confederate troops march to
    Gettysburg, 158, *161*, *165*
  Culp's Hill, 166, 168
  dedication of Maine monuments, ix,
    341–43, *342*
  Devil's Den, 175
  fiftieth reunion of Union and
    Confederate veterans, 374–75
  "Fredericksburg to Gettysburg" map, *161*
  Law's Brigade, 166, 169, *173*, 174
  Little Round Top, ix, xvi, xviii, 168–69,
    169, 170, *172*, 175–79, *179*, 186,
    191–92, 194, 335, 366, 415n65
  "Little Round Top Day 2: July 2, 1863,"
    173
  local citizens and, 164

ABOUT THE AUTHOR

RONALD C. WHITE is the *New York Times* bestselling author of the biographies *A. Lincoln* and *American Ulysses* as well as three other books on Lincoln, most recently *Lincoln in Private*. White earned his PhD at Princeton, has lectured at the White House, and has spoken about Lincoln across the world. He is a senior fellow of The Trinity Forum in Washington, D.C.

This book was set in Baskerville, a typeface designed by John Basker-ville (1706–75), an amateur printer and typefounder, and cut for him by John Handy in 1750. The type became popular again when the Lanston Monotype Corporation of London revived the classic roman face in 1923. The Mergenthaler Linotype Company in England and the United States cut a version of Baskerville in 1931, making it one of the most widely used typefaces today.